The Draft, 1940–1973

Modern War Studies

Theodore A. Wilson
General Editor

Raymond A. Callahan
J. Garry Clifford
Jacob W. Kipp
Jay Luvaas
Allan R. Millett
Series Editors

THE DRAFT, 1940–1973

George Q. Flynn

 University Press of Kansas

© 1993 by the University Press of Kansas
All rights reserved

Published by the University Press of Kansas (Lawrence,
Kansas 66049), which was organized by the Kansas Board
of Regents and is operated and funded by Emporia State
University, Fort Hays State University, Kansas State Uni‑
versity, Pittsburg State University, the University of Kan‑
sas, and Wichita State University.

Library of Congress Cataloging-in-Publication Data

Flynn, George Q.
  The draft, 1940–1973 / by George Q. Flynn.
    p.   cm. — (Modern war studies)
  Includes bibliographical references and index.
  ISBN 0-7006-0586-X (alk. paper)
  1. Draft—United States—History.   I. Title.   II. Series.
UB343.F59   1993
355.2′2363′0973—dc20   92-31081

British Library Cataloguing in Publication Data is available.

Printed in the United States of America

10 9 8 7 6 5 4 3 2 1

For Mary Ann R. Flynn
1939–1990

The miracle is
that she was

We few, we happy few, we band
    of brothers.
For he today that sheds his blood
    with me
Shall be my brother. Be he ne'er so vile,
This day shall gentle his condition.
And gentlemen in England now abed
shall think themselves accurs'd they
    were not here,
And hold their manhoods cheap
    whiles any speak
That fought with us upon Saint
    Crispin's day.
Henry V, 4.3.60–67

Contents

List of Illustrations   xi

Acknowledgments   xiii

1   Introduction   1

2   Creating Conscription,
       1940–1941   9

3   From Pearl Harbor to D-Day   53

4   Truman, UMT, and the Draft   88

5   Korea   110

6   The 1950s and Military
       Manpower   134

7   LBJ and Vietnam   166

8   Protest and Reform   188

9   Nixon and the Draft   224

10   The AVF and the Future   259

Notes   283

Bibliographical Essay   351

Index   363

Illustrations

World War I lottery drawing   12

Roosevelt signs Burke-Wadsworth
    Act   17

Drawing capsules for draft lottery   23

Sgt. Alvin C. York chairs local board   26

A family of conscientious objectors   46

Draftees undergoing physicals   55

Roosevelt registers with the draft   63

Truman signs the bill for a new
    draft   104

Protesting universal military
    training   125

Students tested for deferment   143

Testing for deferments   146

Draft protest in the 1960s   174

Burning draft cards   175

Evading the draft   213

General Hershey and protesters   217

Protest during Nixon's
    administration   237

More protests   238

General Hershey with his fourth
    star   244

Nixon tries a lottery   247

Curtis Tarr stirs the last capsules   255

Nixon renews the last draft   257

Now machines do it all   280

Acknowledgments

Over the past several years I have accumu-
lated many debts in the writing of this book. By mentioning these people
I have little hope of liquidating these obligations and no plan to burden
anyone with responsibility for the following pages, but I want the institutions and individuals who helped me to know that I remember and
appreciate that help. On an institutional level, I thank Texas Tech University for providing me with a 1984 faculty development leave, the
Texas equivalent of a sabbatical; the Department of History, which
helped with clerical assistance by Joan Weldon and Peggy Ariaz and two
fine research assistants—Jerry Shepherd and Peggy Hardman—and the
librarians who went out of their way to obtain material for me. On the
national level I am indebted to the American Philosophical Society for
a grant in 1988–1989, and I also received small but vital grants from the
Military History Institute, the Harry S. Truman Library Institute, and the
Lyndon B. Johnson Library Foundation.

Librarians and archivists are historians' most essential friends, and I
benefited enormously from the professionals at the Nixon Presidential
Materials Project in Alexandria, Virginia, the Kennedy Library in Boston,
the Roosevelt Library at Hyde Park, the Truman Library in Independence, the Eisenhower Library in Abilene, and the Johnson Library in
Austin. In Washington, D.C., I profited from the efficient staffs at the
National Archives, particularly Frederick W. Pernell, and the Library of
Congress. Mary Ann Higdon and Thomas Rohria of the Texas Tech
Library and David Coons of that university's computer center provided
excellent support, and my thanks also to Lewis C. Brodsky of the Selective Service System for an informative briefing and access to valuable
photographs. Professors Dan Flores and Ronald Rainger of Texas Tech
and John Chambers of Rutgers read the manuscript and made several
helpful suggestions.

On a more personal level I wish to thank several people who made my research financially possible and socially enjoyable. My daughter Kathleen, a reference librarian herself, provided assistance in obtaining rare material in Washington, D.C. Terry Gough of the Office of Military History in Washington time and time again responded with special information at my request, and Alice Norris was kind enough to allow me to house-sit in her Washington home while I worked in the files. The same courtesy, plus professional aid, was extended by Margaret Melun and Ky Thompson on another occasion, and similar facilities were offered by Paul and Cilla Reising, my brother-in-law and his wife, in the Boston area.

These people helped me to remain focused after the death of my wife of thirty years, Mary Ann Reising Flynn.

Paris, the Left Bank, 1992

1

Introduction

Historians, like other people, enjoy being needed. In recent years military historians have experienced a modest renaissance in the profession. After the nadir of the Vietnam years, when mention of the military might provoke a riot on a campus, the field has rebounded. A sign of this new vigor is the appearance of several historiographic appeals concerning the proper focus for research in military history, and the new calls are not for the old heroic military history of gunsmoke and battles but for socially oriented studies. Arthur Marwick, Richard Kohn, and John W. Chambers II have emphasized our ignorance of how the military experience influences society, and Walter E. Kaegi warns us that we must study soldiers with the same techniques we use to study civilians. We should not merely assume that military institutions reflect the larger culture.[1]

In this book, I attempt to contribute to the new military history by focusing upon the draft in the United States from 1940 to 1973. A leading military historian Russell Weigley writes: "The historic preoccupation of the Army's thought in peacetime has been the manpower question: how, in an unmilitary nation, to muster adequate numbers of capable soldiers quickly should war occur."[2] Turning civilians into soldiers involves political and social issues more than military strategy.

Conscription, or the draft, has been the solution to the manpower problem in the twentieth century, but as war is as old as human society, so is conscription. The idea that all able-bodied men owe an obligation of military defense can be traced to the dark caves of prehistory. The militia principle has survived in various forms, including the National Guard in the United States, but a conscripted force is different. Unlike the people who serve in the militia, draftees usually have no prior military training and are trained by a cadre of professionals to prepare for

1

distant battle. The power of the state to conscript is as ancient as the city-states of Greece and the Roman Republic, where citizenship and military duty were closely intertwined. In modern Europe the idea of conscription coincided with the idea of a national state, and the professional military caste of the Middle Ages soon collapsed before the mass armies of the new nation-states.[3]

The French Revolution launched the military modernization in Europe. In December 1789 a committee report to the French National Assembly put the principle in blunt terms: "Every citizen must be a soldier and every soldier a citizen or we shall never have a constitution."[4] The success of the French armies under the Assembly and later under Napoleon showed the other European nations the power of conscription. Above all, the draft provided mass numbers of troops, which France used successfully to crush opponents.[5] Although the alliance finally defeated the French and Napoleon, the idea of a draft had arrived to stay. By the 1870s Prussia had adopted a similar system, and as one scholar writes, "no army since the beginning of the nineteenth century has fought a major war successfully without calling into service vast numbers of civilians."[6]

The draft resulted in more than the winning of battles; it also had political and social consequences. The existence of a reservoir of manpower allowed for a reduction of standing professional forces and, consequently, the reduction of state expenses. Also, although the main reason for conscription was the need for masses of men, as soon as the idea was put forward it was accompanied by political rationalizations that, in time, became part of a powerful myth called the "citizen-soldier concept." The new system seemed at one with a new tide of democracy, with a wider franchise for citizens. In Germany and England the adoption of conscription contributed to political reforms that spread the vote more evenly in society. Friedrich Engels, the German socialist, wrote, "Contrary to appearance, compulsory military service surpasses general franchise as a democratic agency." When signing the 1940 draft bill, Franklin Roosevelt announced that by adopting the law in peacetime, America "has broadened and enriched our basic concepts of citizenship. Besides the clear and equal opportunities, we have set forth the underlying other duties, obligations and responsibilities of equal service." In April 1967 President Lyndon Johnson announced that "the Selective Service System is a part of America, a part of the process of our democracy."[7] Because all males were subjected to the service requirement, their status as citizens was enhanced; as defenders of the realm they had a claim upon the privileges of the state, including the privilege of voting.[8]

Equally important in rationalizing the draft was that it overcame dangers to the state inherent in maintaining a mass army. Drafting civilians could secure the state against militarism because by infusing the armed forces with a leaven of civilians, the state insured itself against right-wing coups.[9] In addition, just as the armed forces were infused with the culture and values of the civilian state, the army taught values useful for state welfare. The French looked upon the army as a school of citizenship, and the repeated calls for universal military training in the United States have all echoed such a sentiment. According to this argument, military training provides for a healthier, more disciplined youth for the nation. In World War I Chief of Staff Hugh Scott stated, "Universal military training has been the corner stone upon which has been built every republic in the history of the world, and its abandonment the signal for decline and obliteration."[10] Archibald MacLeish, poet and Librarian of Congress, asked during World War II: "How do we give the people of this country the conviction that this is their war . . . and not the generals' war—not the admirals' war?" One obvious answer is to draft the people, and such an approach insures an army of high morale.[11]

The emergence of the draft reflected not only the growth of democracy, but also the modernization of the state apparatus.[12] Several features of modernization contributed to the growth and development of the draft: increased professionalism, expanded and efficient use of technical skills, centralization of power through growth of a bureaucracy, and development of planning and management skills. As General William Westmoreland explained to Congress in 1964, "It is very hard to define where the military begins and the civilian leaves off in our form of government."[13]

Another feature of modernization manifested in the draft was the state's ability to develop rational and orderly use of manpower. The draft meant the power to plan how manpower was mobilized. Planning required the growth of a bureaucracy, and to be efficient in national mobilization, it had to share another modernizing trend, centralization of authority.[14]

The response to modernization by American mobilizers offers some insight into the limits of this process. The twentieth-century bureaucratic planner in the United States sought to construct a draft system that dealt with America's pluralism of values and vibrant individualism. In the process of modernization and planning for total war the army manpower experts offered a selective service system that placed power in the hands of local community draft boards, minimizing the centralized bureaucracy. Despite the trend of modernization, American localism remained strong. More than reflecting an anachronism, local draft boards expressed the continued strains of pluralistic values and individualism. Selective Service showed how the "ideal of voluntary cooperation among dedicated professionals could combine order and efficiency without coercion." In a 6 March 1967 message on Selective Service, President Lyndon Johnson said: "The draft board concept is built on a uniquely American belief—that local citizens can perform a valuable service to the Government and at the same time personalize the Government's procedures. . . . We cannot lightly discard an institution with so valuable a record of effectiveness and integrity."[15]

Ironically, shortly after Johnson's speech, the draft began to disintegrate. This collapse occurred in a decade of challenge to the centralizing feature of modernization. Disillusionment with the draft was part of a larger disillusionment—especially by youth—with authority. In the 1960s the revolt against authority contained contradictory impulses. Even as some young rebels demanded that local authority be overturned, that federal civil rights laws be enforced against racist sheriffs, others ranted against central authority controlling the lives of the poor in urban centers and called for empowering local groups. The draft, however, was criticized because of the absence of national guidelines, because the local autonomy of draft boards reflected local prejudices in decisions.

The draft also had an effect on social modernization. If, as one scholar writes, "the mass army as an institution is on the way out,"[16] the disappearance of the draft has more than military implications. The social impact of using a force of volunteers has drawn the attention of many critics. One fear is that the force will be drawn from a narrow, lower-class, ethnically homogeneous section of the population. But, if an all-volunteer force leads to a stratified military service, did the draft contribute to a more socially integrated army?[17]

The social impact of the draft differs in different cultures and contexts. Whether these cultures are industrialized or pastoral, homogenous or pluralistic, is important. One theorist argues that a military draft tends to "flatten stratification" in an oligarchy but heightens stratification in democratic and egalitarian societies.[18] Should the drafted mass army be used in a major war, the promotion of social mobility is enhanced because the military participation rate increases, and replacements are drawn from a wider range of social classes.[19]

As mobilization after World War II in the United States reached fewer people, the drafted population became less representative of the population as a whole. The drafted population during World War II, however, was more representative than that during Korea and Vietnam, even though the selection system remained about the same through all three wars. Induction standards rose after World War II, and the draft was forced to select from a more narrow range of the population. Similarly, the surge of science after the war led to deferments for researchers, further narrowing the pool. Despite this narrowing, however, the armed forces from World War II to 1970 came closer than ever before to being representative of American society. As compared to other nations, the United States had a large variety of classes serving, due mainly to the draft.[20]

Of course the draft did not fall equally upon all segments of society, even in the massive mobilization of World War II. The primary reason had little to do with the mechanics of the draft, but occurred mainly because the classes did not all have equal qualifications for service. It is simply impossible to insure equal risk to the draft given the needs of the armed forces and the vagaries of the civil population. Even the use of a lottery fails to achieve equal risk because the population at risk is already distinguished by age, health, and sex from the population at large.

Although an old and widely used system, the draft came late to the United States. In colonial America there were numerous laws requiring militia duty but nothing resembling the system of national conscription which arose in Europe in the nineteenth century. Not even the American Revolution reversed this local, decentralized concept of militia duty. The American army under Washington was modeled on the professional armies of Europe. Until the Civil War, national military mobilization policy was guided by distrust of professional armies and a desire to keep them small and under civilian control. By 1835 only five-one-hundredth of 1 percent of the population was in the Regular Army. Geographical location and weak neighbors made it unnecessary for America to develop a mass army. By the time the Mexican War began in 1846 the militia had been replaced by a state national guard service of volunteers. Although a national draft did appear during the Civil War in both the North and South, it was used primarily as an inducement to raise bounties for volunteers. Use of substitutes and buying exemptions insured that the draft had only minimal effect on society.[21]

By the end of the nineteenth century several military planners were considering conscription. Emory Upton's writings on the Civil War made clear the value of being able to draft masses of men for the slugging tactics of modern war, and Elihu Root, appointed secretary of war in 1899, promoted recognition of the National Guard as the first line reserve of the Regular Army with the Dick Act. In the period before World War I, General Leonard Wood proselytized the idea of a mass army which would be filled through a national draft with a two-year tour of duty for the draftee.

As planning proceeded in the new General Staff of the army, certain key ideas emerged on how an American draft could work. Planners stressed that the draft had to be decentralized rather than run entirely from Washington, a characteristic drawn from the militia tradition. Also, the draft had to be run at the local level by civilians, not by military men as had been the case in the Civil War. Such an arrangement would draw into the system the power structure of local communities and would play upon the myth of everyman being able to make government decisions. Finally, drawing upon the myth of egalitarianism, the draft should offer no class or group deferments, and no substitutes or bounties should be allowed.[22]

The draft used in World War I grew out of these ideas and the desire of a new power elite in the nation to insure protection for the American economy. A selective draft made possible the efficient use of manpower, in keeping with the ethos of modern business, and also allowed for a mass army. The Selective Service System created at that time was the precursor of the system that functioned from 1940 to 1973.[23]

From 1940 to 1973 the draft system worked almost continuously, even when the nation was at peace. A study of this draft should reveal insights into the larger political culture.[24] The following pages will consider several paradoxes of the American draft. How was it that an institution that forced men into military service endured for so long in a culture that worshipped freedom? One can understand conscription in time of national emergency, such as World War II, but the American draft system lasted for over thirty years. This institution existed in a state of perpetual tension with American culture, yet the tension was manageable. In the following pages I explain what devices, compromises, and adjustments were used in different historical contexts to avoid rupture of the association between conscription and culture. The following is an account of a system based on principles of local control, of decentralization, and of nineteenth-century values, a system that responded to pressure from various interests by continually modifying the ideal of universality of service.

An ambiguity of the draft is evident in the very name of the institution that ran it—"Selective Service." The name implies scientific management of manpower as promoted by the efficiency experts of modernization, although at the same time it conveys the universal obligation of service. Both principles, scientific selection and egalitarian service, represent basic values in the culture of twentieth-century America. Keeping these two principles in uncomfortable union was possible until 1970. Even then, the system could have survived, but a new political context led to the triumph of the democratic idea of egalitarianism in the form of a volunteer force. Yet the survival of the draft for so long reveals much about how American culture, in its political, military, and social dimensions, operated to accommodate such a contradiction of values.

Many obvious questions arise in trying to understand the durability of the draft. Who was drafted, and who escaped the draft? Is it possible to distinguish between the social impact of war and the impact of the draft? What do we mean by politics influencing the draft? How did the system function under the influence of several different types of politics: bureaucratic politics in struggles with the armed forces, for example? presidential politics, as each leader saw the system fulfilling different needs? interest-group politics, as educators and scientists fought to protect their clients from conscription?[25]

Perhaps most vexing was the problem of measuring the success of the draft. An enormous amount of ink was spilled during the 1960s and 1970s over the inequity of the draft. Critics denounced it as promoting injustice by taking certain men and deferring others. Military strategists called the draft an anachronism from the age of mass armies, an age made irrelevant by the development of nuclear missiles. In reply, defenders pointed out that the draft had always met the demands of the armed forces to defend the country. Both sides were right, and both were wrong. Their answers reflected different points of view about the role of the military, about current military policy, about foreign policy, and about social justice.

Deferment policy was a particularly troublesome topic. There were only so many eligible men, and if the draft allowed one person to stay in school, then another person had to go instead.

Another problem was explaining the rapid decline of the draft, which had existed since 1940 (except for 1947). Polls indicated high approval by the public, and draft renewal passed Congress every four years with little partisan opposition. The draft had met the calls by the armed forces and had proved remarkably flexible. An English scholar wrote in admiration: "The U.S. can raise or lower the number of men it keeps in uniform with much less effort than most other countries can."[26]

Deferments allowed the draft to live up to its "selective" title. Economic, scientific, and educational institutions saw their interest respected in regulations. Congress approved of the draft for various reasons, but that it was inexpensive was a particularly strong selling point. Compared to the cost of higher pay for enlisted men, the draft simply taxed young men a service time in exchange for the security that had been bought by earlier generations of males. The presidents and the military felt the draft was successful, and even the young draft-age men seemed to think the system was fair until the 1960s. The draft seemed to have a strong claim to legitimacy as a permanent American institution, yet by 1973 the draft was dead.

Knowledge of how the draft worked in a variety of historical contexts cannot answer all these questions, but it can lead to informed judgment on the institution. As a history of the draft, this study assumes that any evaluation reflects the dynamic qualities of the institution, of the society, and of the historical context.[27]

2

Creating
Conscription,
1940–1941

In the 1930s most people in the world were concerned with economic problems. For Europeans the concern had begun in the 1920s; for the United States in the 1930s. The world economic crisis had contributed to the rise to power of Hitler in Germany, Mussolini in Italy, and militarist rule in Japan.

Few Americans saw any reason to worry as Germany occupied the Rhineland, the Japanese annexed Manchuria, and Mussolini attacked Ethiopia. When war finally came to Europe on 1 September 1939, as German troops invaded Poland, the Regular Army of the United States of America consisted of 187,893 men. Behind this paltry array stood 199,491 partially trained members of the National Guard. The entire force was spread across the nation and the Pacific. Equipment was obsolete, and training readiness was marginal. When President Franklin Roosevelt declared a limited national emergency in September 1939, American military expansion began in earnest. By the end of November Congress had authorized expansion of the Regular Army and enlisted strength rose to 200,390. This modest increase probably did not impress Hitler who had used 63 divisions to overrun Poland in a month.

By 22 June 1940 the formidable German force had achieved one of the most impressive victories in European history. Hitler's troops swept through the low countries and overran France in less than two months, and the rapidity of the advance against the supposedly formidable forces of France and Britain sent a shock wave through America.

President Roosevelt had begun even earlier a process of educating his fellow citizens to the interrelationship of international and domestic events. Altogether it was a stumbling and indifferent performance, but the increased belligerence of the Axis powers provided incentive when FDR proved hesitant. Roosevelt began to talk rearmament to Americans in early 1938, in an annual message to Congress and at press conferences, but he offered little hope to those, American and European, who wanted a huge ground army capable of intervening in European affairs. Roosevelt promoted hardware rather than manpower. When asked by a reporter if his plans included "drafting manpower, capital and manufacturers," he replied that he disliked the word "drafting" and preferred "mobilization."[1] The president had privately pushed for expansion of the military in November 1938. Unfortunately, his ideas, which stressed the rapid buildup of the army airforce and the navy, clashed with the balanced buildup envisioned in War Department plans.[2]

In May 1940, when enlisted strength in the Regular Army stood at 242,000, the president asked Congress for authority to federalize the National Guard. In the War Department, however, the newly appointed Chief of Staff George C. Marshall revived General Douglas MacArthur's old notion of expanding through the use of volunteers, and a civilian volunteer effort was launched, which, incorporating modern media techniques, was supposed to obtain 400,000 volunteers. Marshall's reason for advocating this outmoded technique of expansion rested upon several premises. He had no desire to call the National Guard to active duty because he did not wish to waste regular cadre or equipment in training. As for using conscription to obtain men in more orderly fashion, neither he nor Roosevelt—both of whom understood the political currents— thought the public or Congress would accept a draft before a declaration of war. Indeed, all planning by the Joint Army Navy Selective Service Committee (JANSSC) of the War Department assumed that the draft law would be passed after war began.[3]

In mid-July 1940 Franklin Roosevelt accepted the nomination of his party for an unprecedented third term, and in his acceptance speech, he remarked that most Americans "are agreed that some form of selection by draft is necessary and fair today as it was in 1917 and 1918." At last the president had publicly endorsed the draft, but neither he nor the War Department had plans for an interventionist army.[4] Defense of the Western Hemisphere was the priority, yet if intervention was required, as became more probable after the fall of France in June, Roosevelt hoped that the American role could be limited to supplying arms. Public opinion, although sympathetic to France and England, supported Roosevelt's position. In this climate neither the president nor the War Department promoted conscription.[5]

Promotion of the draft depended primarily on a small group of eastern elitists who had played a similar role in World War I mobilization. Led by Grenville Clark, prominent eastern attorney and anglophile, and including such nabobs of eastern society as Ralph Lowell of Boston, James Bryant Conant of Harvard, and Harold W. Dodds of Princeton, this group tried to push the president into supporting a draft. When that failed, the Clark lobby worked on Congress until a bill emerged under the sponsorship of Senator Edward R. Burke and Representative James W. Wadsworth.[6]

The Clark effort represented the old Wilsonian anglophilia which had played such an important role in intervention in 1917. The group believed it was the moral responsibility of America to help preserve English civilization from a new barbarism, even if it meant sending boys to fight in Europe. They thought the best method of obtaining the men for a new expeditionary force was the draft. The draft recommended itself on both political and eugenic grounds. Politically, it suggested that the duty to serve was the responsibility of all, or at least all young males. Eugenically, by broadening the base of the force, the United States could avoid the disastrous effects of volunteering by the best and brightest. Economically, the draft provided for government control over who fought in Europe and who contributed at home.[7]

Whatever their motives, the Clark lobby did yeoman work in selling the draft. They worked inside and outside the government. Within the administration, they promoted the appointments of Henry L. Stimson and Robert Patterson as secretary and undersecretary of war, both of whom were sympathetic to the views of Clark. General John M. Palmer, a former associate of Marshall, testified before congressional committees. With the help of Julius Ochs Adler of the *New York Times*, the lobby spread the word across the country to trade papers, American Legion posts, state legislators, chambers of commerce, universities, Rotary clubs, and radio stations. By July 87 percent of the newspaper editors in the nation favored the draft.[8]

When the Clark lobby introduced its draft bill in Congress it met opposition. As late as 14 June 1940 the president still insisted that the "time is not ripe yet." Gallup polls of the same month reported 64

World War I lottery drawing (1918). Courtesy, Selective Service System National Headquarters.

percent in favor of one year's compulsory military training at age twenty for males. Roosevelt's own mail, however, still ran two to one against the draft.[9]

From the perspective of the president and the War Department the introduction of a draft bill would merely provoke isolationist opposition to more essential legislation pending in Congress—legislation providing a budget to purchase arms. But with the fall of France on 22 June 1940 and the appointment of Henry L. Stimson as secretary of war on 20 June a change in planning seemed necessary.

If there were to be a draft bill, Marshall hoped to insure that it was consistent with the draft ideas his staff had been preparing since the mid-1920s. He felt it would be a disaster if all the plans and training done by the JANSSC were made obsolete because the meddling of Clark led to a bill inconsistent with the prior plans.[10] To avoid this catastrophe the War Department established liaison with the Clark group and testified vigorously before congressional hearings on what the final form of the bill should be.[11]

In early July, War Department officials, led by Major Lewis Hershey, an ex–National Guard officer from Indiana, worked out a revision of the initial bill to conform with JANSSC planning. The service liability age was narrowed to 21 to 45; length of training was extended to 12 months; and selectees were all to be given the same pay and benefits. The Clark group did succeed in retaining the provisions for a wide registration, of ages 18 to 65, but the army planned to call only those aged 21 to 31. Most important, the army insisted on cutting the Clark provision for special occupational deferments. No blanket deferments were to be offered.[12]

The principles and ideas behind the Selective Service bill had emerged in 1917, had been refined in the 1920s and 1930s and remained until 1973. First, planners wanted to be fair and democratic, not least of all to ensure votes in Congress. But the terms were useless unless they fit in with specific dimensions of the culture. The first test was whether a productive economy could be maintained as thousands of men were drafted. The basic idea of a "selective" draft was to insure that the home economy would be protected from the reckless volunteering that had caused problems in England. The World War I experience in the United States also revealed many economic errors in mobilization. Planners for the new draft believed that manpower had to be better controlled. They believed, for example, that when the draft began, all volunteering for the service should end.[13]

Army planners called for some central control of manpower, but they did not want a civilian director of labor to have control over military manpower. Planners understood that the draft apparatus would have a serious impact on the work force, but they did not think conscription should be used to control directly civilian labor. They specifically rejected drafting strikers to insure labor stability and believed attention should be paid to the newly acquired political strength of organized labor. In World War I the American Federation of Labor (AFL) had been given a seat on appeal boards of the draft. Planners in 1940 insisted that, while labor might again be officially recognized at the appeal level, the local draft boards should not consist of representatives from economic interest. Such a special interest approach would conflict with the notion of social consensus that the local boards were supposed to embody. The very notion of "selective service" implied that some draft deferments had to be extended to key workers, but planners insisted that the deferments be based on individual merit and decided by the local board.[14]

Such ideas reflected the democratic ideology of planners but said little for their economic wisdom. The American economy had become increasingly complex and interconnected in the twentieth century, and Labor was even more specialized. To expect that local boards, filled with community leaders, could make sensible decisions on economic deferments was unreasonable. Similarly, it was wise for the military to admit that both civilian and military manpower were key ingredients to mobilization. Yet to insist that responsibility for the two be kept distinct only invited problems. One such problem involved the desire to avoid deferments for young male students because such deferments had created trouble in World War I. Yet modern technology had developed rapidly, and both industry and the armed forces required the services of trained, specialized personnel who were products of extensive schooling. There seemed little point in granting a deferment to a technician if there was no protection for someone learning the same technique.

The second test of draft universality involved the social norms of the United States. Planners stressed the importance of universality of service, as befitting a democracy, but certain social as well as economic realities had to be acknowledged. Young married men and fathers posed problems for implementing a universal draft. In World War I much confusion had arisen over claims of dependency by the recently married. Jack Dempsey avoided the draft by claiming to be the sole support of his wife; a claim she disputed. The planners opposed any statutory deferments for fathers or married men, but permitted local boards to acknowledge dependency hardship in individual cases.[15]

Maintaining the spiritual strength of America represented another social consideration of planners. From colonial militia duty through the 1917 draft, the state had accepted the need to provide exemptions for religious ministers and for individuals claiming conscientious objection to killing.[16] While such recognition reflected the importance of religion in the social fabric, refusing to offer a similar avenue to men with religious scruples invited resistance to the draft effort. Drafting pacifists in World War I had proved an administrative burden to the armed forces.[17]

Initially the JANSSC planned to provide religious exemptions through regulations for "duly ordained ministers" of recognized churches.[18] But Army officers soon discovered that the issue was too sensitive to escape a statutory mandate. On 21 November 1939 Monsignor Michael Ready of the National Catholic Welfare Conference approached Secretary of War Harry Woodring to request statutory exemption of ministers and divinity students. Similarly, a pacifist lobby led by Paul C. French argued for expanding the CO clause to men outside of traditional peace churches. The army resisted, but the draft bill was revised in Congress in 1940 to provide for exemption of ministers and divinity students, and the CO provision was broadened to include those who were members of pacifist sects and those who objected because of "religious training and belief." These changes were minor but did remove some flexibility from the execution of the draft under Selective Service. [19]

Another social ideal that controlled planning on the draft was more odious than the special treatment for religion. This ideal was racism. America had continued the racial patterns established after the Civil War with the Jim Crow system, and the armed forces were no different than any other institution in establishing segregated units. In World War I black draftees had provided loyal service, but after the war, the navy had no place for them. In 1932 they were permitted to volunteer only for mess duty. In World War I, a statistical study of draft board action in southern states revealed that blacks had been called at a higher rate than whites. In Alabama 63 percent of the white male population within the eligible age cohort was registered; only 37 percent of the blacks in the group was registered. Yet 27 percent of the white group was inducted, but 32 percent of the black group was called up. A similar pattern emerged in Florida, Louisiana, and South Carolina. Colonel John Langston, a draft official, admitted that the figures suggested that local boards "exaggerated black participation." In 1940 blacks represented 10 percent of the total male population eighteen and over and 8 percent of the 20 to 34 cohort—racism posed a mobilization problem. [20]

When the draft bill arrived for congressional debate Negro leaders pressed for changes. They pressured President Roosevelt into promising black access to all branches and to officer status. The president also promised that blacks would be drafted only in proportion to their percentage in the population, a figure he estimated at 10 percent. In Congress Senator Robert Wagner (D-N.Y.) pushed through an amendment to the draft bill prohibiting any racial bias in the right to volunteer for service, and in the House Representative Hamilton Fish (R-N.Y.) obtained an amendment providing that draftees would be selected without any racial prejudice. In spite of these changes, Jim Crow did not end, although the president met with several leaders, made promises, and appointed one black leader, Dr. Channing H. Tobias, to an executive committee studying proposed draft regulations. [21]

Despite the efforts of civilian and military leaders to accommodate economic and social culture, pushing the draft through Congress was no easy task. In staunch opposition to conscription stood organized labor, most of the major religious groups, and many educational institutions.[22] James F. Byrnes (D-S.C.), Senate majority whip, insisted a peacetime draft did not stand "a chinaman's chance." Opponents resurrected the arguments that had been used in World War I: a draft was unconstitutional; it would destroy democracy and promote militarism; it would encourage war; it meant the end of free labor. John L. Lewis of the Congress of Industrial Organizations (CIO) added that volunteers would suffice and that a draft would interfere with economic mobilization. Dorothy Day, Dorothy Detzer, Oswald G. Villard, and other members of the peace movement added their opposition. The educational community was split, with leaders of elite, established schools supporting the bill and more marginal institutions fearing loss of enrollment.[23]

Attendance in Congress also suffered because debate on the Burke-Wadsworth bill took place during the hot Washington summer. In the Senate several amendments emerged, but only a few survived. Of those that prevailed the most important established a narrow range of registration: ages 21 to 31. Senator Wagner obtained his antidiscrimination clause, and Senator Henry C. Lodge (R-Mass.) succeeded in limiting service of draftees to the Western Hemisphere. Another amendment gave the president power to seize plants needed for defense. Several attempts were made to delay implementation of the draft for up to 60 days, in hopes that voluntary recruitment would remove the need for conscription. But the delaying tactics were rejected, and by the end of August the Senate passed the draft bill 50 to 35.[24]

The House, which had waited for Senate action before even taking up the bill, moved rapidly in early September. The lower chamber retained the administration's wider range of registration at ages 21 to 45. Representatives then rejected the plant seizure amendment adopted by the Senate. More significantly, on 5 September, representatives adopted an amendment by Hamilton Fish of New York to delay the draft for sixty days while seeking 400,000 volunteers. When the bill went to conference, however, the Fish amendment was deleted and the age range was fixed at 21 to 36. After some further modification of a mandatory plant rental clause, the conference bill was passed on 14 September. In the Senate the vote was 47 to 25 and in the House 232 to 124.[25]

Roosevelt signs Burke-Wadsworth Act, 16 September 1940. Courtesy, Selective Service System National Headquarters.

Although the Clark lobby was important, the passage of the peacetime draft bill was mainly a response to the rush of European events. As Germany conquered France in June and began an aerial bombardment of England, American sentiment, in and out of Congress, became more receptive to the draft. The tallies showed party affiliation to be more important than geography and ethnicity, despite studies linking the latter two variables with isolationism. In the Senate 40 Democrats and 7 Republicans supported the bill. In the House 186 Democrats and 46 Republicans approved. Approximately two-thirds of the Republicans in Congress opposed the conference report on the bill.[26]

Yet the passage of the draft bill in September 1940 hardly represented a triumph for executive or party leadership. The War Department had been planning a draft since the mid-1920s, but continued to believe, with Roosevelt, that approval could only be achieved after a declaration of war. Even as Congress debated the bill, Marshall and Hershey expected a voluntary recruitment campaign to precede the draft. Indeed, Hershey had to rewrite quickly all the regulations to accommodate the new reality of a peacetime draft. Similarly, Franklin Roosevelt displayed little leadership in the draft campaign. He did nothing to push the bill through Congress, remaining skeptical of the idea until the last minute. He was campaigning for a third term in office against Wendell Willkie, a popular opponent. Roosevelt had no desire to give Willkie the opportunity to paint the Democrats as a war party because of the draft bill. Although the president endorsed the draft on 19 July when accepting the nomination, by mid-August he was waffling. He encouraged the idea of a delay for volunteers and insisted he preferred a national service bill with men going into a Civilian Conservation Corps. After Willkie finally endorsed the draft bill on 17 August, Roosevelt wrote to a Democratic editor on 26 August that he shared "doubt as to whether a limited form of selective draft will be popular. In fact, it may very easily defeat the Democratic National ticket." But he went on to explain that a recent observation of troop manuevers in upstate New York had impressed him with the need for more equipment, training, and men. The U.S. Army, he was convinced, could not stand up to the Germans because the men were too soft.[27] Before they could be toughened with training, the men had to be drafted.

The draft became law on 16 September 1940. This legislation created a system that continued to exist with one short interruption for over 30 years. By and large the War Department was happy with the coverage in the law. The act was designed to raise a large army: a maximum of 900,000 men could be drafted in peacetime. The prologue of the act stated that military service "should be shared generally in accordance with a fair and just system of selective compulsory military training and service." Every male in the United States, including aliens, between the ages of 21 and 36 had to register for the draft, and each was liable, if called, for one year of active duty followed by 10 years of reserve duty. Those inducted under the draft could not be used beyond the Western Hemisphere except in U.S. possessions, including the Philippines.[28] Anyone eligible could volunteer before being called. Volunteering for regular military duty continued even after the draft passed, but one had to volunteer for three years rather than just one year.

To manage the recruitment, the act created a system of selection. There was to be no racial discrimination in the selection and training. Quotas were established for each state and territory based on a formula that provided credit for those already on active duty and based on the total number of men eligible and not deferred. Deferments were offered for certain public officials and whoever the president authorized for the "maintenance of the public health, safety or interest," such as farmers and industrial workers. Religious ministers and those studying for the clergy were also exempted from service, but not registration. All deferments, except those specified in the act, were made on an individual basis. For students the law provided a temporary deferment for one academic year if called prior to 1 July 1941. This exceptional group deferment ended on that date.[29]

Conscientious objectors (COs) were recognized and offered noncombat or alternate civilian service. The justification for a CO claim had to be "by reason of religious training and belief," and it was not limited to members of traditional peace churches. An appeal system was also erected to allow men to dispute all classification by local boards.[30]

The law also provided for reemployment rights for inducted men. Those called up were to be "considered as having been on furlough or leave of absence during his period of active military service" and were to be "restored without loss of seniority" and to benefit from any increases which had accrued during his absence. The director of Selective Service was to oversee this provision and provide reemployment assistance. As for industry, the act empowered the president to require the cooperation of any industry for defense production, which had to take precedent over all other jobs. If denied cooperation, the president could take possession of the plant with just compensation.[31]

To administer the statutory provisions, the act authorized the president to create a Selective Service System. Here the law followed closely the recommendations of the JANSSC. Civilian local boards were established and given responsibility for classification and calls. The law declared that "the decisions of such local boards shall be final except where an appeal is authorized in accordance with such rules and regulations as the President may prescribe." The director of Selective Service could be a military officer detailed to that duty.[32]

Any person who violated the law or regulations prescribed, by refusing to register, or to serve, or provided false information to a local board, or even "knowingly counsels, aids or abets another to evade registration or service" was liable for a fine of not more than $10,000 or imprisonment for five years or both.[33]

The new law resembled the World War I draft, but there were some differences. In contrast to the language of expediency found in the prologue of the 1917 law, the 1940 law suggested that the draft was based on democratic principles and was consistent with those ideals. The reemployment rights granted in the new law were unique. Penal provisions under the new law were to be enforced by civilian agencies rather than the War Department. Provisions for religious exemptions and CO defer-ments were broadened considerably in 1940 and a system of alternate civilian service spelled out in the act. Finally, the president was granted new authority to conscript industry as well as manpower.[34]

Given the history of conscription and the tradition of European mil-itarism, the American draft seemed a model of civilian control. But the law meant little until put into practice by the new Selective Service agency. With the task of drafting almost a million men while the United States remained at peace, the agency anticipated some problems.

Thanks to a civilian lobby, planning by the War Department, and pressure caused by the rapid collapse of France, a draft law existed. The law operated for 14 months before the United States entered World War II, which provided time for the virtues and defects in the Selective Service System to surface. The institution affected every aspect of American life, from the caliber of major league baseball to the reputation of the medical profession, from the survival of liberal arts colleges to the rate of pro-creation by American males. A political scientist observed cynically that the Selective Service was created primarily, according to one theory, to insure public acceptance, with the assumption that efficiency in obtaining men would emerge incidentally.[35]

The theory of draft organization represented a triumph of Jefferson-ianism. Because Americans had great faith in local government and local solutions, the draft was run by local boards, "little groups of neighbors." The first director of the system, Clarence Dykstra, said it was best seen as "supervised decentralization—the selection of men by their neighbors and fellow citizens." National headquarters provided only guidance and general rules.[36]

A national draftee quota was broken down into state quotas and then to local board quotas based on various extenuating circumstances in the smaller units. The values of American society received endorsement through deferments for fathers and married men. The deferment of key workers, religious ministers, and conscientious objectors also fit national mores. Finally, an elaborate appeal system helped to insure that the draft would mesh with existing notions of judicial administration.[37]

The same concern with cultural consistency and public acceptance appeared in launching the draft. After signing the bill into law on 16

September 1940, the president appointed a special advisory committee to scrutinize the plans drawn up by the War Department. But the committee, under the chairmanship of Frederick Osborn, provided only a cursory screening, having been informed that the bill should receive "the quickest possible checks." The momentum of mobilization overcame any serious revision of the War Department plan.[38]

On 16 October 1940, over 16 million young men appeared at precinct election boards across the country to register with the Selective Service. In his proclamation establishing registration day, Roosevelt said the action would proclaim "the singleness of our will and the unity of the nation." The older generation saluted the young in an action that strengthened the resolve to "hold high the torch of freedom in this darkening world." Male citizens between the ages of 21 and 36 were put on the draft rolls.[39]

Once the men had registered, 6,400 local draft boards went into action. The War Department had selected the board members months earlier from lists sent in by governors and state adjutants general. The boards' first step was to send out information forms to each draftee to obtain data needed to classify the men into draft categories.[40] After the classification procedure, each potential draftee received an order number to be used in the national lottery to establish a random selection sequence.

Scheduling the lottery, however, generated some political nervousness. The president was worried about the possible political backlash of holding the lottery so close to election time, because Wendell Willkie had increased his popularity by accusing Roosevelt of leading the nation into war. After signing the draft regulations into law on 4 October, the president inquired about changing the lottery dates of 23 to 28 October to a time after the November election. James Rowe, White House political advisor, and Harold Smith, director of the budget, explained that the public was aware of the planned date and that changing it would only provide Willkie with a chance to "make political capital out of the postponement." Besides, local boards would not use the lottery sequence for draft calls until 8 November, after the election, and any delay would interfere with the army's mobilization schedule. The arguments convinced Roosevelt, and he agreed to participate personally in the lottery on 29 October 1940.[41]

Selective Service organized the first lottery with the panache of a Hollywood awards ceremony. No pains were spared to convey an image of fairness, integrity, and national importance. Every local board had been limited to a roll of no more than 8,500 registrants, and the purpose of the lottery was to establish the selection sequence to be followed at the local level. The drawing thus had to provide 8,500 random numbers. To be on the safe side, Selective Service decided to provide 9,000 numbers. Clerks stuffed opaque capsules with the numbers 1 to 9,000 and then locked them in government vaults until lottery day.[42]

On 29 October 1940, the Selective Service auditorium was filled with reporters and dignitaries. The War Department arranged for war planes to fly over the scene, and some 500 veterans provided an honor guard for those carrying the capsules. President Roosevelt appeared to offer a benediction on the proceedings. He referred to this "most solemn ceremony," calling it a muster of resources and the democratic means of mobilizing. He also read messages from individuals representing three major religious groups in the country, all of whom endorsed the proceedings. The scene resembled a liturgical ritual of national faith. The capsules went into the same fishbowl used for selection in World War I as officials stressed historical continuity. Secretary Stimson, slated to draw the first number, was blindfolded with cloth taken from a chair used at the signing of the Declaration of Independence, and the ladle used to stir the capsules was made from the wood of one of the rafters of Independence Hall. The scene reeked with American heritage.

Stimson reached into the bowl and withdrew a capsule from which the president read the number 158. In the audience, an ineligible female greeted the number with a screech. After the first number the president and Stimson departed and lesser dignitaries filed forward to pull additional numbers. As each number was called it was recorded by a camera and then placed on a sheet of cardboard in a continuous sequence. The cardboard was also photographed. This master record, with 100 numbers to each sheet, would guide local boards. Seventeen hours later, Hershey selected the last capsule. To insure integrity, officials had not permitted any break in the proceedings, saying the drawing "must go on in full view of the multitude until it is completed." Unfortunately, when the lottery ended, six numbers remained unrecorded. Hershey quickly wrote down the errant numbers and held a mini-lottery. Despite the theatrics and precautions, there had been a snafu. Statisticians also complained that a random selection was impossible with a constantly shrinking total of capsules. Rumors arose that a Detroit youth who had number 158 might sue for a recount. What had begun in the grandiose had ended in farce.[43]

Secretary of War Henry Stimson draws capsules for draft lottery (1940). Courtesy, Selective Service System National Headquarters.

Lieutenant Colonel Hershey had been running the draft bureaucracy with an unofficial mandate from Roosevelt through Stimson, but after the law had been passed and inductions were about to begin, the president had to pick a permanent director. The law allowed either a civilian or a military man, and in the end the president decided to pick a civilian because he wished to emphasize that the draft was a civic operation, not a military one. Draftees remained civilians until inducted by the armed forces. On 12 October Clarence Dykstra, president of the University of Wisconsin, accepted Roosevelt's offer of the directorship. Dykstra had credentials as a progressive and had been active in both academic and civic affairs. So routine was the choice that the Senate barely mustered a quorum to confirm him on 15 October. At Stimson's urging, Roosevelt appointed Hershey deputy director.[44]

Ironically, national headquarters had already been organized by the War Department, and it consisted of military officers earmarked earlier for this duty. Dykstra was a civilian sitting on the top of a military cadre. But because of the decentralized character of the draft much responsibility fell to the governors. Roosevelt wrote them in late September and called upon them to appoint state directors and local board members who had the confidence of the local communities. In fact, this directive was mere window dressing as the War Department had worked with state adjutants general and had developed a list of potential local board members throughout the country. The volunteers came from a variety of local organizations, some religious, some ethnic, but most from the American Legion and the chambers of commerce. Even local political organizations provided names. In a few areas, such as New York City, the mayor had to appeal publicly for men to accept this nonpaying, thankless task. When the all-male character of the membership drew complaints, Dykstra explained to Susan M. Kingsbury of the National Committee on Economic and Legal Status of Women, that "at times the work of the members of the local boards may become quite strenuous and . . . it would be inadvisable to impose such obligations upon women." Also, members had to check on delicate physical defects of draftees. But the law itself did not limit membership on the boards to males.[45]

The mechanics of obtaining men through local boards was straightforward. The War Department informed the director of the total number of men needed for a particular month. Generally, this figure arrived six weeks ahead of the date for induction. The director applied a formula to determine how many men would come from each state and each local board. The gross quota for a particular state came from dividing the sum of all men available for military service, after credits for deferments, by the sum of men available from all states. From the gross quota was subtracted state citizens in the National Guard or reserve or those on active duty. The resulting figure was multiplied by a fraction, the numerator of which was the number of registrants in any one local board area and the denominator of which was the number of registrants in the state. These estimates were sent to the War Department, and each corps area was authorized to call upon the states in its area to provide their quota. The state director of Selective Service, using a similar formula, broke up the corps requisition into quotas for each local board.[46]

After assigning a local draft call number based on the master roster, the local board mailed out a questionnaire to each registrant. This form asked for data on marital status and dependents, prior military service, present occupation, education, court record, and physical condition. Based on the information supplied by the registrant, the local board classified each registrant according to availability, with 1-A representing those immediately available and 4-F representing those unfit to serve. Men with dependents, vital jobs, or other qualifying characteristics which might limit their availability fell into intermediate categories.

A classification was dynamic. For example, in one sitting of the local board for Franklin County, Massachusetts, the members shifted one registrant from 2-A to 1-A because his brother had gone back to work. Another man was put in 2-A to finish a college course. Another was held in limbo while the board awaited a confirmation of his student status from a college. There was little urgency in classification action at that time because the nation was at peace and several hundred thousand men had already volunteered. In Washington, D.C., the local quota was for 51 men but over 1,000 volunteered.[47]

Draft officials went to extraordinary lengths during the first months of operation to insure that the system met the expectations of the American people. Chief among these expectations was that the draft represent a democratic approach to selection. With the draft a reality Col. John D. Langston reminded the War Department of the need "to mould public opinion in support of Selective Service." Above all he urged a constant stream of press releases on how well the system was doing.[48]

As part of the selling campaign, the local communities and the War Department cooperated in staging elaborate ceremonies celebrating what the *New York Times* called "the pioneers of a mighty army." At Fort Dix, New Jersey, the first draftees were met at the train by a regimental band and a color guard. Down south Clyde O. Brown, a farm boy from Georgia, received the honor of representing the inductees from eight southern states. The governor and thousands of VIPs joined in the celebration. Unfortunately, Brown turned out to be no raw recruit but a grizzled veteran who had served several years in the infantry and been honorably discharged. Other promotional efforts included a comic strip entitled "Draftie." Bob Hope and Dorothy Lamour appeared in a movie called *Caught in the Draft*, which one critic called a "wacky farce" on the futility of avoiding the call. A public poll in December 1940 showed that 92 percent of the population felt the draft was being handled fairly and 89 percent thought it was a good idea. A year earlier only 35 percent had approved of the idea. A poll of draft age males found 76 percent approving the draft. Older people felt it would help the boys mature and solve the unemployment problem.[49]

Building on the good will, Selective Service publicized the effect of the draft on both the low and the mighty in American society. Americans

Sergeant Alvin C. York chairs local board. Courtesy, Selective Service System National Headquarters.

laughed to read that young King Peter of Nazi-occupied Yugoslavia vowed never to dance again until his nation was free. But in New York City, Wong Yee Choy, a Chinese baker who spoke no English, was so anxious to fight the Nazis that he volunteered as the first draftee at local board number 1. Press coverage also followed the appearance of Benson Ford, Henry Ford's grandson, before a local board. His rejection for physical reasons was announced to the world, as was a deferment for Nelson Rockefeller. But Selective Service inducted William McChesney Martin, the president of the New York Stock Exchange. He exchanged his salary of $4,000 a month for a private's pay of $21 a month. The *New York Times* editorialized that the public needed assurance that the draft was "absolutely democratic and made no distinction between men of different social ranks or economic status."[50] Information used for claiming deferments became public knowledge.

The press and public took a lively interest in the draft status of athletic heroes and movie stars. When the draft first began, baseball owners offered the usual expression of patriotic pieties. Warren Giles of Cincinnati swore that the star would "go just as quickly as the bat boy," and that baseball wanted no special treatment. Harry Grabiner of the White Sox, however, pointed out that the public still needed some amusement. Tom Yawkey of the Red Sox opposed exemptions but worried over the loss of Dom DiMaggio and Ted Williams. The owners voted on 11 December that any player subject to the draft should go on a national service list so that clubs interested in buying or selling such an individual would know of his vulnerability. Men on the list would not count against the club player limit.[51]

Bob Feller of the Cleveland Indians and Phil Rizzuto of the Yankees were classified as 1-A. Probably no star received more attention than Hank Greenberg, the Detroit slugger and most valuable player. When first asked, Greenberg admitted being 1-A and insisted he would not ask for a deferment. Then reporters discovered that he had asked for an occupational deferment or a delay so he could play the entire season. The local board denied the application, and Greenberg, although 30 years old and scheduled to earn $55,000, was inducted. Fighter Joe Louis, the Brown Bomber, lost his dependent deferment when his wife began divorce proceedings. Joe reassured his fans that "I'm ready to go anytime. I'll take anything they give me." On a less serious note, in Austin, Minnesota, the star high school fullback had to leave town when his draft board reported he was playing under an assumed name and was in reality 23 years old.[52]

As the stars began disappearing, several baseball owners began to reconsider their initial enthusiasm for the draft. Larry MacPhail of the Brooklyn Dodgers told the press that the draft was unfair to players, depriving them of a substantial income. In his opinion, baseball players should be given the same deferment privileges as scientists and physicians. Clark Griffith of the Washington Senators wrote to presidential aide Gen. Edwin M. Watson suggesting that a drill sergeant be assigned to each club so that the players could pick up military training while continuing to play. After all, he wrote, "baseball is a semi-public institution." At first Selective Service seemed receptive to such arguments and sent out a memo to local boards saying that players called for induction during the season might be granted a 60-day postponement because of hardship. But the public denounced such special treatment, and the War Department finally adopted a policy which allowed them to take some celebrities even if they failed to meet all standards, thus serving public opinion and preserving the myth of egalitarianism. [53]

Preserving myths proved difficult because of the reality of the war. It was true that, of voters in their twenties, 86 percent favored the draft, while only 14 percent opposed it. But other polls showed that 90 percent of all youth were opposed to entering the war. A Youth Congress in Washington and a Youth Committee against War opposed the draft as a threat to civil liberties. Several divinity students in New York refused to register, and Norman Thomas, leader of the Socialist party, called for repeal of the law. In January 1941 5,000 students formed the Student Defenders of Democracy to resist induction. [54]

Arguments against the draft ranged from threats to civil liberties to violations of the Constitution, although the Supreme Court had upheld the constitutionality of the draft in 1918. In 1941 the courts reaffirmed the right of the government to impose conscription even though there had been no declaration of war. The Third Circuit Court of Appeals held that the nation was "not precluded from preparing for battle . . . until such time as our preparations would be too late." The court upheld the conviction of five draft objectors for failure to register. [55] Legal protesters were few. More problems arose from those who simply tried to evade the system.

Selective Service relied more upon peer pressure than law to force men to cooperate, and sometimes the pressure bordered on vigilantism. In World War I civilians took suspects into custody for the police. Mass raids were conducted in some urban centers to round up men, who were then held until they could produce their draft cards. In November 1940 teams of volunteers assisted local boards in checking on men within the liable age categories. The director of the New York City draft used members of veteran organizations such as the American Legion to help. One official said "It will be a grand thing to get one conviction."[56]

By June 1941 the government had obtained only 116 convictions for violations of the act after over 10,000 investigations. The theory behind prosecution was not punishment but social coercion. Selective Service gained little from putting men into jail, and in January 1941 Roosevelt signed an executive order providing parole into the Armed Forces for any man convicted of violating the draft law. Selective Service wanted cooperation from the Justice Department, but local boards were instructed not to aid in apprehending fugitives. For example, boards should not draft a man wanted for forgery just to permit apprehension by the sheriff.[57]

Local boards had enough problems without having to act as deputies. Behavior patterns of those trying to avoid the draft ranged from threatening physical violence to draft officials to outright bribes. In several cities relatives of draftees offered from $100 to $1,000 to local board members to obtain deferments. In Philadelphia and New York local board clerks extorted money from registrants with promises of deferments. One local board chairman received a two-year jail sentence for accepting bribes. But incidents of this sort were relatively rare.[58]

Serious problems arose from the decentralized nature of the system and from attempts made to minimize the draft's impact on the existing social structure. Thousands of registrants had to be processed and classified. Classification was made more difficult as a variety of groups demanded blanket deferments for their workers, students, or husbands, although such an action was specifically prohibited by the law.

The Jeffersonian strength of the system, which invested classification power on local boards, insured that the landscape of decisions reflected the many terrains of the nation itself. Variations in interpreting the rules and variations in local conditions led to different priorities in each area, and appeal boards, one for each 600,000 of the draft population, were supposed to smooth out any inconsistencies. The system must have worked satisfactorily, because by March 1941 only 10 draftees out of some 2.6 million classified had appealed their classification to the final authority, the president.[59]

But the myth of an egalitarian draft barely survived the passage of the law itself. The first and most troublesome conflict in values arose over the principle that all men were equally liable. All men were not even eligible. The law specified that the draft should apply only to men in a specific age group. Within the male age cohort of liability (21 to 36), however, the law made provisions for the president to offer deferments on the basis of social and economic values. Section 5e of the law authorized the president to provide deferments "of those men in a status with respect to persons dependent upon them for support which renders their deferment advisable."[60]

Selective Service interpreted the language of the law to mean that single men were called first. In 1941 the inequity of the policy drew little attention. The scheme reflected deeply held values of American society: women were too weak to fight, and the American patriarchal home was the bedrock of the Republic. Mayors, social workers, Eleanor Roosevelt, and army officials all supported the deferment of married men. Although there was no official group deferment, married men were usually granted deferments if they could establish that others were dependent upon them for sustenance. Local boards at first considered a working wife evidence of no dependency, but Major Gordon Shaw of Selective Service (SS) headquarters explained that "to say that a man is to be called because his wife and children would not starve is to deny that the wife and children depend upon him for more than his pocketbook. It is to deny his moral leadership and protection." Headquarters urged local boards to be lenient with heads of families. If a man married after registering for the draft the board should assure itself that this step was a natural one and not one made just to avoid the draft.[61]

Such a policy was popular with the military because the army had little interest in older men or men with dependents. But by November 1941 the deferment rate for dependency was running at 70 percent, and Hershey warned that the American family must assume more responsibility for national defense. Local boards were inconsistent. One board in Cleveland insisted that all men with working wives should be drafted. In North Carolina local boards, demanding more than mere marriage, insisted that there be a harmonious relationship and that no wastrels be deferred just because they had wives. In another state a local board removed a dependency deferment when the draftee's mother complained of failure of support. In 1939 there were 1,404,000 marriages of those of all ages. In 1940 among the age cohort 18 to 29 there were just over 5 million marriages.[62]

The draft also affirmed traditionally held American values about women. The law specified that only males were eligible for the draft.

When Eleanor Roosevelt and other female leaders sought a larger role for women in the operation of Selective Service, they met a stone wall. Hershey kept insisting that women should concentrate on running their homes and setting moral examples. Dykstra explained that women could not serve on local boards because physical questions would prove embarrassing for them. At best women might serve as clerks and as associate members to advisory boards. Much consternation arose when a woman from Austin, Minnesota, managed to register for the draft. For the duration of World War II, conscription was a male enterprise.[63]

Although the draft affirmed some traditional values, its impact in other areas was radical. For example, it had several implications for American medicine. First, the draft threatened to reduce the number of civilian physicians and medical students. Second, the local physician became an appendage of the draft apparatus, performing examinations on inductees for local boards. Finally, American physicians again confronted the threat of a national health program. Most Americans in 1940 believed that they enjoyed the best health and medical care in the world. Such pieties had been a constant refrain from the American Medical Association (AMA) for years, and longevity figures were frequently displayed as final proof. This rhetoric had helped to derail President Roosevelt's attempts to incorporate a health insurance program in his New Deal in 1935.[64]

The inauguration of the draft in late 1940, however, had raised a disturbing specter. Induction involved submitting each draftee to a physical exam at the local board level. These exams were initially comprehensive and conducted by volunteer local physicians. The standards of the exams followed the guidelines for eligibility established by the armed forces. If the draftee passed this initial screening, he was sent on to an army induction center where another exam was conducted by military personnel. This double examination, in theory, was to help insure that the World War I waste caused by in-service disability would be reduced. Early reports on the results of these exams shocked many Americans. Army induction authorities, receiving men already passed by local board physicians, had expected to weed out only about 2 percent more. Instead they found about 15 percent of the new men failing the physical and mental exams. More astonishing, local boards had already weeded out over 40 percent for obvious physical reasons. Local board physicians reported that many early volunteers were so anxious to pass their physicals that they concealed defects. The rejection rate was 50 percent of selectees by the summer of 1941. In the period 15 May to 15 July 1941 some 93,111 registrants in 47 states were rejected for failing to meet the fourth-grade-level literacy requirement established by the army. In some southern states rejection for syphilis ran almost 30 percent among Negroes. Men under 26 were rejected at only a 24 percent rate.[65]

There were many different reactions to these figures. Hershey and other public officials called the results "a national disgrace." Eleanor Roosevelt said she hoped that the information would "give impetus to the movement for a comprehensive and nationwide health program." The president must have been reminded of his early failure to achieve such an objective. Walter West, executive secretary of the American Association of Social Workers, blamed the rejections on "inadequate public assistance programs." Lloyd R. Williams, a Connecticut agricultural official, insisted that more food production was the only solution. The national nutritional conference argued that lack of attention to a proper diet was to blame. The medical profession responded by blaming everything but deficient medical care, and Dr. Morris Fishbein of the American Medical Association claimed that army induction standards were too high. Dr. Roger I. Lee, president-elect of the American College of Physicians, also said regulations were "too rigid." Where Surgeon General Thomas Parran saw a "national disgrace," Lee saw picky rules on teeth and eyesight. The steady fall in death rates, he insisted, showed that "the American people today are healthier than ever before." The argument over cause and remedy continued throughout the war with only a modest effect upon the health delivery system.[66]

Selective Service went about improving its liaisons with the medical profession. A medical advisory council appeared at national headquarters, and field organizations of medical examiners and medical advisory specialist boards were formed in each state. By the summer of 1941 some 33,000 physicians and dentists were working with the draft, and an effort was made to have the local board exam correspond more closely to the military exam. Too many men were passing at the local board, resigning their jobs, and then being turned back by army physicians. Most men were being rejected because of poor teeth, eyes, feet, or illiteracy. On 13 March 1941 dental standards were lowered. A dentist was appointed to every local board and a committee on dentistry emerged at national headquarters.[67]

In short order a system was established to mobilize physicians. The armed forces offered commissions to physicians, but those who remained at home enjoyed protection from the draft. Selective Service, despite the prohibition against blanket deferments, provided deferments to most local physicians, to faculty of medical schools, to medical students, and even, for a few years, to premed students. Such protection flowed from the close association and cooperation that developed between the draft agency and the medical profession. Perhaps no other profession enjoyed such advantageous relations with the government or experienced so little dislocation as a consequence of mobilization.[68]

The government tried to launch a rehabilitation program to salvage more men for the draft. To many citizens and to the officials of Selective Service an obvious remedy for physical problems was a tour in the army. Early reports from boot camp indicated that men gained weight and were in better condition than when they left civilian life. But Secretary Stimson and other military officials had no interest in using military resources to improve national health. Neither would the War Department consider lowering induction standards.[69]

By summer 1941, however, public pressure demanded action on rehabilitation. National headquarters informed local boards that, with the consent of the draftee, information could be released to social agencies working to rehabilitate rejectees. By August the rejection rate had climbed to over 40 percent and the Commission on Physical Rehabilitation of the Federal Security Agency (FSA) began urging a national program. Paul McNutt, head of the FSA, also spoke up for a national program when he found that the Army refused to lower standards and had no time for in-service treatment.[70]

Finally, on 3 October the president addressed the issue at a press conference. He had found the rejection figures so disturbing that he asked for a recheck. Now the figure had reached 50 percent of those examined, which was a 20 percent increase since July. Roosevelt rejected the argument made by Dr. Fishbein and others of the AMA that the army standards were too high. Some 1 million men had been rejected out of the first 2 million examined. Hershey wrote Roosevelt that approximately 20 percent could be rehabilitated for general service because the defects were mainly hernias, bad teeth, bad eyes, and other minor defects.[71]

On 10 October 1941 Roosevelt announced the launching of a national program of rehabilitation for draft rejectees. The target was the 200,000 men who had been certified by local boards as suitable for full recovery and induction. Local physicians and dentists would give treatment at the expense of the federal government. The president insisted that this was merely a first step and that something broader and more permanent would follow. The draft had thus helped resurrect the idea of a national health plan.[72]

At first Roosevelt wanted McNutt and a special committee to assume responsibility for the rehabilitation program and use the facilities of the Civilian Conservation Corps. But Selective Service had already established a plan with the close cooperation of AMA officials. Hershey explained to the president that it was not "practical to use two agencies simultaneously in the limited field of rehabilitation." Instead, Hershey offered an executive order which authorized the Selective Service to plan, establish, and carry out the program and even engage in education rehabilitation. When the Japanese bombed Pearl Harbor the plan went on the shelf, but continued high rejections insured that this social issue would reemerge after the war.[73]

In addition to the impact on social institutions, the pre-war draft also affected the economy. In 1940, despite New Deal efforts, there were still 8,120,000 people unemployed in the United States, about 14.6 percent of the entire work force. Most experts expected the draft to affect most young unemployed men. Alvin E. Dodd, president of the American Management Association, warned businesses to continue to hire and train young males even if they were liable for the draft because trained manpower would be needed to cope with the expansion of defense industry.[74]

Despite planning by military leaders, America embarked upon the draft with few clear ideas on how the conflict would affect the burgeoning war economy. With remarkable indifference, the administration launched a process by which thousands of young men were soon withdrawn from the work force. Symbolic of this carelessness was the very structure of government manpower management. The military draft under Selective Service was totally independent of the government agencies responsible for industrial production and manpower. As withdrawals began from the private work force, many big companies established programs by which drafted employees could continue to receive compensation while training. Henry Ford announced that "every young man taken out of a good job for compulsory military training should be paid $5 a day." Such generosity continued even as the draft made more serious inroads into industrial personnel. On 28 October 1940 Director Dykstra assured employers that their production would not be hurt by the draft because local boards knew that defense production had priority. But this idealism soon ended.[75]

By early 1941 employers began to complain at the loss of key workers. Local boards apparently refused to give industry the type of priority promised by Dykstra. Social values, such as dependency, carried more weight with the government than economic factors. Selective Service headquarters reacted to the problem by issuing a stream of directives emphasizing the need for "selective" manpower management. As Hershey explained, the system was in a position to impose manpower controls over the entire economy. But such power had to be exercised with recognition of the need for key workers as well as for soldiers.

Few signs of such recognition appeared. Local boards refused to relinquish their classification authority to Washington, even at the behest of the president and military officials. Although elaborate forms and procedures were established to insure that job deferments went only to the deserving, the complaints continued throughout the war. Sidney Hillman of the Office of Production Management complained that skilled metal workers were being drafted, and Secretary of Agriculture Claude Wickard worried at the loss of vital farm workers.[76]

Planners of the draft had assumed that voluntary cooperation would insure compliance with directives from Washington. Management would cooperate by requesting deferments only for essential, irreplaceable workers. Local boards would cooperate by offering deferments on an individual basis to key workers in industry. Blanket deferments for workers were forbidden by law, and the government expected local boards to exercise skill in selecting only those men whose induction would not adversely affect the economy. Such cooperation was to flow from the decentralized organization of the draft. Local boards were staffed by community leaders, many of them businessmen who would recognize those who were indispensable in the local plants. The boards were authorized to offer delays or postponements to key workers so that replacements could be trained. Regional appeal boards had representatives from labor and industry, and all drafted workers were guaranteed reemployment in their old jobs when released from training.[77]

In practice, however, managers sought to protect all of their workers, rather than just a few key men. War contracts rolled in and plants began to expand. Managers sought to hoard workers for the expected boom years ahead. Local boards, although filled with business leaders, displayed a ruthless social bias and refused to offer deferments to key workers if it meant that a young father or married man had to be inducted. As for reemployment rights, in practice it proved impossible to guarantee a returning veteran his old job because many plants had been reshaped by military contracts.

Organized labor had opposed the draft. Conscription historically fell disproportionally upon the working man, and labor leaders had no reason to expect any changes in the new system. During the debate on the 1940 bill William Green and John L. Lewis had both been strong opponents.[78] As the draft got under way, labor leaders saw their worst fears realized: the Selective Service system proved no friend of labor.

Draft planners in the 1930s had recognized the importance of obtaining cooperation from union leaders. But the military officers emphatically rejected establishing draft boards on the basis of class. Hershey argued convincingly that board members should see themselves as representing America first and not certain classes. Patriotism and unity were the watchwords for mobilization. Yet the very system of selection for local board members insured that business interests were overrepresented and labor underrepresented. This arrangement reflected the distribution of power and influence in communities. Businessmen on local boards, of course, were not supposed to act as businessmen but as Americans.[79]

This idea was not easily accepted. When Governor Lauren D. Dickinson of Michigan failed to appoint any labor leaders to local boards, unions complained to the White House. The president asked the War Department to obtain fair representation. Director Dykstra, simultaneously, warned local and appeal-board members against "occupational partisanship." Only state appeal boards were supposed to have membership from various sectors of the economy and society. Even here Dykstra emphasized that this did not mean "that the member appointed from labor is appointed simply to represent the interests of labor, in the sense of being the partisan advocate of labor." The same was true of the business representative. But not all states complied with the requirement of having various interests represented on appeal boards. One governor appointed as the labor representative a man who had at one time been a worker.[80]

Such an attitude insured that, as new war industries cranked up in 1941, labor disputes multiplied. Almost immediately local draft boards became entangled in the unrest. When the Congress of Industrial Organizations (CIO) threatened to strike the Ryan Aeronautical Company of

San Diego, the local board chairman threatened to draft all strikers. Richard Frankensteen, CIO negotiator, protested to Roosevelt, who passed the complaint on to Hershey. Admitting ignorance of the details, Hershey insisted it was "obviously untrue" to say that a worker automatically lost his job deferment if he went out on strike. Deferments were granted for skills as well as jobs. The man who struck retained his skill and did not quit his job in conventional terms. The Selective Service, said Hershey, was not designed to intimidate workers.[81]

Hershey's attempt to curtail antistrike activity by boards moved against a tide of public and congressional opinion. Even when he ordered state directors to investigate actions by local boards, he found his influence limited. Local board chairmen and some state directors still drafted strikers. National headquarters might insist that the striker still possessed his skill and should be deemed only temporarily out of work, but local boards refused to cooperate.[82]

By spring 1941 several congressional bills were awaiting action, all aimed at using the Selective Service to crush labor unrest. Senator Tom Connally of Texas wanted to amend the Russell-Overton bill to permit the government to take over any plant in which either labor or management hampered production. Other pending resolutions made it illegal for draft-age men to strike. Representative Hatton Sumners (D-Tex.) said his judiciary committee would recommend the death penalty for any man interfering with defense industry.[83]

But Roosevelt had no intention of allowing Congress to run amuck with antilabor legislation. Without waiting for a reckless bill which he might have to veto, the president issued an executive order on 9 June 1941 authorizing federal troops to occupy a strike-bound aviation plant in Los Angeles. Stimson, meanwhile, put pressure on Hershey to insure that the draft would in fact be used to frighten workers away from strikes. On the same day as Roosevelt's executive order, draft headquarters issued orders to local boards to reclassify any registrant, deferred for his occupation, who ceased to work. Daniel Omer, the legal counsel for Selective Service, said the policy was consistent with congressional opinion and would avoid public and political criticism of the system. The draft could not be a haven for strikers with deferments. Even men who had a dependency deferment would be reclassified if they went on strike.[84]

Roosevelt's actions succeeded in deflecting anti-union legislation and reducing labor unrest. The number and size of strikes declined. In June there had been a total of 377,700 man days lost on military contracts. By July the War Department reported 28 strikes in progress involving only 12,600 men working on military items. The American Youth Congress complained that the draft was being used to break strikes and "to deny workers, in effect, the opportunity of improving their conditions."[85]

Neither the president nor Hershey wished the draft to be identified as a tool of management. Labor had convinced the National Defense Mediation Board that in some cases strikes occurred because management had failed to follow government guidelines on wages and hours. To draft striking workers in such cases seemed to be punishing the wrong men. In two strikes during the summer, at Curtiss Wright Propeller Plant and the Kearney Shipbuilding and Dry Dock Corporation, both in New Jersey, Hershey acted to prevent local boards from reclassifying "pending clarification of the situation."[86]

Despite such orders, local boards continued to threaten strikers with reclassification. One local board in Fort Myers, Florida, informed the president that it would issue no more induction papers "as long as John L. Lewis dictates the labor policy of the United States." When Walter P. Reuther, executive with the United Auto Workers, obtained a deferment, public protest reached a crescendo. A Gallup poll of November 1941 revealed that 86 percent of the public thought defense workers should lose their job deferments and be drafted if they struck. Over 70 percent of the public favored passing a law to prohibit strikes in defense plants.[87]

In contrast to labor relations, the draft offered more favorable treatment to the education establishment. The theory behind the draft, in both World War I and World War II, remained consistent. Conscription was sold on the basis of the ideal of equality of sacrifice and on the practical basis of efficient and selective management of manpower. These two notions frequently warred against one another, and nowhere was this more evident than in dealing with education. The 1940 law made clear that, although everyone was liable to serve, the president could provide deferments for men who were "necessary to the maintenance of the public health, safety, or interest." Also, the law specifically provided for temporary deferment, up to 1 July 1941, for men enrolled in colleges for the academic year 1940 through 1941.[88]

When the original draft bill was debated in Congress not all educators sought special treatment for students, but surveys showed a clear majority of presidents of liberal arts colleges favoring the bill. Testimony did reveal division among the faculty, however, less enthusiasm by presidents of state schools, and the expectation of some special defense role for colleges.[89] The American Council on Education published a plan which called upon the government to conserve educational "values and resources and personnel" and said that the excitement of mobilization should not disrupt education.[90]

But after the law went into effect, educators began clamoring for special treatment. New York City found that almost 3,000 of its teachers were draft eligible. The National Association of State Universities came out in "unalterable opposition" to any blanket deferment for students, but a concerted movement for just such treatment was soon launched. Charles Seymour, president of Yale, called on the government to institute a special program by which college students could fulfill their draft obligation by serving four months in the summer at the colleges. He insisted that it was "short-sighted" to draft men who were well along in their training. Seymour's statement was soon followed by cries from professional groups representing engineers and physicians seeking protection for their students, all in the interest of national welfare. As for the students themselves, a poll by the American Association of Junior Colleges found that most believed that they should be deferred through graduation.[91]

The law had provided a postponement only for the school year 1940 through 1941, which was fast coming to a close. But what of the next year? If the draft drained off students and teachers in the summer, many colleges would have to close their doors. Democratic national committeeman Charles Sawyer, thinking of votes, appealed to the president to extend the deferment for the next school year. Charles L. Parsons of the American Chemical Society declared that the draft threatened to deplete the nation's supply of technical and scientific brains. A Gallup poll in April found some 69 percent of the population favored allowing students to graduate before being drafted. The American Council on Education (ACE) urged college officials to work closely with local boards to insure continued deferments through the summer months. Dixon Ryan Fox, president of Union College, appealed to an alumnus, Undersecretary of War Robert Patterson, to save American colleges from destruction. The trustees of over 60 colleges and universities called upon Roosevelt to extend the blanket deferment for another school year and not reduce the draft age to 18.[92]

The administration resisted initially this call believing that granting a special deferment to college students would set a bad precedent and create public relations problems. The issue became pressing when General Hershey and other military leaders began to advocate that the draft age be lowered from 21 to 18. The high rejection rate for physical disabilities was directly traceable to age. Men over the age of 26 were proving almost useless to the army. In a speech in Chicago on 29 March 1941 Hershey recommended that the special temporary deferment for students be repealed because young, bright men were needed in the army. Roosevelt agreed. "Certainly," he wrote, "we do not want to provide that the mere matriculation into college can serve as a means of evading the compulsory military training." At the War Department, Patterson dismissed the fears of faculty. Deferments or drills for college students smacked of special privilege for the rich. For Patterson the only justifiable deferments were for men currently producing military munitions and equipment. College boys should line up to volunteer.[93]

Yet, even as the administration talked tough, students were being deferred. A survey of 105,000 college students age 21 on or before 1 July 1941 indicated that only 8.4 percent had been classified 1-A. These figures were virtually meaningless, however, because by law all students who requested a deferment to 1 July 1941 had to receive it.[94]

As summer arrived, students flocked to jobs and vacations and administrators were busy protecting their institutions against the draft. The ACE vowed to continue to monitor local board action during the summer to insure that vacationing students were not gobbled up by the military. A group of several hundred liberal arts colleges, including Columbia and Harvard, offered a new three-year curriculum which would allow their students to graduate before being inducted at age 21. Some educational leaders bombarded Congress with pleas for a law specifically deferring students until graduation. The AMA was first with a bill offering a blanket deferment of all medical students. After physicians got, rather than a bill, new regulations offering more protection for medical students, other professions began lining up. As K. C. Leebrick, president of Kent State University, explained to Senator Elbert D. Thomas, the student deferment bill was not class legislation. He believed it was necessary because saving colleges meant saving democracy and helping the defense program. The range of rationalizations was wide, but it all added up to the same parochialism—the draft theoretically required equal sacrifice, but it was also selective, and students needed to be selected out.[95]

The administration reacted to this campaign by offering a series of compromises. On 15 July Hershey made an impassioned appeal to Roosevelt to resist tampering with the decentralized classification system. According to Hershey, students fell into three distinct groups. First were those students in special fields such as engineering and medicine where all signs pointed to shortages. To provide for such students Selective Service had issued a series of memos to local boards urging special consideration for extending deferments after 1 July. Second were those students who might be useful for defense, and thereby eligible for deferment under the "national health, safety," category but were not so easily identified. The third group was all draftables. Hershey urged that local boards be allowed to exercise their judgment. He argued that offering a blanket deferment to all college students would destroy the draft and harm the reputations of the colleges.[96]

The draft had been sold as a democratic mechanism. Giving a blanket deferment to those privileged enough to attend college contradicted this idea. Did the nation want laws or regulations that sent the message that "prior calls shall be made upon the uneducated to defend America." "Is the college student, per se," Hershey asked, "of more importance than the automobile mechanic or farm laborer who is now working and producing?" Selective Service answered by informing local boards that to obtain a deferment the student had to prove that finishing his courses would "make him of more value to the defense program and that there will be a shortage in the field." In cases of hardship for men who entered college and were then called, the local board could offer a postponement to the end of the term or semester, but group deferments remained forbidden.[97]

Educators were still dissatisfied. When the new term began in the fall their worst fears seemed realized. New York University reported a 10 percent fall in enrollment, and similar reports came from around the country. Dean Herbert E. Hawkes of Columbia and others testified before the Senate miliary subcommittee that thousands of potential students were hesitating to enroll because of the uncertainty of their draft status. Senator William Langer (R-N.Dak.) introduced a bill in November 1941 to postpone until the end of the academic year the induction of all college students who had finished one year and were working toward a degree.[98]

To forestall such congressional action Selective Service again bombarded local boards with a series of memos explaining that while a deferment could be granted only for the national interest, a postponement to finish the semester could be obtained on the basis of individual hardship. Not student status but the shortages in a particular field should indicate whether a deferment should be offered. The War Department supported this policy, and the president thought all students should hold themselves ready to serve where needed. Not even the entrance of the United States into war ended the pleas for special treatment made by educators.[99]

Despite all the rhetoric of sacrifice and talk of efficiency that accompanied the adoption of the draft, when the chips began to fall, Americans seemed reluctant to concede any of their existing institutions or attitudes. This reluctance was true of families, factories, and schools; it was also true of racism. America was a racist society in 1941, and the draft had to accommodate itself to this social reality.

Accommodation had been the rule in dealing with blacks since the development of Jim Crow in the late nineteenth century.[100] Draft planners were aware of the potential problem of racism, and the 1940 bill had been revised to specifically prohibit discrimination based on race. The president had made a few token appointments of blacks to his draft advisory board, to the War Department, and to Selective Service, and at his suggestion, Judge William H. Hastie was appointed as special assistant to Secretary of War Stimson on race affairs. Major Campbell Johnson accepted a similar post at national headquarters of Selective Service. As these appointments were intended for image rather than substance, neither man was able to achieve much. Hastie became so frustrated at the refusal of the War Department to accept blacks at the rate promised that he eventually resigned in disgust in January 1943. Johnson, however, remained for many years at Selective Service and eventually witnessed the adoption of more liberal policies.[101]

Unlike the armed forces, Selective Service did try to promote black participation. Hershey personally lobbied many southern state directors to appoint a few blacks to draft boards for the sake of public relations. In early 1941 the system conducted a massive investigation on black participation. Although not all states bothered to reply, the results indicated that thousands of blacks had acted as registrars and advisory personnel but few were serving on local boards. Mississippi replied proudly that "outstanding Negroes in every community are serving in advisory capacity to local boards." But the survey found that in 33 states plus the District of Columbia only 250 blacks served on local boards, 624 were acting as advisors, 30 as government appeal agents, and 486 as examining physicians or dentists. Major Johnson, ever one to put the best gloss on the situation, reported that over 30,000 blacks had participated. Privately he lamented the lack of blacks serving in the South but continued to urge leaders to cooperate with the system, especially in the South. [102]

No matter what the law said about discrimination, the draft did discriminate to fill the ranks of a Jim Crow army. In 1940 the army had only about six black units consisting of 4,450 black soldiers. Blacks could only fill vacancies in these units. Other units were planned, but it took time to build the separate mess and housing facilities required by the segregationist society. In the meantime, the army had no place to put black draftees, so when calls were issued to the Selective Service they were race-specific calls, with few blacks required.

The calls created special problems for local boards. Puerto Rican draft officials had to revise their forms because the initial registration had not distinguished on the basis of race. Now the government wanted 2,100 Caucasians and 300 Negroes from Puerto Rico. A memo from the War Department of 23 December 1940 indicated that the army would be guided in their choice by the "little group of neighbors," the draft board. Some local boards used their order numbers to inform all registrants, black and white, when they could be expected to be inducted. Men left jobs and waited. In some communities large numbers of whites marched off to war while blacks remained at home. [103]

Such actions caused concern. Johnson assured the press that the problem was being worked out "very carefully and with satisfactory progress." Officials denied discrimination and promised that the next month there would be more blacks drafted. Several eastern states failed to meet their quotas for December because they sent blacks who were then rejected on the basis of race by the army induction center. Privately, Dykstra wrote to the secretary of war of the "potentially serious public relations problems" emerging. The delays in inducting blacks were causing more whites to be called early and he feared the situation might lead to a court challenge. In New York state 800 blacks, selected in January and told they would be inducted in February, waited until late March. Over 1,100 whites from Washington, D.C., were drafted but no blacks.

Nationally, only 18,033 blacks were called in March. A general uproar soon emerged. [104]

By March 1941 the problem endangered mobilization. The National Lawyers Guild threatened legal action because of the discrimination. In Connecticut state director Col. Ernest L. Averill protested when black selectees were returned home. Averill insisted that under the law the army had only the right to request a certain number of draftees from each state. He promised to pay no attention to special calls for Negroes. In North Carolina the state director complained that the calls allotted to his "black counties" were six to one in favor of white registration. National headquarters recommended that the director not call any men from these areas until he had a black quota to fill. But Johnson, returned from a trip to the South in late summer, reported that blacks' morale was falling as they were passed over in large numbers. A few southern boards refused to assume the burden of deciding on race, even as Hershey insisted that they had to make a decision based on how the person was accepted in the neighborhood. [105]

By September Hershey asked the secretary of war for relief. Although Selective Service had worked closely with the army on the problem and understood its position, 28,000 Negroes had been selected but denied a call-up. Hershey insisted that the "time has come when the Army must revise its procedure to receive men in such order, without regard to color." Stimson, however, refused to budge, and Hershey appealed to the president: "It is obvious we must sooner or later come to the procedure of requisitioning and delivering men in the sequence of their order numbers without regard to color." But Roosevelt made no change in the system during the war. The military draft merely reinforced racism in American society. [106]

Officials recognized the need to work with existing institutions and prejudices to gain acceptance of the new instrument for mobilization. This conforming attitude also found expression in the way the draft treated American religious institutions and beliefs. Surveys showed that Americans in the 1930s were generally a church-going, religiously dedicated population and American politicians respected the power of ministers to influence citizens on a variety of public issues. During the draft of 1917 administration leaders sought and received endorsements from leading prelates of all faiths. No one, however, went quite as far as James Cardinal Gibbons of Baltimore who announced that, in adopting conscription, "the members of both Houses of Congress are instruments of God in guiding us in our civic duties."[107]

When the draft bill of 1940 first appeared before Congress it drew opposition from many church leaders. Peace churches succeeded in obtaining a clause which provided CO status on an individual basis, based on religious training and belief but not requiring, as had been the case in 1917, membership in a historic peace church. Ministers were exempted from the draft, although they did have to register.[108]

Effectively, the administration had forged a partnership between the draft and religious leaders. This partnership became evident on 30 October 1940 when President Roosevelt read statements of endorsement from leaders of the three major faiths just before he pulled the first capsule for the first draft lottery. Archbishop Francis J. Spellman wrote: "It is better to have protection and not need it than to need protection and not have it." Reverend Frank C. Williams of the New York Methodist Church told his congregation that "the conscription act will have a salutary influence on many young lives stalled by inaction." Reverend Dr. Henry Sloane Coffin, president of Union Theological Seminary, assured the government that his faculty intended to screen applicants carefully to insure that no one used ministerial training as an escape from the draft. And several rabbis praised the draft as a warning to Hitler.[109]

In the year before the attack on Pearl Harbor, Selective Service tried to cooperate with churches. Draft authorities stopped inductions on high holy days for both Christians and Jews. National headquarters implemented the ministerial exemption in the law by establishing that to be eligible an individual had to dedicate himself to this role "to the substantial exclusion of other activities." By January 1941 the exemption had been extended to men studying for the ministry and to lay brothers of the Catholic church. Officials of the Salvation Army and missionaries of the Mormon Church enjoyed similar exemptions. Selective Service provided exemption to many members of the Jehovah's Witnesses, but this sect created problems by claiming all members were ministers.[110]

Equally troublesome for government officials were the men who claimed CO status. Instead of merely establishing membership in a peace church, the candidate had to prove his sincerity and that his belief was associated with religious training and faith. Each registrant was required to fill out a questionnaire (DSS form 40) which provided personal information to aid in classification. On this form was a section where a man could claim CO status. If he made use of this option, he had to fill

A family of conscientious objectors during World War II. Courtesy, Selective Service System National Headquarters.

out another more detailed form (DSS form 47) which asked questions on his religious beliefs and their origins and proof of when the beliefs were adopted. Because national headquarters did not provide more than general guidelines, local boards had to make their own decisions. Sincerity was more important than official church membership and the candidate had to be opposed to war in general, not just the current one.[111]

Civil libertarians were suspicious of the procedure. They pointed out, correctly, that local board members were generally veterans with little training in theological niceties and little sympathy for pacifism. Although the description was accurate, in the year before the bombing of Pearl Harbor the system operated with a degree of liberality. Hershey had sent instructions to all local boards that they were to interpret the provisions of the law broadly. "It is general policy," wrote the director, "to show leniency in handling of conscientious objectors and while regulations stipulate 'by reason of his religious training and belief,' such training might even be given in the home, and it is not necessary that a conscientious objector be a member of any recognized religious sect." Such liberal policies insured a degree of acceptance for the system.[112]

COs had two options when faced with the draft. They could accept military service but foreswear fighting, in which case they were assigned to noncombat task within the armed forces. Or they could refuse to participate in any military duty and be assigned to camps and required to perform civilian, alternate service to insure equal sacrifice. The law asserted that all draft liable citizens should provide some service to the nation, regardless of religious convictions.

The alternate service program was put together casually. Roosevelt had washed his hands of the problem and delegated it to the director of Selective Service. Draft officials consulted with peace church representatives and managed to create a hybrid system which was neither public nor private. Peace churches, anxious to control the treatment of COs, agreed to help finance the camps by paying for staff and supplies. The government assumed overall direction and used deserted Civilian Conservation Corps camps and surplus equipment to set up the camps. COs were supposed to be engaged in work of national importance, but for the first year their tasks seemed nothing but a repetition of the make-work policies of the New Deal.[113]

Such a Rube Goldberg approach to alternate service began generating problems before the nation went to war. The peace churches found that they were paying for the upkeep of nonmembers. Church officials also resented the overall direction of the camps by military men such as Lt. Col. Lewis F. Kosch of SS. COs themselves griped about the insignificant work, and the public began to read stories of how one camp had COs working in "idyllic setting," meditating on philosophy and served by college coeds. There was little discipline in the camps. Men came and went as they pleased and ignored rules on clothing, health, and property. Kosch reported that the "general attitude of the assignees is that they are there for furthering their own beliefs and doctrines rather than doing work of national importance." The program was a time bomb waiting to explode, but at least religious sensibilities had been recognized.[114]

With all of the adjustments of the draft to American cultural sensitivity, the main mission of filling the armed forces with men should have suffered, and it did. Despite all the publicity and the atmosphere of crisis generated in late 1940, the draft unfolded at a decidedly slow pace. Initial plans called for an increase in the armed forces from an October total of 471,000 to a projected total in the army alone of 1.4 million by 30 June 1941. Some 630,000 draftees were supposed to contribute to this total. But only 19,700 men were called in November 1940. The army reduced the draft call because of a rush of volunteers who flocked in to avoid the reserve obligation of the draft and to benefit from priority in assignments. The volunteers continued to appear even when their tour of duty was increased to three years. The rush allowed the army to declare a holiday for draft calls during the Christmas season from 15 December to 3 January, yet the draft was falling behind schedule.[115]

Induction quotas had begun to lag behind schedule in December 1940. By 1 February 1941 only 100,000 of a projected 240,000 had been inducted. Some of the difficulty came from the high rejection rate and the need to impose racial quota, but the main problem seemed to be the inability of the army to prepare training facilities fast enough. Construction of cantonments fell behind by about 28 percent. Selective Service provided better manpower management than the volunteer approach, but due to the emergency neither the military nor President Roosevelt wished to cut off volunteers. Capitalizing upon patriotism and enthusiasm, and assuming a better quality of recruit, the administration deliberately allowed this amateur mobilization to flourish, despite its dangers for the economy and its interference with the draft. Roosevelt personally urged the navy to continue its recruiting of volunteers rather than depend on draftees.[116]

By late March 1941 the draft machinery could call as many men as the army required, but the army was bogged down with the men already called. On 19 April the director informed local boards that quotas would be reduced because of the large increase in volunteers, yet on 1 July a second registration, for men who had attained the age of 18 since 16 October 1940, was held. The president also authorized the induction of an additional 900,000 men for the next fiscal year. Over 700,000 men registered, and a second lottery was held on 17 July to mix the new men with those in the old pool not yet called.[117]

After six months of operation, the draft had mixed results. Some 4 million men had been selected and classified, but only 402,000 were inducted. In the 1.4 million projected strength of the army by 30 June 1941 there were supposed to be 630,000 draftees. In fact, the actual strength was 1,351,000 with 606,915 draftees. But the failure to enroll an adequate number of draftees was not a failure of the system. Rather

the army and the president had insisted upon continuing to take volunteers, and the army had fallen behind in construction of training facilities
and had maintained high physical standards and put strict limits on black
draftees. Despite these problems, the administration began to revise the
system, which had not been allowed to function as planned originally.
The president mentioned in April the possibility of reducing the draft age
to 18. Major General Robert C. Richardson of the War Department told
the press that big changes in the draft were planned. Selling these changes
to Congress, however, proved rather difficult.[118]

Calls for revision of the draft had emerged as soon as the original bill
had passed. The problems that arose in the first six months were varied.
There were a few charges, some sustained, of corruption by local board
members. Mayor Fiorello LaGuardia of New York City complained because national headquarters refused to follow local boards. LaGuardia
had been after a group deferment for his firemen and policemen, but was
frustrated by Hershey. In contrast, several Republican senators, led by
Arthur H. Vandenburg of Michigan, denounced the system because national headquarters allowed local boards too much freedom. The American Legion introduced a bill to provide universal military training to all
men from ages 18 to 21.[119]

By the spring of 1941 the army agreed that the draft did need some
change. Specifically, trainers and other officials realized that the original
age estimates for draftees had been much too optimistic. Rejections at
induction stations and the results of boot-camp experiences convinced
the army that draftees over the age of 26 were virtually useless. The best
soldier was a young man 18 to 21. By May the administration began
seeking the power to defer men by age group, to exclude older men from
the pool. Although the Senate acted rapidly to approve such an amendment to the draft, the House stalled. The issue became confused with a
congressional drive to provide a group deferment for all married men,
all medical students, and other special interest groups. Finally, on 2 July
1941, Director Hershey simply instructed local boards to defer men 28
or over for 30 days or until Congress could act.[120]

Revision of the draft unfolded parallel to dramatic world events. By
the spring of 1941 Germany had overrun France, bombed England close
to submission, and invaded Russia. In the Pacific the Japanese were in
Indochina and boasting of a new co-prosperity sphere in Asia under
Japan's leadership. On 27 May 1941 President Roosevelt proclaimed an
unlimited period of national emergency. In early July American troops

occupied Iceland and extended naval patrols into the mid-Atlantic. Secret staff talks had been held with British military officers to insure coordinated action in both the Pacific and Atlantic when, not if, war came.

Officials felt that when war came men must serve longer than 12 months. The authors of the draft law had always wanted more than one year of compulsory training. Political circumstances in 1940 made any longer commitment impossible, but the expanding war changed the context. When the rumor reached Congress that the army might seek to extend the tour of the draftee beyond one year and "for the duration of the emergency," several senators and congressmen denounced the idea. General Marshall explained on 13 June that a few selectees might be held beyond a year, but he would prefer to retain the National Guard and Officer Reserve candidates. He explained to reporters that one value of the draft was a circulation of new, untrained men through the training facilities. The aim of the draft was to build up a large trained reserve, and trained men had to be released to make room for new untrained men. But in a few days Marshall began changing his tune. [121]

In May 1941 the Japanese moved into French Indochina. Germany invaded Russia on 22 June 1941. On 3 July Marshall recommended to the president that both the geographic and the time restrictions on the use of draftees be dropped so that the army could reach a strength of 2.3 million and be used more effectively. The president had already authorized American forces to occupy Iceland, but under the current law, no draftees could be used in the occupying force. At his press conference of 8 July the president approved Marshall's request and urged action upon Congress. Within days a bill amending the draft law to extend the draftee's tour to six months after the end of the national emergency reached the Senate. Marshall presented secret information to Congress and cited the need to use forces to occupy outlying defensive positions in both the Atlantic and Pacific oceans. Undersecretary Patterson informed House Speaker Sam Rayburn (D-Tex.) that to allow such demobilization would be "to court disaster." [122]

On 21 July Roosevelt sent a special message to Congress urging immediate action on Marshall's request. Despite the press of world events, Congress received the message with skepticism. Republicans vowed to vote in a block against this violation of the contract made with the first draftees. Senator Robert Taft (R-Ohio) wanted only a short extension until the draft could be revised with more specific classification catego-

ries. Senator Walter George (D-Ga.) suggested that draftees be first allowed to extend their service voluntarily.[123] Taft accused Roosevelt of
violating the Constitution by sending troops to Iceland. Even Democratic
leaders, such as Robert R. Reynolds in the Senate and Rayburn and John
McCormack in the House opposed the revision. Isolationists such as
Robert E. Wood and Senator Burton Wheeler joined Socialist leader
Norman Thomas in denouncing the move.[124]

Wheeler went further than most by inviting servicemen to write in
about the extension. The army had argued that the troops were ready to
remain on duty, and an army survey showed that 75 percent of the
draftees were willing to stay on and serve overseas. But the public soon
heard another opinion. Troops from New Jersey, Maryland, and Virginia
sent telegrams to Congress denouncing the extension. When the army
took steps to punish them for violating regulations, recruits resorted to
dropping notes from truck convoys on the way to maneuvers. The notes
demanded an early release, threatened OHIO (over the hill in October),
criticized army brass, and asked civilians to deliver the word to the press.
Such actions created an embarrassing atmosphere for congressional
action.[125]

Public opinion was divided. A survey of hundreds of editorials revealed that over 63 percent or 792 editorials favored the extension. Only
101 or 8.1 percent of the sample opposed the idea. Yet when George
Gallup surveyed men on the street he found more division. On the
question of extension, 51 percent favored it but 45 percent felt the men
should be released. Only 37 percent favored using draftees outside of the
hemisphere, while 50 percent opposed.[126]

Congressional debate reflected this split in public opinion. The fight
became as heated as the Washington weather of July and August. Roosevelt insisted that, without the amendment, some two-thirds of army
strength would go home and then have to be recalled in an emergency.
Such a procedure threatened havoc with army effectiveness. Marshall
complained that many draftees were mixed in units with regulars. But
Republican congressmen and senators were not impressed. Japan seemed
bogged down in China, and Germany was fighting Russia so they felt the
United States was in no danger of invasion.[127]

Eventually, Senate leaders had to compromise. Rather than an extension for the duration of the emergency, they accepted 18 months. Even
with this revision and a pay raise for the draftees, the House voted only
203 to 202 for the extension. In the Senate the vote was 45 to 30. On

18 August Roosevelt signed the extension and issued an executive order putting it into effect and deferring from service those who were 28 or over on 1 July 1941.[128]

Many editorial writers, and later historians, assumed that the amendment involved the survival of the draft. They lamented compromise at a time of international tension. Subsequent students have focused upon the one vote margin in the House as evidence of the strength of isolationism and also insisted that the draft was "renewed" by only one vote. In fact, the existence and continued functioning of the draft were never at stake. If the amendment had been rejected, the Selective Service could have continued to draft men for one year of service. The only issue at stake was an "extension" of the tour of men already in the service, men who had been drafted for a one-year tour. Both opponents and proponents were disappointed at the final measure. One chaplain wrote that the troops would desert in droves over the issue. And Marshall still faced the problem of using men who had only a limited tour.[129]

Another continuing problem concerned the number of draftees who should be in the army. On 19 August the War Department announced that it planned to release both draftees and National Guardsmen after they had served 18 months, and a furlough was planned for Christmas. Selective Service explained that if these men were released it just meant that more new men would be drafted. Local boards expected calls of about 70,000 a month. But the army continued to plan on a huge release of troops by December, including some 200,000 who were hardship cases, married, or over 28. Reserve officers also learned that they were not needed. But Congress had just fought hard over the idea of extending the tour of draftees. To start releasing troops would send the wrong signals to the public. When asked if Congress should allow draftees to be sent anywhere in the world, 53 percent of the public said no and 42 percent said yes. In the fall of 1941 the military seemed undecided on strength levels, and the draft seemed a transitory and experimental tool for military manpower mobilization. But the Japanese bombs falling on Pearl Harbor made it necessary to settle matters.[130]

3

From Pearl Harbor to D-Day

After what President Roosevelt called "a date which will live in infamy," the entire nation confronted the reality of war. The make-believe aspect of military preparation fell away. To be drafted meant more than just a change in clothing, work habits, and sleeping conditions. American servicemen died at Pearl Harbor, and more were soon dying in the Philippines.

From the president to the man in the street came pledges of total commitment. General Hershey said "all requirements of the armed forces [will] be met without delay." Herbert Hoover said, "We must fight with everything we have." The rhetorical commitment was to total war, total effort. In appearance, all citizens and institutions stood ready to serve full-time to defeat Japan and Germany, to return the world to peace, and the United States planned to mobilize its entire society, much as the British and Russians had already done. But appearances were deceptive.[1]

In the next four years the United States put 12 million men in uniform, almost 10 million entering through the draft. Washington adopted new controls over the economy. Historian Walter Millis has written that during World War II "one salient and shocking fact was to emerge: the almost unbelievable power of the modern centralized, managerial and nationalistic state to drain the whole physical, intellectual, economic, emotional and moral resources of its citizens to the single end of military victory." The thesis of the following pages is that this statement is largely nonsense. A study of the military draft reveals that the mobilization was far from total. Many individuals and institutions fought the war on terms far removed from the spirit of Pearl Harbor rhetoric.[2]

In manpower there was a failure in centralization and management and a triumph of localism and the politics of special interests. Throughout the war parochial interest remained strong and effective against pressures from a divided central government. Not even the military was able to get its way. As for the "physical, intellectual, economic, emotional and moral resources" of the nation, they remained fragmented and in many cases as self-serving as ever. In retrospect, the fears or hopes of the war leading to a centralized state seem grossly exaggerated.

The problems facing centralizers emerged when the draft became operational to replace volunteering. For Clark and Stimson the draft represented a scientific means of mobilizing a modern society. As Roosevelt explained when the draft was adopted in 1940, volunteer enlistments endangered the selection principles because many men with special skills ended up in the wrong jobs.³ Only by controlling inductions could the economy be properly mobilized. For Hershey "the primary task of this system (SSS) is to determine the place in which a given individual can best serve his nation." Conscription should not disturb vital industry or disrupt "the basic social fact in American life, the family."⁴

Congress, however, had not intended to give either the president or Selective Service total control over manpower. As for the military, while there was general recognition that the draft should be the exclusive means of obtaining men, when war came the rush of enlistees to the colors proved so fruitful that recruitment of volunteers continued. The army recruited to defend itself against the navy, which had Roosevelt's blessings to gobble up men regardless of their special skills. Secretary Frank Knox informed the press in September 1942 that the navy would continue voluntary recruitment as long as "we can get them. And we are getting them in a very satisfactory number."⁵ Not until December 1942, a full year after the attack on Pearl Harbor did the services end recruitment. And this hardly meant the triumph of central controls.

The law itself reflected an ambiguity in the nation toward centralized conscription. Congress based the draft upon a universal obligation to serve. In a democracy any other notion was politically unacceptable. But having stated a mass obligation, the law then provided for a "selective" mechanism which allowed deferments for economic and social purposes, at the discretion of the president. Problems were bound to arise. As Arthur Krock, political journalist, observed, the public wanted little interference with life style but also wanted no deferments. Citizens wanted movies and baseball to continue, but no deferments for stars of screen

Draftees undergoing physicals during World War II. Courtesy, Selective Service System National Headquarters.

or diamond. Americans wanted plants to produce, but no deferments for young, single workers. Even in the army itself the theory of efficiency created problems. The public believed the army should take everyone, but if the army took specialized workers for the infantry, it was accused of malutilization.[6]

Naturally the war caused some tightening up. Soon after Pearl Harbor Congress acted without debate to cut the prohibition against draftees serving overseas, extended the tour of duty until six months after the war was over, and lowered the induction age to 20.[7] The logic of centralization and universality also pointed to the next step: a national service law and a national agency to draft men for both military and civilian duty. The "corporate elite" who sponsored the draft bill in 1917 and 1940 saw clearly this need. Stimson and Patterson both agreed it was needed. Hershey at SS told the press that such a central allotment agency was inevitable, but such ideas raised no enthusiasm in Congress.[8]

Given the negative political atmosphere, Stimson encouraged Hershey to use SS as a substitute for national service. The agency, however, had been created by Congress with a narrow military goal. Attempting to transform and magnify its mission was not easy. A favorite tactic adopted was to threaten "work or fight," take a war job or be drafted. Before any national effort was made along these lines Mayor F. La Guardia of New York City tried it on the local level. His city patrol corps, a semicomedic civil defense patrol, had trouble recruiting volunteers. To solve the problem, the mayor sent out letters in envelopes franked by SS to all men deferred for dependency (3-A) warning that they faced reclassification as 1-A if they did not cooperate. This action had no basis in law or regulation, as even the city draft director, Colonel Arthur V. McDermott, admitted, but not surprisingly, 90 percent of the 7,000 who received the letters immediately applied for duty with the city patrol. Soon national headquarters began issuing statements that men could enhance their deferred status by shifting from nonessential to essential work. But the draft had definite limits as a means of controlling civilian workers.[9]

Rather than face up to these limits and the need for national service, having SS draft for both the armed forces and industry, President Roosevelt adopted his usual tactic of approaching the problem obliquely. Although opponents accused him of plotting a dictatorship, Roosevelt was strongly opposed to centralized manpower controls and fought against a national service law when such a bill appeared in Congress in 1942. Rather than a new law, the president attempted a temporary agency of coordination, and in April 1942 he created by executive order the War Manpower Commission (WMC) under Paul McNutt of Indiana. Originally designed merely to coordinate the use of civilian manpower, the rule of the WMC was soon expanded to fit the ambitious shoulders of McNutt.[10] But despite his efforts, even when American troops finally engaged Germans in North Africa in November 1942, the manpower situation was still a mess.

Testimony before congressional committees demonstrated that mobilization was creating havoc in the civilian economy. The armed forces continued to recruit volunteers from war industry and labor-short areas, and civilian workers were migrating to high paying jobs even if it meant leaving vital work in farming. Accordingly, at McNutt's urging, Roosevelt issued a new executive order on 5 December which ended all military recruitment, excused men over 38 from the draft, and gave McNutt more control over draft policy.[11]

When McNutt sought central control of all manpower he ran into opposition from Congress, the army, and SS. Within one year the WMC had its power reduced by congressional legislation. Although another attempt at national service surfaced in early 1945, it also failed in Congress, and manpower mobilization remained in practice unscientific and uncentralized. The explanation for this failure of theory can be found in the reality of American politics.[12]

Several powerful forces warred against centralization. To begin with, the SS System itself represented a bureaucracy founded on the principle of local decisions and control. Such a system did not mesh well with theories of bureaucracy. According to social theorists, a bureaucracy emerges in any social structure by the creation of formal divisions of work and authority—including the rationalization of procedures through rules and regulations—the purpose of which is to minimize arbitrary, individual, or local judgment in acting.[13] A major result of bureaucratization in the modern state, according to these theorists, is to expand central control through implementation of common rules by local units. Theoretically, during World War II the SS was to build upon the social consensus to obtain approval for national manpower goals and the efficient use of personnel. The growth of central power, in this scheme, emerged because of a process of modernization unfolding.[14]

Interpreting SS based on this social theory, some students argue that the agency did grow into a means of national control. This control served supposedly to "isolate local boards from sentimental considerations" when they engaged in classifications. Originally local boards reflected local interest to national headquarters, but by the end of the war a reversal had occurred, according to these scholars, and the local agency was an instrument for integrating the community into a national plan. Rather than assume the blame for drafting one man and deferring another, local board members pointed to national regulations. (This trend is explained by a natural desire of men to avoid responsibility.) This, in turn, led to professionalization, with more reference to national guidelines and less to individual prejudices.[15]

However logical this argument of modernization may seem in the abstract, it fails to explain what happened in World War II. SS changed rules repeatedly during the war, sometimes to reflect new national policy but often as a reaction to local pressure. National changes included reducing the draft age, narrowing registration and service obligations, and shifting deferments away from dependency on jobs, among others. But, despite these changes, the operation of the draft also reflected politics which emerged from the local value system. The creation of special deferred categories and the pace of induction of certain social types can best be explained by pressure from below rather than above. SS may have been designed as a rational bureaucratic organization, but it soon became a political institution—"a natural product of social needs and pressures—a responsive, adaptive organism."[16]

During the war the SS proved a major barrier against centralization because of the theory embodied in the law itself. On one hand the law announced a general duty to serve, on the other hand it specified that eligibility had to be determined on an individual basis and prohibited any group deferments. On one hand the national government directed mobilization; on the other hand local boards were responsible for classification. Local boards represented local interests. Board members were civilian volunteers, local elites, who had grass roots power, independent of their role in SS. Such membership placed definite limits on how national headquarters could function. When national headquarters issued rules considered capricious or opposed to local best interest, the local board resisted or reinterpreted the directives. Hershey sent out "advice" to local boards. He was keenly aware that a national policy which violated local opinion could lead to rebellion, and without the volunteers, the draft could not operate.

At its peak, the system depended upon over 184,000 volunteers serving as local board members, most of whom had been identified in the 1930s even before the draft law was passed. The adjutants general of each state had used the National Guard and the Military Training Corps Association to identify local men noted for their patriotism, character, and "standing in the community," and local American Legion posts also furnished names. The standing of these men represented deferential politics in the local community. In rural areas and small towns the board did resemble the theory of "groups of neighbors," people familiar with the draftees; in large cities more anonymity prevailed.[17]

Classification by local boards was theoretically straightforward. National headquarters, following presidential policy, established the order of call and the priority of classifications. The classification system was revised throughout the war but certain general categories remained constant. Class 1-A referred to men immediately available for service; class 2 contained men with some deferment—for example, 2-B meant deferred for an essential job. Class 3 contained men deferred because of dependency or hardship; Class 4 designated men unqualified for service because of age, health, or some other factor. The local board had the job of putting each registrant into the appropriate class while simultaneously seeking to fill induction calls sent out by the armed forces.

The average local board at maximum strength during the war consisted of about 17 volunteers and four part-time workers. Usually the board met at least once a week and sometimes daily. A high percentage of classification actions were automatic and made without a board meeting. A paid clerk merely made the entry on the form. In mid-war one month saw 4,190,536 classifications, but 716,508 were merely inductions of men or changes from 1-A to 1-C. But when a man classified 1-A sought a job or other type of deferment, the local board had to meet. It was in these cases that the local power of the system became manifest.[18]

The action of the local board involved individual consideration. Local board 104 for Franklin County, Massachusetts, considered the case of Joseph Zewinski who sought a dependency deferment. The board refused to take Joseph's word and requested an investigation of the man's home status by a welfare officer who reported back to SS. Sometimes local businessmen appeared before the board to argue cases for occupational deferments for their workers. In fact, most requests for job deferments came from employers rather than selectees. Boards usually required proof beyond the employer's word on essentiality before granting industrial or agricultural deferments.[19]

Actions of the boards were hardly bureaucratic routine. In the course of their work local board members became involved with the family, work, health, and educational background of the registrants. Formal hearings, which might consider several dozen deferments, occurred about three hundred times each year. If a registrant appeared, which was not required, his testimony was under oath. Local welfare, police, educational, and other agencies provided information. Sometimes community pressure became intense. One study found 38 local board members reporting attempted bribes, and in several cases selectees tried physical intimidation on the board.[20]

Despite such pressure local board members derived great satisfaction from their work. When, two years after the war was over, SS conducted an extensive survey of local board members, the findings confirmed all wartime impressions. Some 58 percent of all local board members said they were extremely satisfied with their work; another 37 percent were quite satisfied. Only .1 of 1 percent said they were not satisfied. Asked their opinion about state and national headquarters, from 92 to 94 percent said the relationship was satisfactory or better. This merely meant that neither national nor state headquarters violated the autonomy of local boards. About 77 percent of all local boards said higher headquarters "never" encroached on local prerogatives. On relations with local communities, 97 percent reported a satisfactory or better climate.[21]

For many of the civilian volunteers classification responsibility was their major contribution to winning the war. They took it seriously and cherished the power they possessed, as was shown by the low turnover rate.[22] A majority of them had little enthusiasm for big government and favored rapid demobilization of war agencies. Instead of becoming government bureaucrats, these men remained local leaders anxious for a return to peace.[23]

Although the statutory independence of local boards threatened any move toward national control, the law did create a check on rampant localism. There were numerous advisory boards in the states to provide advice on special deferment questions in industry, farming, and health. Also, an appeal system existed on both the national and the state levels, although local board classifications were seldom overturned. Some 243 appeal boards appointed by the governors handled over 4,300,000 appeals. At one point in 1943 one out of every six inductions went to appeal. The vast majority of these cases, some 65 percent, came not from the registrants themselves, but from their employers. In over 69 percent of the cases the decisions of the local boards were upheld. Little wonder then that only 3 percent of all local board members expressed dissatisfaction with the appeal system.[24]

Occasionally a governor asked the state director to investigate a local board that publicly disagreed with national policy. But Washington appreciated that any attack on the autonomy of local boards could bring the entire draft to a halt. Roosevelt himself never tried to reverse a local board decision. The presidential appeal board was handled by Hershey within national headquarters. Less than 10 percent of local board 1-A classifications were appealed, and in two-thirds of the cases the local board decision was upheld.[25]

From October 1940 to 31 March 1947, when the draft finally ended, SS registered 49 million men, selected 19 million, and saw 10 million inducted. The draft had only been used twice before in the nation. During the Civil War it had produced riots, and during World War I considerable opposition had arisen. The World War II draft had been designed to deflect opposition by using local volunteers. Public support was important to the draft, and the system of unpaid local volunteers was designed to bind local leadership to the draft, but it also bound national leaders to local opinion.[26]

One internal memo explained, "if the principal criterion of deferment should shift from dependency to occupation, assiduous efforts to win public acceptance for this policy are probably in order." Throughout the war the administration conducted opinion surveys through the Office of War Information to check on public attitudes toward the draft.[27] National headquarters geared its operations to convince the public that the draft was fair and deserved support. The policy of publicizing the selection of prominent personalities from entertainment, sports, and business reflected this strategy. When the nation went on full war footing and information on the number of men called was considered secret intelligence, Hershey continued to have local boards publish lists of names of inductees and encouraged news stories on the draft of the famous.[28]

Such actions paid off. Throughout the war the public's approval of local board fairness never dropped below the 75 percent mark. As Gallup admitted: "Few programs in the nation's history have ever received such widespread favorable reaction from the people as the handling of the Selective Service draft." This positive response had geographic, demographic, and ethnic uniformity. Males were favorable by 80 percent; women 75 percent; whites 78 percent; blacks 83 percent; farmers 72 percent; urbanites 81 percent; men under 38 by 77 percent; and men over 38 by 80 percent. Editorial writers praised the fairness of local boards and called for more freedom from national guidelines.[29]

Naturally criticism also appeared. Ernest K. Lindley of *Newsweek* and Senator Robert Taft, among others, found fault with the decentralization of classification. They believed such a policy led to an unscientific draft with skilled men called before the unskilled and single men called before fathers. The charge was true. Local control did lead to unscientific classification, but the results had public approval. An unscientific father seemed more valuable to the public than a bachelor chemist.[30]

Supervision from the top, by the appeal system, could insure individual fairness in particular cases but could not insure central control of the draft. Despite the presence of General Hershey and military officers at national and state levels, civilian volunteers ran the draft. Theoretically, local board members could be fired for failing to carry out national policy, but throughout the war only 124 members were removed and most of those separations involved cases of dubious ethics rather than rebellion against rules. During the war, classification definitions became more rigid as the manpower pool shrank, but local boards still applied principles in their own way.[31]

Occasionally draft officials reversed rules because of adverse public reaction. In February 1942 Hershey ruled that motion pictures and newspapers were essential activities, allowing deferments for actors and reporters. A public outcry soon led to a clarification. No replaceable man could be deferred, and no one expected local boards to defer movie stars. Although at first professional baseball enjoyed some draft protection, by 1943 all professional sports were deemed unessential.[32]

Most remarkable, the system managed to remain popular while simultaneously responding to fluctuations in its primary mission of providing men for war. The system resembled a man juggling two varying sets of balls simultaneously. One set represented the military demands on the draft. As the war unfolded, these demands shrank or expanded in size. The other set of balls represented available manpower and was also constantly in a state of expansion and contraction as deferments shifted, Congress intervened, or lobbyists succeeded in obtaining protection. The system displayed amazing dexterity with its juggling as the military expanded.

From a prewar total of 188,000 men the armed forces rose to an eventual size of 12 million men. The increase occurred much as a balloon expands as blown up by a man with hiccoughs. In the autumn of 1941, before Pearl Harbor, the army had 520,000 regulars, 256,000 National Guardsmen, and 712,000 draftees.[33]

After the attack on Pearl Harbor military plans focused on an 8-million-man army. Registration for the draft expanded to cover all males from ages 20 to 44, putting about 25,829,788 in the pool. Stimson wanted a total of 3.6 million in the army by December 1942. With existing deferments for dependency and occupations, plus a 50 percent rejection rate, the goal seemed beyond reach. Men over 25 were physically suspect, usually married, or in a deferred job.

By the summer of 1942 pressure appeared to call some deferred types. In June 1942 registration was expanded to cover males 18 to 45, yet Congress opposed drafting teenagers or family men. Undismayed, Stimson projected a total of 7.5 million men in the army by December 1944. In 1942 the navy also began using the draft which increased the pressure. Joint induction centers were created for the armed forces in early 1943,

Roosevelt registers with the draft (1942). Courtesy, Selective Service System National Headquarters.

and draft calls in 1943 were projected at the level of 3.5 million. Some 12,000 men were being inducted daily by early 1943. By April 1943 the projections were for 11 million in the armed forces by the end of the year.

To meet the demand Hershey had a draft pool of 22 million men 18 to 37, but 7 million were already in the service, and eight million were unfit, leaving only 7 million available. Of this total, some 1.7 million had job deferments, and 1.5 million were deferred farmers. Only 3.8 million were available in the pool, and out of this total the draft had to find 2.5 million fit men from May to December. Something had to give.[34]

The number of those called was unaffected by the course of battle. Casualty rates did not reach levels affecting manpower projections until well after the landings in North Africa (Operation Torch) of November 1942. The fighting in early 1943 failed to engage large American forces against German forces until after the invasion of Italy in September. When Italy surrendered, Hershey expected some drop in the size of draft calls, but the Joint Chiefs focused on troops needed for the main battle in Europe which was yet to come. The projected date of invasion of the continent had slipped repeatedly, but the North African and Italian battle experiences convinced planners that many more men would be needed. By September 1943 some 8,717,000 men had been inducted. The draft pool seemed empty, and Hershey projected a deficit of 446,000 if calls continued at the same rate and fathers remained deferred. The combined army and navy call for January 1944 was 300,000, the same rate as for November 1943.[35]

The draft then began to fail in its primary mission. By January 1944 Roosevelt complained to McNutt and Hershey that a shortage of 200,000 men had developed in meeting calls. The president called for tightening all deferments—those for jobs, dependency, and agriculture. Marshall explained to James Byrnes, director of the Office of War Mobilization, that the army had tried to accommodate the "special interest" in the nation by reducing calls by 548,000 since July 1943. But new missions were needed, and the army required another 714,000 troops.[36]

One new mission was the invasion of Europe. On the eve of the mightiest battle in the history of American arms, the chief of staff complained at the failure of the draft to provide the needed manpower. Yet the nation still had millions of civilian males aged 18 to 36. How had such a situation developed? It was partly due to the rejection rate, which was high because the armed forces refused to reduce standards and were upheld in their decision by a presidential committee. The situation was also due to the army's insistence on using very young men for combat. But the main reason was the deferment system, a system created as part of an effort to manage scientifically American manpower. By 1944 the system had become a mess of special interest despite early patriotic cries for total mobilization for total war.

From the earliest days of the draft, the rule was special as opposed to equal treatment. The farmer represented the first and most successful exception to universal service.[37] In fairness, farmers did a remarkable job of increasing production to meet domestic and foreign needs during World War II. Crop production rose almost 20 percent during the period 1940 to 1945 and productivity per worker rose about 25 percent. In fact, by 1944 American officials became concerned with food surpluses. The increase had occurred partially because the farmer in America suffered less from labor dislocation than did industry. The induction rate for farmers was only two-thirds of the proportion they represented of the entire male work force. Their rate of voluntary enlistment was less than one-third as large as the percentage of the entire population. When farmers did leave the farm, twice as many left for higher paying industrial jobs as for the armed forces.[38]

The reason for the stability in the agricultural work force was a generous deferment policy by SS. The law provided deferments for men "whose employment in industry, agriculture, or other occupations" was needed for "national health, safety or interest." By 1 July 1944 some 17 percent of all male farm workers aged 18 to 35 were deferred. Only 9 percent of the same cohort in nonfarm work enjoyed job deferments. In January 1945 some 1,634,936 farmers were deferred, and three times as many males under age 26 were deferred for farming as for nonfarming jobs.[39]

The success of farmers in obtaining deferment from the draft illustrated how the system functioned in harmony with decentralized social values. The draft was controlled not only by upper-level decisions on manpower needs, made by the president and military advisers, but also by pressure generated by political interest groups at lower levels, working through Congress and public opinion.

The draft had hardly been launched and the nation remained at peace when, in June 1941, several Congressmen expressed concern at the loss of farm labor. Such a loss reflected not merely draft withdrawals but the new economic opportunity for higher wages in industry. In 1940, according to government reports, there had been 2.5 million farm workers in excess of need. The director of the Agricultural Adjustment Administration had urged the millions of sharecroppers to take new jobs in industry, and by the end of 1941 some 1 million croppers had taken this advice.[40]

In early 1942 complaints began arriving in Congress that cotton, corn, and wheat farmers could not find workers. The farm operators were being outbid in wages for labor by industry, and they placed the blame on local draft boards. SS headquarters informed local boards that farmers could be deferred if they produced a needed crop, had a high skill level, and were in a labor-short area.[41] John Moses, the governor of South Dakota, however, wanted local boards to fill their quotas by drafting only men who had recently left the state for better jobs.[42]

Here was a theme that proved popular in the farm belt. The draft should be used to overcome the natural operation of the labor-wage market, to freeze workers in low-paying farm work. If a man stayed on

the farm he was deferred. If he left, he was drafted. When this use of
the draft was first suggested in industry, Congress and unions raised
considerable opposition. But farm labor had less effective representation
than industrial unions and farm operators in Congress.

The pressure for special treatment continued in 1942. Dairymen from
the Northeast insisted they did not want a blanket deferment but some
plan to encourage workers to stay put. From Omaha came word that
labor shortages as high as 40 percent could create a planting crisis in the
spring. In Washington, members of the House Agriculture Committee
demanded that Hershey draft men to work on the farms. Governor
Moses continued to badger the president and called for a blanket deferment for farm labor in his state. Some 50,000 workers had left the state
since 1940, half of them going to do war work. Without a blanket
deferment the greatest crop in South Dakota history could not be
harvested.[43]

The solution was a law that would grant the government power to draft
workers for jobs in industry or agriculture and freeze them in such positions by use of a threat to draft them into the military. But the notion
of "work or fight" was not popular. Unions opposed the idea, as did
management, and the War Department had no interest in using military
service as punishment for obstreperous workers.

So the administration was left with largely verbal solutions. Hershey
arranged with Secretary of Agriculture Claude Wickard to have state and
county war boards provide data to local draft boards on production
goals, size of farm units, and labor requirements for farmers across the
country. A special team from SS headquarters went west to meet with
Governor Moses and work out a solution that would not impair military
quotas. But verbalization had limits. When the state director of Texas
overrode a local board's classification of a ranch hand as 1-A, the entire
Rotan board resigned in protest.[44]

By the fall of 1942 the protest from farmers had reached a level which
required congressional action. Governor Harold E. Stassen of Minnesota;
Edward A. O'Neal, president of the American Farm Bureau; the National
Catholic Rural Life Conference; and several senators publicly demanded
a blanket deferment for farmers. According to James G. Patton, president
of the National Farmers Union, only 25 percent of farm labor had any
protection because local boards did not understand farming.[45]

Seeking an understanding, SS had Col. Frank Keesling meet with
Senator Millard Tydings of Maryland. The senator offered a farm defer-

ment rider to a bill reducing the induction age to 18. Although a friend of the draft, Tydings explained that he had to do something to relieve the pressure from farmers. At first reluctant to cooperate, Hershey managed eventually to limit the damage of Tydings's rider. As passed it merely restated existing guidelines. A farmer who worked "in an agricultural occupation or endeavor essential to the war effort, shall be deferred . . . so long as he remains so engaged and until such time as a satisfactory replacement can be obtained." Since this formula advised local boards, it did little more than add congressional advice to Hershey's advice. Eventually SS provided a list of farm activities considered essential and non-essential with an elaborate system of work units required for deferment. Even tobacco was included as an essential crop.[46]

The Tydings rider was, according to Hershey and Stimson, no more than an expression of congressional opinion, but it did create problems. Congress assumed that the farm labor problem had been solved. Local boards, maintaining their classification discretion, assumed the amendment was merely another bit of discretionary advice. Organized labor, represented by Philip Murray of the CIO, immediately asked Roosevelt for parallel protection for industrial labor. General Marshall complained that deferring another 50,000 farmers would mean curtailing the creation of several divisions. To cope with an expected short number in the fall, the War Department began accelerating calls and cutting postinduction furloughs in half.[47]

Farmers continued to be drafted. Local boards refused to excuse single, young farmers if it meant drafting older married men. In early 1943 five major farm organizations met with Congress to demand a blanket deferment. In short order Senator John H. Bankhead (D-Ala.) and Rep. Paul J. Kilday (D-Tex.) drafted such a bill. Senator Ellison Smith (D-S.C.), chairman of the Agricultural Committee, denounced as "nonsense" the military ambition of creating an armed force of 11 million men. The Bankhead bill passed the Senate by 50 to 24 on March 18. At the same time several state governments took independent action. Governor John C. Vivian of Colorado ordered an end to all inductions of farmers in his state, and the California legislature passed a similar resolution. Public opinion surveys found 27 percent of all farmers denouncing the draft, as compared to only a 6 percent negative rating among all other occupations. The draft mechanism seemed a victim of grassroots rebellion.[48]

The administration quickly put down this rebellion by concessions.

Hershey reduced the amount of farm work needed to qualify for deferment as a full-time farmer. Roosevelt stood by the plan for an armed
force of 11 million but was sympathetic to furloughing soldiers to bring
in the crops, something Stimson opposed. Administration officials testified against the Bankhead bill as class deferment. Some 550,000 farm
workers, age 18 to 37, had already been deferred, and a projected 3
million more would be deferred by the end of the year. On 30 April
Roosevelt created a war Food Administration with the idea of mobilizing
a land army of 3.5 million volunteers to help on farms.[49]

The Bankhead bill was tabled in the House, but farmers did start to
receive more deferments. By 1 February 1944, 1,689,458 single and
married farmers were deferred, and farm deferments became so attractive
that single men left jobs in the war industry to return to the farm. When
a presidential commission that was considering lowering induction standards asked Hershey if he had trouble drafting single farmers, he admitted it was his toughest job. Everyone wanted single men to be drafted
before fathers, but the farm lobby had managed to convince the public
and local boards that starvation threatened if a single farmer was drafted.
Getting single men from the war industry was easier than getting a farmer.
On 1 February 1944 FDR called for a tightening up of all deferments,
but even so, a new bill deferring all farmers was sponsored by Rep.
William Lemke (R-N.D.) and passed Congress. Truman eventually ve-
toed the bill in May 1945, but such congressional action seemed consistent with public views as some 71 percent of the public agreed that young
men should be kept on the farms.[50] The farm lobby had demonstrated
how to deal with a decentralized draft, and the case of farm deferments
was only one of several examples of national manpower policy falling
before the force of locally fueled values. Equally frustrating for the administration was the struggle over drafting men with dependents.

Devotion to family found expression in draft regulations, which announced that "the maintenance of the family as a unit is of importance
to the national well-being." Hershey promised in early January 1942 that
married men with dependents would not be called for some time. Such
men went into a special "hands off" 3-A classification. When local
boards in Canton, Ohio, drafted a few married men, Senator Robert Taft
demanded an investigation. SS looked over Canton and found that of the
79 men delivered for induction, 62 were single, 2 divorced, and 15

married. Of the married men, 13 had wed when called by their draft boards, and the other two were in jail for nonsupport.[51]

Special treatment of married men with dependents caused special problems. From 1939 to 1943 the male population from age 20 to 34 rushed to the altar at a high rate. In 1939 the marriage rate per 1,000 of the population stood at 10.7; by 1942 it had climbed to 13.3. Married men represented 54 percent of the white males in age group 20 to 34 in 1940. Before Pearl Harbor a total of 15,418,710 registrants had been classified. Some 10,160,000 or 84 percent of all men deferred were in 3-A. Only 2,070,000 were left available for induction and other deferments.[52]

In striving to maintain the American family the government had created a dilemma. Early instructions to local boards had insisted that a wife was a dependent even if she held a job. Also, the date of marriage was unimportant. After the attack on Pearl Harbor these policies changed. Now a draftee had to prove his quick marriage was not an attempt to defeat induction. Originally a man deferred for dependents could be engaged in any or no job. But in April 1942 the 3-A classification was split into those men in nonwar jobs (3-A) and those in war-related jobs (3-B). Theoretically, this discrimination allowed local boards to pressure married men out of frivolous jobs. National headquarters warned that men with only financial dependents would be called in the fall. By July the order of call had been revised to the following sequence: single men sans dependents; single men in non-war-related jobs with dependents; single men in war-related jobs with dependents; married men in non-war-related jobs with wives only; married men in war-related jobs with wives only; married men with wives and children and no war-related jobs; married men with wives and children and war-related jobs.[53] In addition, a man wed before 18 September 1940 was now considered after those married later. Notwithstanding these rules, pro-family sentiment in the community remained unchanged. A local board memo of 23 June 1942 reminded everyone that "the necessity for giving adequate consideration to the family unit where a child or children are involved cannot be over emphasized."[54]

Refinements in the rules merely insured that local boards were more than ever forced to make individual distinctions. A typical case raised the following questions for classification: was the registrant legally married? did his wife work and how much did she make? when was the marriage consummated? any children and how old? was the registrant in a war-related job? The particular answers to these questions did not lead inevitably to a particular classification. Another variable was the character of the local manpower pool. If there were single men available, their presence influenced how tough the board was on married men. As national headquarters admitted, no single policy could be applied to all parts of the nation.[55] Dependency was itself redefined by the passage of the Servicemen's Dependents Allowance Act on 23 June 1942 which provided government support to wives and children of enlisted men.

Despite the new rules, when SS sought to push fathers into war work, strong resistance appeared at the grassroots and in Congress. Instead of males shifting to war-related jobs, some 500,000 wives quit work to enhance their husbands' dependency status. A Gallup poll of 23 March 1942 found 71 percent of the public favoring "a plan to draft men who have dependents if this would be necessary to win the war." But few, including government officials, thought it necessary.[56]

Congress began trying to protect fathers when debating the bill to provide allowance for dependents of servicemen. By the summer of 1942, draft calls were running 300,000 a month. Senator Robert Taft and Representative Andrew J. May (D-Ky.) began a campaign to protect the family, but from different perspectives. Taft was upset because he expected the armed forces to grow to 10 million men by 1944 and that meant that fathers would have to be drafted. May, in contrast, predicted that the war would end soon, probably in 1942 and "unquestionably in 1943." He therefore saw no reason to draft men with dependents. But such men were already being drafted in a few areas. Congress received complaints that thirty-year-old fathers were being called before younger single men. Definitions of dependency seemed to vary from one week to another, and some boards denied that status to men with working wives. Because the new G.I. dependents allowance bill might be construed as removing dependency entirely, Congress included a provision that the draft should still take single men before those with dependents. But this provision was merely advisory to local boards.[57]

To congressional complaints Hershey responded merely that "the circumstances particular to each individual's case affect the board in its determination of classification, and no absolute date can be permitted to govern exclusively in the making of these determinations." He did recommend that states try to create pools of single men to insure that they would be called before fathers and also asked boards to reopen all class 3 files and reshuffle them to insure more protection for fathers with children under 18. But boards were also told to "make every possible effort to insure that . . . calls . . . were met on schedule."[58]

Few fathers were drafted in 1942, yet the threat to take them directly affected the question of taking 18-year-old single men. The threat by Hershey and others that fathers in nonessential jobs might be called helped the administration obtain congressional approval to draft at age 18 rather than at age 20. Military leaders had promoted this idea from the beginning of the war, but Congress had resisted because of fears that the public would disapprove of sending such young boys to combat. Originally the obligation to register existed for men 18 to 64, but induction threatened only those 20 to 44.[59]

By 1942, however, the rate of induction calls, rejections, and deferments all pointed to the need to expand the pool of potential soldiers. In June Hershey explained to the president that the 4,375,000 registered men, aged 18 to 20, comprised the cream of the nation's manpower. All draft experience showed "that men are emotionally, intellectually and physically fit for service in inverse ratio to their age." Only 33.49 percent of men aged 35 were qualified; 84.3 percent of volunteers aged 18 were qualified. Moreover, the public now supported the draft of 18 year olds. In September the public voted six to one to draft 18 year olds rather than fathers. When offered the option of taking 18 year olds or childless married men, the public was divided in half. One month later the margin favoring the draft of 18 year olds without qualification had reached 81 percent.[60] Hershey warned that if he did not call young men, he would have to take over 1 million married men. On 12 October Roosevelt recommended the draft of 18 year olds to fill combat units headed overseas.[61]

This move was not accepted without some opposition. Several psychiatrists protested that the drafting of emotionally immature boys would be a mistake. They believed that fathers should be taken instead. But another group of psychiatrists, true to the splintered character of that discipline, insisted that no emotional harm would come to young men serving in the armed forces. All of the branches of the service accepted volunteers of that age anyway. But Congress still disliked the idea of sending such young men into immediate combat, and educators testified that their students should be allowed to finish their training before being called. When the bill finally reached the president on 23 December 1942, young farmers were protected by the Tydings amendment, and another provision allowed students to finish their academic year if called after school began. But Congress approved drafting 18 year olds mainly to gain some protection from the draft for fathers and married men.[62]

Shortages in industrial labor, especially on the West Coast, combined with the November 1942 invasion of North Africa and subsequent casualties convinced military leaders of the need for more troops and once again put the draft spotlight on young married men. On 31 January 1943 Hershey sent a memo to local boards telling them to disregard dependency deferments in order to meet calls. General Millard G. White of the War Department told Congress that the protection of fathers had forced the army to take illiterates, victims of venereal disease, and general undesirables. Stimson also warned that deferring fathers would interfere with winning the war. There were already 8 million men deferred in 3-A, and 6 million of them had children under 18. Paul McNutt announced that draft boards were going to call 3-A types who remained in unessential jobs. The WMC immediately published a list of nonessential jobs or a nondeferral list.[63]

The attempt to coerce fathers into key jobs fell flat. Few fathers bothered to change jobs, even after Hershey's memo ending dependency classifications. Officials had been predicting the draft of fathers since October 1942. Such cassandra calls had little impact on job shifting but did provoke a reaction in Congress. Unimpressed with the dire warnings of military experts, Congress insisted that the draft should not be turned into a tool for controlling civilian labor, and boards continued to take single men before fathers.[64]

Illustrating the problem, in January 1943 an Office of War Information (OWI) survey of public opinion concluded that more education was needed to prepare the people for a draft of married men. The education had to start in Congress. In response to McNutt's pronouncement of work or fight, Rep. Paul J. Kilday of Texas charged that the draft was becoming a threat to "the preservation of the family in American life." To save the institution he offered a bill insuring that no father could be drafted before a single man in any state. A few days later Senator Wheeler offered a similar measure in the Senate. The administration explained that by the summer there would be no one but fathers left in the pool of draftables. As for organizing all married and all singles within a state, Hershey thought the idea was "a hopeless administrative proposition." Indifferent to the facts, on 12 April the House passed Kilday's bill by a vote of 143 to 7. Fortunately, the Senate Military Affairs Committee tabled the measure on 28 May.[65]

The defeat of Kilday's bill, however, was another spurious victory by the administration. SS retreated again. Hershey announced that he was putting off the draft of fathers until July. Later he spoke of August, then October, procrastinating not for sentimental reasons, but because throughout the country local boards protested the induction of fathers. In some cases the boards decided to post the names of all single men with deferments. This "rat file," as it was called, was to alert the public that fathers were being called to protect the single men. In other cases the boards resigned or threatened to quit. A few boards merely announced that they planned to take no fathers while single men were deferred. In Oklahoma City, J. B. Watson, chair of local board 3 said fathers would not be drafted until "this mess is straightened out." Richard K. Mellon of a local board in Pennsylvania called for a "complete house cleaning of industry as regards all single men of draft age."[66]

Warren H. Atherton, commander of the American Legion, urged that "every eligible single man that can be replaced" be removed from government and industry before drafting fathers. The commander of the Army-Navy Union agreed, and the ex-warden of Sing Sing prison insisted that prison inmates be drafted rather than fathers. Mayor La Guardia of New York feared such a draft would cripple his police force. On 15 September 1943 the Gallup poll reported that 68 percent of the public preferred to draft single men from essential war work rather than draft fathers.[67]

When SS informed local boards that some 446,000 of the 6,559,000 men deferred as fathers had to be called before the end of the year, Congress rebelled again. The Kilday and Wheeler bills were revived amidst general hearings on manpower. Senator Wheeler denounced McNutt and the threat to fathers. Taft, Sheridan Downey (D-Calif.), and Harry Truman joined in the protest. They felt that McNutt was twisting the purpose of the draft by threatening to call up fathers who worked in unessential jobs. Downey announced that few draftees were needed because the air force could bomb the enemy into submission. Representative May insisted the military wanted too many men. The surrender of Italy in September added fuel to these arguments. And Senator Taft continued to call for splitting the draft pool at age 30 with all below that age being called before any above.[68]

In short order the Wheeler bill appeared in the Senate and a revised Kilday bill in the House. Both measures required that the draft of pre–Pearl Harbor fathers be delayed. Wheeler wanted a temporary delay, but the Kilday-May bill required a permanent exclusion. Congress at that time threatened to control manpower policy by statute, bringing chaos to administration plans. In response the administration paraded a series of witnesses before congressional committees. McNutt, who had lost all credibility with Congress, warned of disaster if all fathers were deferred and essential workers called instead. Hershey, who had good rapport with politicians, argued that the pool of single men was dry. In a patronizing tone, Lt. Gen. Joseph T. McNarney told the senators: "Whoever initiates such a change must assume the grave responsibility for ignoring the considered judgment of our military leaders arrived at after careful and prolonged study." Marshall and Admiral Ernest J. King both spoke against the threat. Bernard Baruch, the leading mobilizer of World War I, bluntly told senators either to support Marshall or fire him. The president hinted at a veto.[69]

This phalanx of opposition took its toll on the bill in the Senate. When the vote came, the Senate unanimously rejected the Wheeler bill and offered a substitute which allowed the induction of fathers but increased government allowances for child support. When the measure reached the House floor, however, it was revised. Supported by the farm lobby, the House drafted a new bill which stripped McNutt's power over the draft, cancelled the list of unessential jobs, and deferred all fathers until all other eligible men were taken. To the administration's disgust, the House version prevailed in the conference committee. The final bill specified that pre–Pearl Harbor parents were to be deferred as long as possible "without affecting the usual, regular and orderly flow" of men.[70]

The president's early inclination to veto the measure was eroded by political considerations and he signed the bill on 10 December. The measure had passed by a wide margin and a veto would probably have been overridden. Still, Roosevelt could not resist deriding the measure which said, in essence, that fathers should not be drafted unless they had to be drafted. "What kind of legislation is that?" asked the president. The answer, of course, was political legislation.[71]

No amount of political legislation could protect the family from the impact of the war. Dependent deferments shrank from 8 million in 1943 to less than 100,000 by 1945, but the draft was only one of many forces upsetting family life. Married women joined other women in employment outside the home, and by 1944 16.5 million women made up 36 percent of the entire civilian work force. Of the total, one-third had family responsibility. Juvenile delinquency skyrocketed during the war years, and the divorce rate rose dramatically, from 16 per every 100 marriages in 1940 to 27 per 100 in 1944.[72]

The family was only one of several institutions which frustrated the scientific management of manpower during the war. Equally stubborn, when confronted by war and the draft, was education. Good manpower management required deferments for scientists and others with knowledge valuable to society. Deferring such people represented another challenge to the egalitarian rhetoric used to pass the draft.

Draft officials expected problems with the educational institutions in the country. With few exceptions both teachers and students had opposed the adoption of the draft in 1940. Students shared with most other Americans a rather low opinion of military life, and in the interwar period there had been a positive correlation between years of education and pacifism.[73] Accommodating the opposition of students and teachers had led to a provision in the original law allowing a student to be deferred until the end of the academic year, 1940 through 1941. The law also provided for deferments for scientists, reflecting the effectiveness of the education lobby and the concept of efficiency in manpower management.[74]

Yet even with the provisions and before Pearl Harbor, college enrollment began to drop. Professional schools were hard hit. For example, law school enrollment dropped by 25.2 percent from 1940 to 1941. There was also a sharp decline in enrollment at the undergraduate level with a 22.3 percent drop in agriculture and business enrollment from 1938 to 1942. The draft had only a limited impact on enrollment before Pearl Harbor. The decline came as many young men volunteered for the service or found attractive jobs in war industry.[75]

Even two months after America entered the war there seemed little pressure on education through conscription. In February 1942 SS sent out two questionnaires, one to students and another to administrators. Some 1,450 colleges and 150,000 students responded. The students reported that local boards were generous in granting postponements. Only 9 percent of those who replied were in class 1-A, and 47 percent were in 2-A or 2-B. About 50 percent of all college males had deferments because of their special training. If both the school and the student requested a deferment, the odds were three to one that it would be granted.[76]

Students in medical science and health fields received most of the deferments. About 81 percent of men with these majors reported being in 2-A or 2-B. Similar high percentages existed in engineering (71), biology (46), chemistry (69), physics (59), and geology (56). But many liberal arts and social science majors were in 2-A and 2-B. Of all class 2 deferments, health fields had the highest rate of deferent, about 75.5 percent and liberal arts the lowest at 21.4 percent.[77]

College administrators reported only a modest impact from the draft, in that they had to spend time requesting deferments for their students. Some 37 percent of all full-time students who responded to the survey said the colleges had initiated their deferment requests. In addition, 31 percent of the 856 administrators who responded announced the implementation of an accelerated degree program. In the four New York City colleges the credit hours for a degree dropped from 138 to 116. As the draft was taking men no younger than 21, the schools expected to graduate most students before induction.[78]

Yet despite the slight impact of the draft, college leaders anticipated further problems and pushed a program of special draft protection. The draft law might state a universal obligation to serve, but several academic leaders warned of disaster if their students were taken. Dr. George B. Cutten, president of Colgate, wanted all promising students deferred until graduation, even if it meant drafting forty year olds. The American Chemical Society warned that the draft of chemistry students could cause America to lose the war. Dr. James B. Conant, president of Harvard, pleaded with Roosevelt in March 1942 to treat colleges as vital war industries, with protection from the draft. Others wanted colleges used to rehabilitate men rejected by the military for illiteracy, and a conference of 50 West Coast academic leaders blasted the administration's failure to utilize colleges in national defense and the trend to draft future leaders.[79]

But not until the fall of 1942 did the draft threaten to create serious problems for colleges. As Marshall called for younger soldiers and as dependency deferments ate into the manpower pool, the only logical reservoir of suitable draftees became men 18 to 20. When administration leaders introduced a Senate bill reducing the induction age to 18, some education leaders began to protest. They sought an amendment which would defer all graduate students to the end of the academic year. Others argued that college students should not be drafted as privates but commissioned as officers upon graduation, and engineering deans denounced the threat to America's technical capabilities.[80]

Administration spokesmen tried to defend the age revision. Hershey called deferring college students discrimination on an economic basis.

Patterson denounced colleges for insisting on business as usual. They felt that a blanket deferment for students threatened military morale and would deprive the armed forces of many capable soldiers. As for commissions, Patterson emphasized that colleges were not needed to produce officers because there was already a huge stockpile of such men.[81]

But the clamor continued. One college president predicted the closing of hundreds of schools. President Joseph A. Brandt of the University of Oklahoma called the threat the gravest since the Civil War. Speaking before deans of engineering colleges, A. Potter of Purdue said all engineering students should be deferred. Colonel Edward A. Fitzpatrick of SS tried to explain the impossibility of protecting all vital men and at the same time finding soldiers to fight. As it was, engineering students received deferments at a rate only a little below medical students.[82]

Only after concessions had been made to the education establishment did an amendment pass creating induction liability for 18 year olds. The amendment passed on 13 November 1942, but a month earlier the president had asked the secretaries of war and the navy to develop a plan to use the colleges in the war effort. Guy E. Snavely of the Association of American Colleges submitted such a plan to Eleanor Roosevelt. Roosevelt passed it on to his military leaders and reminded them that drafting at 18 would "greatly deplete all undergraduate enrollment." Also there was great training potential in the equipment and faculty at the colleges. Why not train men on the campuses?[83]

Military leaders resented the president's request because it favored social priorities over military efficiency. Patterson complained that training was more efficient in the service facilities than on idyllic campuses. Lieutenant Gen. Lesley J. McNair, commander of the army ground forces, was appalled at Roosevelt's idea. McNair faced a general shortage of some 300,000 men and a declining level of quality in infantry units. Now, he moaned, "We are asked to send men to college!"[84]

Despite the protests, a program was created and launched in early 1943. Called the Army Specialized Training Program (ASTP), at its height it involved 150,000 men and was a source of derision by the military and SS. Inductees as well as enlistees were eligible for the program, and local board members were cynical about the sudden thirst for knowledge that promptly sprang up among 1-A types. When commanders delayed assigning soldiers to colleges for special training, however, Marshall applied pressure. Yet within a year even he had second thoughts, and by February 1944 the ASTP had been cut by some 80 percent.[85]

Writing after the war, Major General Harry L. Twaddle emphasized that the ASTP program had been dumped on the army. "The underlying reason for institution of the ASTP program," wrote the general, "was to prevent some colleges and universities from going into bankruptcy. From a strictly mobilization viewpoint, the value of the program was nil."[86] The general was bitter but on the mark. The men would have been more quickly trained in the military, and the withdrawal of men with high aptitude scores contributed to the continued decline in quality of American ground forces. But the program did provide a subsidy to American education during the war.

Even with the subsidy, American higher education administrators continued to complain. By the fall of 1943 enrollment in graduate schools and professional schools had plunged about 30 to 40 percent. True, female enrollment jumped, but mainly in liberal arts. In June 1943 some 17,000 male engineers were scheduled for graduation but 6,000 were already committed to the army. Over twice as many college men were already serving as draftees as had served in all of World War I. In November 1943, 585 colleges reported a full-time civilian enrollment of 373,993. This represented a 38 percent decline from the total of 603,558 in November 1942, but the blow had been softened by the assignment of 288,000 military students to the colleges, 140,000 from ASTP alone.[87] This decline was serious, but so was the loss of millions of lives on the war front.

The administration accepted, and the draft law recognized, the need to defer some students. But the rub appeared over which students merited this privilege. The War Department, represented by Stimson and Patterson, accepted the need for a few deferments for highly specialized students, but Paul McNutt of the WMC had other ideas. He wanted to protect as many students and schools as possible. Paterson complained that if McNutt had his way, thousands of young men majoring in accounting and forestry would be protected at a time when the army needed them, and parents would be able to buy their sons out of the service by paying college tuition.[88]

Under pressure from both the civilian education lobby and the calls of the armed forces, the SS adopted a modified student deferment program in spring 1943. To merit deferment, a student had to be majoring in one of twenty special fields useful for defense, and the school had to certify that the student was in good standing and would graduate before July 1945. SS hoped to keep the total of such deferments under 27,000.

In addition, the ASTP was launched. Soon 80 percent of all students in medicine and 76 percent in engineering were under an obligation to serve after graduation in exchange for their deferment.[89] But many in the scientific community still considered these programs as too little protection for a vital resource; others considered all deferments unjustified.

In early 1944 all deferments came under criticism from the president. The armed forces needed younger men as the buildup for Operation Overlord, the invasion of France, continued. Marshall decided to end the ASTP, and after conferring with industrial and educational leaders, SS issued a bulletin, effective on 15 February, tightening quotas on colleges. Seniors graduating before 1 July 1944 who majored in one of the special fields remained deferred. Among nonseniors, only 10,000 deferments were to be granted for the entire nation, and they were limited to the fields of chemistry, engineering, geology, geophysics, and physics.[90] Young scientists also had some limited deferment, and the War Department obtained a blanket deferment for 10,000 men under age 26 who were working on secret projects, including radar and the atomic bomb.[91]

The reversal of policy only enraged the science lobby. Charles L. Parsons of the American Chemical Society and Frank B. Jewett of the National Academy of Science warned Roosevelt that the nation's supply of trained scientists was threatened by the new draft regulations. Parson feared a loss of production. Jewett acknowledged that up to March 1944 he had been impressed with the "remarkable understanding" shown by local boards in granting deferments to young scientists. But the current plan to take all men under age 26 meant "real damage" to war work. These science spokesmen took little solace from Roosevelt's reassurances that deferments would continue for a limited number of specialists.[92]

Until 1944 America's draft policy was very protective of students. Some of the protection came incidentally, because of the reluctance of Congress to take men under age 21, but the cry to protect special talent and training also had its effect. SS directed local boards to be liberal with deferments in a variety of educational fields. Such policies, together with the ASTP program, helped colleges survive. After the war 75 percent of local boards expressed satisfaction with how the college deferment system had operated.[93] Other deferments were less satisfying.

Unlike the sentimental value of the home and the potential value of the school, the industrial economy required protection because of its direct role in the war. The economy had been staggered by the depression of the 1930s—in 1939 about 17 percent of the work force (over 8 million) remained unemployed, despite the New Deal, and research and development as well as modernizing had all been postponed. After the war began, industry began galloping at an unprecedented pace, and the draft arrived on the economic scene with the impact of a Saudi prince at a fire sale. Thanks to the draft and war contracts, unemployment disappeared and labor shortages became the problem.[94]

Long before the passage of the 1940 bill, military and other planners recognized some of the implications of the draft for the economy. The United States Employment Service anxiously offered to share with military planners a roster of some 7 million unemployed men who might be taken in a draft, but such a simple approach to drafting military manpower was unrealistic and unscientific. Provisions in the law specified that men could be deferred if engaged in war work. To planners, such provisions seemed pregnant with power to overhaul the entire economy for war and were consistent with theories of modernizaton. The deferment power of the draft could be used to insure an efficient relocation of workers from unessential to essential tasks. Industries that refused to contribute to the war, or did it poorly, could be penalized by withholding draft protection from their workers. A new level of national economic management seemed possible.[95]

But the idea was unrealistic. Men were to be drafted or deferred according to the needs of the armed forces. This meant that many workers were rejected, some 47 percent of all industrial workers whatever their job. After being declared 4-F a man lost all fear of the draft and worked where he wished. Also, Congress in passing the draft bill had specifically rejected any broad powers over the economy. At no time during the war did Congress support a true national service law that would authorize the type of mandatory control of civilian labor that planners desired. True, at various points during the war the administration tried to use the military draft as a civilian workers draft, but Congress always resisted, with the encouragement of organized labor and management. Due to rejection rates, to the selectivity of the draft, to public and presidential distrust of national service and the opposition of unions, the draft failed to revolutionize the economy.[96]

The modern, universal draft failed, for example, to reverse the historic relationship of economic class and military service. In a survey of a northern community during the Civil War, one historian observed that the draft operated according to a skill and class bias. Men without property served at a higher rate than those with property. Men with professional skills served at a lower rate than unskilled or unemployed men. Despite all the changes made in creating a modern, twentieth-century draft that sought to avoid the mistakes of the Civil War, a similar pattern emerged in World War II.[97]

Occupation was a direct influence on vulnerability to the draft. Semiprofessionals such as clerks and dancers suffered heavily from the draft. Among laborers, carpenters and plumbers were taken while machinists and printing craftsmen were deferred. Deferments were also related to work status. The higher the job status, regardless of its relation to war productivity, the more likely the irreplaceability of the worker. Operators and laborers made up only 2.5 percent of all working males 18 to 44 in 1940, but this cohort furnished 41 percent of all men inducted to June 1945. Clerical and sales personnel contributed 12 percent. Yet the draft was supposed to defer men on the basis of their contribution to defense industry, not on the status of their jobs.[98]

What had happened to the idea of occupational deferment, the heart of selectivity in SS? Several months before the draft bill was enacted, Capt. Joseph F. Battley, a War Department planner, warned that local boards might not accept the idea of job deferments.[99] In 1940 industry expanded by drawing upon the surplus work force. Calls were moderate, and induction standards were high. But after the attack by the Japanese on Pearl Harbor, workers flocked to volunteer despite Hershey's admonition to "stay at your job until called." Draft calls increased, and induction standards were lowered. SS reminded local boards of their responsibility to be selective and protect vital war workers, even apprentices. Employers were asked to screen their workers and request deferments for only irreplaceable men.[100]

The War Department and the War Production Board (WPB) cooperated with SS in identifying key industries that required special treatment by local boards. SS began certifying classes of workers in various industries that merited deferments, but the task was soon taken over by the newly created WMC under Paul McNutt, who began issuing lists of essential occupations meriting deferments. The army announced that certain key workers in the aircraft and ship industries would be rejected as volunteers without the permission of their local boards. But volunteering continued, and by the summer of 1942 the scheme of selective deferment was in trouble.[101]

Complaints cropped up from all sides. Colonel Arthur V. McDermott of the New York City draft office demanded that industry "tighten its belt, face the facts and do some housecleaning." Thousands of young men had to be called, and he thought women and older men should be used to replace draft-eligible single men. Congress and local boards complained that married men were threatened because of excessive job deferments.[102]

Industry, in turn, grumbled that too many men were being drafted. The National Maritime Union wanted all seamen deferred. A steel manager predicted that, at the current draft rate, his industry would lose 25 percent of its work force by the end of 1943. Shipbuilders announced that their workers were being drafted as fast as they were trained. And V. E. Doonan of Ford Motor Company said local boards were stripping his plant of all mechanics.[103] In 1943 the WMC continued to issue bulletins on vital men who should be deferred, but a House Committee on Small Business in February reported that such action had failed to provide any substantial relief from the indiscriminate drafting of vital workers.[104]

The WMC appeared to be a failure. By May 1943 some 5,500 businesses employing 3 million workers had filed replacement schedules with WMC to provide for orderly withdrawal of workers. These schedules were guides that told local boards when particular men could be called. But several local boards vowed to ignore the information if it meant drafting fathers before single men.[105] McNutt issued a nondeferrable job list to force men into war jobs, but it just created more confusion. Production of the B17 by Boeing was cut back because of worker shortages, and Robert E. Gross, president of Lockheed Corporation, pleaded with Congress to provide leadership and decide if the nation needed planes or soldiers.[106] In September 1943 a freeze was implemented on draft calls for the West Coast under the orders of James Byrnes at the Office of War Mobilization, which was supposed to provide overall supervision of the economy.[107]

By fall the situation had reached crisis proportions. Hershey continued to threaten to draft fathers; industry continued to complain at losses; local boards denounced hoarding of single men by industry; and Congress denounced McNutt for trying to impose national service through the military draft.[108] Then Congress pushed through the Kilday bill, revoking most of McNutt's powers and giving added protection to fathers. By February 1944 the president complained that SS had been too lenient with deferments, but tightening up deferments proved difficult. The military itself set a poor example. The naval installations at Pearl Harbor refused to cooperate with local boards who wished to take young single workers from port facilities.[109]

The American public, reflected through local boards, simply refused to sanction any radical solution to the problems. Before the attack on Pearl Harbor over 60 percent of those polled favored greater government control of unions, but this did not translate into a labor draft. During the war the public consistently favored national service when the question was posed independently. In December 1942, 56 percent approved; in February 1944, 65 percent; in January 1945, 55 percent. When the question was qualified by asking whether fathers in nonessential jobs should be called rather than single men in war jobs, the public preferred to take single men by 68 percent to 24 percent. A survey of March 1942 found 61 percent in favor of drafting men and women for war work, but in April 1943 only 37 percent thought there was a shortage of such workers. In February 1944, 65 percent said "draft war workers if needed," but only 16 percent said there was a need. In January 1945, 55 percent approved the national service bill, but 39 percent favored voluntary methods. Whenever the idea arose it met opposition in Congress and finally died in early 1945.[110]

Given public opinion, the administration preferred to try indirect means to insure a stable and adequate work force for war industry. SS became such an indirect agent for keeping labor in line. Organized labor had originally opposed the draft for precisely this reason. After labor's hope to have representation on each local board was defeated, as a violation of the community notion of Selective Service, major unions appointed liaison officials to national draft headquarters. Despite public objections, Hershey authorized deferments for leading union officials, explaining that labor leaders merited deferments because they promoted production efficiency in war industry. Both the AFL and CIO were embarrassed at this recognition and denied requesting special protection. But at least in early 1942 a surface harmony existed between the draft and organized labor.[111]

As military calls increased, as war production expanded, and as the labor force sought to make the best of a booming economy, dissonance replaced harmony. Management began using the draft to control labor. For example, California shipyards flushed out weak workers by sending their names to local boards for reclassification. Such actions were licit because local boards awarded deferments only at the request of management. Also, when unions began to strike over the layoffs and other issues, the government tried to use the draft as a weapon to curb the actions. War and navy officials, including Stimson and Knox, recommended to Roosevelt that SS should withdraw job deferments if a union struck in defiance of a War Labor Board decision.[112]

Reluctantly, on 12 September 1942, Hershey announced that when headquarters advised that a group of deferred workers were adversely affecting the war effort, boards should immediately terminate deferments and reclassify the strikers. Similarly, if workers in a vital industry, such as nonferrous metal mining, left jobs without approval, they should be reclassified into 1-A. Hershey worried that such actions were of questionable legality and might harm the community consensus upon which the success of local boards rested, but he acted under strong pressure from Stimson and Congress.[113]

In Congress during 1943 Senator Warren Austin and Rep. James W. Wadsworth, the original sponsers of the draft, introduced a national service bill. In the House Lyndon Johnson offered a bill calling for draft reclassification of all war workers who had a record of absenteeism. And on the local level, draft boards began acting against workers without the aid of legislation.[114]

Such actions did little to prevent labor disturbances, many of which arose inevitably from the dynamic war economy. Some disturbances arose over trivia, and some, such as the grievances of the coal miners over wages, hours, and safety, had been growing for several years. Reaction to the miners' strike began at the local board level and later spread to Washington. Without waiting for national direction, Gen. Ben Smith, state director of Alabama, ordered local boards to reclassify strikers in several war plants. Governor Prentice Cooper of Tennessee did likewise for striking coal miners after having been told by local board members that they would draft no additional men "until our government has taken adequate steps to meet this [strike] situation." Col. T. J. Johnson, Tennesee state director, told local boards to begin reclassifying miners.[115]

In Washington there was more caution. Roosevelt issued an order that the miners return to work. When union leader John L. Lewis ignored the order, Roosevelt did not call for a draft of the strikers. The president had no desire to antagonize labor and was unsure of the legality of drafting the strikers. He also thought that given time, Lewis would offend the public with his cavalier attitude toward the war effort. The solicitor general reassured the president that if he raised the draft age from 38 to 45 he would pull in most of the miners. As for legality, SS regulations provided for the cancellation of deferments for groups "adversely affecting the war." Also, to prevent miners from moving to other jobs, the WMC could direct that strikers be barred from new jobs, as President Wilson had done in World War I. Finally, the SS could be ordered to reclassify miners with a 4-F classification into 1-A and the armed forces asked to take them as limited service types.[116]

Heartened by the advice, Roosevelt finally acted. First, he had Harold Ickes, secretary of interior, begin talks with the recalcitrant Lewis. Second, he asked Congress to raise the draft age to 65. If Ickes failed to find a solution, Roosevelt planned to issue a work-or-fight order to miners, cancel occupational deferments, and have the army waive physical requirements. He informed the army to be prepared to take in 250,000 miners between the ages of 38 and 45 and another 50,000 up to age 65. At the same time, Congress passed the Smith-Connally act on 25 June over the president's veto. It made strikes illegal in plants seized by the government and made unions liable for damages. Finally on 18 August the president issued an executive order authorizing SS to cancel the deferments of striking workers. These tactics worked, and the strike was over by the end of the year, although Lewis had won some wage concessions.[117]

Miners returned to work, but strikes continued on a reduced scale throughout the war. Local boards continued to threaten strikers with reclassification, but mere reclassification failed to intimidate labor for several reasons. Many strikers had deferments unrelated to their jobs— through age, physical condition, or dependents. Furthermore, despite distaste for strikers, military leaders had no desire or room to induct marginal men. Stimson thought the threat of induction would suffice, although General Hershey, himself a conservative Republican, discouraged the use of the draft to control labor because he felt it was an inappropriate expansion of govenment power. The entire experience demonstrated that the military draft was an inappropriate instrument to control labor.

Despite all the deferments and disputes over discrimination, when the war finally ended, the draft had succeeded in achieving its original objective. During the war the nation had peacefully registered 49 million men, selected 19 million, and inducted 10 million. A postwar survey of local board members found that 92 percent were satisfied with the policy of occupational deferments.[118] In 1940 pro-draft advocates had constantly argued that it was the most democratic means of raising an army. Although the vagaries of military assignment and economic need precluded the imposition of a truly universal draft, although social priorities precluded the use of women, the aged, and fathers, the draft did contribute to an egalitarian and diversified armed force.

A massive postwar survey of 13 million men below the grade of commission officer, all of whom served between 1940 and VJ Day, supports this conclusion. Despite deferments, the best and brightest did not evade service. The average serviceman had more education than the civilian male cohort. Some 56.8 percent of enlisted men (ems) had finished at least one year of high school and 12.3 percent had at least one year of college. Only 40.6 percent of the civilian cohort could say the same. Soldiers averaged one more year of formal schooling. Even black servicemen averaged more education than the total white male population.[119]

Thanks to the system of distributing calls by state, soldiers came proportionately from each state. Only a few industrial states provided more than their proportion of males of service age according to the 1940 census. This anomaly arose because many such states enjoyed an influx of workers from rural states, but these workers were still carried on the draft rolls of their original home. Across the vocational spectrum, the percentage of manual workers from urban areas who served was more than their percentage of the 1940 male work force, while professional, managerial, service, and farm workers served less.[120]

In physical and social makeup the armed forces were not representative of the entire population, but within the cohort there were few radical differences. Thanks to the screening by SS and the armed forces, the physical and mental status of soldiers was better than that of the civilian cohort. By the end of the war, almost 50 percent of all who served were still under 26 years old. But only 29 percent of the total male population was under 26 in 1940. Only 8.5 percent of the ems who served were black, but blacks made up 9.5 percent of all males 18 to 44 in the population of 1940. Thanks to the pro-natal policy of Congress and SS, soldiers were mostly single men. Over 70 percent of army inductees were men without any family ties when drafted, although some 60 percent of the entire male cohort was married, widowed, or separated. Still some 3 million married men did serve as ems, only 28 percent of the total. The nation had drafted its manpower without upsetting its demographic character.[121]

Neither had the draft upset the political structure of the nation. The war had begun with gruff cries for total war, total sacrifice, and academic theories of modernization promised more regimentation from above. The reality, however, was more prosaic. The supposed march of centralization was not advanced by conscription as practiced in the United States. The entire process of mobilization had to accommodate itself to the political consensus.

4

Truman, UMT, and the Draft

In 1945 the war ended in Europe and the Pacific; the draft continued. Americans had never tolerated a peacetime draft before 1940, and before either Germany or Japan surrendered in 1945 a debate began over how long this alien institution should continue beyond the ceasefire. Willard Waller, a sociologist, wrote that renewal of the draft, due to expire on 15 May 1945, seemed a prudent idea because it would keep the United States strong, the only nation "with idealistic and humane principles in its foreign policy." America needed to remain strong because her riches would prove a tempting target for future enemies. On the other side of the debate Norman Thomas, leader of American socialists, wired President Roosevelt on 21 January 1945 supporting a worldwide move to end the draft because "no nation will endure the costs of general universal conscription except as it is tied up with militarism and imperialism."[1]

Roosevelt died before the war ended, and when Harry Truman became president on 12 April 1945 one of his first acts was to sign a one-year draft extension. He explained that the draft was needed to continue military actions in Asia. Congress, already seeking to reestablish its independence, passed the extension easily but inserted a provision which required that all inductees under the age of 19 be given six months' training before going overseas. Neither Truman nor General Marshall liked this revision because both General MacArthur and General Eisenhower were short of replacements. Marshall explained that victory over Germany did not remove the need for replacement troops while Norway, Denmark, and Holland remained filled with fanatical Nazi troops, but Congress was unmoved by his pleas.[2]

Five months later, after Japanese officials trod gingerly across the deck of the USS *Missouri* to sign the surrender documents, Americans in and out of the service demanded an immediate demobilization. Almost 80,000 letters arrived on Capitol Hill, all urging an early end to the draft.[3]

The public's position on the draft seemed clear: bring the troops home immediately and stop taking boys through the draft. But such a procedure made little sense in view of American occupation commitments made in the peace treaties. The soldiers abroad also wanted to come home immediately, but they realized that their chances of rapid demobilization were influenced by the availability of replacements. Troop opinion, therefore, supported a continuation of the draft.[4]

On 9 May 1945, one day after the surrender of Germany, Truman signed Public Law 54, which extended the draft for one year. Congress and the public supported this action because war continued against Japan. But in August 1945 the Armed Service Committee of the House began hearings on demobilization. Several representatives, including May, Thomas, and Kilday urged Truman to cut in half all induction calls, and by VJ Day leaders in both the House and Senate opposed continuing the draft. They particularly wanted an end to induction of men under age 20.[5]

Congress was reacting in traditional fashion to the pressure of constituency opinion, but this attitude created problems for the administration. General Hershey informed the White House that he expected draft calls of at least 63,000 in September. Recruiting volunteers could not furnish enough troops as replacements for occupation forces. Provisions in the draft extension PL 54, which removed 18 year olds from the draft pool, were also creating problems. Hershey urged an extension of the draft beyond 1946 as a means to "reassure the peoples of this country and the rest of the world that the United States government is determined to fulfill its obligations in securing the peace for which we fought."[6]

To complicate matters even more, Hershey's attitude lacked the unanimous support of the military. Given the opportunity, many military leaders preferred a force of volunteer professionals, backed by a training program to create a reservoir of militia for emergency call-up. As early as 23 August the navy informed Truman it wanted to stop using draftees and rely exclusively on volunteers. The army had devised an elaborate plan to promote volunteer recruitment with the early efforts aimed at promoting reenlistments of veterans. Congress contributed to the effort by passing a law on 6 October which authorized enlistment tours of 12, 18, 24, and 36 months for men as young as 17, even as draft power over 18 year olds disappeared. Liberal reenlistment furloughs and cash bonuses were also offered.[7]

Prudent military leaders, however, realized that the move away from conscription had to be accomplished slowly. In May 1945 Stimson had begun to phase out the system of taking marginal men to prevent relocation of valuable civilian workers. He insisted that the army needed only young, physically fit types. When Japan surrendered, the army announced plans to draft only for replacement purposes. Stimson projected that the force would be cut to 2.5 million men in the next 19 months and would require 50,000 men a month from the draft, "in proportion of 45,000 white and 5,000 colored." Also, the army wanted only men below age 26. Truman approved the decisions, which met praise in Congress.[8]

President Truman's attitude toward the draft was as ambiguous as that of the military. His ideas were based on his own experience in World War I as a National Guard officer and his work as a senator during World War II. First, he wanted to adopt a system of universal military training (UMT). On the surface UMT seemed to be no different than the current military draft. But, as articulated by administration leaders for the next several years, UMT meant merely calling young men for a short period of training, generally six months. A system such as SS could be used to call the men into training, but they never went on active duty with regulars. The draft pulled men from civilian life into military life and into regular duty. UMT, in contrast, was more of an elaborate summer camp to train young men, much like the Plattsburg movement of pre–World War I days.

Truman believed UMT would aid the nation as well as the armed forces. Through UMT the president hoped to improve the health, education, and citizenship of youth. Incidentally, and this was the part approved by the military, a huge reservoir of trained manpower would be created. The entire idea resembled the old nineteenth-century militia program, except it would be run by the national government rather than the states.

As for the current draft system, its days were limited. Truman had little use for continuing it after the Japanese surrender. In the afterglow of atomic explosions at Hiroshima and Nagasaki, the president told his cabinet that SS was "unimportant for longrun military security." He felt it more essential for the next war that the United States recruit scientists and invest in scientific methods of war. Long before Dwight Eisenhower or John Foster Dulles spoke of massive retaliation, Truman was thinking in similar terms.[9]

But despite this lack of enthusiasm from the military and the president, the regular draft had to continue for a time. General Marshall made that clear in discussions in early August. He believed it was unfair to retain men who had fought and won the war as an occupation force. Those men had to be released early, and, to prove the point, they soon began rioting to get out. The army estimated that it required some 1.2 million men for European occupation and the same in Asia. While these figures were soon scaled back to a total of 1.55 million, even that total could not be achieved without the draft. UMT had to be designed from scratch and Congress sold on the idea. Recruitment of volunteers was not going well, although both Patterson and Secretary of the Navy James Forrestall still preferred to use the volunteer system. Only Postmaster General Robert E. Hannegan, with an eye to political problems, urged an immediate end to conscription.[10]

Accepting the inevitable, Truman had prepared a message to Congress in early September calling for a continuation of the draft. His justification reflected both civil and military motives. To Governor Olin D. Johnston of South Carolina the president explained that the men who fought the war should be discharged and young men drafted as replacements. "It is not going to hurt some of these kids between the ages of 18 and 26 to do a little bit of work. It will be good for them physically, teach them some discipline."[11]

Military officials supported the president. General Marshall promised to push volunteers but warned that only the draft could furnish enough men. As for UMT, Patterson cautioned the president that trying to slip this plan through Congress would only create a crisis. If asked to adopt UMT, politicians might use the occasion to end the draft. The War Department hoped by spring 1946 to have better news on volunteers, which would make a gamble on UMT more reasonable. When Eisenhower became chief of staff in November 1945, he supported UMT but still preferred a large active army. Both he and Patterson felt the army had to remain at 1.6 million through the summer of 1946 "to maintain our international and domestic commitments," but they expected a maximum of only 500,000 volunteers.[12]

Logic, however, carried less weight than the cries of constituents. Truman's call for draft continuation met opposition in Congress, in the homes of draftees, and also in the Office of War Mobilization and Reconversion (OWMR). John Snyder, as director of OWMR, was acutely aware of the need to end the draft. As the manpower pool shrank during the war, more and more essential civilians had been drafted. In late 1945, the draft threatened to take key personnel who were playing a vital role in reconversion. Snyder's office estimated that only 300,000 men, age 19 to 25, remained to draft. He urged the War Department to limit inductions to young men just reaching age 18, which was the group Congress sought to protect. And there was simply no way in which the army could reach its projected strength for 1946 by drafting only 18 year olds. Marshall and Patterson both informed Snyder that the army had to continue drafting those aged 18 to 26. They needed a minimum of 50,000 per month, and only 35,000 men reached 18 each month.[13]

As the new year began other military manpower figures revealed that both the president and the War Department had seriously miscalculated the availability of men, both volunteers and draftees. In early 1946 the entire demobilization program verged on collapse because of a crisis in military manpower brought on in equal shares by Congress, the president, and the War Department.

On New Year's Day the press revealed that SS had failed to meet its quota of 50,000 men per month. On 3 January the War Department announced that the rate of demobilization had to be slowed because of the failure of the draft and the absence of volunteers. The news upset everyone: families; Congress feeling the heat of public rage; SS; and the troops expecting to return from overseas. In Germany GIs wired the *New York Times* that SS should find replacements with the speed they found fighters during the war. In the Pacific troops rioted.[14]

As usual, no one wanted to claim responsibility for the snafu. Administration and military figures pointed to the inconsistent behavior of Congress, but Congress refused to accept the blame. A special Senate subcommittee on demobilization, chaired by Edwin Johnson, launched hearings by calling upon General Hershey to explain the failure of the draft. Hershey, who prided himself on good relations with Congress, was at pains to reassure the senators that they alone were not responsible. There was blame enough to go around.[15]

Hershey had informed the White House that on VJ Day the draft should be reduced to men under 26. In such circumstances the maximum he could draft was 50,000 a month. Then Hershey found, because of congressional and presidential decisions, that he had to work without 18 year olds, with competition from armed force recruiters, and with continued deferments for scientists, farmers, and educators. Senator Johnson had suggested that the president could easily remedy the situation by authorizing the drafting of men up to age 45 and by forcing the military to take in some 4-F rejectees. But the War Department had increased standards for induction after VJ Day and had launched a massive recruitment drive. These actions had made the draft pool smaller and led to the deficit in December 1945.[16]

The deficit was an embarrassment to everyone. The draft was scheduled to end in May 1946, but the War Department said it had to hold troops in the service to meet occupational duties. Some senators suspected that the entire crisis was manufactured as a means of extending the draft. Patterson came back from a tour of the theaters complaining that the army could not fulfill its duty without more draftees. To ease SS's task, the president ordered the induction of men 26 to 30 and the War Department again lowered physical standards to take illiterates and men with hernias, crooked spines, and even psychoneuroses. Hershey informed prison wardens that he wanted more parolees made available for the draft. Senator Johnson informed Hershey, "You are on notice that May 15 is the deadline" for ending the draft.[17]

The Senate Subcommittee on Demobilization and the House Military Affairs Committee both told Hershey that the draft could not be extended, but the White House refused to listen. On 21 January 1946 Truman announced his postwar military manpower program. He wanted UMT, but settled for a call to renew the draft because the services could not rely upon volunteers. The public and Congress, nevertheless, required more motive than a presidential call before reversing the tradition of no peacetime draft. The motive soon appeared.[18]

On 15 March 1946 Winston Churchill spoke at Fulton, Missouri, on the dangers of Communism and Russian expansion. The administration had realized the need for a peacetime draft even before the cold war had become a reality, but arguments based on maintaining armed force strength for occupation purposes had been unconvincing to the public. Only when the administration tied the draft to the threat from Russia did support for such a draft emerge.

According to reports by the Gallup poll, the American public was disposed to a large armed force. As the war ended a sizable 30 percent of those polled did not think the United States could trust Russia to cooperate during peacetime. About 47 percent did not think the atomic bomb made a large armed force unnecessary, and at least 70 percent favored one year of military training for all young men. The public also felt the draft should not take men under the age of 20. But by March 1946 some 65 percent favored a continuation of the draft for one year. Some 71 percent of the public also disapproved of Russian foreign policy.[19]

Throughout March the administration rallied public opinion to convince Congress of the need for draft extension. Eisenhower, Patterson, Secretary of State James Byrnes, and Hershey all argued for the extension. Their arguments varied only slightly. The army said it could not get enough volunteers, and Byrnes spoke of the unsettled conditions of world affairs. Less talk was heard of replacing veterans and more of obligations under the United Nations for maintaining peace. Soon the press reported that the "Russian situation" had convinced senior members of both parties of the need for extension. On 5 April Truman emphasized that the United States policy was to support the United Nations, even if a conflict broke out between Britain and Russia over the Near and Middle East. But the UN could not operate unless Congress passed UMT and a draft extension. Neither the British nor the USSR had demobilized as fast as the United States.[20]

All through April Congress debated the draft extension measure. The House offered a bill suspending inductions for several months to see if enough volunteers would appear; in contrast, the Senate was more receptive to administration arguments. Secretary of War Patterson campaigned among veteran groups to gain support for extension. As was often the case during such debate, final manpower figures were confused and different men offered different figures. The Senate finally offered a six-week draft extension but cut liability to men aged 20 to 30. The House immediately accepted this compromise bill.[21]

Truman thought it was a bad bill. The new age limitations would cut the monthly pool from 30,000 new men to 5,000, and men over 25 were generally not acceptable to the service. The terms meant that the draft was hanging by a thread, nor did the bill send a message of reassurance to Europe about America's willingness to play a large role in the postwar world. In the end Truman signed the measure on 14 May because Congress remained strongly opposed to peacetime conscription. It was to take a more significant shift in international relations to change this attitude.[22]

The shift soon came. Soviet obduracy over German unification and threats in the Middle East convinced Truman that a tougher stance was needed. On 27 May the United States announced a suspension of reparation payments in equipment from West Germany to Russia. Soviet troops in Iran began a slow withdrawal after signing an oil agreement with the shah's government. In Greece the British continued to assist a right-wing government fighting leftist guerrillas aided by Tito. A foreign ministers' council, meeting in Paris, recessed on 15 May after failing to reach agreement on European peace treaties. Generals MacArthur and Eisenhower both announced that the ability to garrison effectively the defeated nations required the continuation of the draft.[23] Senator Warren Austin, Truman's newly appointed delegate to the United Nations, told the press that failure by Congress to pass a significant draft extension would seriously hinder the ability of the nation to achieve its foreign policy objectives and would "nullify our obligations to other countries." John Foster Dulles, an assistant secretary of state, reminded the nation that not one peace treaty had yet been signed with America's former enemies. Finally, industrialists, scientists, and former officers joined in calling for draft extension. The only dissenting voice came from union leaders and the Socialist party.[24]

Even more persuasive than geopolitics were petitions pouring into Congress from the troops overseas. From Japan 208 enlisted men wired senators urging the draft of teenagers. Another 323 wrote the *Stars and Stripes* calling on all soldiers to wire their congressmen to support such a draft. During the war the young men had been considered old enough to fight; surely they were old enough for occupation duty. The War Department not only failed to reprimand the troops for involving themselves in politics, but also released information that showed that some 61 percent of all enlisted men polled felt the draft should be used to supplement volunteers.[25]

The campaign succeeded. On 25 June Congress sent Truman a bill providing for further draft extension to 31 March 1947. It exempted all 18 year olds, but made men 19 through 34 liable. Fathers were exempted and the tour of duty cut to 18 months. The bill also included a pay raise for service men, to aid in recruiting volunteers, and provided a two-month moratorium on inductions. Although superficially a victory for Truman, the bill was hardly satisfactory. The removal of 18 year olds from the pool meant a serious problem. Men over age 25 provided few draftees because of health problems and dependency status. Yet SS was expected to furnish some 300,000 men before the expiration of the draft on 31 March 1947. It could accomplish such a goal only if all occupational deferments were ended and it drafted veterans who had not served outside the United States.[26]

Revision of the second extension, however, seemed unlikely given the final vote in Congress. In the House the vote was 259 to 110, and there was only one negative vote in the Senate. The only consistent opponents of the draft were midwest isolationists in the House, but Republican Senator Vandenburg, formerly a leader of this group, now supported the amended draft bill.[27] This half-a-loaf draft provided clear warning to Truman that further extension seemed unlikely in the absence of an actual war and that the War Department should proceed swiftly with plans to recruit volunteers.

During the last months of 1946 and early 1947, the War Department tried to move toward an all-volunteer system. Patterson had already launched the recruitment drive. Truman also continued to push his UMT program as a means of establishing a viable reserve without a draft.[28] The goal for mid-1947 was an army of 1 million men fed by a volunteer enlistment rate of about 40,000 a month. To achieve this goal Congress had provided a pay increase, yet pay had little bearing upon whether or not a man reenlisted because the economy was booming and civilian jobs were plentiful.

Despite extensive advertising in various media, the War Department found it difficult to reach its goal of volunteers. Some months it did better than needed. For example, when the GI bill benefits were about to expire, a huge group of volunteers entered the service. But on average the totals were below the 40,000 needed. Eisenhower warned that the draft might have to be renewed or extended beyond March 1947, but Patterson concluded, using bizarre reasoning, that the presence of the draft hurt the army's ability to get volunteers. He recommended to Truman that the draft be allowed to expire, saying the time was right to see if volunteers could be found to maintain an army of over 1 million men.[29]

On 3 March 1947, Truman, following the advice of the War Department, recommended to Congress that the draft be ended as scheduled. What was the Selective Service System became the Office of Selective Service Records (OSSR), a small operation designed as caretaker for draft records. The decision had been made although public opinion polls indicated support for a peacetime draft and the president began designing his program of containment of communism and aid to Greece and Turkey, steps that launched America's cold-war policy. The armed forces went looking for volunteers as Truman went looking for a means to contain alleged Soviet expansion. Something seemed skewed in American behavior, at least to other nations.

The decision to end the draft sent a somewhat muddled message to Europe, especially Greece.[30] General Marshall, the new secretary of state, wanted a permanent military training program to insure international security and motivate disarmament. But Truman had decided to dump the draft. He explained to Karl Compton that the Joint Chiefs felt "the international situation we now face requires regular forces in being and a capability for rapid mobilization much in excess of any previous U.S. experience." Such rapid mobilization, in Truman's and the military's opinion, was better served by volunteers and a UMT program than by the draft. The president also gambled that by ending the draft he would help obtain passage of UMT.[31]

The decision turned out to be a mistake; there had been plenty of indications that it would. Military planners had pointed out that in the next war the United States could expect to be the first target. Marshall, in his final report as chief of staff in 1945, had predicted that the army would need a minimum of 4 million men within one year of mobilization. Without a draft only half of all reserve units could be filled. Patterson and others might have thought that SS could be quickly reinstituted in an emergency, but such thinking was not shared by draft officials. Lieutenant General J. Lawton Collins testified in December 1946 that the army preferred volunteers and UMT, but that for the immediate future the draft was needed. Eisenhower felt the air force was whistling Dixie by assuming that big bombers could replace ground troops. Fans of air power "argued that Russia could be reduced by long-range aircraft," but Eisenhower had found those assessments "completely unrealistic." He had been convinced as late as February 1947 that large ground forces would continue to be needed, yet in the next month Truman had dropped the draft.[32]

Even members of the President's Advisory Committee on UMT had recommended against this course of action. After hearing testimony and making studies, the group concluded that the army, unlike the navy, could not recruit enough troops to maintain an adequate force level. Since public opinion supported a continuation of the draft and even enlisted men favored the idea, the committee urged that the army first get an extension. After this was achieved, the push for UMT could be conducted without a sense of urgency.[33]

The presidential decision to end the draft in the face of such testimony raises doubts that Truman had already developed a fixed position on the cold war. Containment policy flowered in 1947, as Truman scrapped the one proven mechanism for maintaining the armed forces at a level consistent with a belligerent posture. Some of the inconsistency can be explained by a closer look at Truman's options. On the one hand, he could fight Congress for draft renewal, despite the advice of Patterson that the army was ready to try a massive recruitment of volunteers. On the other hand, he could accept the end of the draft and concentrate on pushing volunteers and UMT. Truman always preferred UMT because taking young boys after high school for six months training required less accommodation by society than the draft.[34]

Truman's willingness to end conscription probably also arose from the simple fact that the draft was a political headache. The president recalled the contentious social impact of the draft from his senatorial years and the early years of his presidency. Its widespread impact on domestic institutions had been tolerated during the war, although even then special interest groups fought for protection and privilege. During the postwar period the peacetime draft became a target for protest from scientists, educators, and pacifists. More important, the draft was opposed by two politically potent members of the Democratic coalition: organized labor and the black community.[35]

Of the many groups opposing a continuation of the draft, none was more vigorous than organized labor.[36] Unions still recalled with some bitterness that the draft had been used during World War II to prevent workers from shifting to better-paying jobs and to crush strikes.[37]

Truman himself had considered using the draft to overcome the labor unrest which had arisen during demobilization in 1946. His major foe had been the United Mine Workers under John L. Lewis; miners were in and out of the mines all year, even after the president had seized them. Railroad workers and longshoremen had also threatened walkouts. In May 1946 Truman had asked Congress for more power to control unions. Secretary of War Patterson had suggested that Truman amend the draft age eligibility range beyond 30 years to make it more effective in curbing labor.[38]

The House had rushed to support Truman and immediately passed a bill by a vote of 303 to 13. This measure allowed a temporary seizure of industries essential to national security and also provided that workers who continued to strike after the seizure would be fired and subject to immediate induction. But the Senate had proved less cooperative.[39] Senator Robert Taft, noted for his antiunion bias, became a hero to the working man by attacking Truman's proposal. Charging that the measure violated civil liberties, a coalition of union members, southern Democrats, and all Republicans defeated the bill by a vote of 70 to 13. Only thirteen Democrats had voted for the measure in the Senate. Thirty-three others joined 36 Republicans in opposing it. After the 1946 elections created a Republican majority in both houses, the Taft-Hartley act provided increased presidential power over unions, but without any draft punishment.[40]

Another social headache which ended with the draft concerned African-Americans. The draft law contained a nondiscrimination clause, but the nation sank below the letter of the law to conduct a Jim Crow draft for a Jim Crow armed force.[41] Even before the end of the war Roy Wilkins of the NAACP had informed President Roosevelt that the American Negro opposed the idea of a peacetime draft which continued the old pattern of segregation. The humiliation of suffering such treatment while German-Americans and Italian-Americans were integrated into the armed forces could not be tolerated. If a peacetime draft was needed, Wilkins insisted that it be color-blind. The Fraternal Council of Negro Churches also announced opposition to any draft continuation if segregation remained in place.[42]

That such concern seemed justified was supported by SS statistics on the effect of wartime draft segregation.[43] Through 1 November 1946, SS reported that since 1940, 1,162,873 blacks had enlisted or been inducted into the armed forces. This was 7.4 percent of all registrants. A total of 1,074,398 blacks had been drafted, and 88,475 had enlisted. Of the 11,896 conscientious objectors during the war only 122 were blacks. Blacks made up 10.6 percent of all registrants and 10.7 percent of all inductions. Some 800,000 had served overseas.[44]

Within the SS System itself only 250 blacks served as local board members. Another 30 acted as appeal agents and 624 as advisory board members, including 486 physicians and dentists. Altogether some 1,800 black civilians worked as volunteers in the system—mostly in the North and the West—and had little say in the operation of the system, even with Campbell Johnson at national headquarters.[45]

Notwithstanding this invisibility in the system, during the war the black press refrained from criticizing the SS. Gallup surveys in June 1945 revealed little black animosity toward the system. In fact, they were slightly more favorable on the question of the fairness of the draft system than were whites. Whites rated the draft handled fairly in 66.7 percent of all cases; unfairly in 19.2 percent. Blacks ranked the draft fair in 69.6 percent of responses and unfair in 14.7 percent.[46]

This complacency ended when the thousands of blacks who had served overseas returned with greater expectations of American society. When Truman first began campaigning for a renewal of the draft in 1946, the new militancy revealed itself. Even Campbell Johnson, a staunch moderate, called for an end to racial calls in any new draft.[47]

Truman himself was sympathetic about ending segregation after the war. In December 1946 he created the Civil Rights Commission to study the "American dilemma." The report of the commission, issued in 1947, called for an end to segregation in the armed forces and several other measures. The Truman bill for UMT, introduced in Congress in 1947 as a substitute for the deceased draft, contained no provision for segregating training units by race. In an address to Congress in February 1948 the president called for an end to discrimination in the armed forces and on 30 July 1948 issued Executive Order (EO) 9981 to implement this concept. Truman received a report from the services on the greater efficiency of integrated units, but he was also influenced by political considerations and pressure from the black community.[48] Whatever his motives, postwar America seemed a better place because of Truman's actions.

With the draft ended, America in 1947 appeared poised on the edge of a new era. Demobilization had been largely achieved. American employment reached a high of 62 million. And the booming prosperity, which would continue for the next 12 years, had only begun. Total armed force strength, however, was down to 1,445,910, after a high of over 12 million in World War II. Out of a population of 149,188,000 an estimated 1.1 million males reached 18 each year and were contacted by military recruiters. But almost all these young men turned a deaf ear to offers to see the world in navy blue, or learn a trade in army khaki. Too many opportunties abounded in the bustling civilian scene. By 1 March 1948 the army stood 129,000 under its authorized strength of 669,000.[49] Jobs were too plentiful, the pleasures of peace too seductive.

But peace was becoming increasingly problematic. In 1947 relations between the Soviet Union and the United States began deteriorating. General Lucius D. Clay in occupied West Germany started to build up a new Germany to confront the Soviets. Truman issued a doctrine in March, which committed the United States to a world-wide role of peacekeeping. George Kennan at the State Department explained that the theory behind the Truman doctrine was containment of revolutionary Russia. Congress appropriated aid in support of the idea and continued the aid under the guise of the Marshall Plan the next year. But federal spending on national defense dropped from $44,731,000,000 in 1946 to $13,015,000,000 in 1948 while the average military strength of all services declined from 7,545,000 to 1,460,000.[50]

The spring brought not only cherry blossoms and showers to Washington but an immediate need to reassess the nation's military readiness. On 28 February 1948 the Communist party in Czechoslovakia, with support from the Soviet Union, gained control of the government. Another Soviet satellite joined Poland and most of eastern Europe. This episode, together with Russia's earlier refusal to join the Marshall Plan and bellicose statements by Stalin, focused Truman's attention on the state of American preparedness for war and draft renewal.

The president had little desire to foist the draft upon the American people again, but, in a sense, he was hoist with his own petard. He had a romantic view of the military, probably a result of his uncritical reading of history and his service as a National Guard artillery officer in World War I. Out of his experience he derived a consistent disdain for professional military men, with the one exception of George Marshall. One scholar, observing Truman in action from 1945 to 1950, accused him of all but "wreck[ing] the conventional military forces of the United States." While this judgment seems too severe, Truman did pursue a policy of drastic budget cuts. And his enthusiasm for UMT was less a reflection of his desire to expand trained reserves than of his interest in the social value of putting young boys through a regimen of exercise and close order drill.[51]

He had ended the draft in 1947 because of his preference for UMT and the military's desire to go all-volunteer. But he had also become increasingly bellicose in dealing with foreign affairs. By early 1948 he confronted some hard decisions. Both the UMT plan and the all-volunteer plan were failing. Secretary of the Army Kenneth C. Royall informed him in mid-January that manpower levels were dangerously low. Volunteers were down to 12,000 a month when 30,000 were needed. Similar warnings came from Secretary of Defense James Forestall. Truman also learned that the stockpile of atomic weapons, which supposedly made the United States master of the postwar world, consisted of only a dozen World War II bombs. UMT languished in Congress with much opposition and little support.[52]

If Truman continued cuts in the Pentagon budget, at a time when Soviet actions were in the headlines, it would destroy the credibility of his bold statements of 1947, and play into the hands of Republicans who accused him of being "soft" on communism. Also, the Marshall Plan would have difficulty achieving economic restoration in such an atmosphere. If the military was to be kept up to the programmed level of 1.3 million without sufficient volunteers, Truman had to find an inexpensive means of achieving defense readiness.

Returning to the draft, however, presented serious political problems, which Republicans hoped to use. The president also had to contend with new militancy among black Americans, voters that Truman needed for election in November. In addition, resurrecting the draft meant facing again the opposition of educators and the calls for special protection from the scientific community.

When, in early 1948, Truman did call for draft renewal, A. Philip Randolph created the Committee against Jim Crow in Military Service and Training to lobby against segregation. Working through the Republican majority, and particularly through Senator Robert Taft, Randolph unified black opinion, especially young blacks against racial discrimination and segregation in the armed forces. The proposed plan to reiterate the nondiscriminatory language of the 1940 draft law failed to satisfy Randolph. Polls showed over 70 percent of black college students supported Randolph's call for a boycott of any racial draft calls.[53]

Not even Truman's call of 2 February 1948 to end discrimination in the armed forces placated Randolph. The Committee against Jim Crow in Military Service demanded that Truman issue an order ending segregation immediately and support integration in any new draft bill. Truman's equivocation provided additional reasons for blacks to oppose any renewal of the draft. And at first blacks were denied interviews at the White House and opportunities to testify before congressional committees.[54]

When Randolph finally did appear in late March 1948 before congressional committees, fireworks went off. Senator Wayne Morse of Oregon appeared shocked when Grant Reynolds and Randolph both insisted that they would openly counsel black youth to resist any Jim Crow draft. If the nation were at war, warned Morse, such an act would be treason. Even the NAACP drew back from this bold position. But Randolph had good reason for his extreme action. Pious words had meant little during World War II, and Jim Crow calls had occurred despite the language of the draft law. He repeated his demands to Truman at an interview on 22 March, but the president insisted he was doing all he could do.[55]

As Congress debated draft renewal, Randolph kept up his pressure. He arranged for Issac Woodard, a black GI who had been brutalized while in uniform by South Carolina police, to sit in the Senate galleries as a reminder of the failure of the system during the war. He also called upon black youth again to refuse to accept draft into a Jim Crow army. But all his work was in vain. Secretary of the Army Royall was satisfied with a reiteration of the antidiscrimination clause of the 1940 bill. Truman sought to soften the blow by insisting that he saw no distinction between discrimination and segregation. Southern leaders, including Vinson in the House and Russell in the Senate, had their way. The new bill duplicated the language of 1940. But on 26 July 1948 Truman issued EO 9981 which stated: "There shall be equality of treatment and opportunity for all persons in the armed services without regard to race, color, religion or national origin." But would the order have any impact on the reality of life in the draft and in the armed forces?[56]

The 1948 draft law merely banned discrimination, not segregation. Truman's EO seemed to assume that one followed the other, but the idea was presumptuous. Reports from the field seemed contradictory. Secretary Royall told the press that he was personally opposed to a repeat of the racial draft calls of World War II, but that no final decision had yet been made. General Omar Bradley, while addressing the press at Fort Knox, Kentucky, made clear that the army could only follow civilian society on the issue of integration. In explaining this diversion from White House policy, Bradley explained to Truman that he had been misquoted, or quoted out of context, but he still believed that it would "be hazardous for us to employ the Army deliberately as an instrument of social reform." Bradley, it seems, had not known of Truman's new executive order.[57]

In contrast to the hesitancy of the army, the SS moved aggressively to end racial draft calls. These calls had been the bane of the system during World War II, imposing impossible burdens on local boards, and Her-

Truman signs the bill for a new draft (1948). Courtesy, Selective Service System National Headquarters.

shey acted mainly out of a desire to improve draft efficiency rather than concern with racial justice or fear of a black boycott. SS had already ended racial classification on its forms. The official agency position was that the armed forces should use all available men "without regard to race or other distinctions or other minority group affiliations." When the 1948 bill was debated in Congress Hershey informed the Pentagon that SS intended to select men by date of birth "without regard to race or color." The Pentagon agreed with this procedure, "provided the Secretary of the Army was allowed to make the announcement." But by spring 1949 there was hesitancy by the services to use blacks, which Hershey insisted was contrary to official policy. Certainly, including minorities made it easier for SS to fill calls.[58]

Although SS initiated the end of racial calls without approval from the Pentagon, and prodded the services to use blacks, within the draft system itself minorities continued to face barriers. Local draft boards still reflected community prejudice. In Texas, Mexican-Americans complained that the governor refused to name any Latin Americans to draft boards. And across the South a similar pattern prevailed and led to a crisis during the increased calls in the 1960s.[59]

But overall the Army did a much better job of promoting integration than civilian society did. Although draft calls remained small, black volunteer enlistments jumped to 22 percent of the total by April 1950 and 25 percent by July 1950. This prompted the G-1 (personnel) of the General Staff to request a reinstatement of racial quotas in September 1950, but the secretary of the army rejected the idea. In July 1951 the army announced that the last all-black unit was to be disbanded. Integration of the army seemed complete by April 1952.[60]

In 1947 Truman had accepted the death of the draft in part because of pressure for special treatment for special groups. In retrospect, World War II, because of massive mobilization, appeared a triumph of draft egalitarianism. During the 1960s critics accused the draft of discrimination based on wealth and talent, but during World War II complaints arose that the system was too equitable, too egalitarian. SS had cast its net widely and dragged into the service the chemist and the street cleaner, the physicist and the plumber, the biologist and the bookie. Truman had supported this approach and had refused to interfere in the operations of a government committee that proved parsimonious with science deferments. Edgar F. Puryear, committee chairman, saw as his task to "eventually eliminate from the government rolls every single male employee under thirty years of age."[61] In the postwar world, however, such equity frightened the educated elite who worried about the future of the nation.

The war had no sooner ended when leading science politicians, such as Vannevar Bush, began a campaign to protect science from the egalitarian impact of the draft. Bush and others complained that, unlike other nations, the United States had rejected scientific manpower mobilization for the "shibboleth that all men are to be treated alike regardless of talent." The political value of equality had triumphed over scientific efficiency. But, according to Bush, civilian scientists had proved decisive in winning the war and would be equally decisive in maintaining the peace. He estimated the deficit of science students who should have earned a B.A. at about 150,000 by 1945. By 1955 he predicted a deficit of 17,000 advanced degrees. In science, the triumph of equity equaled disaster.[62]

Science lobbyists suggested several methods to avoid the disaster. If the draft could not be ended, it should cease taking bright young scientists into the army where their talents were wasted. Also, those scientists already in the service should be given an immediate release. Bush pushed these ideas upon Undersecretary of War Patterson and President Truman even as the rubble at Nagasaki continued to smolder. Patterson was easily won over. He had fought hard to insure that scientists working on defense projects received deferments and also planned to continue the close cooperation between defense and science in the postwar world. He supported the deferment of young scientists but rejected, for morale reasons, the early release of scientists already in uniform.[63]

Selective Service officials pointed out that the system already offered deferments to medical students and fathers and included a delay in call for high school students. If the draft began deferring all young men who wished to study science, the 400,000 returning veterans who were expected to return to school might be squeezed out. Hershey predicted that, rather than a shortage, colleges would soon be inundated by applicants, even without more deferments. Finally, the deferments made it difficult to meet War Department calls for occupation troops, and by the end of 1945, SS was already running 15,000 a month short.[64]

But the atomic bomb had provided a graphic example that science provided the key to the future. By early 1946 influential voices in the educational and scientific communities made themselves heard in favor of discriminatory drafting. George Zook of the American Council on Education argued that enrollment in engineering schools was only one-fifth of normal and that science B.A.s were down 40 percent, M.A.s 30 percent and Ph.D.s, 20 percent in physics and chemistry. The only solution to the crisis was to allow colleges to certify 18 year olds for deferments if they majored in such fields as biology, chemistry, engineering, geology, physics, or other sciences. Howard A. Meyerhoff, executive secretary of the American Association for the Advancement of Science, urged Truman to support a law that would draft gifted men into a student corps. He and others recommended that men 18 to 26 "shall be allocated to the colleges, university, and technical schools after induction rather than through deferment."[65]

When Truman asked for a draft extension in 1946 the science community had Senator Warren Magnuson add a clause providing deferments for young student scientists. Although this clause was dropped in a conference committee, pressure from the American Physics Association, chemists, and others continued unabated throughout the year.[66] Within the administration Patterson at the War Department and John R. Steelman, director of the Office of War Mobilization and Reconversion, added their voices in the same cause, but neither Truman nor Hershey felt it was a good idea to offer such special protection. Hershey felt it wrong "to discriminate in favor of individuals financially better situated than other persons." When the draft ended in 1947 the entire controversy became moot.[67]

Truman's call in 1948 for draft renewal resurrected the issue of deferments for scientists and students, the best and the brightest. The nation had accepted the claim, as made by Bush and others, that American scientists had been drafted and wasted during the war, but the claim was dubious. More chemists entered the service through the reserve than through the draft. Despite these facts, the American Chemical Society (ACS) and the *New York Times* both complained about the draft stealing scientists from civilian laboratories.[68]

By 1948, with draft renewal in the air, this seed of discontent had blossomed into a flower of discrimination. The Department of Defense (DOD)[69] created a special commission under Alexander Wetmore to make recommendations. SS also appointed an advisory committee of educators to solve the problem. Both of these groups came to the same conclusion. There should be no blanket deferments, but deferments for students and scientists should be offered on a selective basis. The deferment of students was to be based on academic performance, as measured by a national test and by class ranking. Soon the administration had in place a system for deferring gifted individuals, a system that was bound to channel men into certain fields. Manpower experts rejoiced at this victory of scientific management over romantic concepts of equity and individual equality.[70]

On 15 March 1948 the Joint Chiefs of Staff recommended immediate reenactment of the draft. Two days later, while speaking to the Friendly Sons of St. Patrick in New York City, Truman called for passage of UMT and a temporary renewal of the draft. The temporary nature of the draft received emphasis because both Truman and Congress had repeatedly called conscription an unfortunate wartime necessity. Yet here he was, scarcely six months after ending it in 1947, calling for a resurrection.

Representative Leo Allen, chairman of the Rules Committee of the House, recommended instead that the army beef up volunteer recruiting by offering a bonus of $1,000 to $1,500. Although this idea of buying volunteers became acceptable in the 1970s, in 1948 it smacked too much of the disastrous scheme of the Civil War. It also warred against Truman's desire to cut spending, hence his response that the suggestion was "asinine."[71]

But if buying an army was out, how could Truman obtain draft renewal? In his earlier struggle to obtain aid for Greece and Turkey and pass the Marshall Plan, the president had beat the drum of the Communist menace. Once again this instrument was played, and the American public responded to the rhythm. A Gallup poll on 24 March found 63 percent in favor of conscription, and General Marshall and others lent their support before hearings. After considerable wrangling and disagreement, Congress voted finally on 24 June 1948 to renew the draft. At the same time the politicians buried Truman's call for UMT.

The report of the House Armed Services Committee of 7 May 1948 made congressional reasoning clear: "This recommendation correctly reflected a serious deterioration in the international situation over the months . . . and constituted the necessary response of this government to specific, aggressive, and dangerous actions on the part of the Government of the Soviet Union." The report then cited the coup in Czechoslovakia, Soviet pressure on Finland, and restrictions on American forces in Berlin and Vienna. Incidentally, military testimony revealed that the armed forces planned to expand to 2 million by mid-year but recruiting was down. Strength levels had already fallen some 129,000 below authorized numbers.[72]

The new draft was hardly new. It simply resurrected the Selective Service System from its standby status as the OSSR, and the major organizational components remained identical to those created in 1940. A few changes were made in eligibility requirements. All men ages 18 to 26 not in the service were required to register and were liable for a tour of twenty-one months. Although inductees had to be at least 19, an 18 year old was allowed to enlist for one year with a commitment to six years in the reserve. College students were allowed to postpone their induction until the end of the academic year. The president was authorized to make all needed rules to protect vital manpower through deferments, but again the local boards made the final decisions about classification. Veterans who had served over one year after 16 September 1940 were not liable for induction.[73]

Conscription had seemed an orphan in Washington, but once it was adopted it proved a stimulant to high-quality volunteers. In the immediate aftermath of World War II, when Patterson and others had been confident of the attractiveness of military service, the army had moved to upgrade its manpower quality. After taking virtually any young male in World War II, the army raised its minimum acceptable intelligence test score for enlistees from 59 to 70 and in 1948 raised it again to 80. These higher standards cut voluntary recruitment to dangerous levels.

With the new draft law in place, volunteers with high scores flocked to the colors. For the first six months after draft renewal, the army found all its slots filled with volunteers, about 200,000 more than projected without the draft. But the new draft was more a threat than a reality. By 30 January 1950, SS had registered over 10 million young men, but drafted only 30,129, in four different calls. Some 368,000 men had successfully volunteered for the army. The air force, navy, and marines satisfied their requirements with only volunteers. By 1950 half of all local draft boards operated on a part-time basis. Congress cut fiscal year 1950 appropriations for SS in half. The selective manpower mobilization system seemed redundant, a relic of an old-style war.[74]

Neither Truman nor the recently created DOD had any plans for containing communism by any means short of all-out, total war. When Louis Johnson became secretary of defense in March 1949, he began paring down the military establishment. The organized reserves of the armed forces declined from 746,000 in June 1948 to 600,000 in June 1950. The Regular Army had an authorized strength of 677,000 in 1949 and declined to 591,000 by mid-1950. At the end of 1949 all services halted voluntary enlistments. This gesture took place even as Russia exploded its first atomic bomb and Mao Tse Tung took control of the Chinese mainland. Containment had led to military aid for Greece and Turkey and economic aid to western Europe, but it had no appreciable impact on the readiness of American military manpower.[75]

5

Korea

In his state of the union address on 4 January 1950, President Truman explained with understatement that the world was "unsettled" and called for another extension of the draft, despite the fact that no one had been inducted in 1949. He said the draft was needed to maintain a "strong and well-balanced defense organization." At that time about half of all local draft boards functioned only one day a week. In the same breath Truman sent Congress a budget request that aimed at reducing armed forces personnel by 190,628. The total military budget was $13.5 billion. Why then call for an extension of the draft?[1]

Truman's motives were economic and political. Expanding the military manpower pool through volunteers obtained by the draft threat represented a means of assuming a strong defense posture that was much cheaper than trying to buy volunteers with increased pay and benefits. Draft extension, urged by the army with hopes of stimulating recruitment, also made Truman look tough in the face of countercharges by Republicans. Finally, the Department of State was urging a major buildup of American defense capability.

A team from the departments of Defense and State drafted a long-range plan for American strategy at Truman's request. By 12 April he had read what came to be called National Security Council (NSC) 68, an expansive and expensive program to build up America's defense establishment with the view of convincing the Soviets that their ambitions were unrealizable. The report envisioned spending some $35 billion a year and as much as $50 billion if necessary to rearm the nation. Truman, who had been cutting military budgets, had little reason to endorse such a grandiose scheme. The plan would surely placate red baiters at home, but Truman refused to release the document, fearing that it would stimulate needless apprehension. Instead, he continued his tough rhetoric and pushed for draft extension from a reluctant Congress.[2]

Congress appreciated the budgetary arguments. The draft was a powerful means of insuring full subscription to the armed forces, even when no one was drafted. Without having to offer college scholarships, special bonuses, trips to Europe, and in-service training, and without spending millions on recruiting ads, the armed forces found men beating a path to their door. These men were anxious to take up a three-year assignment at very low wages rather than be drafted for a 21-month tour of duty followed by five years in the reserves.

Still, the administration had to offer something beyond monetary savings to obtain congressional approval for draft extension. In 1940, even while war had raged in Europe, many viewed the draft as a violation of American traditions. In 1950 there was the peril of communism, but congressmen had doubts about the need for an agency which seemed to function by not functioning. There were some in Congress who agreed with former Secretary of War Robert Patterson, that only atomic bombs and missiles could contain the communists. The president himself had privately expressed this opinion. Why load up a ground force which would be superfluous in the next war?[3]

Truman's halfhearted commitment to the draft became clear during negotiations with Congress. Representative Carl Vinson, head of the House Armed Services Committee, attacked Secretary Johnson's request for extension and made a counterproposal. Congress would approve draft extension, but only if a rider were attached to the bill prohibiting any inductions without separate legislative action. At first Johnson resisted this infringement on presidential prerogative. George M. Elsey, a Truman aide, warned that such a rider would "negate the purpose for which we seek extension," but Truman agreed to accept the check of a concurrent resolution before inductions began. The president did prefer a provision allowing him to begin drafting if, after consultation with the National Security Council and military leaders, he found that the international scene demanded resumption.[4]

Several thousand miles to the west the People's Republic of North Korea began massing troops behind the 38th parallel, the artificial boundary with South Korea. The division of Korea, an artifact of World War II, had always been an uneasy one. Various guerrilla actions had taken place since 1945, and both the Russian-supported government in Pyongyang and the American-backed state in Seoul were committed to unification of the peninsula nation. When the invasion from the north came on 25 June 1950 (Washington time) Truman, under the urging of Acting Secretary of State Dean Acheson, pledged America to defend South Korea.[5]

The president's action represented a reversal of both diplomatic strategy and military planning. After spending several years cutting conventional military power, and only recently endorsing an offshore defense line in Asia, Truman proceeded to throw American forces into a ground conflict of confused civil origins. In his announcement of the decision, Truman cast the conflict in terms of the worldwide struggle with communism, but this fight hardly satisfied the apocalyptic character the public had come to expect of such a conflict. Because of the Truman Doctrine, Marshall Plan, and NATO, the eyes of Americans were focused on Europe, and because of administration rhetoric, Americans had expected nuclear bombs to fall. Now the American public was forced to take a new view and to accept a new principle of conflict—limited ground war in Asia.

Congress was confused by this rapid reversal of policy, a reversal that occurred without their collaboration. One day Truman seemed content to accept a standby draft, ceding induction authority to Congress, but the next day a new war required a new draft policy. General Douglas MacArthur in Japan had discovered that defeating the North Koreans required much more than he could commit from his garrison forces. On 27 June a conference committee of the House and Senate adopted a proposal for extension of the draft without any major changes. Representative Dewey Short of Missouri, who had been a strong opponent of the draft, rose to admit his past error and embrace conscription. On 30 June 1950 Truman signed a draft bill which continued the old system. The SS had to do more than scare recruits into volunteering because the armed forces required immediate inductions and even called up reserve forces.[6]

After the debacle of Vietnam in the 1960s conventional wisdom argued that the draft was inappropriate for limited wars. SS had been designed for mobilizing mass armies, critics emphasized. To use it in fighting a guerrilla war courted disaster. The French, for example, had refused to use conscripts in Indochina, after a bad experience with them in Algeria. But the United States did use draftees in Korea and, although the general mobilization for that conflict was clearly confused, without SS the United States would have fared worse. With Korea the draft became an accepted part of the political landscape. Also, during the conflict an elaborate system of deferments went into action, a system which revealed American values and priorities in the cold war. Finally, with Korea African-Americans became integrated into the military establishment.[7]

As the war began, an air of unreality seemed to prevail at the White House. At a cabinet meeting on 8 July General Omar Bradley, chairman of the Joint Chiefs of Staff, reassured everyone that the decision to commit troops to Korea was well received in Europe. Yet within months he began explaining to MacArthur that the commitment to Korea had to be limited because of needs in Europe. England and France were concerned over the extent of America's commitment to the Asian theater. In contrast, Secretary of Defense Johnson urged the immediate drafting of 100,000 men. Truman hesitated because such a step might suggest "we are on the verge of war." To the president, as to most Americans, war meant total war, total mobilization, using all the weapons in one's arsenal. The next few years educated Truman and the public about a new kind of war.[8]

The same dated concept of war pervaded the army's mobilization plans. As a consequence, mobilization during the remainder of 1950 was ill-conceived, poorly executed, and damaging to conduct of the Korean conflict. In contrast to romantic illusions of the air force and the president, the army's basic plan involved war against a superpower, cooperation with European allies, and a slow, three-year expansion of forces through the draft and volunteers to a total of 6.3 million men. World War II veterans were not to be recalled for duty. Within a few months all those ideas proved false.[9]

The first revelation occurred in Japan. MacArthur originally assumed that he could defeat the North Koreans with the forces on hand in Japan. Yet his four divisions were all under strength and garrison soft. He soon began petitioning Washington for more troops. On 3 July Johnson informed the press that mobilizing the reserves was not under consideration "at the present time." But the reality of Korean warfare soon forced reconsideration.[10]

By 9 July 1950 Congress had authorized an extension of the draft and a call-up of reserve forces. This last action proved a political and manpower disaster. The army at first invited volunteers from the organized reserves, but few appeared. By 10 August involuntary reserve call-ups began. Officers, medical specialists, enlisted men, and World War II veterans returned to the colors. By the end of August over 600 reserve units had been recalled and most proved useless. Rather than sending units to MacArthur, the army ended up sending individuals. Soon the general reserve in the United States was dangerously depleted, and Mac-Arthur continued to demand more forces. Theoretically, the reserve forces should have been used to train new inductees, but by the time the draftee was ready to fight, the war in Korea might be lost. So the training base in the United States was stripped to beef up MacArthur's forces. Weekend warriors were taken from their civilian positions, and veterans found themselves heading once again to the front. Complaints poured into Washington.[11]

When the war had begun in Korea the United States Army had ten divisions, five of which were in the general reserve, four under MacArthur in Japan, and one in Germany. None of the divisions was up to full strength, and the garrison troops were not combat tough. The situation was not surprising. In Washington the Truman administration had spent the last few years cutting away at the military budget, but due to the war, the cost of defense rose from $12 billion in the second quarter of 1950 to $50.5 billion in the second quarter of 1953.[12]

In the midst of the muddle, the one bright spot was the operation of the stepchild of Truman and Congress, the draft. Without the draft the nation would have faced disaster in Korea. General MacArthur found that his forces made little impression on the North Korean Army. Even with the use of reserves, the general found it necessary to fill half the Seventh Division, used at Inchon, with South Korean troops. Other American divisions also had to use Koreans. The Department of Defense issued draft calls of 50,000 each for September and October, 70,000 for November, and 40,000 for December 1950. The calls were programmed on the basis of available training capabilities, which had been seriously sapped to augment MacArthur's immediate needs. Truman announced that he expected the armed forces to total 3 million by the end of the fiscal year. But Hershey told the House Armed Services Committee that the existing draft pool made such a target unreachable.[13]

When the draft began, the pool of manpower seemed impressive, more than large enough to fill Truman's goal. But as was always the case, raw figures of registered men were deceptive. Although there were over 9 million registered, the figure shrank rapidly when the deferred (1.2 million), veterans (2.7 million), those already enlisted (870,000), and the disqualified (900,000) were subtracted. SS estimated that for each month it had a working pool of qualified and available men of perhaps 200,000. The immediate needs for Korea were easily satisfied by the draft. It provided 180,000 men in the first three months of the war—which was more than the DOD had requested—and could have called more, but DOD was limited by the shortage of training personnel. To increase the flow of men, the army cut basic training for draftees from 14 weeks to six weeks.[14]

The move was fortuitous because in November 1950 thousands of Chinese volunteers hit MacArthur in a surprise attack. The general wanted an immediate reenforcement of 74,000 men from the United States. January and February calls were raised to 80,000 men each, which was more than double the original requirement. The high level of calls continued with 80,000 for March and April, 60,000 for May, and 40,000 for June.[15] Unfortunately, the authorized strength of the army for fiscal year (FY) ending 30 June 1951 was 1,552,000. But if the SS filled all the outstanding calls, the army would be over strength by several tens of thousands.

The draft's efficiency had outrun the administration's plans. Part of the confusion came from the crisis atmosphere created by MacArthur's reaction to the Chinese offensive. Another incentive for large calls was the desire of the administration and the army to demobilize reservists and veterans who had been called up in the emergency of June through September. These men were valuable fillers, but they were politically expensive. The White House had been bombarded with complaints from dependents and employers over the injustice of taking veteran reservists before new men. Finally, the Army was attempting to stockpile for the future. By calling large numbers in early 1951, the Army could insure that the trained manpower in the United States would increase, even after replacements for Korea had been used.

Such over-calls created serious problems. The army lacked authorized money, space, and training facilities to handle these men. The embarrassing facts of the situation became clear to Secretary of Defense Marshall by early March 1951. After conferences and recriminations between General J. Lawton Collins and Assistant Secretary Anna M. Rosenberg, Marshall made clear that the calls had to be cut.[16]

But cutting already announced draft calls created more public relations problems for the administration. At a time when fighting continued intense in Korea, when European threats were receiving new attention, when, on 11 April, Truman was relieving MacArthur because of public disagreement over America's commitment to Asia, when Congress was debating a new draft bill, the army had to admit that it did not need so many men. From Capitol Hill Senator Lyndon Johnson, Speaker Sam Rayburn, and others sent word that such action was bound to harm chances of passing another draft bill. Rosenberg, however, informed Hershey that DOD had to cut its call of April from 80,000 to 40,000. The official justification for the cut was an increase in volunteers and fewer casualties. The real reason was sloppy administration.[17]

For the duration of the war the draft continued to provide more than enough men for the armed forces. By the end of June 1951 local boards had delivered an average of 5.5 percent more men than requested. And at no time during the Korean mobilization period was the draft ever in danger of failing to meet calls. Rosenberg informed Truman in October 1952 that the draft could meet calls through June 1954 without any major changes in deferment policies. In June 1952 there were 13.2 million registered, minus those already in the military or veterans (3 million), those exempt or overage (3.4 million), those rejected or deferred (4.6 million), and those under age 19 (.4 million). SS estimated that the pool of available men was about 1.1 million. At the end of fiscal year 1953 there were 14.4 million registered, but almost 9 million were deferred or exempt, and another 3.8 million were veterans. The available total stood at 938,137.[18]

The draft system had once again met the needs of American military mobilization. The Korean War draft was similar to the operation of World War II, but there were also important differences.

The draft law which operated during the Korean War had been created in 1948. Under its terms all men aged 18 to 26 were eligible for registration, and men 19 to 26 were liable for induction for a tour of 21 months. To a remarkable degree, the same men who had started in 1940 continued to run the system. Hershey continued as director, and there was a high level of continuity in state and local board personnel. The local boards continued to be manned mostly by veterans and local middle-management leaders. In Texas, for example, only eight of the 137 boards lacked veterans.[19] The SS remained independent, directly under the president, and operated with decentralized decisions. Local board actions were again final, unless appealed.[20]

Because the SS had been created to insure a scientific use of manpower, the classification procedure was an essential task. The local boards guarded jealously this responsibility. As the local board decision was final, except for appeals, the burden of proof for any challenge rested with the registrant. The board assigned the registrant to the lowest, or least liable classification for which he was eligible. The class designations listed below changed very little over the years.

Draft Classifications

1-A	Available for duty
1-A-O	CO, available for noncombat
1-O	CO, available for civilian alternate service
1-S	High school student
1-Y	Physically and mentally qualified only in war
2-A	Deferred for civilian occupation
2-C	Deferred for agricultural occupation
2-S	Deferred as college student
1-D	Member of Reserve or ROTC
3-A	Father or has dependents
4-B	Deferred official by law
4-D	Minister or divinity student
4-F	Physically, mentally, or morally disqualified
4-A	Veteran or sole surviving son
5-A	Over age of liability
1-C	Member of armed forces

After classification, the local board monthly prepared a list of registrants listed in order of birthdates with the oldest first. The classification status was attached to each name so that calls could be made by going down the list from oldest to youngest. This list created a pool of manpower, available at different rates for military duty. Within 10 days of receiving his induction notice the registrant reported for a physical check. A man could be ordered for induction only after his acceptability had been determined by this preinduction physical. If a registrant refused to report, the board called the local U.S. attorney to start prosecuting the delinquent.[21] As deferments were temporary and new registrants appeared each day, the state of the manpower pool was in continuous fluctuation. A major change occurred when draft eligible men volunteered.

Studies repeatedly demonstrated that men volunteered, not because of enthusiasm for military life, but to avoid the draft. In 1947, in the absence of a draft, total enlistments ranged from 9,000 to 14,000 a month, but first-time enlistments were only 4,000 to 10,000. After Truman asked for a new draft in March 1948 enlistments jumped to 20,000 a month, of which 15,000 were first-timers. When enlistees were polled about the reason for their action, about 40 percent admitted they had entered to avoid the draft. Yet the differential between the number of volunteers with no draft and with the draft was about 60 percent.[22]

As the draft expanded for Korea, voluntary enlistments caused problems, as they had in World War II. When young men received their draft notice, they rushed to volunteer in the service of their choice.[23]

As Table 5.1 shows, the official percentage of first-time enlisted men rose during the Korean conflict. In fiscal year 1951 some 587,000 men were drafted, representing 32.1 percent of the total. But this was merely the official percentage. Between 40 and 60 percent of the 630,000 non-draftee volunteers were draft motivated.

To stabilize the draft pool, SS called upon the military to end the recruitment of volunteers. In World War II the War Department had eventually ended its recruitment of volunteers, but it did not in the Korean War.[24] By early 1951 several congressmen began calling for a cessation of volunteering. Representative Gerald R. Ford of Michigan informed Secretary Marshall that such recruitment of volunteers was expensive and the result was confusion, since it kept local boards from knowing accurately the size of draft pools. In one Michigan county there were uniformed men on recruiting duty as well as two local draft boards. Besides the use of regular army personnel, the army and air force spent some $7,110,963 in fiscal year 1951 on advertising, and in the same period, the navy and marines spent $1,136,789 for the same purpose. Over $8 million went into obtaining men who were scheduled to be drafted anyway.[25]

Secretary Marshall and Assistant Secretary Rosenberg sought to defuse the attack against recruitment by reiterating the old arguments. Conscription was against American tradition, while volunteering was part of that tradition. The enlistee spent one year more than the draftee in the service, so he was cheaper in the long run. Volunteers had higher morale than conscripts. Without volunteers the draft calls would have to grow larger, meaning an end to deferments for husbands and students.[26]

Most of these arguments were dubious. A study of some 2,291 men

Table 5.1. Enlisted Men, Entries by Source (in thousands)

FY	Totals	Enlistees	Draftees	Reserve	Percentage of Draftees
1948	281	281			
1949	398	368	30		7.5
1950	182	182			
1951	1,826	630	587	609	32.1
1952	991	532	379	80	38.2
1953	961	397	564		58.7
1954	647	382	265		41.0
1955	695	480	215		30.9
1956	583	446	137		23.5
1957	576	396	180		31.3
1958	453	327	126		27.8
1959	451	340	111		24.6
1960	439	349	90		20.5
1961	446	386	60		13.5
1962	715	409	158	148	22.1
1963	447	373	74		16.6
1964	527	376	151		28.7
1965	454	351	103		22.7
1966	933	598	335		35.9

Source: Morris, Thomas D. "Report on Studies of the Draft," in Martin Anderson, ed., *The Military Draft* (Stanford: Hoover Institute, 1982), 550.

in Korean combat found that the draftee was less delinquent, more ef-ficient, and more apt to finish his full term of service than the recruit. The draftee contributed more in two years than the enlistee in three years. Volunteers had lower educational achievements, lower mental test scores, and lower physical standards. The draftee was always closer to the civilian norm for the draft-age cohort in education than was the enlistee. In the pre–Korean War volunteer infantry battalion, there were few high school graduates, low technical proficiency, and high court-martial rates. Testimony by officers in Korea continually emphasized the superiority of the draftee to the enlistee, in line and command functions.[27]

As for the cheapness of the volunteer, the estimate of cost ignored the generally lower level of performance provided. True, the volunteer did reenlist at a higher rate than the draftees, but if the army really sought a professional force, it would do better to recruit from the high quality manpower provided by the draft. As many of the volunteers were draft induced, their morale seems likely to have been no higher than that of the draftee. The draft had been conceived originally as a means of insuring efficient manpower mobilization. It had been successful in World War II by use of deferments and because volunteering had ended early. In the Korean War the continuation of volunteering made manpower efficiency impossible.

Another source of confusion in the pool size was the formula for deciding the number of eligibles in each state and local board area. Officially the armed forces notified immediately the local board if a registrant was acceptable and inducted. SS then adjusted its pool status accordingly. But in practice the military frequently delayed over 60 days in reporting the status of draftees to SS, and consequently calls were made based on inaccurate statistics. Congressmen frequently complained, with some justice, that their state was serving up a disproportionate number of men compared to another state.[28]

The pool also suffered from constant revision of its internal character through appeals for reclassification. Each registrant had the legal right to appeal any classification assigned by the local board. As a first step the registrant requested a personal appearance before the board, where he presented additional information to substantiate his request for a change of status from 1-A to a deferred category. The additional information might simply be a letter from a college registrar saying that the man was enrolled, or a statement from a local minister saying that the man was a conscientious objector. The request could be made at any time, perhaps if the man received a new job assignment. No classification was permanent. Should the local board fail to agree with the registrant after a hearing, a written appeal could be submitted within 10 days to the state appeal board. If the action of this state board was less than unanimous, the registrant could appeal to the presidential board. The process took time and delayed induction.[29]

Although a source of controversy in later years, the appeal system seemed to function fairly well during the Korean War, and the period before the war saw few appeals. From 1948 to 30 June 1951 only one in every 200 registrants appealed his classification, and there were 10,862,546 classified registrants. In fiscal year (FY) 1949 only 7,000 appeals occurred, and the number dropped to 2,200 in FY 1950. But with the huge inductions for Korea, appeals climbed rapidly. There were 32,000 in FY 1951, 49,000 in FY 1952, 51,000 in FY 1953, and 46,000 in FY 1954. Registrations and classifications had also climbed so that appeals applied to only one of every 140 men classified. From November 1948 through 30 June 1952 only 2,640 men carried appeals as far as the presidential board. As for disposition of appeals, state boards upheld local boards in about 80 percent of the cases. Of the cases that reached the presidential board, some 28 percent received new classifications. Over 70 percent of the cases involved claims for occupational defer- ments, since industry had the organization, staff, and money to challenge the system. An individual seeking reclassification for his own personal benefit was at a considerable disadvantage.[30]

The low number of appeals reflected public approval of the system. Polls conducted during World War II on the fairness of the draft ran from 93 percent approval in 1942 to 79 percent in May 1945. But Korea was a far cry from the crusade against the Axis. Limited war meant limited mobilization and only a two-year tour of service. But once again public opinion rated the draft highly. When Robert Borchardt, a German observer, spent six weeks traveling around the country in 1952 he failed to hear a single complaint about the draft. Gallup documented the same approval. In April 1953 over 60 percent of the public gave draft boards a high vote of confidence. Only 10 percent registered any dissatisfaction, and this approval rating remained consistent across a variety of ages and incomes. Those with a lower income showed more approval than those making more.[31]

The favorable public consensus translated into bipartisan political ap- proval. In congressional voting from 1946 to 1960 the SS System over- came party lines and enjoyed a high index of support from both Democrats and Republicans. Defense officials praised the rapidity with which the draft had obtained the men for Korea. Secretary of Defense Robert A. Lovett congratulated Hershey on 31 July 1952 after the draft had inducted 1 million men since 23 June 1950, and President Truman commended Hershey on a job well done.[32]

The draft had succeeded in filling military calls while executing the mandate of planners to be selective in a limited mobilization. Lovett was particularly impressed because the draft had achieved success "without disrupting other phases of our national life." In contrast to the massive mobilization of World War II, the Korean draft was a minor operation that met with little opposition. The efficiency seems surprising because the system was designed for total rather than limited mobilization and during this period SS erected the elaborate deferment arrangements, later a target for protest.[33]

There was no protest during the Korean War. The draft worked and was popular with both the public and Congress. The bipartisan strength of SS became especially apparent when a revised draft law was debated in 1951. This legislation became more than a routine renewal of conscription because President Truman used the occasion for a last ditch attempt to gain approval for his old ideal—UMT.

By 1950 several constituencies had coalesced around UMT and the draft. James B. Conant of Harvard and other university presidents came out for the idea, Conant believing it essential for the United States to resist "Communist domination" of Europe by maintaining an armed force of from 3.5 million to 5 million for a period of ten years. Such a force could not be raised by merely continuing a peacetime draft. Only an effective UMT could solve the problem of training young men. The Association of American Universities also called for a ten-year extension of the draft with a 27-month tour and no deferments, except for the physically disabled.[34]

In December 1950, as American forces staggered under the onslaught of Chinese troops in Korea, General Marshall met with his advisers to plan on extending the draft in 1951. A DOD report on manpower mobilization called for a system which could continually increase "our mobilization potential through training and educational programs to expand our supply of persons with highly developed skills essential to civilian and military activities." The planners at DOD emphasized that "we must rely heavily on science and technology." Marshall agreed but also commented: "I do not believe we can continue with our present policy. We cannot continue to make short-term plans for emergencies which are followed by periods of radical demobilization and the termination of authority to train men for military service."[35]

The subsequent draft bill was called Universal Military Training and SS. It asked for a continuation of the draft with a tour of 27 months. All eligible men would be inducted, nearly 80 percent of the 1 million reaching age 18 annually. A small group of some 75,000 would be selected for specialized professional training, future military scientists, and would be required to finish their tour of active duty after their schooling. In addition the bill proposed an eight-year training obligation for all youth, who would enter the reserves after a short period of military training. This UMT dimension would be implemented after the fighting in Korea was over. Rosenberg explained to the Senate Armed Services Committee that rather than just a continuation of the existing draft, UMT guaranteed a regular flow of men into reserve components. This big reserve would allow for a smaller active force to operate and avoid waste and insecurity.[36]

The administration began its campaign for universal military training as war news became more encouraging. By January 1951 the new commander in Korea, Matthew Ridgway, had established some stability at the front. The Joint Chiefs concluded that a line could be held on the peninsula with the seven assigned divisions. Truman made clear, by relieving the general, that he rejected MacArthur's program of concentration on Asia for the containment of communism. But in maintaining manpower levels the armed forces again in April called up reservists. During the entire Korean War some 243,300 reservists and 138,597 National Guardsmen were activated.[37]

The proposed UMT envisioned creating an even larger reserve force which could be called in an emergency, but the experience with such call-ups during the Korean War created public relations problems. At the same time unwilling reservists and veterans were being recalled, the draft calls for 1951 were reduced and deferments offered to farmers, students, and married men without children. However, a reservist who was both a student and a father could be and was recalled.[38]

Given the unsatisfactory experience with mobilizing reservists in 1950, critics wondered why defense officials should persist with the plan to create a new system of UMT, which would ensure even greater reliance on such types in the future. Official justifications sounded shaky. Korea was an emergency, and trained men were needed fast. The draft provided untrained men. As for cutting draft calls, Marshall informed Congressman George P. Miller that "it is mandatory that schedules set by the Joint Chiefs for expansion be adhered to." This arid answer hardly helped the congressmen; more satisfying was the promise by DOD to return reservists to civilian life as fast as possible.[39]

To ensure passage of the bill, however, the administration had to once again play its anticommunism card. A Joint Congressional Committee on Armed Services announced that since 1939 some ten nations "have fallen under the boot of international Communism," and Russia now had the atomic bomb. "The grim fact is that the United States is now engaged in a struggle for survival." How could America compete with the 795 million people in the Communist world, when the free world had only 725 million? Marshall played up this theme, writing to senators that we must not "provide them with an opportunity to achieve their goal of world domination."[40]

Congressmen believed in this threat, but the belief would not translate into support for the new bill without revision. The idea of using 18 year olds seemed to threaten the American home, and mothers bombarded Congress with protests. Congress also objected to 27 months of service and the size of the armed forces, and providing a special deferment for students seemed unfair. Alfred O'Gara, chairman of the Business Men's Committee, complained to Senator Taft that the bill represented the "boldest steps toward totalitarianism yet proposed." He envisioned the measure as a means of building up a "political aristocracy of college-trained new or fair deal thinkers who would have it in their power to perpetuate the chains of dictatorship." James G. Patton, president of the National Farmers Union, in a less hysterical response, felt UMT would be an inefficient means of dealing with manpower. "Selective Service," Patton wrote to Taft, "is infinitely preferable to U.M.T."[41]

On 19 June 1951 Congress passed a bill by a lopsided vote with strong bipartisanship. It was not the bill Truman wanted, but he had to sign it. The law lowered the effective age of induction to 18.5 years, but all eligible older men had to be called before local boards would be allowed to tap the younger group. In addition the law provided for 24 months' active duty to be followed by six years reserve duty, lowered the aptitude standards for qualification, created a 5-million ceiling for the armed forces, and deferred college students to the end of the year or until they dropped out, whichever came first. Any person receiving a deferment, however, remained eligible for the draft to age 35. The regular maximum age of liability remained 26.[42]

The law, called the Universal Military Training and Service Act, did provide that men under 19 were liable for training in a National Security Training Corps (NSTC), but Congress had to authorize specifically such training. In addition, the act created a National Security Training Commission of five members to plan for UMT. Truman quickly created the commission, and it reported favorably to Congress in October 1951, although by that time all sense of urgency had disappeared. Fewer troops were needed in Korea, inductions were cut back, and traditional opponents of UMT were vocal. Although congressional hearings on the report began in early 1952, the House voted to recommit the UMT proposal to committee. The Senate took no action.[43]

UMT was stillborn, but the draft had been renewed and had delivered the men requested by the armed forces for Korea. Cold-war fever contributed to support for the draft, but its new popularity was also owing

Protesting universal military training (1951). Courtesy, Selective Service System National Headquarters.

to the unprecedented amount of selectivity it adopted during the conflict. In the limited Korean War, SS reflected more clearly the type of scientific management of manpower that experts had hoped for as early as World War I. In the absence of massive mobilization, such as that in World War II, the system offered deferments for social, economic, and educational reasons to insure minimal disturbance to civilian society. So sensitive was the system that it came to meet little overt opposition from a culture supposedly dominated by concepts of antimilitarism and volunteerism.

Draft protest had collapsed during World War II before the danger of fascism. In the period before Korea cases of delinquency ran low because draft calls were low. From 1948 to July 1950 there were only 204 cases filed by U.S. attorneys out of 10,750,000 registrants. With the increased calls after June 1950, cases of delinquency rose. By 30 June 1952 some 20,072 cases had been referred to the Justice Department. Overall, there were about 12,000 delinquencies for each 12 months of the Korean draft. These figures did not accurately represent draft protest, however, because many men were merely careless about reporting changes of address or were late in reporting. The Justice Department was able to close over 20 percent of all cases without any prosecution, but those actually charged with violating the draft totaled 4,490 in 1950, 3,680 in 1951, 5,610 in 1952, and 6,300 in 1953. For each year respectively the number of men convicted was 1,750, 1,560, 3,130, 3,450.[44]

Although popular surveys continued to show little enthusiasm for the war or military life among youth, there was no organized protest against the draft, and young men reported when called. In *Estep v. U.S.*, 1951, the Supreme Court declared that Congress had excluded the draft from judicial scrutiny of administrative action. If a draftee sued, courts were limited to judgment of whether a local board acted in conformity with the regulations. If the local board action had conformed, the case was thrown out. Local board classification decisions were final unless there was no basis in fact for a classification.[45]

The support of the draft remained strong even amid charges of a social bias in operation. As was true in World War II, the lower classes provided a disproportionate share of the casualties in Korea. After the war, an Eisenhower appointee, Assistant Secretary of Defense John Hannah, announced that Korea was a "poor man's war." Edward R. Murrow also claimed that the draft offered protection to an "intellectual elite." Two sociologists conducted a study in Detroit and found that casualty rates in eight different income areas became progressively lower as the value of homes rose.[46]

But these generalizations disguised a complex experience. Without question military assignment, controlled by the armed forces not SS, to a combat arm correlated with education, which correlated with income status and race. But whether or not a man ever entered the military through the draft concerned less bias on education and income. During the Korean War the social class of a family was a weak variable in predicting military participation. Only sons of farm workers had significantly less military experience than other groups. A combination of the draft, volunteering, and reserve options such as ROTC insured that a high percentage (75) of sons of both blue- and white-collar workers entered the armed forces. Even professional and managerial fathers had 67 percent of their sons in the military. If only participation through the draft is considered, however, a class bias did appear. But since the draft was also responsible, indirectly, for encouraging volunteers and reservists, it indirectly contributed to a lessening of class bias in all military participation. At its high point the Korean War saw 3.7 million Americans serving. Only one-third of those without a high school education served; only one-fourth of those with graduate training served. Since the vast middle class provided most of the men, glaring bias in service was avoided and protest minimized.[47]

Another reason for the lack of protest of the draft was that the public felt the draft deferment policies were biased, as they had been in World War II, to protect the sacredness of the family and religion, the long-range value of education, and the importance of a sound domestic economy.

Since 1940 the draft had reflected the nation's strong commitment to the traditional family. During the Korean War, Marshall had wanted to reduce the draft age to 18, but during congressional elections in 1950, Democratic leaders urged an end to all talk of drafting such youngsters because Republicans were using it to win votes. Few military leaders agreed with the image of an 18-year-old as a "youngster," but they had to bow to political reality. The same reality protected women. During World War II there had been talk about drafting female nurses, but nothing came of it. During the Korean War the Department of Defense rejected such a move, and public surveys in both 1950 and 1951 indicated strong opposition to a female draft, even if women draftees were limited to noncombat roles. Similar sentiments spilled over to concern with fathers.[48]

Under the 1948 draft law, which was merely extended in 1950, husbands without children were offered a deferment in class 3-A. The 3-A class had grown dramatically after World War II so that in the year prior to the Korean War there were 402,000 men in this category. In the 12 months after the invasion, the class grew by 381,000. After the law was revised in 1951, so that men without children could be deferred only under extreme hardships for a wife or other dependent, the group grew by only 117,000 in FY 1952. On 30 June 1951 there were 1,139,514 or 14.7 percent of all classified men with such a status.[49] The SS tried to tighten up the classification by qualifying only fathers who maintained "a bona fide relationship in their home" with a child, but the class continued to grow. By April 1952, among the 20,925 men who entered 3-A that month, some 493 were former 2-S, or students who had used up their education deferment. Local board members complained that marriage and children were becoming means of pyramiding protection from the draft.[50]

Military leaders had little sympathy for the sanctifying of fatherhood, but Truman accepted reality. In April 1952 a Gallup poll found that 48 percent rejected the drafting of married fathers, although 43 percent approved. As elections approached in October 1952 SS warned about the need to call fathers. The president asked Rosenberg if they were really needed at that time to meet the new calls. Rosenberg reassured him that such a step might not need to be taken until the summer of 1954, and even then it could be avoided by cutting student and occupational deferments. By January 1953 there were 1.4 million fathers deferred.[51]

The nation also determined to protect religious leaders as well as the family from the effects of conscription. During and after World War II draft laws provided recognition for the role of religion in society. Regular and ordained ministers were exempted, not merely deferred, from the draft, and even students preparing for the ministry were granted deferments. In the school year 1951 through 1952 there were about 54,000 such male students, of whom 30,000 were deferred in 4-D. More directly, the draft recognized the importance of religion by continuing the tradition of deferring individuals with conscientious objection to war.[52]

Great Britian offered protection to COs merely by simple application and appearance before a tribunal. The United States, however, recognized only objectors who based their claim on traditional religious feelings, and after the Korean War began, required that the CO perform alternate work. The 1951 draft law specifically made the CO liable for civilian work in the national health, safety, or interest. Boards usually ordered COs to jobs which were mutually acceptable. Although the officials of the American Friends Service Committee and the National Service Board for Religious Objectors both preferred an absolute exemption without any work requirement, they went along with the law. Roger W. Jones of the Budget Office felt that the CO organizations "are generally very well pleased with the outcome and that so long as there is no formally organized federal work program they will be able to work out with General Hershey" any problems. The small numbers involved helped avoid problems. In 1950 there were fewer than 12,000 COs out of 9,239,000 registrants, and the total classified as CO declined to 8,000 in 1951 and 5,000 in 1952. Although not as generous as some other nations, the American system of treating COs was more liberal during the Korean War than in World War II.[53]

Also liberalized was the treatment of black Americans. During World War II the draft had conducted racial calls and generally cooperated in maintaining a Jim Crow defense system. During the Korean War things changed. The system itself, with its decentralized state and local boards, continued to reflect the Janus face of American society on race. For example, local boards in the South remained all white. But in the execution of the draft the system anticipated the end to the Jim Crow army. Truman had begun the process by issuing his executive order of 26 July 1948 banning discrimination in the armed forces, and the draft bill passed in 1950 reiterated that there should be no discrimination on the basis of race in the execution of the draft. In 1950 SS eliminated all racial information on its forms, but only after exhausting the old forms. The services opened enlistments to blacks who flocked to join in such numbers that the G-I had second thoughts. By March 1951 all training units were integrated and no racial calls were made.[54]

Equally consistent with American values was the elaborate planning of the draft to protect the economy, education, and science from the dangers of reckless mobilization. SS was designed to manage mobilization so that it had a minimum impact on vital components of the economy. Some of this mission had been obscured by the politically essential idea of a universal draft, with all eligible men being draftable. The draft law of 1948 reemphasized such universality. The reality, of course, was always different, with men avoiding the draft for physical and vocational reasons. Theoretically deferments offered for key workers were temporary (60 days), but in practice they tended to be extended indefinitely.

When the Korean War began the Truman administration once again expected the draft to protect the home economy. On 8 August 1950 the National Security Resources Board (NSRB), created by the National Security Act to oversee vital home front components, met to study the impact of Korean mobilization. Stuart Symington, the chairman, and Secretary of Labor Daniel Tobin both complained that reserve call-ups and the draft created havoc in war industry. Truman directed Symington to work with the secretary of defense and the secretary of labor to come up with some kind of manpower control program, an echo of the War Manpower Commission of World War II. But like that in the earlier conflict, the only real manpower control was provided by the SS and various lists of essential skills and jobs provided by other agencies.[55]

Farming was well protected, although by 1950 American farm production had become so efficient that vast quantities of food were stored in government warehouses. The index of productivity of farm labor climbed dramatically. Farm output per manhour (base year of 1967 = 100) jumped from 27 in 1945 to 35 in 1950. Fewer farmers were producing more goods than ever.[56] Given such a record, young male farmers should have been more draft eligible than ever, but such was not the case. Politics, more than economic statistics, governed deferment policies.

When the Korean invasion began, the United States population stood at 150,696,000. Of the total work force some 59.5 million were in construction and industry and 12.85 percent or 7,628,000 were in agriculture. Of all draft registrants, about one-eighth were farm workers. From 1948 to 1 December 1951 SS granted some 84,864 male farmers aged 18 through 25, nonvets and nonfathers, deferment in class 2-C. These men were supposed to be producing for the market substantial quantities of farm products needed to maintain the national health and safety. In FY 1952 the number of 2-C deferments rose by 19.6 percent to 98,865. By the end of FY 1952 the total was 99,000, an increase of almost one-fifth from 30 June 1951. Yet total deferments and exemptions in the same period had grown only one-sixteenth. Several hundred thousand farmers were also deferred as fathers, veterans, or overage. Nonfarm occupational deferments, 2-A, stood at only about 20 percent of farm deferments. Farm deferments were not temporary, and by November 1953 only three of every 10 such registrants had entered military service, a much smaller percentage than the 2-S or 2-A types. Nearly 30 percent of the farm deferees under 25 remained in that classification for three or more years. No other occupational group did as well in avoiding the draft.[57]

The triumph of the farmer over the draft was a victory of political lobbying, a continuation of his achievements during World War II. Even as farmers became more efficient and fewer were needed, they became less draftable. The major farm organizations such as the American Farm Bureau Federation and the National Grange had opposed the draft renewal in 1948. Major complaints, however, did not begin until the calls for Korea. James G. Patton, president of the National Farmers Union, joined congressmen and individual farmers in protesting the draft. The protest covered familiar grounds: it was destroying family farms; dairy herds were being sold off as workers were either drafted or enticed to better-paying city jobs. These complaints came from an industry which was producing so much it was necessary for the government to store the surplus.[58]

The lobbying consistently focused upon social goals such as preserving the family farm, but equally important was the threat to the cheap wage structure in agriculture. A shortage of labor should have driven up cost, but this trend was minimized by offering a deferment rather than a raise. The lobbying worked despite surpluses, despite the reduction in number of farmers, and despite public opinion. Public polls in 1952 and 1953 showed little support for deferments for young, single farmers, but Congress and the president were more understanding.[59]

After Truman complained about drafting farmers, SS conducted an exhaustive survey on farm deferments. The survey showed that farm production had increased while farm population had decreased. The young farmers who left went to industry, not the armed forces. Of the 700,000 who left farm areas for the service, some 437,000 volunteered before being drafted. Armed force recruiters were very active in rural areas. Only 276,000 farmers were ordered for induction during the period since 1948 when 6 million left the farm. The local boards, filled with veterans, resented this excessive protection of farm boys. It seemed to be always the son who was claimed for deferment rather than the tenant or hired hand. The overage worker, veteran, and rejectee simply refused to stay on the farm because of the low wage rates. Hershey concluded: "there is help if the farmer is willing to pay more."[60]

Truman saw the survey but still wanted local boards to work closely with county agricultural mobilization committees to protect the proper farmers. By late June 1952, the president adopted a recommendation by the Office of Defense Mobilization which required that SS provide 2-C deferments for essential farm labor and work with state and county mobilization committees to measure quantities of farm commodities produced for market by each deferred registrant as compared with the average annual production per farm worker from a local average farm. The Department of Agriculture and the Department of Labor also had to furnish information on production and availability of replacements. The president also instructed the armed forces not to recruit among farm workers. Under failed farmer Harry Truman, farmers remained one of the most protected segments of the economy.[61]

In contrast, SS limited severely nonagricultural job deferments. In June 1951 only 24,403 men held 2-A deferments for key jobs in industry. The nonagricultural part of the nation's work force was growing rapidly, but the percentage deferred was declining. To some degree, however, the 2-A figure was distorted because it did not include the young men in training or in school who received a 2-S deferment. By June 1952 a total of 32,000 held 2-A protection, but the increase had come mainly by the decision to drop protection of 3-A from men who had wives but no children, although many of these men successfully claimed 2-A status.[62]

As mentioned earlier, the draft law provided that the president could defer men in key jobs who were essential for the nation's welfare. Classifying the men and defining the positions was the responsibility of local boards who were supposed to be guided by a list of essential activities issued by the Secretary of Commerce and a list of essential occupations issued by the Secretary of Labor. The first occupation list was issued on 3 August 1950. It was followed in April 1951 with a list which grouped essential activities under 25 broad headings. The executive order amending draft regulations defined necessary employment as a job in industry, science, etc., considered "to be necessary to maintenance of national health, safety, or interest" and the registrant could not be replaced because of a shortage in the field or removal would cause a material loss of effectiveness in such activity.[63]

For the most part this system worked well and generated few political or economic problems. As it had during World War II, American industry cooperated by depending upon the vast labor force beyond the reach of the draft. Occasionally a complaint arose over 2-A deferments only in the case of highly trained specialists in 1952 and 1953, but generally there were few men under age 25 who were deemed irreplaceable by management. In the fall of 1951 a critical shortage arose in the machine tool industry, a shortage probably more related to efforts to automate than to the draft. But SS sent alerts to all local boards to ease up on drafting those in such occupations. Truman issued an executive order in June 1952 on industrial apprentices which authorized local boards to defer qualified young men under rules stipulated by Hershey. The director assured Truman that these regulations would provide for a regular flow of required machinists, mechanics, and other skilled workers.[64]

The decision to protect highly trained specialists, key scientists, and future scientists reflected achievements in the World War II draft and the fear of Communist masses in the cold war. Some scientists and other members of the public felt that science had won World War II for

America. This simplistic idea was given considerable support by the dramatic atomic conclusion to the war. In truth, the war had been won by masses of armed men fighting traditional battles, but science had contributed and was certainly the beacon of hope for the world in the post-1945 period. With the threat to the United States of the masses under Communist control in Russia and China, science was even more vital in balancing the scales of power. The nation could not match the Asiatic hordes man for man but could destroy them effectively with new wonder weapons.

The draft during the Korean War accommodated the idealization of the scientist. The chairman of the NSRB urged Truman early in 1951 to create a national scientific personnel board to protect key scientists. Truman informed all departments and agencies of the need to defer them. An interdepartmental committee on scientific research and development arose under the chairmanship of Hugh L. Dryden to oversee a uniform policy of deferment for government scientists, but deferment was hampered by the decentralized nature of the draft which led to a lack of uniformity among local boards in dealing with deferment claims. To overcome the problem the SS appeal system worked closely with the Scientific Manpower Committee to insure protection.[65]

A more serious dilemma arose because the educational-scientific establishment convinced the government that young men studying for a career in science should also be protected. In August 1950 the Naval Research Advisory Committee, headed by W. Albert Noyes and including such prominent men as Leonard Carmichael of Tufts, L. A. Dubridge and Robert A. Millikan of Cal. Tech, J. R. Oppenheimer of Princeton, Lewis L. Strauss, and A. H. Compton implored the president to protect not just scientists, but graduate and undergraduate students in science and engineering—the future of science. The lobby called for creating a special class of young men immune to the universal obligation to serve.[66] Out of such concern arose an elaborate student deferment program which grew in the 1950s as Dwight Eisenhower replaced Truman in the White House.[67]

6

The 1950s
and Military
Manpower

The age of Eisenhower, the 1950s after
Korea, has become the good old days not merely in the mind of the
person in the street but also in the writings of historians.[1] Americans
remember the low inflation rate, the absence of official American wars,
and the stability of traditional institutions—despite the jarring appearance of Elvis Presley and rock and roll. The absence of draft protest fit
the absence of all protest. The ship of state sailed a serene sea guided by
a wise helmsman. But despite the absence of high draft calls, lists of
casualties, and other features that later made the 1960s so tumultuous,
there were important political battles over the shape of conscription
during the 1950s. The outcome of these battles shaped the national
manpower institution that Eisenhower eventually turned over to the
Democrats. In 1953, however, few Democrats were around as the first
Republican since Hoover took the oath of office.

Dwight Eisenhower had been thinking about soldiers and how to obtain them longer than most Americans. He had witnessed the evaporation
of armies after World War I and had experienced the problem of recruiting in the 1920s and 1930s. The mobilization problem of World War
II had finally been solved by the passage of the Selective Service Act, but
Eisenhower had faced troop shortages while directing the Allied conquest
of German-occupied Europe in 1944–1945. After the victory in Europe
he had returned to the United States as chief of staff, offering his ideas
on how to insure sufficient military manpower for the future. Like most
military leaders, he had been appalled at the hasty drive by Congress and

the public to demobilize. He, General George Marshall, and others had pleaded with Congress to maintain the draft and slow down the stripping of American defenses.[2]

Throughout his stay at the Pentagon Eisenhower remained wedded to an unpopular idea. Although he publicly supported both UMT and the draft, he much preferred a system of universal military *service*, rather than just the training of a huge reserve force. He wanted a large army in being, and he preferred that it be filled with professionals rather than con-scripts. In February 1947 he dismissed as "completely unrealistic" the ideas of air force lobbyists who felt America could control the Soviet Union with long-range bombers. His personal experience in Europe and his study of Pacific campaigns had convinced him "that any army in being of the sort contemplated under UMT represented the minimum for safety in the face of any serious military threat." Depending entirely upon conscripts, however, struck him as a very expensive proposition because of the constant turnover of men with only a two-year obligation.[3]

When Truman tried to resurrect the draft and UMT in 1948, Eisen-hower appeared before Congress to support the measures. Senator Rus-sell of the Senate Armed Services Committee asked him to choose one or the other idea. Eisenhower at first equivocated but then admitted that the draft was most essential, but he hoped Congress would also adopt UMT. Privately, after leaving office, he continued to insist that universal military service was the "only democratic way" to meet international obligations. He so informed Secretary of Defense Louis Johnson in July 1950. Such a force would also depend upon short-term draftees at nom-inal pay. As president of Columbia University he had joined James B. Conant, president of Harvard, in pushing UMT. When the Chinese en-tered the Korean conflict, he replaced his academic regalia with the uni-form of an American commander in Europe and warned that we might have to put all men in uniform.[4]

By 1952, however, as he entered the presidential campaign, Eisen-hower confronted a new situation. The mobilization for Korea had gener-ated enormous political controversy, particularly the recall of veterans. The reversals on the battlefield, the removal of MacArthur, and the limited tactics all contributed to increased public disenchantment with the conflict. Korea became a useful target for Republicans bent on cap-turing control of the government. Truman had pushed through the draft law of 1951 with a provision for UMT, but Congress had merely autho-rized a study while continuing the draft. A poll in the March 1952

Scholastic magazine of high school students found young males favoring UMT by 53.36 to 35.88 against.[5]

During the campaign Eisenhower explained to representatives Cole and Johnson that UMT service was "an obligation that every citizen owes the nation." At a press conference he admitted that he did not understand how both UMT and the draft could operate "hand-in-hand." He spoke of UMT but thought of universal military service. That is, he expected the young men to be trained in units on active duty, not in a half-way house with a quick return to civilian life. Presumably, since the obligation would be universal, there would be no need for "Selective" Service. Still he endorsed Truman's UMT because he thought it would be a tragedy to send untrained men into battle. He also felt that the program sent the message to the world that the United States, much like ancient Rome, was a "serious sober society that's doing its best to protect its own systems."[6]

After Eisenhower's triumph at the polls in November 1952, those men who had favored UMT and a strong military force took heart. The members of the National Security Training Commission (NSTC), created by the 1951 law, immediately began lobbying the president elect to make UMT a priority item on his agenda for 1953. The commission assured Eisenhower that both the draft and UMT could operate simultaneously. The draft alone, however, had too many loopholes. Some 2 million qualified men were deferred from the draft and had no reserve obligation. Yet 640,000 World War II veterans had been recalled during the Korean War. National leaders also lobbied for UMT. Senator Russell called it essential for national security, and Senator Lyndon Johnson complained that men were avoiding Korea because we lacked the guts to require training after World War II. General Marshall labeled the system "inadequate and ruinously expensive." General Bradley called UMT "the most effective use of our manpower and monetary resources."[7]

The first manpower project on the president's agenda, however, was to plug loopholes in the current draft. The public and the local boards had complained for several months that offering deferments for fathers was unfair, because they felt that many young men were marrying to avoid military service. A young man in school supposedly held a temporary deferment, but when he married he obtained a permanent one. The same pattern occurred in occupational deferments, where a defense worker could marry, have a child, and then find a new job, secure in his new deferred status.

These inequities seemed unacceptable as the cold war heated up. At a cabinet meeting of 12 February 1953 Secretary of State John Foster Dulles warned that "the situation has never been so grave as it looks today." Dulles pointed to Russian ambitions toward Berlin and Chinese mobilization over Korea.[8] If the United States hoped to stand firm around the world its military manpower system needed improving. One of the most disturbing issues, in the president's mind, was the massive loophole which allowed thousands of young men to avoid all military training. Under the 1951 law every draftee became obligated to six years reserve duty after his active service. If Eisenhower could close the loopholes which allowed some 400,000 young men to avoid conscription, SS assured him that the draft could be an instrument for achieving UMT without additional legislation.[9]

At his first meeting with congressional leaders, the president pressed for action to cut draft deferments and make induction a more universal experience. Unfortunately, his desire to expand the draft ran counter to his desire to cut the budget. Throughout his presidency he cut back on the authorized strength of ground forces as a means of saving money and balancing the budget. But if the army needed fewer men, draft calls had to fall and more men had to be deferred. This problem surfaced slowly. When Ike first took office he pressed his congressional leaders to act on the draft. Senator Leverett Saltonstall (R-Mass.) explained patiently that Ike did not need congressional action because many deferments were under executive control.[10]

And the idea of cutting deferments seemed popular. Local boards and congressmen both heard complaints about the unfairness of the draft. The universal obligation of service in the law seemed contradicted by student deferments and deferments for marriage and fatherhood. The 3-A, dependency classification, at that time held over 1 million men. Some 185,000 were in 2-S (college students), plus another 333,000 were in ROTC or other reserves.[11] The army's strength declined from 1,447,992 enlisted in 1942 to 1,388,182 in 1953. Under the system then in place, if an emergency occurred the deferred men would need a year of training. To meet immediate needs, the government would again have to call up veterans and reservists.[12]

By June 1953 the draft pool had suffered a massive leakage of manpower through deferments. The 3-A class was increasing at the rate of 12,000 to 14,000 each month, or up to 14 percent of each male cohort reaching 18.5 years. Such deferments were virtual exemptions from induction. Another 200,000 were in 2-S, 100,000 more in farm deferment, and 30,000 in other occupational deferments. The 3-A deferment created the worst publicity because in many cases it demonstrated a pyramiding strategy. All deferments were being jeopardized.[13]

Despite the figures, Arthur Flemming, head of the Office of Defense Mobilization (ODM) manpower committee, found it difficult to obtain a consensus on reform. Almost everyone agreed that pyramiding had to stop, but there was disagreement over how to stop it. Republican congressional leaders wanted the president to avoid the political risk associated with attacking privileges of the American family. The DOD wanted to end dependency deferment only for men who had initially claimed 2-S status. And still others argued that the order not be limited merely to students, but cover everyone in the pool, including men who left defense jobs after fathering a child.[14]

Finally, on 11 July 1953, a few weeks before a Korean armistice, Eisenhower issued EO 10469, under which all men at that time deferred in 3-A as fathers were continued as deferred. But after 25 August 1953 any new registrant not already holding 3-A was ineligible for it unless he could show that his induction would create an extreme hardship. For a man to slip into 3-A before the deadline he had to present evidence to the local board that his child was conceived before August 25. The order covered all registrants, not just students.[15]

Fifteen days later, on 26 July 1953, the United States signed an armistice in Korea. But for the rest of the decade the cold war remained a major focus of the public and the administration. Several incidents, such as the shelling of Quemoy and Matsu, the collapse of the French in Indochina, and a Berlin crisis, contributed to continued tensions between the United States and Russia. But after the Korean armistice the Eisenhower administration concentrated on a new defense style that put the draft in limbo. With the president paying more attention to the use of covert operations and building up an intercontinental bombing and missile force, draft calls fell to only 11,000 per month by the end of 1954.

At the end of fiscal year 1953 there were 14.4 million men registered for the draft and 13.9 million classified. Among the classified over 9.1 million were either deferred or exempt. Of the remaining 4.8 million 3.8 were either already in the service or veterans. A little over 938,147 men were available for immediate call. The deferred category included over

1.1 millon dependent types (3-A), 162,000 in college (2-S), and 1.7 million rejectees (4-F).[16]

Throughout the remaining years of the decade draft calls continued to decline, with the slight exception of 1958.

Inductions by Calendar Year

1953	472,000
1954	253,000
1955	153,000
1956	152,000
1957	139,000
1958	142,000
1959	96,000
1960	87,000[17]

The calls declined despite the annual prediction by General Hershey that the SS would have to call more men in the near future.[18]

Such contradictory information was the natural outcome of a paradoxical manpower policy. Even as Eisenhower shifted strategy away from mass armies, he insisted upon retaining the draft device as insurance and as an incentive to volunteers. General Carlton S. Dargusch of the ODM explained to Flemming that the draft "is bound to be with us for a long time, certainly so long as the cold war continues." The strength of the armed forces had been cut to under 3 millon in 1955 and would be cut to 2.4 million by 1960. The army, the main user of the draft, shrank from 1.5 million in 1953 to 873,000 in 1960. As needs were reduced, calls were lowered and the pool of eligible draftees rose. SS drafted the oldest eligible men first to insure they did not escape at age 26. But when the average draftee age reached 23 and above, the army complained. Older men were harder to train and created more problems.[19]

Other, more-long-range problems originated because of reduced calls and draft renewal. An estimated 1 million eligible men escaped the draft each year. The men who had received some military training grew older and fewer young men were being trained. But the Pentagon was more concerned with raising induction standards so that a higher quality recruit could be obtained from the surplus manpower. By January 1959 there were 1.3 million men registered for the draft who had no classification at all.[20]

Given the reduction in calls, the task of SS should have been easier, but the agency remodeled its mission. Following a bureaucratic law of long standing, headquarters became a beehive of intrigue and activity. Denied release in its primary mission of mobilizing men for combat, the agency assumed a vast array of personnel management tasks.

Bureaucratic problems multiplied. The Korean armistice had hardly been signed before an internecine conflict erupted between the director and the National Appeal Board.[21] This fight required presidential intervention. In addition, the reduced calls also made SS more expensive to operate, an ironic and simple rule of bureaucracy. The agency was designed to draft men into the armed forces, and its structure was geared to this end. When, in the 1950s, drafting became secondary to deferring, costs went up. A survey covering the period 1948 to May 1955 showed that it cost only $41.16 to classify a man in 1-A. But the elaborate procedure required to classify a man as 1-W (CO in alternate service) ran to $128.88 per man. To reclassify a man as 2-S (deferred for college) cost an additional $24.98. If he was reclassified to 4-F, it cost another $23.68. In return for this spending not one soldier entered the armed forces.[22]

SS, denied its primary mission, made a virtue of the secondary mission. Since the ideal of a "universal obligation to serve" was a dead letter, the agency began to exaggerate its selectivity and management of personnel. Although the redefinition may have pleased those interested in government manpower planning, it was bound to generate political opposition from those who accepted the draft only because of its egalitarian obligation. The expansion of deferments had been slow during the Korean War, but it was the wave of the future. Hershey urged draft officials to forget the total mobilization concept of World War II.[23]

By 1958 SS was boasting about its new role. "The only reason the Nation is not short 40,000 or 50,000 engineers today," read a press release, "is because they were among the approximately 1,100,000 students deferred by SS in 1951, 1952, and 1953, during the Korean War." The agency had become "the means of channeling people into engineering, into physics, and many other pursuits which have to do with this atomic age." Hershey informed Congress that "inducting men is now only a collateral, almost, you might say, a byproduct of its operation." Local boards who had originally demanded proof that a man should be deferred began to seek excuses not to draft men. Such a conversion meant the United States had a universal military obligation and a draft, but two-thirds of all men reaching 18½ avoided military service.[24]

Administration decisions on defense strategy combined with demographics and pressure from industry, science, and education to shape the draft into a channeling agency. Hershey boasted that "educators love the system and tell me we are doing well." The army reported no morale problems about the inequities of the system among those who were drafted. In February 1959 some 4.4 percent of the army's enlisted men were college graduates, a peacetime high. All the other services, which did not rely on the draft, had less than 1 percent of such men. Everyone seemed happy, but Hershey warned that if he ever had to pull in the deferred men, "all hell will break loose."[25]

The system and principles guiding the new channeling had arisen before the Korean War and were consistent with ideas of efficient manpower management. By fall 1948 several dozen specialists in various fields had arrived in Washington and began meeting under the auspices of SS. Although initially there were six committees dealing with humanities, engineering, physical sciences, biological sciences, social sciences, and healing arts, within a few days the entire group had merged.

The committee faced two major problems: how to maintain the supply of young scientists by deferments for training and education, and how to insure the utilization of men already trained. Most of their effort went into the first problem. In short order they realized that the best approach was to concentrate, not on specific fields, but on registrants whose aptitude recommended them for continued preprofessional and professional training. The final plan covered all fields, not just science and engineering, and recommended that students be deferred based on their class standing and their performance in a national examination. The committee report took an unabashed elitist approach to deferments and justified the stand on the basis of cold war exigencies.[26]

Although the plan was initially confidential, news of it soon spread in the education community. Not everyone was happy with the elitist approach. James B. Conant of Harvard wrote Eisenhower who was president of Columbia at the time, "I am very much inclined to oppose the whole business of deferment of students." He warned that colleges and medical schools would soon become havens for draft dodgers. The American Association of Universities, representing 34 colleges, passed resolutions in December 1948 opposing any deferment for students or any men under age 22. A resolution signed by Conant, Eisenhower, Herman B. Wells, Karl Compton, Harold W. Dodds, Charles Seymour, and others recommended that the military use the draft to induct key men and then assign them to colleges in areas where there was a defense need. But this approach was at odds with the SS committee plan.[27]

The entire issue became moot when Truman failed to act upon SS's recommendation. As draft calls were low and all induction scheduled to end in June 1950, the plan was filed for later reference. When the Korean War began, it was resurrected by the White House.[28]

Truman issued an executive order on 31 March 1951 creating the student deferment program. Regulations governing the system emerged on 10 April, and by 30 June there were 77,513 students classified 2-A(S). By September all deferred college students were assigned classification 2-S. A student became eligible for such a classification by scoring 70 or 75 on the Selective Service College Qualification Test (SSCQT) or by performing in the upper half of his class.[29]

The program placed the burden of action on the student. If he wanted a 2-S classification, he had to request it in writing from his local board. After finishing his first year, the student had to ask the college registrar to certify his status on an SS form and had to take the SSCQT. If the student wished to change his major subject he had to consider whether this would lengthen his stay and thereby jeopardize his classification. The SS expected the student to take no more than four years to obtain a bachelor's degree, two years for a master's, and not more than four years beyond the bachelor's for a doctorate.[30]

The SSCQT represented a novel means of national evaluation of students. Designed by the Educational Testing Service of Princeton, New Jersey, the test was first offered on 26 May 1951. There were about 1.4 million male students in college full time, but not all had an incentive to take the test. About 575,000 were either too young or too old to be drafted or were exempted as veterans or divinity students or had dependents. Another 275,000 were in the reserves or ROTC. This left only 550,000 as a potential draft pool. Of the 550,000, almost 400,000 took the multiple choice exam.[31]

A high percentage of eligible students benefited from the program. About 78 percent of those who took the first exam qualified for deferment. In one midwestern state, almost all of the 14,275 male nonveterans attending college were deferred in January 1952. By the end of the 1952 through 1953 school year about 20 percent or 240,000 of nearly 1.2

Students tested for deferment. Courtesy, Library of Congress.

million male students were either in 1-S (high school) or 2-S. The American public approved, despite the apparent contradiction between universal service and protecting college students, and the impact of Korean mobilization on reservists. Polls reported that in January 1951 46 percent of the public felt students in college should be deferred until graduation and 38 percent were opposed. By April 1951, after the SS program was announced, 55 percent felt those who passed the test should be allowed to stay in school and only 36 percent opposed. By April 1952, after the program had been operating for a year, some 69 percent favored allowing students with good grades to graduate before being drafted and only 24 percent opposed. During the Korean War an estimated 75 percent of the draft-age cohort served in the military. Of the 25 percent who escaped, two-thirds were 4-F rejectees and another one-third were deferred, 909,000 for dependency, 110,000 for occupations, and 850,000 for school.[32]

The creation of an acceptable student deferment program during the Korean War was a reaffirmation of America's commitment to education. The system flourished despite the disapproval of the leaders of SS and President Eisenhower. A survey of male students at 11 major universities in spring 1952 showed 73 percent favored the new arrangement, reflecting the growing disenchantment with the Korean action. In 1952, 83 percent of the males polled had a "negative attitude toward service." In 1953 some 26 percent of college students were strongly opposed to the war and 36 percent had reservations. Almost 96 percent polled said they seldom felt guilty about their status, and less than one in 10 felt he was getting privileged treatment. Over 90 percent felt that the deferment was merely a postponement and that they would eventually serve.[33]

But did they serve? Was deferment only postponement? In the spring of 1953, SS studied the education level of its pool of registrants. Using a sample inventory total of 110,897 men from 18 through 28, the study found that 18 percent had only attended elementary school, 10 percent had attended junior high school, 16 percent attended but did not graduate from high school, 20 percent graduated but went no further, and 16 percent had some college education. About 12 percent failed to report their education status. According to census reports for 1952 the percentage of male population finishing grammar school was 20.2, high school 20.7, and 16 percent attended college.[34] The education level of the registrants in the pool was fairly consistent with that of the civilian cohort. But how were the registrants classified?

A study of the classification history of registrants by education revealed several interesting patterns. As education level increased, so did the percentage classified 1-A. Only 9.6 percent of those with elementary education were classified 1-A; 11.6 were 1-A if they attended high school but did not graduate; 17.5 if high school graduates or beyond. Conversely, the lower the level of education, the higher the percentage classified 4-F: 40 percent with elementary education and 15 percent for some high school. Similarly, the percentage of men volunteering for service increased with the amount of education.[35]

The Eisenhower administration feared that college students were escaping service entirely by pyramiding deferments. But the study of 1953 found little evidence of such a trend. Of 225 registrants in class 1-S (high school) in April 1952, some 40 percent were in 2-S a year later, but 38 percent had entered the armed forces. Of those 11,079 classified 2-S, a year later 20 percent had entered the armed forces, but more than 50 percent remained in 2-S.[36]

Another study was conducted in 1953, by the Scientific Advisory Committee of Selective Service. Taking a random sample of 400 students from the universities of Indiana, Michigan, Minnesota, and Boston, the study found that over 70 percent of those who left school during World War II either returned to the same school or attended another one. Interrupted veterans had a "survival to degree" percentage which was higher than that for the nation as a whole. Boston University students entering in 1947 and 1948 survived to graduate at the rate of 43 and 54 percents. Interrupted veterans graduated at a 71 percent rate. The study concluded that interruption of college for military duty "does not seem to decrease the chance that the student will eventually attain his degree. There is some indication that it increases it."[37]

Whatever the concerns of local boards and politicians, students, educators, and the public endorsed the college deferent plan. Not many students were pyramiding their student deferments into dependency deferments. The manpower needs of the armed forces had stabilized and calls were being cut. Yet despite these encouraging signs, administration leaders continued to bemoan the inequity of the arrangement.

Their concerns sprang not from statistics on manpower or military needs, but because of the tension between a selective draft and an egalitarian society. At the heart of the complaints was the supposed antidemocratic bias inherent in any such deferments. Such a bias was basic to any "selective" system. In the case of students, however, the selection had led not to the excusing of a few key workers, or older men, or sick men, but to a large crop of healthy young Americans whose parents could afford to send them to college. The problem worried congressmen and local board members more than it did the public. But critics felt that the program made it necessary for the poor to fight while the rich stayed home.[38]

The Scientific Advisory Committee and other defenders insisted that the continuation of the program contributed to national defense by enhancing the defense technology of the nation. Also, college was not merely for the rich. Because of higher rejection rates, the poor were not drafted at any higher rate than the rich. But politics, not for the last time, triumphed over statistical reality. Ignoring the arguments and favorable polls, Eisenhower eventually issued an executive order ending dependency deferment for 2-S types and raised the standards for graduate students. And Hershey dismantled the Science Advisory Committee, which had failed to respond to his prompting about further reduction of the system.[39]

Yet these actions were political window dressing. Complaints from educational and scientific lobbies grew shrill when any threat to draft

Testing for deferments. Courtesy, Library of Congress.

graduate students appeared. Education leaders wanted even more done for their community.[40] And SS continued to cooperate. On the state level committees of scientists and educators offered advice on deferment requests from industry, and the college deferment program expanded. By spring 1955 SS convened a new national scientific advisory committee, staffed by government insiders and chaired by Dr. Leonard Carmichael. By a unanimous vote the group approved the program and also supported an "internship" for science and engineering graduates. The internships allowed graduates time to obtain a deferable job. The government was supporting the pyramiding of deferments.[41]

The pool of student registrants grew even larger by 1955. In 1954–1955 there were some 37,426 people aged 5–34 enrolled in schools across the country. This total represented about 23 percent of the population. Of the total only about 50 percent finished high school and only 2 of 5 enrolled in college. Of this small group only two-thirds graduated. Only 25 percent of students who started grammar school graduated from high school, and not more than 1 in 12 graduated from college. About 1.2 million male full-time college students were registered for the draft. Many of them were not classified 2-S, as they went into ROTC (190,000) or other classifications. Among the 150,000 2-S types, length of deferments varied. Some 23.4 percent were in the classification less than one year; almost half were in between one and two years; 23 percent were in two to three years; 2.5 percent were in three to four years; and only 0.9 percent were in four or more years.[42]

Over the following several years the draft became less and less a threat to college males. The total number of men classified 2-S remained around 150,000 to 154,000 but was a smaller percentage of the male cohort 15 to 24 which was in college. This group, 15 to 24, of the total male population rose from 16.5 percent in 1948 to 20.4 percent in 1958. In 1958 about 2,415,000 young males were in college and annual inductions were only 142,000. The next year less than 100,000 were called up. In 1960 only 3,316 college males bothered taking the SSCQT. As local boards were not calling men until they reached age 23, a de facto blanket deferment of college students existed. The Pentagon kept insisting that the odds were 99 to 1 that a young man would be called before age 26 if he had no deferment, but an increasing number of students felt it was worth the gamble. If a man accepted a 2-S deferment, he extended his liability to the draft to age 35, although few men over 26 were called.[43]

Support for the blanket protection of an educated elite expanded in October 1957 when Russia launched the world's first earth satellite— *Sputnik*. A poll of high school students in 1959 found almost 80 percent of the 15,000 polled favoring military service for all, but 64 percent also favoring college deferments.[44] Colleges increasingly assumed the program was designed to provide blanket protection of their enrollments. Some deans, anticipating the 1960s, objected to assigning class standing to students. With calls so low there was little incentive to follow strict guidelines. The SS was in a poor position to punish uncooperative schools, but ranted about the dishonesty of some college officials, warned about future accountability, and used the FBI to investigate careless schools. But in reality the program had gained too much momentum to control.[45]

Leading scientific organizations had supported the transition of the SS into a manpower channeling agency because they supported special treatment for scientists. Having a national agency provide protection for their constituents was more efficient than having to deal with thousands of local boards in thousands of communities across the nation. Selling the idea of privilege was easier at the top than the bottom. Although the law spoke of equality of sacrifice and Hershey insisted that "both the learned and the unlearned" must serve, in the 1950s the draft reflected another reality.[46]

The scientific community believed their special knowledge was the key to national power, and equality of sacrifice was rejected as an outmoded idea and replaced with belief in a meritocracy. Howard A. Meyerhoff, executive director of the Scientific Manpower Commission, explained that a GI could be trained in a few weeks and was easily replaced, but a physicist required five years' training and was virtually irreplaceable. Leonard Carmichael of the Smithsonian explained that equality of sacrifice was not "necessarily desirable," when it conflicted with efficient utilization of talents. Major Lenox R. Lohr, president of the Society of American Military Engineers, insisted that "equality of sacrifice is incompatible with the demands of national security." Industrial leaders such as L. J. Fletcher of Caterpillar Tractor Company also called on the nation to accept unemotionally the incongruity of equity of service with "equity of survival."[47]

The reason for the inequity of service was the existence of a worldwide threat of communism, which might exist another 50 years. The free world could not match the Communist countries in manpower so must resort to scientific methods of warfare. However, the Communist countries were more advanced in science. According to General Leslie R. Groves, who had presided over the construction of the atomic bomb, the American educational system was failing to produce enough scientists, and those few who did emerge should not be wasted in the ranks.[48]

During the Korean War several solutions emerged to the shortage in scientific manpower. James R. Killian, White House adviser, called upon the armed forces to release serving scientists and engineers not working in their field. He believed emphasis should be placed on "selectivity" of service, with service given a broader connotation than merely carrying a gun.[49] The armed services rejected his idea, but on 22 October 1952 SS issued operations bulletin 42 which emphasized the need to defer scientists, engineers, and draftsmen. The departments of Labor and Commerce issued lists of critical occupations and essential activities to guide local boards in granting deferments. A special survey by SS as of 31 October 1953 found that of the 24,000 men in 2-A some 10,100 were engineers, 2,900 were scientists, and 1,600 were technicians. But only 61 percent of those in 2-A were in defense production. Over 10 percent had held their 2-A status for three years or more.[50]

When the Korean War wound down, Eisenhower ordered a tightening of deferments, and in July 1953 Hershey pushed up standards for graduate deferments. The science lobby protested, arguing that graduate education provided the traditional path to scientific maturity. Several thousand graduate students were called between 1 May and the end of 1953. The chemistry department at the University of Illinois gave half its assistantships to foreign students. Professor Donald S. Clark of Cal Tech complained that local boards in southern California were busy reclassifying as 1-A men accepted in graduate school. The 1951 through 1952 first-year graduate student enrollment in science was 11,721. In twelve months it dropped to 8,000.[51]

Besides the tendency to pyramid deferments, graduate students took a long time to finish their degrees. Most of them were part-time students and taught classes the rest of the time, a violation of draft regulations. Studies showed that only 36 percent of graduate students in science could continue without teaching or fellowship aid, but local boards found the value of pure research too esoteric. Officials argued that the military needed scientists and that discharged veterans could fill the vacated slots in graduate schools. On 20 September 1954 the administration again upped the standards for graduate student deferments. Those entering after January 1955 had to be in the upper quarter of their last undergraduate class or score 80 on the SSCQT.[52]

The shifts in standards created personal problems for young scientists. George E. Kaufer worked with the electronics research laboratory at Columbia University. He had received a student deferment to finish his graduate degree and an additional two-year deferment to finish his research at the lab. When classified 1-A in March 1954 he appealed all the way to the National Selective Service Appeal Board (NSSAB) and was rejected. Lawrence H. O'Neill, head of the lab, complained bitterly. Kaufer had been working on defense contracts involving guided missiles. O'Neill pointed out that Russia had 400,000 engineers compared to America's 500,000 and was producing them twice as fast. The deferment that allowed Kaufer to finish his master's was useless if he could not apply his talents as a permanent member of the lab staff. But despite O'Neill's ardent appeal, Kaufer's reclassification stood.[53] A limerick in the SS *Newsletter* reflected the general sentiment:

> Today in college
> To gain more knowledge
> More and more I strive.
>
> A student deferment
> Is my preferment
> 'Til I reach thirty-five.
>
> But Selective Service
> Has me nervous
> They grant but one degree.
>
> Despite my plea
> for a Ph.D.
> They offer me a P.F.C.[54]

The Kaufer case was an exception. The system usually did grant some protection to advanced students. A survey in 1955 found that there were about 133,034 male graduate students among some 1,730,000 male college students. In 1954 through 1955, 30,874 males received graduate degrees, 20,239 in science. A sample survey in 1955 found that only 2.6

percent of all male graduate students were classified 1-A, while 70.9 percent were deferred, exempted, or unclassified.[55]

After a ringing reaffirmation of equality of service in the 1951 draft act, the system had become more and more disposed to inequality.[56] In a survey in Michigan in 1955, registrants engaged in scientific and specialized fields made up 7.3 percent or 27,250 of the registrants in the state. After dropping those still in school and those about whom information was not complete, SS offered a detailed report on the remaining 13,692. Some 22.4 percent were mechanical engineers, 24.3 were general teachers, 9.6 were electrical engineers, 6.1 were civil engineers, and 6.3 were science teachers. Some 76 percent had bachelor's degrees, 14.6 master's degrees, and 1.9 Ph.D.'s. Ironically, these men worked mainly outside of national defense. Some 88 percent replied that in their opinion their present work was nondefense. Out of the 13,692 some 2,421 had never been in the armed forces, and of the 82 percent who had been in, 68 percent had served in the enlisted ranks.[57] Selective Service channeling was protecting civilian production more than the nation's defense production.[58]

By the end of the decade the science and education lobby could look back on considerable success. There existed a system of deferring virtually all students and teachers, and most scientists were protected. When draft renewal came up toward the end of the decade, Dr. Alan Waterman of the National Science Foundation reported that "scientists had become used to it," and recommended a simple renewal of the program.[59]

Several hundred scientists offered advice to each state draft system about deferments. By 1960 there were over 57,000 men deferred in 2-A because of critical skills, including 3,900 apprentices. The SS found itself boasting about an elite deferment program forced upon it by lobbying and demographics. A press release read that framers of the draft "realized that registrants could be induced by the attraction of deferment to matriculate in colleges and pursue courses leading to degrees in those specialties where shortages exist." The SS had become the "nation's store keeper of manpower."[60]

Besides keeping count in the store, the draft also began playing a role in the quality of the goods, the health of manpower. During the 1950s the operation of the draft influenced the American health system in several ways. The most immediate effect was to cast doubt upon the efficaciousness of the system by turning up a huge number of young men who were physically unfit for military service, the 4-F types. The draft system also had an impact on the providers of health in that the deferment policies adopted by SS influenced the supply of physicians. Finally, the draft became an indirect instrument to force physicians into the armed forces.

Mobilization efforts for the Korean War showed that American youth remained as unhealthy as in 1940. In a report on the period June 1948 to June 1955 the SS found that only 4,321,000 men out of a total of 16,707,000 had been processed for possible duty. Of this group, some 481,000 were rejected by local boards, another 119,000 were rejected at the time of induction, and 1,648,000 were turned down after their preinduction physical. A total of 2,248,000, or 52 percent, were rejected for service. Of 1,418,997 rejections from July 1950 to June 1954 some 44.4 percent failed the achievement test only, and 43.9 failed only the medical test. Another 9 percent failed both achievement and medical tests. Despite a reexamination of those rejected due to failure of the achievement test and a lowering of standards, the 4-F figures proved rather stable.[61]

The following list offers a breakdown of the causes for rejection of SS registrants from June 1948 to 30 June 1955:

Causes	Percentage of Rejections
1. circulatory diseases	15.5
2. bones and movement diseases	14.5
3. psychiatric disorder	13.0
4. digestive disorder	10.5
5. eye defects	7.5
6. ear and mastoid diseases	6.5
7. allergic diseases	6.0
8. congenital malformities	4.5
9. infective and parasitic diseases	3.5
10. neoplasms	2.5
11. miscellaneous	16.0[62]

Projecting these figures onto the national health scene was difficult. The draft pool was not a random sample of all youth 18 to 25. Those temporarily in the 1-A category were a selection of all registrants. The pool of men eventually submitted to military induction standards had already been cut down. It omitted all men who enjoyed a deferment, those who had enlisted to avoid the draft, and those serving in the reserves. An estimated 38 percent of the entire draft-liable pool fulfilled its obligations for military service during the Korean War through means other than the draft. When all these considerations were plugged into the rejection figures, probably only 23.6 percent of all American youth failed to qualify for military service during the Korean War.[63]

After Eisenhower achieved an armistice in 1953 the rejection picture began to change. As induction calls went down and defense budgets shrank, the army rejected more men, although there was no immediate change in standards. Preinduction rejection rates for fiscal year 1954 rose to 40 percent from 31.3 percent in 1953. In 1957 the Department of Defense sought relief from a provision in the 1951 draft law, supported by southerners, which required acceptance of men who scored a minimum of 10 on the Armed Forces Qualification Test (AFQT). Scores of 10 to 30 on the AFQT corresponded to I.Q. levels of 70 to 90. Such men were hard to train. But by 1957 the draft was filling over 40 percent of its calls with such men. The administration needed to find personnel to operate complex weapons. In July 1958 Eisenhower signed a bill permitting higher standards at induction, and by fiscal year 1959 the armed forces were rejecting over half the men given preinduction and induction exams.[64]

The press trumpeted each new advance in medical technology as a breakthrough heralding the end of this or that disease, but the general health of American males seemed unaffected. The issue of public health had an effect on how the draft treated physicians and medical students.[65] Deferments had been extended to medical students until the very end of World War II. In 1941 the ratio of physicians to the population was 1.31 per 1,000; by the end of 1946 the United States population stood at 143 million with 205,000 doctors, and the ratio had climbed to 1.43 per 1,000.[66]

When the draft was renewed in 1948 a special Healing Arts Committee at SS advised the director that national interest required maintaining medical school enrollment. The committee also called for deferments for undergraduate premed majors, and SS complied. The 1951 draft law said that such students should be deferred in numbers adequate to keep the health professions at peacetime strength. This protection of medicine, dentistry, veterinary medicine, osteopathy, and optometry continued throughout the Korean War.[67]

Defining adequate numbers proved controversial because the armed forces also required service from medical personnel. With 48,000 doctors in the Army Medical Corps in July 1945, the ratio of physicians to those on active duty was about 6 per 1,000. The navy had 14,191 doctors in August 1945 but only 6,606 in June 1946. The draft act had been amended in December 1943 to read that "no individual shall be called for induction . . . because of their occupation, or by occupational groups . . . except pursuant to a requisition by the land or naval forces for persons in needed medical professional and specialists categories." A medical draft had not been needed during World War II, and the 1948 draft law omitted this provision. But with the Korean War things changed.[68]

In September 1950 the administration proposed Public Law (PL) 779 as an amendment to the draft act. It provided for a special call of physicians, dentists, and other health personnel. Pentagon officials offered a strong argument for such a special, selective draft. In World War II about one-third of the nation's physicians had served in the armed forces without affecting civilian morbidity and mortality rates. Many physicians had been trained at government expense. The army alone had enrolled 20,000 medical students and 7,700 dental students in the ASTP. The navy had done the same for 11,000 medical and 3,000 dental students. About 8,000 physicians and 3,000 dentists who had accepted training under these programs had never been called to active duty, and many others had seen only limited service. Defense officials argued that such men owed the government service and should be called for service in Korea. The army could not fill its medical corps positions by calling up reservists. In the early months of the conflict it had had to borrow over 300 physicians from the navy.[69]

At hearings before the House Armed Services Committee in late August 1950 congressmen listened sympathetically. Physicians with active reserve commissions had already been called up. Their objections at being dragged away from busy practices added to the general chorus of protest raining down on Congress over mobilization. Representative Kilday argued that such a blanket draft could upset civilian public health, but a majority of the committee felt that civilians should support the military during what they assumed would be a limited war.[70]

In fact, the army did not wish to draft physicians. The idea behind PL 779 was to coerce professionals into accepting a reserve commission in the medical corps with a special $100 monthly bonus. This option remained open to any specialist for 21 days after he was called by SS and received his preinduction exam. The draft was again being employed to channel manpower. The law authorized the registration and call of all males under age 50 in medical, dental, and allied health fields. Health personnel were arranged into four priority groups with first priority given to men who had trained in ASTP or navy V-12 or been deferred during World War II for preprofessional training but who had served less than 90 days on active duty. Priority 2 contained similar types who had served between 90 days and 21 months. In priority 3 were men who had had no active military service after 16 September 1940. Into Priority 4 went men who were not in priorities 1 or 2 and who had active service in World War II or afterward.[71]

President Truman announced that the established priorities seemed to be "logical and fair" when he signed the measure on 9 September.[72] In short order General Marshall requested and Truman approved an SS call of 300 doctors in November, 300 in December, and 322 in January 1951. Some 500 dentists were also to be called during the same period. The SS began registration on 16 October. Some 12,000 physicians and 4,500 dentists went into priorities 1 and 2. In January 1951 another 74,000 physicians and 28,000 dentists went into priorities 3 and 4. But no one was drafted. As expected, the threat of induction spurred physicians and dentists to seek commissions. By the end of January 1951 3,420 physicians and 1,880 dentists had signed up as officers and taken their bonuses. By 30 June 1951 the Department of Defense reported a ratio of 3.78 physicians to every 1,000 troops, a figure slightly higher than authorized.[73]

The draft had succeeded in channeling specialized manpower. But this success had required certain concession to the medical profession. When the doctor draft bill was first debated in Congress authorities in the medical profession emphasized the need to protect civilian health needs. Although the final bill ignored such pleas, Truman appointed a special seven-member national advisory commission on the selection of doctors, dentists, and health personnel to advise him on calls. The committee, headed by Dr. Howard A. Rusk, served under the National Resources Planning Board. Rusk warned young physicians to volunteer. "If they do not," he said, "they will find themselves inducted as privates and subject to a pretty period of scrubbing floors before they can practice their profession."[74]

This was tough talk, but the Pentagon strongly objected to putting civilians, however disposed, in a position to influence military manpower. After much debate the DOD finally accepted that physicians had to be given some advisory role. Besides the Rusk committee, statewide medical advisory committees were authorized by the law to counsel local draft boards on the availability of individual physicians. Calls for medical personnel were screened at the White House level. Although final authority on any draft case remained with local boards and final authority on military calls remained with the secretary of defense, the existence of the state-wide boards insured that the medical profession had a strong influence on who was threatened with the draft. One physican, a loyal Democrat, warned that the committees were staffed by men "opposed to Truman and everything he stands for in a medical or health way and he will crucify himself amongst the profession by letting the A.M.A. or state society officers handle this in the coming draft."[75]

Despite the politics involved, the system functioned well. Local draft boards generally followed the advice of professional boards. By 1953 the armed forces had 3.5 million men, among whom were 13,000 physicians and 6,500 dentists, 8 percent of all the physicians and dentists in practice in the United States.[76] For every 7 physicians in the Regular Army, another 7 had come in as a result of the pressure of the doctors' draft. The army was quite pleased with the results, having obtained young doctors with broad training and good attitudes.[77]

These results, however, were not achieved without political problems, and modifications of the law and policies were soon needed. By 1952 priorities 1 and 2 were exhausted. Only about 50 percent of the men in those categories had actually entered active duty; the other 50 percent had been deferred or rejected for physical defects. The Department of Defense then decided that physicians who could carry on a private practice were fit for military duty. But even with that liberal standard the draft had to move into priorities 3 and 4. There were 33,086 physicians and 13,703 dentists in priority 3, and 51,735 and 17,812 respectively in priority 4. The draft had become a threat to men who had already served or who were much older and had no debt of training from World War II.[78] SS first called priority 3 types who were under age 35, with induction scheduled for December 1952, but soon all ages were made liable for call.[79] Grousing grew but the armed forces again got enough volunteers.

What began in 1950 as an emergency measure became more permanent. The original doctors' draft was scheduled to expire in July 1953, but a proposal for renewal soon appeared before Congress. The Department of Defense had reduced physical standards and had cut the ratio of doctors to 1,000 troops from a World War II high of 6.5 to 3.5 in late 1953. A projected call of 1,800 for the second quarter of 1953 was reduced to 1,200, but an extension of the law was still needed. With an armistice in effect in Korea, the request met considerable opposition from professional associations.[80]

Medical associations insisted that the armed forces could cut further their calls. The AMA called for better utilization of physicians on active duty, or a further reduction in ratio of doctors to troop strength. In particular, the AMA insisted that military physicians not be burdened with care for civilian dependents. Finally, the association wanted better incentives offered to recruit volunteers into the medical corps reserve, such as higher bonuses.[81]

A survey in 1953 of physicians released from active duty found many complaints about underutilization. One physician complained that the entire idea was a conspiracy among his civilian colleagues to take over his practice. Administering the law, even with the cooperation of advisory boards, was a major headache. To threaten a physician with induction could lead an entire community to protest the shortage of health care. One young doctor found himself in priority 2 although he had served over 24 months on active duty during World War II but only 18 months as a doctor. The 1950 law insisted that all who served less than 21 months had to be classified in priority 2. Despite the unfairness and protest, the draft pressure continued. County and state medical advisory boards were as hard boiled as draft boards. General George Armstrong, the surgeon general of the army, advised physicians to take a commission as soon as they got a draft notice. He warned that a few doctors had been ruined professionally by trying to fight the system.[82]

When Congress considered extending the system (PL 84) in the summer of 1953, the AMA advanced various reform proposals even while admitting that a continuation was needed. In the hearings congressmen proved more receptive to testimony from the DOD than the AMA. The law passed on 29 June 1953 extended the basis system for two years with only minor adjustment in priority 4 status. In December, President Eisenhower issued an executive order that stated that physicians and dentists who had 21 months or more of active duty since 16 September 1940 were no longer draft liable. It also stated that priority 2 types were to be selected according to their length of previous active duty with those having the least number of months selected first on a nationwide basis.

Those physicians who had been inducted under the doctor draft for Korea, served 12 months, and were then released were no longer liable, as was the case with other reserve officers.[83]

In 1954 a new problem arose. Secretary of Defense Charles Wilson insisted that reform was needed because of the "vital problem of dealing with Communists." In reality, a few dentists and physicians had used the courts to beat the draft. When faced with induction, they applied for a commission but refused to sign the loyalty form required by the government. (The loyalty form contained questions about affiliations with organizations that had supposed Communist ties.) The army then denied the commission, and the men were drafted as privates. The draftees sought relief from the courts, arguing that the doctor draft envisioned physicians functioning in a professional capacity, which could not be done without the commission. In several cases the court held that if the man was not given a commission he had to be released. On 18 June 1954 Congress amended (PL 403) the doctor draft law to close this loophole. The law then read that such special registrants could be appointed or promoted to any grade or rank, including enlisted.[84]

In 1955 the general induction authority under the 1951 draft law again came up for renewal. There was little debate over the need to continue the regular draft, but the medical profession made a strong case for ending the special draft of physicians. The AMA argued that military needs could be met by young physicians who were liable under the regular draft, without additional liability for older physicians as provided in the doctor draft law. SS responded that one-eighth of all physicians registered under the regular law and one-seventh of dentists so registered were already on active duty. But two-thirds of physicians and three-fourths of dentists were in class 5-A, which made them overage for regular liability. Without the doctor draft these men would have no pressure to enter the service. The DOD predicted a 15 percent shortage of needed health personnel under such circumstances.[85]

Eventually President Eisenhower resolved the issue in favor of national security. The regular induction authority was extended for four years but the doctors draft for only two years. To provide a long-range solution to the problem, PL 118 created an Armed Forces Reserve Medical Officer Commissioning and Residency program, called the Berry plan after Dr. Frank B. Berry, assistant secretary of defense. The Berry plan provided additional incentives for young physicians and dentists to take commissions by allowing those that volunteered to receive monetary assistance and remain deferred through internships.[86]

In 1955, of the 7,000 male graduates of medical schools only 4,500 were vulnerable for induction, and of these some 10 percent would be physically disqualified. This left only 3,500 available for military duty. Yet the armed forces needed approximately 10,000 medical officers on active duty, two-thirds career types. In mid-1956 two-thirds were serving only because of the doctors' draft. Some relief could be provided by calling doctors of osteopathy, who were eligible for the draft under the original law of 1950. But when the issue arose in September 1956, Hershey recommended, and Eisenhower agreed, that osteopaths not be covered by the doctors' draft. Ironically, the success by orthodox medicine in marginalizing competitors led to increased draft vulnerability for regular doctors. In October 1956 Berry warned the AMA that, given the needs of the services and the small number of physicians in the 35 to 45 age group without military service, the doctor draft had to continue. New incentives were offered for physicians under 35 to volunteer, but if they did not, "they will be drafted."[87] But by 1957 the active duty strength of the armed forces had dropped to 2,795,798 from a 1952 high of 3,635,912. The strength of the army alone had dropped from 1,596,419 to 997,994. SS inductions dropped from 552,000 in 1951 to 139,000 in 1957.[88]

In June 1957 the original doctor draft law ended. The DOD could hardly push for renewal when in all fiscal year 1956 there had been only one call for 150 physicians and 10 dentists. In fiscal 1957 the call for 1,130 doctors had been filled by men under age 36. Prospects for the next year were so bright that there seemed no need for a law making physicians and dentists liable up to age 51. The armed forces could fill their needs by using special calls of regular registrants. Here was the rub. Although the doctor draft law expired, there was still to be a draft of doctors but from a smaller pool. House Resolution 6548, approved by Congress in mid-1957, allowed the president to issue special calls for physicians and dentists who were normally liable for the draft. Each year an anticipated 5,000 medical graduates became eligible for service. The DOD expected to select only half this group. Under the Berry plan some 2,100 residents were in deferred status, with another 900 going in each year. Some 500 doctors would enter the armed forces from this program. But the engine which made possible this new program remained the threat of the draft.[89]

From 1958 through 1961 there were no special draft calls for doctors. The Berry plan was working well. In 1960 about 150 too many doctors were due to receive commissions after their deferments through internships. The male medical graduates stood at 7,000 and the needs of the armed forces at 3,000. The AMA immediately called for granting draft immunity to the surplus. More and more young physicians were willing to ignore the Berry reserve program and take their chances with the draft.[90] The medical manpower problem had come full circle. As had been the case with college students, a system of deferments and channeling through the draft had been used indirectly to achieve a manpower objective. And as calls had dropped a similar sense of achievement had descended.[91]

The channeling and protection of elites during the 1950s had seriously compromised the primary mission of the SS—to find fighting men. Few complained because the leadership of Eisenhower had generated a general sense of complacency. With general prosperity, with the development of missiles and atomic bombs, experts predicted that future wars would be fought with machines rather than men. Other contributing causes to the compromise of the draft's mission were demographic concerns, special interest lobbying, and strategic decisions. SS suffered especially from the vacillating manpower policy adopted by the Eisenhower administration.

In November 1953 the Planning Board of the National Security Council offered a top secret report on "Defense Mobilization Planning Assumptions." The major assumptions included the following: there would be a long period of tension and limited wars; global war was unlikely in fiscal year 1954 or 1955, but if such a war came it would come without warning and involve nuclear attacks and "mass destruction of major urban areas"; there would be full mobilization of manpower to fight a coalition war; and, most significant for current manpower planning, "the present UMT and Service Act will be continued for the period short of global war."[92]

Given these assumptions, the administration had to make some hard choices in 1953. The draft law then in effect provided induction authority only until 1 July 1955. Eisenhower was worried particularly about the absence of a trained reserve. The political backlash from calling up more than 700,000 reservists, including many World War II veterans, during the Korean mobilization remained a vivid memory. The president asked the National Security Training Commission to offer proposals for a reserve program. The ensuing report, entitled "Twentieth Century Minutemen—A Reserve Forces Training Program," amounted to a new call for UMT through a six-month training camp plus 7.5 years reserve duty for all 18 year olds. But Congress ignored the report, DOD did not think it timely, and Eisenhower also had reservations. He did not believe that six months of training was sufficient.[93]

With UMT dead in the water, the administration turned again toward the old standby, renewal of the draft. Hannah at DOD recommended that draft renewal be made a legislative priority for 1954, one year ahead of the expiration date. Nothing in the international situation recommended a reduction in the armed forces and only the draft provided the needed men. The president, however, continued to worry about using a draft while allowing so many deferments. "We've got people who have gone scot free and will soon be out of the age bracket," he remarked. He could not understand the need to defer "a man to go to college." But his advisers, particularly Fleming, assured him that his executive order had closed the major loophole. Students eventually served upon finishing school. While he felt these assurances were dubious, Eisenhower accepted the need to push for draft renewal. He had little option.[94]

The Reserve Forces Act of 1955 passed Congress with little debate. It provided for an extension of the draft and included a 24-month active duty obligation. All of the current deferment arrangements were left in place. The only new aspect of the law was a ready reserve obligation of four years for all on active duty. In addition, a special voluntary six-month active duty program was offered for up to 250,000 enlistees a year. These men had an additional 7.5-year reserve obligation.

The president accepted this approach because he was more and more convinced of the irrelevance of a mass army of draftees as a response to a surprise nuclear attack. He wished to cut defense costs and saw that money could be saved by expanding a ready reserve rather than processing short-term draftees in and out of active duty. He was also conscious of increased equity problems as the size of draft calls fell and the age cohort grew. But by 1956 there were signs of weakness in the new reserve program. The six-month program enlisted only 4,000 men a month rather than the 20,000 which had been planned. With draft calls down to less than 12,000 a month, the average teenager preferred to take his chances with SS rather than commit himself to the reserve, even for six months of active duty.[95]

The consistent failure of recruitment for active duty and reserve duty, as well as traditional political reflexes, conditioned the administration's attitude toward the draft during the 1956 presidential election. Adlai Stevenson, once again the Democratic nominee, recognized the need to offer bold proposals in trying to unseat the popular Eisenhower. Stevenson made two headline-grabbing recommendations: end nuclear testing, and end the draft. In a speech at Youngstown, Ohio, the Democratic candidate argued that the draft system led to "incredible waste" and that much time and money could be saved by moving toward a volunteer system.[96]

Privately, Eisenhower had reason to agree with Stevenson's assessment, but politics demanded a vigorous rebuttal. Vice-president Richard Nixon immediately branded the idea "irresponsible." In fact, the administration had adapted to new weaponry by reducing the strength of the armed forces by 20 percent, or 700,000 men, since the end of the Korean War. Draft calls had been cut to 136,000 in 1956 from 523,000 in 1953. The new reserve act offered a new means of service. But despite these steps Eisenhower insisted that the draft remained an "essential stimulant," for both the active force and the newly forming reserve forces. "Loose talk" about ending the draft was "hurtful to America's security interests throughout the world." He also reminded his listeners that "we must not be deceived when communist power adopts a new and smiling tactic. There is no change in its fixed determination to dominate the world." The draft remained "indispensible."[97]

In November Eisenhower easily disposed of Stevenson, but he failed to end growing contradictions in manpower policy. The military participation rate of American young men was dropping drastically. About 1,158,000 young men had reached induction age in the year before the Korean War, and by 1957 some 66 percent saw active duty and about 22 percent were declared unfit. This represented a military participation rate (MPR) of almost 90 percent for the eligible cohort. But because of Eisenhower's success in ending the war and his cutback in defense spending the MPR had dropped drastically by 1957. A special study in February 1957 found that young men reaching draft age had a good chance of never serving. Of the 1.2 million who reached draft age in one year, only 139,000 faced a draft call.[98]

These long odds were about to become even longer. The DOD pushed through Congress a bill permitting induction stations to raise the mental achievement standards required for active duty. Such a step was justified, explained the Pentagon, because of the surplus of manpower. The six-month reserve program was also modified so that volunteers had their total service obligation reduced to five years, compared to the eight years of draftees. Reserve units began to build up.[99]

After stressing the need for the draft in his campaign, Eisenhower recommended to his cabinet that the army be cut further in authorized strength. At the Pentagon, a special study by Ralph J. Cordiner proposed pay increases and additional benefits. Such actions, read the report, could cut turnover and lead to an all-volunteer force. The president recognized the value of an all-volunteer force, not the least of which was the end of an increasingly redundant draft. By early 1958 the army announced a plan to reform into smaller units to cope with the reality of the nuclear battlefield of the future. The proposal called for a cut in both active duty units and reserve forces.[100]

Although a combination of National Guard resistance and a thrift-minded Congress prevented any action on the Cordiner recommendations, the climate of 1958 seemed ripe for ending the draft. Induction authority was due to expire in 1959. But despite the increased problems of equity caused by reduced calls and new defense priorities, the administration decided to ask for draft renewal. The countervailing pressures at work emerged in staff discussions. Both the DOD and SS called for a simple extension of the current program. The Pentagon preferred an all-volunteer force, but the generals found they could not wean themselves from the draft pacifier. Assistant Secretary of Defense Charles C. Fincucane explained that without the draft, the number of volunteers would drop. The SS, he continued, was the "pillar of our ability to mobilize manpower in an emergency."[101]

After 15 years of operation, however, the pillar had cracks. The draft in 1958 was almost identical in structure and rules with that of 1945, but the technology and strategic thinking of the United States had changed dramatically. A staff study by the OCDM suggested that the administration offer a specialized draft, which would zero in on those men with needed skills. Here was a proposal to become truly selective and give up the "universal" service idea. Such a move toward selectivity, however, would compound the problems of equity which existed in the current deferment system. J. Roy Price, of the Office of Civilian Defense Mobilization, reminded the administration that "if the draft continues as is, equity problems which can be serious politically as well as philosophically are bound to arise." With low calls and an increasing cohort, the idea of universality of service was becoming more and more a sham. [102]

Any talk of substantial reform worried the Pentagon. If Congress began a serious review of the draft, SS and DOD officials feared the traditional American opposition to coercion might lead to dumping the entire idea of conscription. These stand-patters argued that ending the draft would have a deleterious effect on NATO allies. [103] The pressure of the cold war, the comfort of living with a familiar system and fear of congressional rebellion decided the day. The 1959 draft law, passed with hardly a second glance, merely extended the existing system. Eisenhower admitted to the press that inequities existed in the system but could offer no solution as he left office.

When presidential candidates lined up in 1960 the draft remained an unsolved issue. Eisenhower's policies and the inexorable increase of birth rates during the 1950s caused the draft to fall far short of reaching the objective of universal service. Around the country educators and businessmen both testified to the impact of the threat of the draft rather than the reality of induction. The draft failed to induct many college students, but graduates were liable. Frank E. Young of the Bank of America admitted, "We usually wait until a young man has completed his draft requirement" before hiring. [104] In conscription appearances and reality were growing further apart.

Democratic candidates sought to capitalize on the issue. Hubert Humphrey was dissatisfied with the law; Stuart Symington called for an all-volunteer force; and John Kennedy pushed the idea of youth service in a peace corps. The leading Republican candidate, Richard Nixon, continued to insist that the draft was indispensible. But the public seemed more concerned with television debates and Kennedy's religion than with the draft. [105]

When Eisenhower had first entered office the nation was embroiled in the messy conflict in Korea. Military manpower policy had proved a shambles in mobilization for the fight. The public and elected officials spoke warmly of the age old concept of "citizen-soldier," calling up trained civilians to fight any war. But during the 1950s, it became clear that it was easier to achieve the citizen role than the soldier role in the old concept. A joint congressional committee report on the 1951 draft act said: "The duty of bearing arms in defense of the Nation is a universal duty. Therefore, we believe that universality, not selectivity, should be the basis of the assignment for military duty." The draft law spoke of a universal obligation, but the system had spent more time on managing civilian deferments, and less on drafting for the armed forces. Active-duty military manpower dropped from 3.5 million to 2.5 million in Eisenhower's two administrations. The number of men in the army, which was the only branch using draftees, dropped from 1.5 million to 860,000. In 1954 some 58 percent of all men entering the army were draftees. In 1961 the percentage was only 22. Even the reserve forces suffered, despite the new law of 1955. With low draft calls, recruitment for reserve duty became difficult. [106]

As John Kennedy assumed office in 1961 the draft was again accepted widely by the public, mainly because few were being drafted. Yet the draft had not provided the initial troops needed for the Korean War. Reservists and World War II veterans had been called up at great political costs. And much rhetoric had been spent on the need for a better military manpower policy for the limited conflicts of the cold war, of the need for a professional, volunteer force. But continuing the draft proved the easy way, and so it was continued. When Lyndon Johnson contemplated reinforcements for Vietnam in 1965 he asked former President Eisenhower's opinion. Eisenhower approved the move, but warned that "sending conscripted troops to Vietnam would cause a major public-relations problem" and suggested using only regulars and volunteers. Unfortunately, because of the manpower decisions of the 1950s, there were too few such professionals, and Johnson used the draft instead, with disastrous results. [107]

7

LBJ and Vietnam

There has been recent public and scholarly interest in the Vietnam War. Memorials have appeared, anniversaries celebrated, institutes opened. A wide range of literature has also appeared. Most of the studies agree that the war created great changes in America and Vietnam, toppled leaders, and revolutionized society.

One of the greatest changes in America was the replacement of the military draft with an All-Volunteer Force (AVF). This shift meant the dismantling of the draft system which had functioned since 1940. Although President Nixon made the shift away from the draft, the system had begun dying during the Johnson presidency.[1]

At first some officials saw the war in Vietnam as the salvation of the draft system. Since Korean demobilization, the draft had remained in place but fewer and fewer men had entered the service through the system and deferments had grown. The problems of surplus disappeared with the war in Vietnam. Once again Selective Service began operating at full speed.[2]

The use of the draft for the Vietnam War seemed to offer several political advantages. On an immediate level, the use of young draftees and draft-induced volunteers avoided the political repercussions which would follow induction of older men in reserve units. Using the draft also posed less danger to the economy. Personnel officers in corporations breathed easier when they learned that key personnel in reserve and National Guard units were not being called. Younger draftees had a high unemployment rate anyway, which could be reduced by military duty. Some military leaders, including Secretary of Defense Robert McNamara, preferred using the regular forces, but there were not enough regulars. The draft allowed Johnson to fight a limited ground war in a distant corner of the world for over six years, but it also contained a political risk. Former President Eisenhower warned that "sending conscripted troops to Vietnam would cause a major public-relations problem."[3]

There was great concern in the 1960s over equity of service and duty of citizenship. The immutable tension of conscription and freedom once again stood out boldly. The equity issue revolved around the reality that the draft was not universal. Even within the male cohort of 18 to 26, specified as liable in the law, many men escaped induction and some escaped all service. The mobilization of World War II had seen some escape service, but in the war of Vietnam, with limited mobilization, the fact that some served and some did not created more political heat.[4] Of course the larger draft calls for the Vietnam War insured less inequity than the small calls of the post-Korea 1950s.[5] But inequity, like most social problems, was less a question of statistics than of perception. No troops died during the post-Korea 1950s.

The criticism of the system's equity came, not from the lower middle class which provided most of the draftees, or the lower classes, but from the upper classes which provided few draftees. After a decade of lobbying specifically for elite protection, some elite figures must have had a guilty conscience. John C. Esty, Jr., headmaster of the Taft School, spoke for the upper class when he testified before Congress that the "present practice makes a mockery of the original intent that every able-bodied man serve his country." Yet the original intent of military planners had been that the draft be modern, scientific, and selective, rather than universal.[6]

The inherent tension between the management goal of selectivity and the political goal of equality of sacrifice had always been present in the draft idea. The heat rather than the terms of debate did change during Vietnam. On one side were those who might be called "pure egalitarianists," who felt that every man in the liable age cohort should have an equal risk of military service. On the other side were those who might be called the "pure merit" types, who argued that a person's value to society, in science, education, or industry should reduce the individual's risk of military service. The notes of the "pure egalitarianist" theme fit the chords of the national political symphony, but the "pure merit" position appealed to those singing of the growing sophistication of war and society.[7]

Similarly, the draft protest which emerged in the 1960s was consistent with a long tradition. In the United States the first national draft during the Civil War provoked a murderous riot and 38 officers of the Provost Marshall General, in charge of conscription, were assassinated and 60 others wounded.[8] Antimilitarism, anticentral government, and pro-individualism, all served to insure resistance to a draft. And not only Americans resisted the draft. Wherever the institution appeared it provoked resistance and evasion, in England, France, and Prussia.[9]

But in America since 1940 draft protest had been only a minor irritant to the government. When induction authority under the draft law came up for renewal in the 1950s and in 1963 it breezed through Congress.[10] The major problem facing SS in 1961 was not draft criticism but an overabundance of eligible young men. President John Kennedy sought to relieve the problem by reversing Eisenhower's order and again insisting that all married men be placed at the bottom of the call sequence. Also, college students were automatically deferred if they passed their courses. The public repeatedly voiced support of a draft system which served mainly to encourage men to volunteer. Average draft inductions from 1955 to 1964 were only 10,000 a month. To better tap the potential of the agency, the Democratic administrations of the 1960s even began using it to help promote social rehabilitation, including the war on poverty.

Things soon changed. In 1964 fires lit in Southeast Asia soon became a conflagration that engulfed the nation, destroyed the political career of President Johnson, and ended conscription. But when Johnson took office after the assassination of Kennedy in November 1963, the military manpower situation looked promising. The active-duty military strength of the nation totaled 2,670,000. Added to this was a reserve force of around 2.7 million and a National Guard strength of over 370,000. These figures were deceptive, however, because they did not represent forces easily committed without significant political shock waves. American commitments stretched from Berlin to Japan. An expansion of military commitment in any particular area meant the administration had to make some difficult choices. To mobilize the reserve or to declare a national emergency might derail Johnson's beloved Great Society program of domestic reforms. But in 1965 when Johnson sent troops to Vietnam he was thankful for the existence of a tried and true instrument for providing cheaply vast numbers of young men, the SS System.[11]

With the Universal Military Training and Service Act of 1951 all men had to register for the draft at the age of 18 and remained liable for training and service from 18½ to 26. After registration a man was examined and classified in order of his potential for induction. The tour of a draftee's active service was set at 24 months. Should a potential draftee receive one of the many deferments available, his liability for induction was extended to age 35. Although SS was a permanent government agency, the president had to obtain new induction authority every four years. Congress had routinely granted such authority in 1955, 1959, and 1963.[12] Congress and the public accepted the draft as a permanent part of the national landscape. Over 61 percent of senior and junior high school students thought the draft system was fair in 1965.[13]

One of the main reasons for the acceptance of the draft in the pre-Vietnam era was the simple fact that few young men were being drafted. From 1955 to 1964 draft inductions averaged about 100,000 a year, but the population in age group 15 to 24 had grown from 21,641,000 to 29,519,000 in the same period. While the draft took fewer men, many more young men became eligible.[14]

This increase of draft-eligible men arose because the United States had experienced a baby boom after World War II and there had not been mass casualties in the Korean War. President Eisenhower had kept peace, and his new defense tactics had cut manpower levels in the armed forces. Deferments had flowed from SS in ever-increasing numbers. The prime draft-age group of 19 to 25 had totaled 8 million men in 1958, but it had increased to 12 million by 1964. By 1974 it was 13 million.[15]

To Johnson, the SS pool must have appeared a cornucopia. In 1964 some 16,835,000 young men were in the eligible age cohort of 18½ to 26, and some 2,000,000 were already classified 1-A, ready for induction. Another 12,800,000 were in various deferment or ineligible categories: 2.3 million were veterans; 2.8 million were already in uniform; 4.9 million held educational, job, or other deferments; and 4.1 million were physically or mentally disqualified for duty. In November 1964 there were 1,276,273 newly registered 18 year olds and all but 200,000 had been classified. Some 190,000 held high school deferments, 294,000 had college deferments, 11,000 had job deferments, 15,000 had dependency deferments, 62,000 were already in the service or reserve, and another 97,000 were either fit only for emergency duty or not fit for any duty. Nearly 500,000 of the 18-year-old registrants were classified as students.[16]

Even considering all deferments, on paper there were plenty of young men available for an expansion of American armed forces. However, the information on individual status was not always current. Also, a serious distortion of the 1-A pool came from the divided responsibility of deciding if a man were physically or mentally qualified for service. In the initial classification step the local boards of the Selective Service could and did disqualify those men with obvious defects. But only the armed forces Induction Station could make a final decision. Past experience showed that, of those men local boards considered 1-A, about 50 percent failed to meet the armed forces standards. A sudden expansion of the armed forces might require that SS revise its deferment procedure and draft men who had enjoyed special protection for several years.

For those leaders trained in the traditions of the cold war—in "defending the rights of free people everywhere" (Truman), "bear[ing] the torch of freedom" (Kennedy), "America keeps its commitments" (Johnson)—the threat in Vietnam provoked a conditioned response. From Truman in 1950, Eisenhower in 1956, to Kennedy in 1961, the United States had committed itself to the creation of a non-Communist South Vietnam. Since assuming office in November 1963, Johnson had learned that the military strategy for South Vietnam was faltering. In November 1963 Ngo Dinh Diem, the former American hope for leadership of this new nation, was killed in a coup by his generals. And the military men who assumed control over the government in South Vietnam proved inept.

In 1964, when Johnson ran as a peace candidate and defeated Barry Goldwater, there were less than 24,000 U.S. troops in Vietnam. By 1965 their commander, General William Westmoreland, was insisting that the United States itself would have to assume a fighting role to save Saigon. In July 1965 Johnson approved sending 50,000 ground troops and implicitly agreed to increasing the total to whatever was needed. The Joint Chiefs recommended a mobilization of reserve units and a call-up of National Guard units, but the president rejected such a step. He remembered the political turmoil which had followed a reserve call-up during the Korean War and wanted to avoid derailing his domestic programs. Instead, he decided to provide the troops through the reliable draft system.[17]

From 1965 to 1968 the armed forces grew rapidly to fight an undeclared war. In 1965 there were 2,655,000 men in uniform. By mid-1968 the total had climbed to 3.5 million. The acceleration had begun when Johnson announced a doubling of draft calls in July 1965. From calling about 16,000 draftees each month, SS began calling 40,000. During fiscal year (FY) 1965 the number of draftees forwarded to examination stations tripled. Boards sent up 399,000 draftees in FY 1966 and 343,000 were inducted. About 300,000 men were drafted annually for the next three years, but at the same time some 2 million new men reached age 18. The SS had a pool of 1,965,000 in 1-A classifications.[18]

This expansion, so impressive at first glance, was rather insignificant when compared to past work by SS. Inductions from mid-1965 to mid-1966 averaged only 28,623 a month. During World War II the military had inducted 200,000 a month; during Korea 80,000. During the Korean War the active force grew from 1.46 to 3.64 million in two years. From 1965 to 1967 it expanded only from 2.65 to 3.38 million. Even as draft calls rose so did deferments. Occupational deferments rose to over 480,000 by 1968. The numbers were historically unimpressive, but the historical context was impressively different.[19]

Draftees accounted for only 40 percent of total accessions of enlisted personnel, and during the entire Vietnam War only 25 percent of the 6 million men who served were draftees. In 1967 some 47 to 49 percent of the army and 16 percent of the total armed forces in Vietnam were draftees. At the high point in the Korean War some 52 percent of the entire enlisted ranks were draftees. In World War II some 15 million served, and 66 percent were draftees. As a percentage of the entire armed forces, the draftee share had declined by the Vietnam War, but this group's combat contribution increased. In 1965, 28 percent of army battle deaths were draftees; in 1966 the total rose to 34 percent, and in 1967 to 57 percent. In 1969 draftees accounted for only 16 percent of the entire armed forces but made up 88 percent of the infantry in Vietnam and accounted for between 50 and 70 percent of combat deaths. Draftees went into the infantry and volunteers into support elements.[20]

This effort by draftees unfolded gradually as Johnson expanded the war. As the draft quotas climbed it was easier to push people into deferrable categories or into volunteering. A 1964 survey indicated that 40 percent of all volunteers were draft motivated, and this figure went up to over 50 percent after 1965. Armed forces recruiters began to have a field day, and membership in the reserves also soared, with about 70 percent of the new reservists being draft motivated. ROTC membership on college campuses suffered a decline during 1960 to 1970, but the expansion of the draft cut the decline by one-third. From 1965 to 1970 the probability of a college graduate's being drafted increased from 3 in 10 to 6 in 10.[21]

Military recruiters filled quotas, but they were playing in a zero-sum game. As reserve and National Guard enlistments grew, the draft pool became smaller. SS now had to revise the liberal deferment policies in place for ten years, but as the draft expanded, interest groups demanded more deferments. The business community worried about losing young technical workers, colleges worried about declining enrollments, and married men worried about their "Kennedy deferments." SS had some 19 million men registered, but the pool of immediately available men was much smaller. Some 2 million students were deferred, another 2.5 million were physically disqualified, and 2.4 million more were below the standards for general service. The law prohibited group deferments, but students, teachers, and married men had enjoyed protection. To meet the new calls arriving from the DOD, the situation had to change.[22]

President Johnson expanded the American commitment in Vietnam by small increments, with a subtlety at first undisturbing to critics. In late August 1965 he revoked the Kennedy order putting married men at the bottom of the ladder, but not before hundreds of men had rushed to marry to beat the draft. The draft quota for December 1965 rose to 40,200. SS easily met the increase and had no plans to draft even flunking college students. The 2 million students and 4 million fathers in the pool seemed safe.[23]

But in early 1966 calls continued to run high. The system began an inventory of those men over 26 who had earlier taken a deferment and of the 1-Y types who scored marginally below armed forces standards on the qualification test. This latter group held some 2.4 million men. The SS wanted to dip into this category before curtailing the student deferments, but the DOD refused to accept marginal types and had little interest in men over 26. By September 1966 local boards once again began tightening up all deferments.[24]

Slowly the draft system shifted from its half-speed posture to launch what some expected to be another success story. But in the 1960s expansion confronted an array of regulations and deferments which were all designed to keep men out of the service rather than bring them in. As the supply of young, single graduates ran out, local boards moved relentlessly toward childless married men, then to college dropouts, and finally to 1-Y types. By the summer of 1966 the draft used the following sequence, in descending order, to call men: delinquents, oldest first; volunteers up to age 26; single and married since 26 August 1965, 19 to 26 with oldest called first; men over 26, youngest first; finally men 18.5 to 19 with the oldest called first.[25]

The first problem SS encountered involved the size of the call, which might vary by several thousand, and the 60-day lead time for delivery.

Calls had to be proportioned to states and then to local boards. Michigan might induct 17,210 in FY 1966, while Texas, with many more people, might induct only 15,156. Each state had a different size pool of eligibles, because of different age, occupation, and educational populations and rejection rates. The boards also had to deal with registrants who showed up newly married, newly enrolled in school, or newly employed in a key job.

Applying all the variables was very much a human endeavor, and the flexibility of local boards, which had long been the pride of the system, now became a source of criticism. In a survey conducted in mid-1966 the local board members made clear their biases. As in World War II and Korea, members were biased toward protecting the home. Fathers got preference for deferments over all other types. Officials were also biased toward education. Of the members surveyed, 71 percent said they preferred to take 1-Y men first to meet the larger calls. Only 14.7 percent preferred to reclassify students. Like most Americans, local board members believed they were acting fairly, but fairness was redefined as the war in Vietnam expanded and protest arose.[26]

Protest had begun with the modern American draft system in 1917. The number of men who failed to register for the World War I draft has been estimated at anywhere from 350,000 to over 2 million, compared to some 24 million who did register. Rather than resist, men tried simply to evade the draft and the Provost Marshall General reported in 1919 that 337,440 were officially charged with "desertion" from the draft. By the end of the war about half of this total had been prosecuted.[27]

Compliance with the draft law improved during the next two American wars. In World War II, from 1940 to June 1947, some 11,879 violators of the SS act were sent to prison, out of an estimated total of over 300,000 violations reported to the FBI. The vast majority of the violations proved to be merely technical. When the FBI checked in large cities it found that few persons of draft age had failed to register. Some 6,812 persons were apprehended, but all were registered without prosecution. After the war an Amnesty Review Board reported that half of all the cases considered involved men with prior records of more serious offenses. The largest group of men imprisoned for resisting the draft in World War II were members of the Jehovah's Witness organization, but their rationale had little to do with disagreement on foreign policy.[28]

Using convictions cited by the Justice Department as a basis, the ratio

Draft protest in the 1960s. Courtesy, Library of Congress.

of convictions during World War II was one for every 2,220 inducted. During the Korean War the figure was only 1 to 10,399 inducted. From June 1948 through March 1961 a total of 250,960 delinquent registrations was reported by local boards. Again, most of these were merely technical. Only about 2,500 convictions resulted under the law. The ratio of convicted to registrants was 1 for each 9,657, out of a total of 24,143,938 registered with SS by the end of March 1961.

Draft protest from 1940 to 1960 was no more than a minor nuisance in the execution of the SS mission. No one in SS or in the White House anticipated that in the next few years resistance to the draft would become a force for reform, contribute to the retirement of a president, lead to a revision of military strategy, and cause the replacement of the draft itself with an all-volunteer military force.[29]

Draft protest in the 1960s took a different form than earlier manifestations and began well before Johnson expanded the American commitment to Vietnam. Expressions of the protest ranged from turning in a

Burning draft cards in the 1960s. Courtesy, Library of Congress.

draft card to destroying government property. In May 1964 in New York 12 men burned their draft cards at a rally by the Student Peace Union. Four others at Berkeley, California, did the same to protest American intervention in the Dominican Republic. Several such rallies were held in the summer of 1965, but not until July 1966 did any protest organization emerge. In the fall of 1967 demonstrations involving card burning took place in several major cities and 1,000 cards were returned to the Justice Department. During the protest at the Pentagon on 21 October 1967 1,000 cards were supposedly turned in but many were merely blank papers. By the end of 1967, SS reported that 618 persons in 46 states had turned in or destroyed their draft cards, but only half were in 1-A. In early 1968 twenty briefcases allegedly filled with draft cards arrived at the Justice Department. With some 35 million Americans registered for the draft, such actions were merely a nuisance.[30]

Harassment of draft officials and picketing of draft offices had little effect on operations at first. In March 1966 when General Hershey spoke at Columbia University, a garden of radicalism, one hundred pickets appeared, but the speech went off with little disturbance. By 21 March 1967, however, Hershey found it more difficult to give speeches on campuses. At Howard University in Washington he was driven off the stage by protesters waving placards bearing slogans such as "Draft beer, not students", and "America Is the Black Man's Battleground." In 1968 FBI agents provided protection when Hershey spoke. After a protester set fire to a Hershey chocolate bar at the University of Tennessee and students at the University of Wisconsin hit his car with a barrage of eggs, he canceled a number of appearances.[31]

Such harassment was tiresome, but other actions were more serious. In the fall of 1965, at the University of Michigan, protesters began using sit-ins at draft boards to disrupt proceedings. And by 1966 occupations of buildings had been supplemented with destruction of draft records. On 27 October 1967 Rev. Philip Berrigan, a Catholic priest, and others entered a Baltimore draft board and doused records with blood from Polish ducks. In 1968 protesters used homemade incendiary devices to burn records in several major cities. Induction stations in California were put under siege and by 1968 disruptions were occurring across the nation. Marine recruiting officers on campus found themselves upstaged by students conducting guerrilla theater. Imitation marines using rubber blades, water pistols, and ketchup bottles "bayoneted and shot" students dressed as peasants. Protest had escalated in response to American involvement in Vietnam.[32]

Defenders of American foreign policy lumped all the protesters together as "bums." But the movement was quite diverse in origins, in motives, and in actions. For some protest was a means to a larger end; for others it was an end in itself. Few protesters came from the lower class blue-collar population, the weekly wage earner group. Most of the actors in the drama were college students from comfortable upper-middle-class homes. Yet many different kinds of men come from such homes. Social classification fails to explain what brought them together under the antidraft banner.[33]

The inspiration for some was classical pacifism, an old and honored tradition in America, even outside of the traditional peace churches. In the 1950s the Committee for a Sane Nuclear Policy and the Student Peace Union were organized on college campuses. Nuclear testing and fallout of stromium 90 from the atmosphere had fed renewed interest in antiwar work. By the early 1960s the War Resisters League and the Central Committee for Conscientious Objectors were once again active.

A peace lobby of some 7,000 students marched in Washington in early 1962.[34]

The civil rights movement inspired others. In the 1950s Martin Luther King launched his crusade for equal rights for black Americans. This movement sensitized and mobilized many young college students to injustice. By the end of 1965 the black-led Student Nonviolence Coordinating Committee expressed unity with draft resisters. To protesters the war in Vietnam seemed a misallocation of resources and a killing ground for blacks.[35]

Another source of draft protest was the counterculture movement on college campuses in the 1960s which was modeled upon Socialist, antiwar, and civil rights groups, but offered a much wider perspective for protest. Members of the movement believed a revolution was needed to counter the burgeoning technological bureaucracy which threatened to stifle all creative humanity. They thought the impersonal treatment of students in large universities, many with defense contracts, was only part of the problem. Critics pointed to the exploitation of the Third World by the industrial and imperialistic powers of the globe, led by the United States. Drawing upon the writings of Mao Tse Tung and Franz Fanon, these radicals denounced the cold war as an excuse to rape and pillage in the underdeveloped areas of the world. Cultural radicals expressed a growing sense of individual moral worth, something on the order of a secular revival. As formal churches became less relevant, personal morality took on greater significance. This new moral sensitivity generated a strong reaction to conscription to fight in Southeast Asia, an area long subjected to Western imperialism.[36]

The diversity of the ideology emerged in individual testimony. For some, draft protest was merely a "surrogate" for opposition to social problems and foreign policy. Dagmar Wilson of the Women Strike for Peace explained to congressmen that her group was not merely concerned with the unfairness of the SS but with the "impact of the draft on the fabric of society." When student radicals issued the statement of the May Second Movement in 1964 they proclaimed "We, the students of the United States, refuse to be drafted." The argument was not against the draft but the authority of the government to direct young lives in defense of a foreign policy of containment which seemed outmoded if not pernicious. When draft resisters were interviewed, some 88 percent justified their action as opposition to the war in Vietnam. Only a little over half were protesting the nature of the draft system itself. This was mainly because very few resisters understood the nature of the draft system. First, a resister identified with an ideology which questioned imperialism, the cold war, social justice at home, the campaign in Vietnam. Only incidentally did he focus on the operation of the draft. To them the draft system was only a symptom of deeper problems.[37]

Attacking the draft system proved an attractive means of recruiting large numbers of young Americans to an ideological cause which few understood or adopted fully. Polls showed that college students exhibited a high degree of patriotism and support of government. But these students had been educated to mass demonstration by the Civil Rights movement. By focusing upon the draft as a threat to continued progress in their careers and upon the forced labor aspect of conscription, radical groups such as the Students for a Democratic Society (SDS) played an appealing anthem. The SDS saw draft resistance "as a handle with which to organize and educate other students about the nature of capitalism and imperialism."[38] One resistance leaflet explained that if large numbers of men would reject government authority, the administration would be forced to change its policy. Arresting huge numbers of middle-class Americans could cause enough political damage to reverse the foreign policy of the Johnson administration.[39]

But draft protest alone remained too diffuse for true revolutionary potential. When a draft conference was held at Antioch College in November 1966 a wide variety of options emerged. Some argued that destroying the draft would force the president and Congress to revise American foreign policy. But others replied that an all-professional military would make easier foreign adventures. Still others merely wanted more recognition of individual conscience in draft classifications. Kingman Brewster told graduates at Michigan State University that an all-volunteer military would end campus demonstrations. In the 1960s students were protesting in other nations that had no draft. The uprising seemed an assault against existing authority. But a study of the American resistance movement found that up to 75 percent of new members rejected larger radical social and political ideology.[40]

Of course self-preservation was an obvious motive for draft resistance, but inadequate to explain the protest. Interviews with resisters found that protest provided a means by which individuals created "fateful experience," and enhanced their moral worth. Only a minority of draft resisters in the New England movement were even in class 1-A and in danger of induction; one-tenth of the Boston area resisters were divinity students who had exemptions. A lawyer who specialized in defending draft resisters wrote, "I have never yet found one that did not have, at the very nub of his feelings, his opposition to the war." It was "the" war in Vietnam, and not all wars which drew opposition. When Dr. Benjamin Spock, overage for the draft, was indicted for counseling against the draft he proclaimed that he was "not a pacifist," but opposed intervention in Vietnam. Repeatedly, resisters drew upon the historical analogy of the Nuremburg trials, with the lesson being that an individual could not violate his conscience about immoral action even at the behest of his government.[41]

Because a majority of draft protesters were motivated not by a coherent and unified ideology, but by moral and religious scruples rooted in individual feelings, the movement became attenuated into gestures of individual witness or into tactics to avoid service rather than laying waste a corrupt SS. The vast majority of draft opponents were satisfied with avoidance of service, which fell far short of radical hopes. And avoiding the draft proved surprisingly easy in the 1960s.

The easiest way to avoid the draft and to satisfy demands of individual conscience was to apply for conscientious objector (CO) status as provided in the law.[42] Pacifists had won recognition in the statute as early as 1940, and during the 1960s this means of avoiding service became increasingly popular. Local boards complained that applications for CO status became routine because of counseling services offered by churches and others. In 1965 the Supreme Court in *U.S. v. Seeger* broadened the definition of eligibility for such status to include a belief that "occupies a place in the life of its possessor parallel to that filled by the orthodox belief in God." From 1964 to 1971 the number of civilian COs grew from 17,900 to 61,000.[43]

The problem in obtaining CO status was that one had to claim opposition to all wars, not just to Vietnam. The notion of selective conscientious objection was upheld by all major religious bodies as consistent with the notion of a functioning conscience. But the law prohibited it as a political, rather than a religious, decision, and the courts upheld this distinction despite all challenges.[44]

For those not willing to claim CO status, a myriad of other methods existed for avoiding the draft.[45] One was migration to Canada. This was a last recourse and one available only to men with some means and strong motives. Estimates vary on the total number of men who took this step, but most studies place the figures at between 60,000 and 100,000.[46]

The easiest means of avoiding the draft was simply to stay in school and make passing grades. Undergraduate deferments remained in place until 1970. Calls by Students for a Democratic Society (SDS) to boycott the SSCQT, used to guide local boards on deferments, fell on deaf ears. An ex-student, when asked why he and his classmates clung to this protection while other boys were called, explained that the privileged deserved their privilege.[47]

Another convenient escape route was marriage and children. During the Vietnam era one study found that one of every eight married men had taken the leap earlier than planned because of fears of the draft. In one week over 40 men in Georgia got married after being ordered for induction. After August 1965 marriage alone was no escape, but having a child provided one throughout the war. For those not ready to take this step one could always improvise to obtain a physical rejection. The armed forces' physical and mental standards were not lowered during the Vietnam War, as they had been during World War II, but nevertheless they were still fairly modest. Alleged tactics used to beat the exams ranged from ingesting bizarre substances to adopting eccentric behavior. But examining physicians retested when lab results seemed inconsistent with physical exams. As the war became more unpopular in the late 1960s, physicians became more sympathetic to evaders. But this dodge did not generate a disproportionate number of rejectees. In the second half of 1968 about 45 percent of all men sent for preinduction physicals were rejected, a figure consistent with figures since World War II. The most common cause for rejection was being overweight, a condition easily proven.[48]

Perhaps the most innocuous tactic of avoiding service was simply to use the system's own elaborate appeal apparatus. With the right legal advice, it was possible to delay a final decision for some time, much like a white-collar criminal in the court system. Once having exhausted appeals within the draft system, one could then use the courts. The men using this tactic assumed that, as the months dragged by, the war might end or they might marry and have children, or they might even become too old to serve. Appeals increased during Korea and Vietnam over World War II. At the end of the Korean War there were 47 appeals per 1,000 compared to 3 per 1,000 at the end of World War II. By mid-1969 there were 98 appeals per 1,000 1-A registrants, or twice the rate during the Korean War. The rate of approval of appeals also increased from 65 percent during World War II to about 80 percent during the Korean War. Although no figures are available for the Vietnam War, the trend seems clear: the more civil dissatisfaction with the war, the more approval of appeals.[49]

Given the ease of avoidance and the mixed motives of the protesters, the system survived the storm. SS continued to meet all calls made by the armed forces until the early 1970s. The protest movement had little impact on the lower classes or the middle class, groups that furnished most of the draftees. The mass of college students were also untouched. The United States continued to fight the war in Vietnam until 1975. While protest was a short-run failure in ending the system, it did have some significant results.

Perhaps most significant, the protest succeeded in convincing elite opinion makers in the United States, especially in Congress and in academe, that the draft operated unfairly and needed major revision. The president reacted to the pressure by instituting a reform attempt and also by trying to use the draft in novel and illegal ways. Much like the U.S. Army in Vietnam, the Selective Service System performed its mission, but lost the war to survive because of political considerations.

Ironically, the draft system was used by both defenders of the Vietnam War and its opponents as a means to an end. Defenders of the draft used it to get troops and to threaten dissenters. Opponents used it as a target to unite radical groups. When draft calls expanded, the base of the antiwar movement also expanded. The aims of antiwar and antiimperialism protesters were too radical for the middle class because they threatened part of the patriotic ethos. Early protest, such as card burning and sit-ins in late 1965 provoked mainly negative reactions. But, by attacking the draft, radicals could recruit threatened students, and by pointing to weaknesses in the draft procedure they could recruit political leaders. Protest was made more legitimate. If the draft was unfair and the draft was needed for the war, then something must be wrong with the war. As the war in Vietnam became more of a quagmire, protest against the draft became more acceptable to larger segments of the public.[50] In the uproar of the protest President Johnson at first assumed that reforming the draft would cure the protest. He mistook an effect for a cause.

Johnson had the reputation of being a master of the political arena, but in his attempts to deal with draft and racial protest he overreacted. The black uprising in the cities was particularly upsetting, after what Johnson thought was substantial progress on civil rights. He reacted to violence in Watts and Harlem by sending in the FBI to search for a conspiracy.[51] His response to draft protest followed a similar pattern of overkill, as did the reaction of draft officials.

SS had always faced some protest, but during World War II and Korea it had been so small as to breed complacency. Hershey had told his state directors in November 1951 not to overreact to protest because it just wasted energy and gave the delinquent a martyr complex. As the protest of the Vietnam War began in 1965 he sought to retain this composure and blamed the behavior on misguided professors who he believed were influencing a small minority. Local boards, already staffed by middle-class figures who resented the entire youth culture arising around them, were clearly more upset at the protest than those at national headquarters. The state directors of Delaware and Illinois both threatened in late 1965 to revoke deferments for protesters. But evaders rather than protesters caused the most serious problems for the system. By 1968 Hershey had to recruit military reserve lawyers to serve in the system because of the number of appeals. Then he admitted that the campaign to frustrate the draft was well planned and aided by the media. Still, as late as April 1968 he appeared sanguine when addressing state directors. Lawsuits would continue and perhaps increase, "but if we have only one for every ten we get in we will be doing well," he explained.[52]

By the summer of 1968 violent protest again arose. Besides being pelted with eggs and booed off platforms, the operators of the system faced bomb threats. By March 1969 one state had some 5,915 delinquency cases pending, either in the SS appeal system or civil courts. In San Francisco alone over 100 attorneys offered free legal services to men seeking to beat the draft. Local board members suffered harassments at home. Morale dropped. One director suggested that the American Bar Association try to disbar attorneys giving draft evasion counsel or prosecute other counselors for practicing law without a license. Many man-hours were spent on the endless appeals. Some local board members resigned under the pressure. The state directors admitted that "harassment has had quite an impact on the system." Ironically, the new surge of protest was a reaction to Johnson's attempt to use the draft to crush dissent.[53]

The character of the Johnson administration's reaction to protest offended not merely protesters but civil libertarians, congressmen, and others. It also distorted the draft in a manner which contributed to its ultimate collapse. SS had traditionally disassociated itself from any responsibility for enforcing the draft law. Such responsibility had created problems during the Civil War. The Joint Army Navy Selective Service Committee of the 1930s stated emphatically that enforcement of the law was "not in the least a function of the Selective Service Administration." Responsibility rested in the hands of the Department of Justice under the statute passed on 16 September 1940. During World War II national headquarters had informed a local board in Louisiana that catching draft dodgers was "not authorized," and that the system "is not a law enforcement or criminal investigating agency." Of course, such a position did not preclude using the draft to pressure individuals. During the war, as we have seen, the threat of induction was used to coerce striking workers and others into vital jobs. And by the end of the war most officials at national headquarters accepted the idea that the draft might be used to induce desirable behavior. The entire deferment system erected in the early 1950s aimed at channeling scientists and students.[54]

By the 1960s SS had an array of powers to channel men, to induce behavior. Regulations made clear that when a registrant failed to perform any duty required by the law, the local board should declare him a delinquent and notify him. The board could then change his classification, lift his deferment, and accelerate his induction. A delinquent was defined as someone "required to be registered under the . . . law who fails or neglects to perform any duty required of him under the provisions of the Selective Service law." Officials gave delinquents first priority in any draft call.[55]

If declared delinquent, a draftee could appeal his status. The vast majority of such cases involved a breakdown of communication and were resolved easily without reclassification or induction. But by 1965 national headquarters had adopted a new philosophy in defining delinquency. Originally a local board considered only positive actions in evaluating a man's eligibility for deferment. Now "certain negative acts" were to be considered harmful to national interest and to be used to lift deferments and create delinquencies.[56]

A protest at the University of Michigan on 15 October 1965 precipitated this change. On that date a group of faculty members and students participated in a sit-in at the local board in Ann Arbor. The action was part of a nationwide protest, and after several hours the 39 demonstrators were removed by police. Almost immediately Colonel Arthur

Holmes, the Michigan state director, called Hershey in Washington. After discussion, they agreed that removing deferments from any protesters
who had them was the proper response. Hershey told Holmes to call for
the files of every arrested protester who was a draft registrant. After
identifying the men, each of their local boards was informed of the arrest
and given the hint that deferments should be reconsidered. Reclassifications took place, but after appeals only six students remained in 1-A. The
students had also been arrested for trespassing, but even before trial they
had been declared delinquent for interfering with the draft.[57]

When some congressmen objected to the way the protesters were dealt
with, Hershey offered a vigorous defense. He informed Congress that
"any deliberate, illegal obstruction of the administration of the law will
not be tolerated." National headquarters held the view, formerly supported by Congress, that when any man violated the draft law he should
be given a chance to enter the armed forces rather than be prosecuted
and go to jail. Reclassifying delinquents, according to Hershey, was old
procedure. Of course, only the local board could make a reclassification.
As Hershey explained in a radio interview, "some boys went to Vietnam
so the boys in Ann Arbor could stay and protest."[58]

Few in SS anticipated the impact of Hershey's action. If any one incident could be isolated as the starting point for the dismantling of the
draft, the reclassification at Ann Arbor would merit priority. But there
were short-run gains from the policy. Despite an occasional spectacular
foray by the Berrigan brothers, sit-ins at local boards ceased to be a
problem.[59] The draft continued to function, and SS complaints of draft
law violations per 100 inductions from 1966 to 1970 remained fairly
modest. In 1966 only four per 100 were registered. In 1967 and 1968
the figure stood at about 6 per 100, jumping to 10 in 1969 and 12.5 in
1970. But at no time was there a shortage of draftees. In FY 1968, after
several years of protest, the system delivered over 1,000 inductees a day;
a total of 340,000 registrants were inducted into the armed forces. In
1966 a survey of student registrants at the University of Wisconsin
found that 38 percent believed any protest against the war meant a loss
of deferment. The same year the system announced a resurrection of the
SSCQT, the test used to obtain college deferments. Over 765,000 young
men flocked to take the exam. Even the SDS realized the futility of asking
students to boycott what many saw as their salvation.[60]

Students clung to their deferments and local boards continued to deliver men, but the use of the draft to curb protest produced a strong

reaction in the older generation. Several colleges relocated armed force recruiting booths to more remote sites on campus, with a consequent falling off of volunteers. Professors began writing the president and congress over the injustice of Hershey's action. Kingman Brewster, president of Yale at the time, told the graduating class in 1966 that the draft had made a mockery of service to the nation. A group of 101 law professors at nine universities petitioned the president to state clearly that the draft was not to be used against student demonstrators. In World War II Assistant Attorney General Tom Clark had called reclassifying delinquents into 1-A "an administrative penalty," but in February 1966 a new assistant attorney general, Fred M. Vinson, Jr., announced that the draft "should not be used to end dissent."[61] When asked about Vinson's statement, General Hershey replied that "a classification process is administrative, not legal . . . and there's no question about who makes that law." Such insouciance came not from arrogance but from the knowledge that SS had support in the White House, in public opinion, and in congress for its actions against protesters.[62]

A debate soon began in the White House. George Reedy, a presidential aide, acknowledged that the reclassification of protesters had popular support, but he warned that it might cause Johnson long-range problems. Student deferments were granted because of status, not because of good behavior. To remove the deferment when the student did nothing to change his academic status was to impose a punishment which properly belong to the courts. The reclassification at Michigan seemed to be an understandable act of anger by local draft officials. But such action, implying military service was a punishment, jeopardized SS's reputation of fairness. Johnson, who detested the protesters, asked Joe Califano, presidential aide, to consult with Cyrus Vance and Hershey for suggestions on the issue.[63]

The young men serving in Vietnam also offered suggestions on ways to handle antiwar protesters: "Draft the son of a bitch so he can find what it's all about." When Lou Harris surveyed the public on antiwar demonstrators in late 1965 he found that 59 percent said one had a right to demonstrate, but 32 percent denied the right, and 89 percent favored the draft system. All the organized veterans' groups supported the draft throughout the war. Polls also reflected consistent intolerance with antiwar protesters, even among college students. From 1964 to 1970, in some 27 different polls, a majority of college students favored the war and more bombing of the North Vietnamese. In the spring of 1965 a survey of 20,000 high school students found 70 percent strongly agreeing that America's participation in the war in Vietnam was a good idea. In March 1966, when the public was asked if involvement in Vietnam was a mistake, some 71 percent said "no."[64]

The SS could also count on important backing in the halls of Congress. In 1965 congressmen made clear what they thought of the protesters. The Gulf of Tonkin resolution on 7 August 1964 had put Congress behind the president, and in 1965 Congress passed the Rivers bill which provided five years in jail for anyone willfully destroying his draft card. Johnson signed this measure on 31 August. In both the Senate and the House leaders spoke out against the demonstrators. Senator Thomas J. Dodd of Connecticut called protests "tantamount to open insurrection." Similar notes of hyperbole echoed from John Stennis, William Proxmire, Thomas H. Juchel, Mike Mansfield, Frank J. Laushe, Everett Dirkson, and Richard Russell. In the House, Rivers led a large chorus of antiprotesters, joined on occasion by Gerald Ford.[65]

During 1966 the House Armed Services Committee called constantly on Justice Department officials to accelerate the rate of prosecution for draft evasion. At one hearing Representative F. Edward Hebert of Louisiana urged Assistant Attorney General Vinson to "forget the First Amendment," when the latter insisted much of the protest was legitimate exercise of free speech. Hebert wanted the courts to decide on what was legitimate, not the Justice Department. Repeatedly, Congress offered to strengthen the hand of draft and justice officials in the battles against resisters, but neither Hershey nor Ramsey Clark wanted punitive legislation, and both took a more sanguine view of the protest. Hershey felt the protesters were vastly overrated and were just a few "misguided kids." Clark insisted that Senate Bill 2975, which made it a crime to take actions to influence men to evade the draft was redundant. The existing law already provided five years in jail for anyone who "knowingly counsels, aids, or abets" anyone in evading registration or service. Similarly, Hershey felt the existing law gave him ample muscle to control the demonstrators.[66]

The congressional consensus against protesters, however, was always subject to the needs of partisan politics. In the 1964 presidential election campaign Barry Goldwater had called for a study of how to end the draft, an echo of what several Republican senators and representatives had urged early in 1964. The issues of college deferments and uniformity in classification provided grounds for discontent. But for the most part the criticism was a sign of Republican desperation for some weapon to attack the increasingly popular LBJ. The president defused some of the criticism in 1964 by asking the DOD to study the draft.[67]

When nothing emerged from the study, Republicans became convinced, correctly, that the president was trying to sidetrack the issue. Then Hershey's actions at Ann Arbor raised the issue of civil rights. Even Democratic Representative Emanuel Celler of New York, no dove, protested this use of the draft. By March 1966 30 Republican representatives had signed a round robin calling for a study of the draft. Republicans complained about student deferments as well as the class bias of the draft.[68]

Bipartisanship on conscription was collapsing. And, to complicate matters, the induction authority of the draft law, which Johnson needed to wage war in Vietnam, was up for renewal in 1967. Renewals had been almost automatic in four-year cycles since 1951, but with protest in the streets and Republicans calling for an investigation, the president realized he had to offer more than rhetoric if he wished a continuation of the procurement system which made possible his escalation in Southeast Asia.

8

Protest and Reform

Nothing provides more reassurance in life than the familiar. Companies such as McDonald's and Holiday Inn motels thrive on the theme. No matter how alien and new the terrain, whether in Europe, in Arabia, or India, the American tourist breathes a sigh of satisfaction at the sight of the old familiar signs, emblems that guarantee a continuity in the American cultural experience. For a veteran of World War II, who joined his son being processed through the draft in the 1960s, there must have been a similar sense of the familiar. The same system which had called and processed the father in 1940 stood virtually unchanged in the 1960s. A few new forms were used, but in most cases the local draft board continued to operate in the same old buildings. Even more striking, the same old faces sat on the boards and the same secretaries did most of the classification work. Few federal agencies had such a remarkable degree of continuity with policy and personnel. But this continuity had become a problem in a decade of challenge to all old forms and policies.

White House officials had been worried about the unchanging draft system long before the increase in calls for Vietnam. The reduced calls of the 1950s and the demographic surge of eligible young men offered a prospect for moving to an all-volunteer system. As early as 1962 the Kennedy administration considered a review of the system. King Carr, a Kennedy aide, admitted that the system functioned efficiently with few problems, "shaped by the views and personality of General Hershey." But the system needed streamlining. Although officially a civilian agency, many of its key positions were held by military men. There was no coordination, however, between SS and other manpower programs such as those in the Labor Department.[1]

Kennedy planners felt SS might play a role in domestic reform programs. Appointing a Task Force on Manpower Conservation on 30 September 1963, the president explained that the draft was needed in case of war, but he worried about the increase in deferments and the charges that local boards discriminated by income in deferments. Six weeks later Kennedy was assassinated and in Wisconsin a draft board was firebombed. Of the many problems Kennedy bequeathed to Lyndon Johnson, one was the future of the draft.[2]

The armed forces, of course, still wanted the draft. In 1963 the DOD had again testified, as it had for several years, that current strength levels could not be maintained by volunteers. Over 120,000 men were drafted in 1963, and the calls were to be higher in 1964. Johnson announced on 18 April 1964 that a comprehensive study of the draft was under way. He had been prompted to act by Senator Barry Goldwater, the Republican presidential nominee, who wanted to end the draft. The draft issue was politically sensitive because of the class bias of the deferment system. As one labor official wrote to the president, "When Walter Reuther realizes his people are doing the dying while the auto executives sons keep getting school deferments, there could be hell to pay." Johnson reacted by trying to remove the issue from the campaign, and on 3 October 1964 he reminded everyone of the pending study from which he expected "good results."[3]

Johnson easily defeated Goldwater, but after several months, the results of the study remained unpublicized. The DOD had conducted a massive survey which had reached McNamara only in April 1965. His report to the president offered little encouragement in changing over to an all-volunteer force or ending draft criticism. Over 40 percent of all enlisted men and junior officers had entered the service because of fear of the draft. Even more worrisome, there was a direct and positive correlation between draft-induced volunteers and technical and professional skills. Whenever rumors arose about ending the draft, volunteering dropped dramatically. Ironically, Johnson's domestic campaign to provide full employment also conflicted with attempts to increase military volunteers. Some 70 percent of all volunteers had lacked full-time jobs when they enlisted. McNamara concluded that the draft had to continue, but he promised to promote volunteering. By 28 July 1965 Johnson had decided to escalate American involvement in Vietnam by using the draft, and McNamara's report remained unpublished.[4]

The delay of draft reform only served to insure a more heated reaction when SS reclassified protesters at Ann Arbor. The unreformed draft system was at the time pulling in thousands. Republicans began demanding to know the results of the Pentagon study. But whatever the report said, it would cause political problems for the president because the draft was becoming uṅpopular. Eric Goldman, Johnson's adviser from Princeton, urged the creation of a blue ribbon Commission on National Service with President Eisenhower as chair, to study the draft and alternatives.[5]

Johnson liked the idea and planned to mention the commission in a speech to the United Auto Workers (UAW) on 20 May. But two days before, Secretary of Defense McNamara stole attention with a talk in Montreal to the American Society of Newspaper Editors. His speech called into question some basic premises of containment. As an afterthought he mentioned the "inequity" of the draft and suggested a system of two years of national service as a remedy. The speech upset Johnson, and when he spoke by phone to the UAW, he failed to mention the draft commission.[6]

Organized draft protests continued to grow, drawing support from black civil rights leaders. Joseph C. Califano, presidential aide, informed Johnson that McNamara "can no longer hold back the draft study." It was released in early July and concluded that the draft was still needed; an all-volunteer force was too expensive. But the study caused more political problems for the president by pointing out the class and race biases of the deferment system. As a remedy Califano and Cyrus Vance recommended that Johnson appoint a commission as had been suggested by Goldman. On 2 July 1966 the president issued EO 11289, creating a National Advisory Commission on Selective Service (NACSS).[7]

Johnson acted for many reasons. Certainly politics was never far from his mind. General Hershey compared the commission to throwing a hunk of meat off a troika pursued by wolves across the Russian prairies, or a wailing wall for "the people who want to yap." But Johnson conceded that the system needed some repair. In remarks to White House interns on 18 August he said: "In many ways it has become a crazy-quilt, applying to some but not to others." The draft was still needed, but the president wanted it to operate fairly, and he resented accusations of discrimination against the poor because they contradicted his domestic efforts.[8]

Creating the NACSS proved easier than adopting reforms. Califano selected the members and cleared their names with both Hershey and

Congress. Burke Marshall, former head of the civil rights division at the Department of Justice, was named chairman.[9] The mandate of the commission was as broad as its membership: to review draft "fairness," military requirements, classification methods, grounds for deferments and exemptions, the appeal system, and how the draft affected society. Califano told the commission that the issue of student deferments was very important. Johnson, according to Califano, had no "predetermined views" on the system. The commission should consider how long the draft would be needed and whether the regulations established in World War II and the Korean War still worked.[10]

With this mandate the commission could and did cover the entire field of military manpower. Very early on the commission adopted a deliberate tone of reform, rather than merely evaluation. Dr. John K. Folger, one of the many outside experts used by the commission, wrote that the best approach was "to design a modified selection and deferment system," rather than try to prove or disprove the fairness of the existing system.[11]

Coming up with a new system would make moot much existing criticism. At the first meeting of the commission Marshall began promoting the idea of national service to replace the existing draft. National service was distinguished from universal military training, an idea already rejected, by allowing for service in civilian ventures such as the Peace Corps and Vista. Kingman Brewster strongly supported Marshall by insisting that American youth were full of idealism and committed to service, but not military service. He insisted that dislike of the draft was independent of the foreign policy objectives of the administration, i.e., the Vietnam War.[12] By the second or third meeting of the commission Marshall and his staff had successfully shifted the focus from a critique of SS toward a new plan for national service.[13]

The commission did an outstanding job of research, and every topic under discussion was documented by heavy files of press clippings. Special experts on manpower, economics, and other topics prepared elaborate staff studies. Seven college students were commissioned to obtain impressions from college campuses on local boards and the draft, and commission members spent much time discussing the student deferment issue. Of the 540 unsolicited letters received by the commission, the majority recommended that all deferments end.

Particular commission members had particular interests. Reverend John C. Murray, a Jesuit theologian, promoted the idea of selective conscientious objection. Thomas S. Gates was concerned with the public relations of the draft. John A. McCone defended the existing student deferment system. Anna Rosenberg Hoffman defended the existing law as the fairest way of obtaining troops, fearing that any call for major reform would only spark more criticism of the existing system. And George E. Reedy also objected to reform. "Almost every criticism that I have heard," Reedy remarked on 18 December 1966, "of the draft structure is not actually a criticism of the draft structure. It is basically a criticism of the world situation." Nonetheless, the commission went about its task of offering a new system. [14]

The work of the Marshall commission stimulated a national debate. Not since 1940, when SS was first created, had the nation considered the fundamentals of military conscription. The debate revealed that there was "vast public ignorance" over how the system operated. Many of the issues raised in the 1960s echoed criticism raised in 1940. [15]

The debate on the draft can be better understood if divided into structural problems and equity problems. The major structural criticism of the draft was its lack of centralization and uniformity of decision. Some states were drafting more of their male age cohort than others. There were also differences in draft rates between urban and rural areas within the same state. Massachusetts, for example, classified 8.9 percent of the cohort as 4-F. But in Michigan only 1.7 percent were so classified. E. L. Keenan, director of the Resource Readiness Office in the Office of Emergency Planning, defended the existing draft. "We believe," he wrote the commission, "that a fundamental objective in the administration of the draft must be the best development and utilization of the nation's manpower resource." These comments echoed the progressive planners of 1916. [16]

But efficiency and planning no longer had priority. The system was suffering because of demographic changes that had produced a huge cohort of draft eligibles and political changes that had reduced the size of draft calls. In the 1950s the growth of the cohort exceeded military demands, which led to a rise in induction age and a growth of deferments. The surplus combined with a new political climate in the 1960s to place less emphasis upon efficiency and more on the fairness of the draft in individual cases. Equity rather than efficiency took the stage. In this new environment several structural aspects of the draft seemed configured to generate unfairness.

The Marshall commission and others focused on local boards for several reasons. One survey of local board members found 25 percent of those who responded asserting that students' self-support in college was important in granting deferments and another 25 percent saying this fact should be ignored. In one state over half the members rejected any deferments for COs despite the law. The notion that local boards were "little groups of neighbors" of draftees proved false. In Chicago the boundaries of draft boards were unrelated to any ethnic or economic neighborhood, but rather tied to old political boundaries. Student surveys at colleges in several states found that few draftees knew any board members.[17]

Neither did local board membership resemble the social and ethnic character of the draftees in other cities. Local board members were almost entirely white, male veterans over 50, with some college education. One positive sign was that the system was slowly increasing the number of blacks on the boards.[18]

The commission concluded that local boards were an anachronism. Members lacked the knowledge needed to provide accurate technical deferments. The boards were designed "for emergency manpower procurement in a relatively rural society." The commission recommended that the president should nominate membership to regional boards, rather than governors nominate membership to state and local boards. It also recommended that retirement age in the system be reduced and no military personnel serve. These reform proposals were carried by the vote of 11 commission members out of 20.[19]

One equity criticism which was pervasive and emotionally effective concerned class bias. Draft opponents argued that the draft sent the poor, the uneducated, the blacks to fight and die in Vietnam while rich, educated whites remained safely at home. Two scholars wrote "We find substantial discrimination along income-lines, by residence or race," in the granting of deferments. James Fallows, a journalist, complained that very few of his Harvard classmates served in Vietnam. Of course social class had influenced military service since antiquity, but Americans in the 1960s were not interested in historical precedent. Democrats squirmed to learn that the higher the level of education the less likely an assignment to Vietnam. The National Guard and reserves offered protection from Vietnam duty, but blacks made up only 1 percent of this group of over 1 million. Studies of Detroit area causalities related to neighborhood income. According to such studies, men drafted during the Vietnam era "came disproportional[ly] from working-class families."[20]

Yet this criticism was misleading about manpower procurement and false about the operation of the draft. The charge of class bias was a simplistic view of equity and draft induction. To those who were male and between the ages 18.5 and 26, it seemed unfair that the nation decided to fight a war. It was unfair that some were deferred. It was unfair if some could not volunteer for the air force. It was unfair if some passed rather than failed the induction physical. It was unfair if, once inducted, some were assigned to a combat rather than a noncombat unit. Finally, it was unfair if some were assigned to Vietnam rather than the Pentagon. In all of these cases, the draft system played a role in only one—whether or not one received a deferment.[21]

A closer look at the draft scene illustrates the simplicity of accusing the system of working on a social-economic bias. The draft deferred more men for lack of education than it did for education. Correlating military participation rate with education illustrates this tendency. In 1964, for males aged 27 to 34, only 41 percent of those with an eighth-grade or lower education served in the military. High school dropouts served at a 70 percent rate; high school graduates at 74 percent. College dropouts served at a 68 percent rate, and college graduates at a 71 percent rate. By late 1967 the relative proportions were as follows: 60 percent of high school graduates, 50 percent of non–high school graduates, and 40 percent of college graduates saw duty.[22]

Problems also arise in correlating combat casualties and class. Even if the draft had inducted a cohort which precisely resembled the income and education averages of the general population for males 18 to 26, the rate of casualties in Vietnam would have been unaffected. The deciding factor in casualty rates was not draft equity but how a soldier fulfilled his military obligation. In an earlier age almost everyone who went into the armed forces expected to engage in combat or be close to the fighting. But by the twentieth century the trend changed, and by World War II less than 20 percent of the U.S. Army actually participated in combat. Assignment policies of the armed forces determined casualty rates. The high casualties among draftees came not because of income level "but because draftees were used mainly as substitutes for high-attrition roles." Unlike those in World War II, the Korean War draftee served for only two years of active duty. This short-term usability of draftees led to combat assignments. As in all wars, personnel policy put the better educated into roles where they were more useful which meant they were usually also safer. Good management meant that those with little education usually ended up in combat roles.[23]

In fact, the American draft system mitigated the usual class effect of warfare in the modern era. By drafting large numbers of citizens—some 2 million from 1965 to 1973—the draft spread the burden of combat over a broad spectrum of the population. True, the least educated still ended up in combat units, but so did those from other segments of society. Social background did have a relationship to service in the armed forces, but it was not a primary factor. The lowest social class did not serve disproportionately under the draft. Men from lower-middle classes rather than the lowest class did serve disproportionately, but the draft produced a "more, rather than less, equitable distribution of the burden across the stratification system," more equitable than the volunteer system of the 1980s.[24]

Neil Fligstein's study of military participation rate of Americans from 1940 to 1973 concluded that "parental socioeconomic status had no effect on the probability of military conscription." Educational level, however, was related to probability of service, but even this varied over time with the relationship strongest from 1950 up to 1964. The relationship was weakest during World War II, because so many served, and Vietnam, because of a huge male cohort of draftable age. The Vietnam-era draft offered the least class bias since World War II. Bias still existed, mainly due to social inequality and armed forces assignment policy, but the draft worked against social inequalities. "The military manpower procurement policies of the past thirty-five years," Fligstein's study concluded, "have been oriented toward providing the armed forces with men and women in the center of the education distribution." Since educational attainment has been increasing in the population, the draft drew mainly from men of working-class and middle-class backgrounds.[25]

The Marshall commission ignored claims of equity achieved through the draft. For political reasons, Marshall sought to change the draft, despite some testimony favoring the status quo.[26] As mentioned earlier, several members of the commission, including Marshall, favored replacing the military draft with a system of universal national service (UNS) for American youth.[27] But such an idea was unrealistic. The idea of UMT had been rejected by Congress, and by church and education lobbies for several years. The notion that military service should be used to teach values or rehabilitate youth seemed a radical departure from democratic social forms. The American Civil Liberties Union felt both UMT and UNS were unconstitutional. When high school students were asked about compulsory national service, only 51 percent favored the idea. Veteran groups had little sympathy for the system which would force some young men to carry rifles in combat while others through the Peace Corps would be allowed to teach naked natives in the third world.[28]

Both UNS and UMT were nonstarters as reforms, but an all-volunteer force had more appeal. The AVF idea was raised several times during the 1960s. Business leaders and economists urged such a system. T. Roland Berner, president of Curtiss-Wright Corporation insisted, against all historical evidence, that the nation had never "really tapped volunteer possibilities." He felt that with better pay, housing, and other fringe benefits, American youth would respond. Economists such as Milton Friedman and Walter Y. Oi and a Harvard draft study group provided elaborate studies on the economic feasibility of an AVF. Some felt the draft was no cheaper than recruiting volunteers. Conscription merely shifted the cost, in the form of lower wages, from taxpayers to the young men drafted. Oi and others insisted that the cost burden should be shouldered by all, not just draftees. Providing cheap labor to the military, Oi insisted, encouraged them to use it more wastefully than could be justified in a market economy.[29]

Such a market model missed several distinctions in the analysis of conscription. Friedman and other economists saw the draft as a tax, much as protesters saw service as a punishment. By considering military service just another job to be quantified like any economic fact, they ignored an important point of social reality. A democratic polity assumed that citizenship involved a willingness to defend the state. Such a defense was emphatically not just another job. If a tax, it was one which each generation paid for the survival of subsequent generations. Much like public duty to serve on juries, the duty to defend the country could not be left to volunteers without a lowering of the sense of "civitas."[30]

Even if one accepted the tunnel vision of the economists, the AVF was costly. Secretary McNamara estimated that an AVF would cost an additional $20 billion. Harold Wool, a DOD official, explained in May 1967 that the "cost of an All-Volunteer force exceeds our capability at the present time." The estimates by Oi and other economists looked good on paper, but civilian labor market forces could not be applied to the military. With an AVF, national security would be tied to the fluctuations in the civilian labor market. Oi had made his assumptions based on a total military force of only 2.65 million men, but in 1967 the United States had a force of 3.3 million. He had also assumed that an AVF would increase reenlistment rates and lower turnovers, but these assumptions were far from proven.[31]

As much as reformers might like the idea, volunteers were draft-induced, especially during wartime. Of the volunteers serving in the 1960s some 40 percent and higher were draft-induced and 48 percent of the men in ROTC were similarly motivated. Neither did the AVF have much support from the public, according to polls. Critics predicted that an AVF could work only if the nation was satisfied with having a military made up of "low aptitude, ill-educated, and older soldiers." The notion of using only volunteers offended efficiency experts who considered it a throwback to the chaotic pre-1917 system.[32]

The issue of inefficiency also entered the discussion of another reform idea—running the draft through a lottery rather than local board selection. Superficially, the notion of leaving the decision to chance was appealing because it removed the alleged class and race bias of SS. If all men went into the pot at age 19 and the government then selected a few by a lottery there would be a gain in equity. If a "loser" was in school he could drop out for service or enter ROTC. Such a system could be operated nationally with state quotas, and all deferments could be ended. Harold Wool, director of procurement for DOD, supported a lottery for a youngest-first draft.[33] Even George Reedy, perhaps the most astute member of the Marshall commission, liked the idea of a lottery. Although he recognized that establishing the pool for the lottery still required rational selection, he felt that a random selection of draftees would minimize equity and political problems.[34]

Both ideas appealed to President Johnson, but there were arguments against a lottery. Such an approach violated the very basis of SS, as created by modernizers and reformers in 1917. A lottery seemed fair, but would the public countenance drafting a nuclear physicist and ignoring a young man on unemployment benefits because of a chance drawing? Such an approach also presented major technical problems. The draft pool or lottery pot had to be created by human judgment, which meant the deferment of special groups would still exist. When the SS had used the lottery to determine the order of call in World War II, the problem of sequencing subsequent lottery results, as monthly draft calls fluctuated, became difficult. But perhaps the most serious drawback to a lottery was its psychological impact. The entire device resembled a gamble in which the losers, despite morale, were supposed to defend the nation against its enemies. Was this the best a democratic nation could devise for national defense?[35]

Such debate by the Marshall commission reflected and contributed to a national confusion on the draft. Then Congress entered the action. Anxious to prevent any infringement on congressional prerogative, Representative Mendell Rivers of the House Armed Services Committee decided upon another draft study. Mark Clark, a retired army general, headed this group. Simultaneously, across the nation several colleges and organizations sponsored conferences on the draft—the most important perhaps held at the University of Chicago in December 1966—which produced a myriad of reform proposals.[36]

The Marshall report, which had the president's initial backing, emerged only after considerable political rehearsal at the White House. On 3 December 1966 the commission concluded that the draft had to be continued. Marshall briefed Johnson, Hershey, Rivers, and Russell on the specific reform proposals at the White House in February 1967. The congressional or Clark report appeared on 28 February 1967. Johnson now had more recommendations than he wanted. Both Marshall and Clark rejected the AVF, recommended extending the draft in 1967, and called for a youngest-first draft call. Johnson accepted these ideas. On the power and structure of local boards, the reports differed. Marshall wanted centralization of power and uniformity of decision, to be achieved by creating regional offices and using computers. Local boards were to be made more representative and limited to five-year terms. Clark, in contrast, praised the local boards and wanted no change. Johnson decided the issue needed more study. Clark wanted to make CO status harder to obtain; Marshall supported the Seeger decision. Both reports dismissed as impractical both UNS and UMT. As for a lottery, which Marshall recommended but Clark rejected, the president approved the principal with the proviso that some graduate or professional deferments be allowed. Finally, Clark favored keeping undergraduate deferments, while Marshall opposed them. Johnson decided this issue also needed more study.[37]

Since the 1950s SS had taken pains to leave the students alone.[38] The original motive had been concern for manpower efficiency. But by the early 1960s a demographic explosion of young men and the reduction in military manpower needs had added a new justification for such deferments. College students were deferred because draft calls were low and there was no place to put draftees. But by January 1966 the picture was changing. In the Ann Arbor incident, SS had given warning that college students who protested the war might lose their deferments. The ACLU reported that the Delaware director of SS wanted to revoke student deferments from all protesters. Local boards also had little sympathy for protesters who held student deferments.[39]

The conflict in Asia insured even less sympathy in the reevaluation of college deferments. More important was the new surge in military requirements for Vietnam. In late 1965 draft calls were rising, and SS expected them to be 60,000 a month. Replenishing the draft pool demanded a look at the 2-S category. In January 1952 there had been only 210,693 men in 2-S; in May 1965 there were 1,659,696. By 31 December 1965 there were 1,834,240 in 2-S or 10.4 percent of all registrants, and the number was growing. In late June 1965 SS had a draft pool of over 2.2 million men. Within the next 12 months the pool was cut to only 1.4 million. Only California and New York City showed a decline in 2-S totals. By January 1966 only 642,000 in the pool were single and eligible. Some local boards began calling married men.[40]

The increased calls by the Pentagon led inexorably to college students. Theoretically, if calls remained at 30,000 or less per month there would be no need to draft full-time students. But the psychology of the Vietnam buildup made it politically impossible to retain a liberal policy toward students. In tightening up college deferments, SS turned to methods first employed during the Korean War. National education associations and DOD agreed that, if students must be drafted, SS should return to the system of evaluating test scores and class standing used in the 1950s. In March 1966 SS announced that the SSCQT was once again to be offered on three different dates in May and June at 12,000 different locations. This system of classifying students had been acceptable and successful in the placid fifties.[41]

But the sixties were different, especially the students. As the new program began, some 150,000 young men were reaching age 19 each month. Colleges were becoming popular as draft havens, and SS sought to weed out marginal students who were merely taking up classroom space. Local boards rose to the task, fired by the belief that some of the radical protesters were maligning the system and the administration from a privileged haven. When asked in 1966 what weight they placed on various factors in classifying or reclassifying students into 1-A, some 70 percent of local boards said they placed great importance on class standing. Some 51 percent felt the same about test scores, and 77 percent about college cooperation. Only 23.5 percent placed importance on whether the student was self-supporting or not.[42]

Students, faculty, and administrators fought against a draft that hoped to gain their cooperation in sending men to Vietnam. The first area of disagreement involved basic eligibility for 2-S. According to draft regulations, a student had to be full time, pursuing a regular degree, and in a senior college. But the definition of full time varied from school to school. The SS expected the student to make regular progress toward his degree. If he was in a four-year program, the student had to complete 25 percent of his courses each year. Junior college students complained when they were made eligible for a 2-A, but not a 2-S deferment. Graduate students who taught part time were also caught in a bind, not eligible for a teacher's deferment, and not full-time students.[43]

Disagreements also arose because students viewed local board members as fossils, aged autocrats with little sympathy or understanding of the problems of youth.[44] College presidents and faculty members resented being forced to play handmaiden to the state system of conscription. Deans disliked the stress on grade performance imposed by the SS. Eventually several schools decided to end class ranking. A dozen schools, including Brown, Columbia, and Wisconsin, released grades to SS only at the request of the student.[45]

The cooperation of college officials and students had always been tenuous and based on self-interest rather than on any affection for the draft. The higher the education level, the less attraction there was to military service. The average college freshman, long before Vietnam, had a negative attitude toward any military service, and at this time the distaste grew. What is remarkable, and frequently ignored, is that despite existing antipathy the system had forced both the educated and the uneducated to serve in the American armed forces. A national survey involving men aged 27 to 34 in 1964 found that some 70 percent had served in the Korean War. They were high school dropouts, high school graduates, college dropouts, and college graduates. Only at the very extremes of the education population, grammar school dropouts and graduate school students, did the military participation rate fall off significantly.[46]

In 1964 about 17 percent of all inductees for the army had some college education. About 14 percent of enlistees for the army came from the same cohort. In the same year about 40 percent of all 26-year-old college graduates entered the armed forces. The annual number of men with college experience who were "indirectly pressed" into the army tripled from 1965 to 1968. Of the 1 million men who entered the military in fiscal year 1965 to 1966, those with some college education outnumbered those with none. As the draft accelerated, the number of students who volunteered increased and the percentage of the cohort remaining for the draft was reduced, so the educational level of the draftee declined. But the draft had induced a highly educated cross section into the military without any reforms.[47] Perversely, this very success in obtaining an educational cross section, a more representative military, prompted more calls for reform.

By the first half of 1967 reform had the attention of almost every branch of government and a considerable segment of the public. Despite the involvement of many powerful figures, both in government and in the public, little significant change emerged under LBJ. Part of the reason for the failure of reform was that President Johnson had conflicting advice on what to do and had difficulty making up his own mind. He detested the protesters but wanted to avoid making martyrs of them. He did, however, issue an executive order on 30 January 1967 which revised SS regulations on violators of the draft law. Under the new regulation a man violating the draft law could be inducted into the service, or be sent to prison. For those imprisoned, the attorney general had authority to grant a parole to permit the individual to enter the military. The order was directed toward men who had violated the law out of ignorance or because of conscience but preferred to serve in alternate service or the military rather than remain in jail.[48] But even as he strengthened SS power to deal with violators, Johnson struggled with the recommendations offered by Marshall, ideas which called for a major overhaul of the system.

Califano urged the president to give full backing to Marshall's recommendations, but Johnson refused to give him a blank check.[49] Two evening meetings were held at the White House. At the first meeting Califano discussed Marshall's report with Hershey and McNamara. Hershey offered little opposition to revision of student deferments, drafting 19 year olds first or using a lottery system, but he had strong objections to Marshall's proposal to centralize classification and weaken the local boards. The president also objected to the centralization proposal. Johnson explained, "I don't believe we're quite ready to walk out on the local boards." He reminisced that his father had been chairman of a local board in World War I and had taken him to some of the meetings.[50]

At the second meeting a larger group gathered to consider the pending report. Marshall presented his report and its arguments to Hershey, Califano, Representative Rivers, and Senator Russell. George Reedy, a member of the commission, also attended, as did the president. Despite Marshall's eloquence, both Rivers and Russell seemed unswayed by the call for major changes in the system, and Reedy added his objections to ending college deferments. As for centralization, Johnson encouraged Hershey to explain the value of local boards. When the meeting adjourned Hershey left with the conviction that centralization was a dead issue and that several other Marshall reforms faced a rough road in Congress.[51]

When the president finally sent his message on the draft to Congress, on 6 March 1967, he did endorse many of Marshall's ideas. He agreed with ending graduate deferments, except in the health field, and also promised to move toward a system of random selection or lottery with 19 year olds being called first. But he asked congressional debate on ending all student deferments and decided to reexamine SS structure, although he insisted that SS had done fine work and all studies agreed that the draft was still needed. He urged Congress to pass a four-year extension. As a crumb to critics, he promised to improve the counseling and appeal systems in the draft and to make local boards more representative of the community, more like a group of neighbors.[52]

Given Johnson's equivocation, Congress had considerable room in which to debate the draft extension bill of 1967. Senator Russell and Representative Rivers still insisted that the draft should be extended without any major changes. But the political scene was changing as the conflict in Asia continued. The actions of the Marshall commission and hearings in the House Armed Services Committee revealed a breakdown of consensus. Draft protest grew. Several Republican congressmen were demanding some changes. By early 1967 Republicans were primed to use the draft against the president, and even some Democrats wanted drastic action.[53]

On 28 February Senator Edward Kennedy offered a draft bill which implemented most of Marshall's recommendations, including a lottery, more centralization, and a six-year term for the director. Kennedy also opposed deferments for jobs, marriage or dependency, and graduate students. He and Senator Joseph Clark of Pennsylvania offered a resolution in the Senate to obtain these goals, and, as a means of publicizing the demands, Kennedy arranged with Senator Edith Green to chair her subcommittee on education. The draft had an impact on education, so Kennedy began hearings on draft reform. He thus circumvented the Armed Services Committee, still dominated by stand-patters.[54]

The Kennedy hearings provided a forum for dissatisfaction. Hershey was the only defender of the SS System as it was. Harold Howe II, the commissioner of education, testified that the draft had the potential for creating "almost unmanageable problems" for universities. These senti-ments were echoed by university presidents, such as Nathan M. Pusey of Harvard, Fred Harrington of Wisconsin, and Kingman Brewster of Yale. Sargent Shriver of the Office of Economic Opportunity testified that the draft had been unfair since 1942 when it first began deferring students and essential workers. Rejecting the entire notion of efficient manpower management, Shriver called for the draft of women and an end to all deferments. Several young draft resisters gave personal witness to the unfairness of the draft.[55]

Such criticism merited a White House response, but Johnson had little enthusiasm for following in the wake of a Kennedy ship. On 6 March 1967 the president informed Congress that he was appointing a task force to review the NACSS recommendations. The task force consisted of Secretary of Defense McNamara, Director of the Budget Charles L. Schultze, and the Director of SS, Lewis Hershey.[56]

The task force staff, under the executive direction of General Carter B. Magruder, began an extensive survey of the system. The final report went to the president on 9 January 1968. Although initially both McNamara and Schultze had serious reservations about the existing sys-tem and favored Marshall's drastic reforms, the task force report proved a vindication for defenders of the status quo. The committee concluded first that the draft appeared "thoroughly competent to carry out any appropriate policy given to it." Second, criticism of the system was often criticism against the war. Third, local board members exhibited compe-tence and patriotism. Finally, the decentralized structure of the system provided an important political shelter belt. Resentment against the draft fell on local agencies rather than on the national congress or executive branch.[57]

A majority of the congressmen who approached draft extension in May and June 1967 already agreed with the conclusions of the task force. The marching and waving of North Vietnamese flags, the actions of Jane

Fonda and other antiwar celebrities merely enraged House members. In fact, at hearings of the Armed Services Committees, Representative Hebert wanted Fred M. Vinson of the Justice Department to prosecute draft protesters under title 18, section 1288 of the U.S. Code. This section provided that when the nation was at war anyone who "willfully obstructs the recruiting or enlistment in service of the United States . . . shall be fined $10,000 or imprisoned for twenty years."[58]

It should have surprised no one when a majority of the House rejected reform and decided to strengthen the existing system. The bill, passed by the House on 25 May 1967 by a vote of 382 to 9 with 6 abstentions, provided a blanket deferment for all undergraduates until graduation. This action ended all testing and ranking problems. The bill also called for drafting the youngest men first, as Johnson had requested, and made it necessary for Congress to give specific approval before a lottery system could be established. All conscientious objectors selected for induction were required to serve in some capacity, and the definition of a CO was changed to overcome a recent court decision making it easier to obtain such status. The bill even required the Justice Department to report to Congress on the disposition of every draft violation case.[59]

The Senate proved just as conservative as the House. The Armed Services Committee agreed with General Clark that the draft was needed for an indefinite period, that a lottery was a bad idea, and that college deferments should be continued. On the Senate floor a proposal by Senator Mark Hatfield to move gradually to a volunteer system was defeated by a vote of 69 to 9, and Senator Ernest Gruening's amendment to make voluntary service by draftees in Vietnam was defeated 75 to 2. Other moves to reduce service from 24 months to 18, to establish a national classification criteria, to exempt Peace Corps members, and to allow legal representation for registrations were all defeated by similarly large margins. The bill itself passed by a vote of 70 to 2, with only Wayne Morse and Gruening in opposition.[60]

The final draft bill, produced by a conference committee, fell far short of a reform of the system but passed on 20 June 1967 by solid margins. In the House the vote in favor was 397 to 29 with 27 abstentions; in the Senate 72 to 23 with 5 abstentions. Such a lopsided vote gave Johnson little alternative, but the bill limited his discretion. By its terms he required congressional approval before launching a lottery system. And he was authorized to establish national standards, but local boards remained free to ignore such guidelines. Undergraduate deferments were extended to all, but a deferred student was ineligible for a dependency deferment. The only hint of reform in the bill was that women became eligible for local board membership. Board member tenure was limited to 25 years, and 75 was the forced retirement age. Despite this paucity of reform, Califano told the president that Congress had gone a "long ways towards meeting his recommendations."[61]

Califano's remark was misleading. The bill created new problems. The deferment of graduate students became limited to those training for jobs necessary for national health and safety. The National Security Council was responsible for identifying such vocations and informing SS. The NSC, however, had no aptitude for the task, and a controversy soon arose with the graduate school lobby. Also, the bill required that the Justice Department prosecute all cases recommended by SS and inform Congress on all exceptions. Rivers, Hebert, and others had an "intense" conviction that Justice moved too slowly on protesters. About this observation, Johnson noted, "I agree." Although the requirement for advance notice before launching a lottery seemed an infringement on presidential prerogative, Johnson accepted it. Neither was he willing to fight over the continuation of governors selecting appeal agents, although this power had led to all-white boards in several southern states.[62]

Running the war distracted Johnson during the debate over draft reform. But his actions throughout the affair, from the appointment of Marshall's commission to the final signing of the bill on 30 June 1967, revealed a man pushed into considering reform because of draft protest and political attacks from Congress and the press. When confronted with a radical proposal for restructuring the system by Marshall's group, Johnson had retreated into still another study. During congressional debate, he did little to lobby for his major recommendations, and in the end he embraced, with almost indecent enthusiasm, a status quo measure offered by Rivers and Russell. The executive order implementing the bill placed a moratorium on graduate and occupational deferment, pending recommendations by the NSC. Johnson's decision to stay with the tried and true insured that the turmoil over the draft would continue.[63]

The decision to reaffirm the basic structure of the SS System generated even more protest. One cause of anger, which cut close to Johnson's domestic reform program, involved the supposed racial discrimination of the draft. It would hardly do for Johnson, who saw himself as the second Great Emancipator, to perpetuate a conscription complex which dispatched American blacks into the jungles of Vietnam at a rate out of proportion to their percentage of the population. National polls conducted in late 1965 and early 1966 indicated that blacks felt they got fairer treatment in the service than in civilian life. Only 18 percent of blacks felt the United States should pull out of Vietnam. While 25 percent felt draft laws were unfair to blacks, some 43 percent supported the system. But black leaders increasingly identified a conflict between the expansion in Vietnam and the hopes of domestic advance.[64]

By mid-July 1966, the radical leaders of the black movement began attacking the draft. Stokely Carmichael of the Student Non-Violent Coordinating Committee (SNCC), Floyd McKissick of the Congress of Racial Equality (CORE), and others insisted that blacks were being deliberately sent to die in Vietnam. Muhammad Ali, heavy-weight boxing champion, refused induction by claiming ministerial status with the Black Muslims. Cleveland Sellers, an SNCC leader, challenged his induction in the courts, saying he had been selected by a system which excluded blacks from local board participation. By spring 1967 even moderate black leaders of the NAACP and Martin Luther King had joined in the protest. King wanted all blacks to claim CO status because the war was a "blasphemy" against American ideals. In Harlem, Rep. Adam Clayton Powell made political capital of the racist draft. Some 200 students of the Society of Afro-American Students adopted a resolution in New England that said: "We believe that America is the black man's battlefield and that the black man must not join the atrocities of this war."[65]

Various studies of the draft fanned the fires of racial discord. In early 1966 an internal audit by SS reported that as of 1 January 1965 the armed forces totaled 2,659,767 with 9 percent or 239,379 being black. The total black male population in the age cohort 19 to 44 was estimated at 3,195,000, although census takers traditionally undercounted minorities. Of this black age group some 239,379 were serving, or 7.5 percent. In contrast, the white male cohort 19 to 44 was 28,242,000 and 2,420,388 or 8.6 percent were serving. Yet blacks made up some 12.2 percent of all enlisted men in the armed forces during fiscal year 1965. In the army some 16.3 percent of all inductees and 14.1 percent of all enlistees were black. By 1968 blacks made up 13 percent of the army, 10 percent of the air force, 8 percent of the marines, and 5.6 percent of the navy. Blacks constituted 11 percent of all enlisted men in Vietnam and 22.4 percent of all killed in action. By 1968 some 30.2 percent of blacks who qualified were drafted, but only 18.8 percent of qualified whites. In 1967 only 316 blacks served on local draft boards, less than 1 percent of all board members.[66]

At first glance such figures justified the charge that the system acted disproportionately against young blacks. A higher percentage of black eligibles than white eligibles was drafted, and a higher percentage of black soldiers than white served and died in Vietnam. But the totals resulted from many forces independent of the draft system. Civilian whites volunteered at a higher rate than blacks and volunteers usually went into either the navy or the air force. Once in the military, blacks volunteered at a higher rate for combat units because of better pay, faster promotions, and higher status. The black reenlistment rate stood at 45 percent of first timers compared to 17 percent for whites. The assignment policy of the military also insured that a high correlation existed between educational achievement and noncombat duty.[67]

The draft system again proved a simple point of protest. In a congressional review of the system in June 1966 representatives Otis Pike and Charles Wilson and Senator Warren Magnuson focused on the higher percentage of blacks being drafted. The SS explained in vain that the enrollment of a larger percentage of minority groups by the armed forces meant very little. Those drafted into the service represented the residue which had been left after the entire cohort pool had been strained by nets created by social and legal priorities. Recruiters took the cream, and whites attended college and found deferable jobs in a higher percentage than blacks. National Guard enlistments were almost all white, with only 1.15 percent black. As deferments and enlistments were disproportionately white, the SS pool of draftables had to be disproportionately nonwhite. "Even a deliberate conspiracy on the part of local board members to draft as many blacks as possible would have little effect within the limitations of the guidelines established by the System," one study concluded. These guidelines had been created by Congress and reflected American society.[68]

American society ensured that blacks fell out of the draft pool by failing to meet physical and mental standards, a trend from the beginning of conscription.[69] By the 1960s armed-force induction stations and local boards combined to reject about two-thirds of the black male cohort, but only 18.8 percent of white males. In 1964 some 53 percent of all 848,000 inductees examined for service failed. About 234,000 failed to meet mental standards; 188,000 failed medical standards and 13,000 failed both standards.[70]

There were many explanations for the high rejection rate and the discrepancy between races. The black population suffered from the American system of health care on a cash basis. Black educational opportunities were also limited, and there was a positive association between mental scores and educational attainment. A study covering the period from 1953 to July 1958 found that on the AFQT white males had a median of 12.4 years of school completed compared to 11 years for blacks. The expected medians on the AFQT were 55 percentile for whites and 15 percentile for blacks. Yet from 1950 to 1966 21.9 percent of whites were rejected on the basis of the physical exam, and only 14.5 percent of blacks examined were rejected for purely physical reasons. The single most common cause for physical rejection was being overweight, which said something about the relative living standards of the two groups.[71]

By the late sixties, nothing had changed. Only one-third of the blacks examined were found acceptable in 1968, but two-thirds of them were taken into the service. Local boards drafted 30 percent of eligible blacks who qualified, but only 18 percent of qualified whites. This imbalance led to charges in Congress of racism, although of the total black population, which was 12 percent of the entire population, only 10.4 percent were inducted.[72]

Ironically, government action to assist blacks contributed to the later charges of a racist draft. High rejection rates for all races had upset government officials for years. President Kennedy had appointed a Task Force on Manpower Conservation in 1963, and from early 1964 through August 1965 SS was engaged in classifying and identifying rejectees for purposes of rehabilitation. Likely candidates were told to get in touch with the Department of Labor, with the Public Health Service, and with other government agencies. About 92,900 showed up for interviews and assistance.[73]

Even the DOD, which had traditionally resisted their role in rehabilitation, came around under the prodding of President Johnson. In August 1964 Secretary of Defense McNamara announced the Special Training Enlistment Program, which provided for the enlistment of a limited number of volunteers who had been rejected for failing to meet standards. An initial group of 40,000 were to be taken into the service and provided with training to bring them up to standards. The program met disapproval in Congress, however, because several senators questioned SS playing a role so distant from its military manpower mission.[74]

When draft calls for Vietnam increased in 1965 pressure increased to expand the pool of eligibles. Daniel Moynihan in the Department of Labor recommended that black male rejectees be allowed to enter the armed forces for rehabilitation. With the best of intentions, Moynihan and others played into the hands of later critics of the war. Attempts to rehabilitate men, especially black men, could be interpreted as seeking to employ lower-class blacks to fight while deferments continued for upper-class whites. In mid-1966 the DOD announced Project 100,000, which aimed at enrolling 100,000 "new standard men" annually. The plan really amounted to a downward revision of eligibility standards for the armed forces. Under the new guidelines blacks found it easier to enter: while over 50 percent had failed the preexisting standards, now only 30 percent failed. White failures dropped from 18.6 percent to 5.3. Of the first 240,000 "new standard" men entering the armed forces between 1966 and 1968 some 41 percent were black, mostly poor, and educational dropouts. While the military had 23 percent of its personnel in combat arms, some 37 percent of the new men went into such arms. McNamara reassured everyone that "the poor of America can be given an opportunity to serve in their country's defense and they can be given an opportunity to return to civilian life with skills and attitudes which . . . will reverse the downward spiral of human decay."[75]

Such lofty sentiments soon seemed singularly misplaced. Although studies showed that even short-term military service had a strong positive effect on socioeconomic attainment, first one had to survive the short term. Black leaders' perceptions focused less on long-term benefits than on short-term risk. Their chagrin increased because the draft apparatus used to pull in these young blacks was another lily-white institution.

The draft apparatus reflected American society. As this society had been racist and segregated when SS was created in 1940, so was the draft. As the society became less tolerant of segregation, so did the system. Under Kennedy and Johnson, Jim Crow came tumbling down in the American South and local draft boards, giving in to pressure by the president, began the painful process of finding black members. A draft system consisting of all-white board members selecting young black men from Harlem or Alabama represented a travesty of democracy in normal times. During the Vietnam War, when casualty lists continued to grow, such a system seemed immoral, but change seemed slow. It took time for national directives to find fruition in local communities.

As the Vietnam era began, SS resembled the public education system in paying only lip service to the concept of integration. In 1962 less than 200 local board members, out of over 12,000, were black. When asked about the situation before the draft reform efforts of the White House, General Hershey expressed regret but pointed to the decentralized character of the system. Like the public school system, local communities ran the boards, and governors appointed the local board members. Few vacancies appeared.[76]

But over the years the membership on the local boards had become what one critic called a "self-perpetuation" of "silk stocking boys." Members served until they died or retired voluntarily. When a rare vacancy appeared, new members were nominated by old members. The entire city of Houston had 13 local boards with a total of 39 members, only two of them black and one Hispanic. By December 1966 there were still only 278 blacks on the 4,080 local boards throughout the nation.[77]

The Johnson administration crept slowly to a realization of the moral and political crisis inherent in the system. Ramsey Clark, the attorney general, reminded Johnson of the political explosiveness implied by such figures. "Negroes can make a strong moral issue of this situation," wrote Clark. With Muhammed Ali making headlines and Medgar Evers urging all Mississippi blacks to refuse induction by all-white boards, Johnson finally acted.[78]

On 6 March 1967 he issued orders that Hershey should work with governors to increase minority representation on local boards. By law the governors had to nominate local board members before the president could appoint them. Only two governors, Paul B. Johnson, Jr., of Mississippi and Claude R. Kirk, Jr., of Florida, refused to cooperate. Over the next several months and into the Nixon presidency, SS strove to obtain more minority representation in the system.[79]

By personal cajolery of southern governors such as George Wallace of Alabama, John Connally of Texas, and Lester Maddox of Georgia, Hershey made progress and was commended by the White House. In less than four years black membership on local boards climbed from 267 to 1,265, a sixfold leap. Increases also occurred in membership by Hispanics and women.[80]

Ironically, the increased percentage of blacks on local boards paralleled an increased percentage of nonwhite draftees. In 1966 less than 1 percent of local board members were black and over 12 percent of draftees were nonwhite. By 1970 local boards were about 7 percent black. The percentage of black draftees rose to 15.8 percent. These figures illustrated again that the black percentage of draftees was an effect not of the racial composition of local boards, but of the national social priorities built into the system. The integration of local boards, however, had little impact on the protest movement. Since much of the opposition was over the war, which continued under President Nixon, integrated draft boards made little difference, and Johnson got little credit.[81]

The government mechanism for enforcing the draft law seemed to be collapsing under the weight of dissent. Both Congress and Johnson became upset when the Department of Justice hesitated to prosecute draft offenders and the federal courts failed to convict. Since its establishment in 1940 the SS had relied upon the Department of Justice to enforce the law. Through the ensuing years the draft had been challenged in the courts on constitutional grounds, but the judges had agreed with Lincoln's simple notion expressed during the Civil War:

The case simply is, the Constitution provides that the Congress shall have power to raise and support armies. This is the whole of it. . . . the Power is given fully, completely, unconditionally. It is not a power to raise armies if State authorities consent; nor if the men to compose the armies are entirely willing; but it is a power to raise and support armies given to Congress by the Constitution without an if.[82]

During the Vietnam War the issue seemed more complex. Early in the expansion of the draft, Justice Department officials called SS's reclassification of men at Ann Arbor a misinterpretation of the law. Hershey responded that Justice was filled with "ACLUers," who refused to prosecute because they lacked sympathy for the war. When draft cards were returned to SS, the agency identified the individuals for prosecution but generally nothing happened. Congress, sympathetic to SS, in the 1967 law directed the Department of Justice to act "as expeditiously as possible to prosecute draft law violators," upon the request of the director. If Justice failed to act, Congress demanded an explanation in writing. Federal courts had to give priority in the dockets to draft law violators. President Johnson agreed with these steps.[83]

But the lack of action by the Justice Department threatened the draft only because of a disturbing evolution in the system. As originally conceived and implemented, the decentralized character of the draft was supposed to be the means of enforcement. Peer pressure within the community guaranteed that the 1940 system worked. The draft of the Civil War had failed because it depended upon enforcement by federal agents. But during the Vietnam years, draft officials began insisting that federal officials again prosecute. Community peer pressure no longer sufficed because community consensus on the Vietnam War had broken down. But if the draft could function only under the influence of such a consensus, there was little point in crying for federal enforcers.

Besides, the Department of Justice was prosecuting violators with unprecedented vigor. Clark ill-deserved the charge of aiding draft dodgers. Three factors were involved in evaluating the work of the Justice Department: the size of the draft call, the number of men who failed to report when called, and the number of prosecutions launched by the department against those who failed to report. The percentage of prosecutions was always small compared to the number who failed to report because most of the failures, as SS itself admitted, were not willful violations of the law (see Table 8.1). Frequently men moved and left no forwarding address or misplaced their induction notice. In such cases it was better to get the man into the service than into the courts.

Prosecutions continued to increase and reached 4,000 in fiscal year 1970. It was true that the vast majority of men accused of draft offenses were never charged, but this pattern was in existence long before Vietnam. Only 25,000 were indicted out of 209,517 charged during the

Table 8.1. Draft Efficiency, 1953–1967

Fiscal Year	Draft Call	Failure to Report	Prosecutions
1953	560,798	22,384	763
1954	268,018	19,698	1,022
1955	213,716	17,183	525
1956	136,580	10,904	277
1957	179,321	9,288	332
1961	61,070	6,968	253
1962	157,465	6,447	322
1963	71,744	3,146	323
1964	150,808	7,389	316
1965	103,328	5,142	369
1966	343,481	7,331	642
1967	298,559	7,234	1,314[84]

Sources: Memos to the president and Selective Service Annual Report 1954 (see note 84).

'WHAT ARE YOU — SOME KINDA NUT?'

Evading the draft. Courtesy, Library of Congress.

entire war, but this percentage was consistent with charges and indict-
ments for all crimes in the American judicial system. It was also true that
the Justice Department did not act on all complaints by local boards. But
by the late 1960s SS was issuing some 20,000 complaints annually. To
investigate all would have required many more field agents than the
department had. With limited resources, the department had to pick and
choose where to act. Finally, the courts, not the Justice Department, had
control over the final disposition of the cases.[85]

At first the courts had seemed sympathetic to the government's position. During World War II, from October 1940 to July 1945, Justice had

investigated some 400,000 cases and had obtained only 19,000 indict-
ments. In fiscal year 1966 Justice launched 642 prosecutions and obtained 366 convictions. In the first nine months of fiscal year 1967 there
were 939 prosecutions and 510 convictions. The rates soon dropped.
The SS had referred over 200,000 names to Justice, but over 100,000
men escaped prosecution because local boards had violated the law in
bringing the charges. Between 1967 and 1975 the percentage of defen-
dants convicted dropped every year. In 1967 some three-fourths of those
indicted were convicted; by 1975 less than 17 percent of draft-law violators were convicted, and less than 9 percent of those went to prison.
Those who did go to jail were usually there because of religious scruples.
As the war became more unpopular, juries became more sympathetic to
evaders, but to President Johnson it looked as if young men were defeating the system.[86]

By 1967 the warm glow of his 1964 election triumph had cooled for
Lyndon Johnson. He confronted a series of problems which bore down
on him with the force of a Texas "norther." The war was not going well,
despite repeated reassurances from administration sycophants. General
Westmoreland kept asking for more troops to put the United States over
the top. But more troops meant higher draft calls, bringing about more
protest. The summer of 1967 was highlighted by black riots in Newark
and Detroit. Martin Luther King, long revered as a moderate, was calling
for demonstrations against the war. Liberal intellectuals, dubbed "ner-
vous nellies" by Johnson, began to oppose the war. Antiwar parades in
1967 drew thousands in the summer, and a special march on the Pentagon was scheduled for late October.[87]

In confronting this crisis Johnson revealed the worst aspects of his
personality. No one had ever called him a cosmopolitan man, but his
distance from the cultural values of most of the protesters was almost
galactic in scope. Although hardly an altar boy himself, Johnson saw the
protesters as dirty, oversexed hippies, with foul mouths and no patriotism. He had no sympathy for their counterculture, preferring Lawrence
Welk to the Beatles, John Ford to Ingmar Bergman, Norman Rockwell
to Picasso, Norman Vincent Peale to Herbert Marcuse. By the fall of
1967 Johnson had convinced himself that the draft was causing the antiwar movement. He also believed sincerely that the protest at home
contributed to the military resistance by the Vietcong in Southeast Asia.
In such a frame of mind he launched a series of ill-advised actions. When

spring finally arrived, optimism about the war was dead, Johnson had decided to leave office, antiwar candidates were capturing Democratic primaries, and the SS System had been discredited.[88]

In 1965 Johnson had authorized the CIA, the FBI, and army intelligence to examine the origins of civil disturbances. By 1967 agents began filing reports on student draft resisters. Johnson wrote Ramsey Clark, Hershey, and J. Edgar Hoover that he wanted progress reports on how they would handle the October demonstration at the Pentagon.[89]

On 16 October several hundred protesters dumped sacks, supposedly filled with draft cards, at the Justice Department. On 21 October over 50,000 demonstrators marched from the Lincoln Memorial to the Pentagon. Met by troops with drawn bayonets, the protesters engaged in a variety of rituals to demonstrate their disdain for the war machine. Johnson watched these events unfold on television. Fatefully, he grabbed the phone and called Hershey, asking what could be done to punish the "s.o.b.'s" causing the disturbance. When Hershey mention the Ann Arbor option of reclassifying and drafting delinquents, Johnson gave verbal approval.[90]

On 26 October 1967, five days after the demonstration, Hershey marshalled a counterattack. In a letter to all members of the SS System, Hershey reminded them that acts which violated the draft law, regulations, or process could not be defined as in the national interest. "It follows," he continued, "that those who violate them should be denied deferment in the national interest. It also follows that illegal activity which interferes with recruiting or causes refusal of duty in the military or naval forces could not by any stretch of the imagination be construed as being in support of the national interest." He said that local boards should begin reclassifying those who interfered not merely with the draft but with military recruitment, including ROTC. Anyone who turned in his draft card should be reclassified and drafted. The Ann Arbor procedure became official policy. All draft agencies should provide information on "illegal demonstrators" to the proper local boards. The boards should then reopen the registrants' classifications and reclassify them as delinquent into 1-A. All men up to age 35 were liable for such action.[91]

These actions only created more political turmoil for Johnson, despite Hershey's attempt to distance the president from the uproar. When asked if he acted with presidential authority, the general told the press that he had called the White House, "just for the courtesy of letting them know I was going to do something" and "not to get their approval." He emphasized that the letter was entirely "my own responsibility." That an old bureaucrat such as Hershey would take such a step without clearance from the White House struck most reporters as dubious. But Hershey stuck to his story. Johnson remained silent, and when Hershey later sought an executive order to confirm his authority, White House aides convinced the president that he should allow the general to "carry the can" alone.[92]

More forthright were the various veterans' organizations and the Armed Services committees. Joseph A. Scerra, commander of the Veterans of Foreign Wars, wrote Johnson, "We are fed up with the groveling paid to those who reject our laws, ideals and flag." A Baltimore television station WMAR ran a survey on 18 January asking if draft card burners should be immediately inducted. Some 85 percent supported the idea. Mail at SS headquarters showed supporters outnumbering opponents by 75 percent to 25 percent. Among college presidents, the elite school leaders protested, but Hendrix College, Henderson State, Ouachita Baptist, and similar schools throughout the nation supported Hershey.[93]

The president received a more negative reaction. Hundreds of letters poured into the White House objecting to the new directive. Hershey had originally admitted that having local boards reclassify men who interfered with recruiting on campus was stretching the law. "It may be that we are assuming just a little," he had told the press. Attorney General Clark thought the assumption was gigantic. Hershey could point to precedents of punitive reclassifying during World War II, but even at that time the assistant attorney general, Tom Clark, had called such action an administrative penalty and illicit. Now his son was attorney general and took the same position. Basically, Ramsey believed that under the law the local board could reclassify only men who did something to violate their own status in the draft. If they committed a civil or criminal wrong, they should be punished by the courts, not reclassified and drafted.[94]

Hershey had issued the order at the president's urging. Both Johnson and those in Congress supporting the war thought drafting protesters was an excellent idea. Mendell Rivers, when he heard of Clark's concern, announced to the press that "if there exists the slightest doubt in the Attorney General's mind that General Hershey's action is not fully supported in the law, he need only say so and I am certain the Congress will correct any deficiency." Califano kept urging Johnson to stay out of the dispute.[95]

Califano wanted Johnson to avoid a controversy which was provoking

General Hershey and protesters. Courtesy, Selective Service System National Headquarters.

considerable protest from public and private sources. Kingman Brewster of Yale, along with the presidents of Princeton, Pennsylvania, Harvard, Dartmouth, Cornell, Columbia, and Brown universities, wrote Johnson, expressing dismay at Hershey's October directive. President John E. W. Sterling of Stanford objected to the denial of due process and claimed the directive would erode the school's disciplinary process. James Perkins of Cornell called to assure the president he had no objection to drafting students who caused trouble off campus, but disliked federal intrusions when protest occurred on campus. And David Truman, a dean at Columbia, said the school would have to ban all military recruitment on campus if Hershey's directive went into effect.[96] Brewster appeared on "Meet the Press" and called the directive "an absolutely outrageous usurpation of power." He warned that if adopted, the policy would disgrace military service and create havoc.[97]

The White House, in the person of Califano, reassured the intelligentsia that there had been a misunderstanding. He arranged a meeting where Clark and Hershey agreed upon a joint statement on draft violators.

The statement, released on 10 December, included the following provisions: a special Justice Department unit was created to prosecute violators; all U.S. attorneys were instructed to expedite investigation and to prosecute vigorously; those registrants who violated a regulation affecting their own status could be declared delinquent and reclassified; lawful protesters were not subject to reclassification or acceleration in the draft; unlawful protesters were to be prosecuted in civil courts.[98]

In addition, Califano wrote Brewster that the president supported the "spirit and letter of due process," a reassuring but gratuitous sentiment. The White House had Hershey's word that lawful protest would not lead to reclassification and that violations of the law were the responsibility of the judicial system. Johnson, however, made no move to revoke Hershey's directive. Neither did Hershey, who defiantly stated that only 15 college presidents had even written on the issue, and not all were opposed to the directive.[99]

Johnson approved the agreement before it was released. He expected it to calm the waves of indignation, but it had the opposite effect. Neil Sheehan of the *New York Times* asked Hershey what he meant in the letter. The general replied that, while Clark and he agreed on most issues, they still had different views of the definition of delinquency. Both agreed that men who destroyed their records were delinquent and subject to reclassification. Men who destroyed the records of others, however, Hershey thought should be reclassified, while Clark felt the crime was punishable by the courts. When Sheehan's story appeared Clark complained to the White House that Hershey had broken the negotiated truce. When Califano tried to pressure Hershey into line, the general cited Johnson as his authority for the original directive. The president never contradicted the general.[100]

Congress, which had only recently voted overwhelmingly to renew the draft without major change, began to protest. In the House, Congressman John Moss of California threatened hearings over the Hershey directive. Rivers and the majority of the armed services committees in both houses remained supporters of SS, but opposition was growing. Senators Edward Kennedy, Philip Hart, Mark Hatfield, Jacob Javits, Clifford Case, and others from both parties offered a bill to overturn the directive. Students continued to protest, and the National Student Association sued Hershey in federal court, claiming his directive was unconstitutional. No one issue led to Johnson's decision to withdraw from the presidential race on 31 March, but the problems with the draft undoubt-edly played a large role.[101]

At the end of World War II some 79 percent of the public had agreed that local draft boards were fair. At the end of the Korean War in 1953, 60 percent had felt the same way. But by the summer of 1966 the percentage had declined. In August some 49 percent said the system was fair, but 37 percent felt it was unfair. In early February 1968 only 35 percent of a Gallup poll approved of Johnson's handling of the war, while 50 percent disapproved.[102]

But the polls provided mixed signals. A Lou Harris poll in February 1968 found that 53 percent agreed with Hershey's directive, and only 30 percent objected. A telephone survey of the Milwaukee area by the local press found that 74 percent thought the draft was fair to minorities, especially blacks, and only 8 percent thought it unfair. The draft itself was approved by 75 percent. When the Youth Council in Oregon sur-veyed 7,700 high school students in December 1967 it found that 68 percent opposed the ending of the draft, and only 20 percent approved the idea. Jim G. Lucas, a reporter for the Washington *Daily News*, tra-veled the country and found that a majority of young men went willingly when called even in centers of protest.[103]

Ignorance of how the draft operated probably contributed to the vary-ing poll results. When George Reedy, a presidential aide, debated the merits of the draft at Brandeis University, he found that his antidraft opponents, Allard Lowenstein and Harris Wofford, were well inten-tioned but "neither of them have the faintest idea of how the Selective Service System works." Over 50 percent of the public surveyed did not even know that a draftee served for two years at that time. This ignorance was shared by many members of Congress.[104]

Other variables having a strong effect on the polls were class and vulnerability to the draft. In one sample some 75 percent felt the military provided a chance for the poor to get ahead, especially blacks. Blacks themselves always gave the draft a higher rating than whites. In contrast, Harvard students felt the draft was a waste because they could contribute more by remaining civilians. Understandably, dissent from the draft was strongest among those who expected to be drafted and weakest among those who planned to volunteer or who expected to enter the service with a commission. A majority of college students supported the student deferment program, but most also opposed channeling by the system, the qualification test, and any type of ranking of students for draft vulnerability. The diversity of local board action and lack of national standards also generated opposition among the least vulnerable class. In contrast, those men who had already served in the military tended to support the draft and the war.[105]

The decentralization of the draft helps explain how military expansion through the participation of civilians on local draft boards helped to erode the traditional antagonism toward service by civilians. The United States fought World War II, Korea, and Vietnam with drafted armies, with civilian armies. After the Vietnamese War, a high percentage of American males had some military experience. The draft had ended the isolation of the armed forces from the larger society.

One of the forces causing opposition to the war in Vietnam was its limited character. The wars in both Korea and Vietnam promoted public dissent and caused presidents Truman and Johnson both to suffer in public opinion polls. The draft system in the late 1960s had also suffered in the polls but more because the war was unpopular than because of any inherent defect in the system. Defects existed, but the intensity focused upon them was a circuitous means of attacking Johnson's war.[106]

Johnson spent much time in 1968 trying to correct some of the system's defects, but critics continued as the war continued. Minorities were moved into local boards under the prodding of the White House, and headquarters issued more pamphlets and information. On the issue of centralization and less diversity of classification, however, there was little change. As Hershey repeatedly told critics, "The lack of uniformity in classification is a reflection of fact and real life. Uniformity is an illusion." Equity was a similar illusion because "people are not equal in capacity, adaptability, or availability."[107]

The failure in Vietnam generated more protest than did the structure of the draft. But the draft brought home to many college students the reality of the war. On college campuses many students who enjoyed deferments protested the war. Strangely, some White House staff members thought the ending of all college deferments and the use of a lottery would defuse protest on campuses. Given the popularity of such deferments, this was a dubious idea. Under Johnson, the idea remained untested. Neither Hershey, Congress, nor the public approved the lottery idea. The 1967 draft law specified that the president could not institute a lottery without congressional approval. A Lou Harris survey indicated that 54 percent of the public opposed use of a lottery and only 31 percent approved. [108]

Johnson began peace talks on 10 May 1968, but military replacements were still constantly needed. The armed forces used a 12-month rotation tour for men assigned to Vietnam. In April 1968 Clark Clifford, recently named to replace McNamara, announced plans to call up 24,500 reservists, but only 10,000 of them went to Vietnam. The others went into the depleted strategic reserve in the United States. The draft had to continue, but Johnson tried to make it more acceptable by cutting back on some specialized deferments. [109]

When the president announced an end to deferments for graduate students, except those in health fields, he met protest from those who preferred a selective, specialized draft over egalitarianism or equity. The response to this "reform" illustrated the amount of self-interest involved in draft regulations. Meeting in February 1966, the SS Scientific Advisory Group concluded that the draft had had "no serious effect" in engineering or scientific fields. The advisors unanimously recommended that class standing and test scores "be the same as used during the Korean War." [110]

The 1967 law provided that the National Security Council (NSC) should periodically advise the director of SS on what graduate fields required deferments. In fact, the NSC had only a vague idea of what fields should be protected. In September 1967 SS sent the NSC a list of critical occupations and fields of study, prepared after consulting with scientific advisers on the national and state level. [111]

Lifting graduate deferments was tricky under any circumstances. The DOD expected to draft 200,000 men in fiscal year 1969. If all graduate school deferments were ended at once, over half of the draft total would be college graduates. But keeping these deferments only fed opposition based on the class bias of the draft. By late November, on the advice of an Interagency Advisory Committee, the NSC issued a memo stating that graduate deferments should be limited to health professionals and a few other critical skills. [112] But Senator Ted Kennedy demanded that all graduate and undergraduate student deferments be ended. In contrast, Nathan M. Pusey, president of Harvard, testified before Congress that ending graduate deferments would mean the loss of countless scientists and college teachers. In February 1968 Johnson approved an order implementing the NSC memo that ended deferments for all graduate study except in health. [113]

The grand reform ideas expressed by the Marshall commission were reduced to a modest cutback of deferments for an educated elite. And even this modest action provoked an outburst of indignation from the educational leaders, some of whom were supporting student protest and student deferments. The anthropologist Margaret Mead predicted the move would cut graduate enrollment in half. The Office of Education predicted a 30 percent drop. President Pusey of Harvard announced that the only men going to graduate school in September would be "the lame, the halt, the blind and the female." One manpower specialist warned that all draftees after May would be college graduates. University presidents pontificated that the action was short sighted and damaging to the nation's technological future. [114]

Such complaints hardly disturbed Johnson, who was preparing his new peace offensive and announcing his withdrawal from the presidential race. Defending the new policy was left to Hershey. The general bluntly dismissed the cries of alarm. He said the educators were basing their projections on all draft registrants in college, rather than just on those who held 2-S deferments. The thousands of students who held married deferments or physical deferments would be unaffected by the order. Also, critics ignored the many veterans returning to civilian life as potential graduate enrollees. Hershey argued that military service would raise educational levels and help reduce crime. A tour in the service would lead young men to appreciate their special advantages and learn about equality. "I have every sympathy with the president of an institution that has gone into the graduate-school business in order to get cheap teachers," he remarked sardonically. [115]

Other government officials were more sympathetic. The Interagency Committee which had made the original recommendation to the NSC decided to monitor the effect of the order, because of the "grave concern" expressed by educators. At the urging of the Council of Graduate Schools, the AAUP, and the ACE, SS informed local boards that a full-time graduate student was entitled to a delay to finish a semester. [116]

But Hershey remained unsympathetic. To a conference of state draft directors in April, he complained, "They [the educators] had lied to me for fifteen years by getting people deferred for two extra years." He thought the graduate students were not students at all, but teachers. "I'll be damned if I am going to have a full-time student being able to be a full-time teacher." Hershey believed graduate students should seek deferments as teachers or researchers. Although he disclaimed any ambition to take over colleges, Hershey warned that "they aren't run by anybody; they've got chaos."[117]

In 1968 Hershey's attitude was shared by an increasing number of Americans. During the presidential campaign Richard Nixon began cultivating this silent majority under what was later called "the politics of resentment." Two respected leaders in the scientific community, strong advocates of scientific manpower management, Leonard Carmichael and Howard A. Meyerhoff, had once felt the draft was dangerous to American science, but now they changed their tune. Carmichael wrote: "My only comment is General Hershey really knows best." Meyerhoff urged Hershey to draft graduate and undergraduate students and most of the faculty, saying students were spoiled brats who raised hell "with gutless faculty encouraging them."[118]

According to one White House aide, it was lucky Johnson had ended deferments for graduate students. If they had remained in place, the huge numbers flooding the schools would have "put a severe strain on present graduate school facilities." In fall 1968 applications ran 10 percent above fall 1967, and at the University of Southern California they were up 20 percent. A check by the Scientific Manpower Commission on 658 chemistry, physics, and psychology departments found a general increase. In chemistry there was a 15.9 percent increase in male graduate students, physics had a 12.5 percent increase, and psychology 13.3 percent.[119]

Once again a changing historical context had upset prophecies. The decision to allow an enrolled graduate student to finish out the semester had encouraged some to gamble for the delay; schools had begun classifying graduate students as full-time teachers, which made them eligible for a different deferment; and draft calls during most of 1968 were well below the DOD's earlier projections. The reduction in calls reflected Johnson's new peace offensive, an action with important implications for the bitter presidential election campaign being waged by Hubert Humphrey and Richard Nixon.

9

Nixon and the Draft

1968 was quite a year. Historians later wrote books on these 12 months. Some of the events that took place were the Tet offensive, the political surge of Senator Eugene McCarthy, the candidacy of Robert Kennedy for the Democratic nomination and his murder, Johnson's withdrawal from the presidential race, the assassination of Martin Luther King, and the seizure of Columbia University by student radicals. Also, from New York to San Francisco protesters burned draft cards and expected to lose their deferred status. The entire question of deferments was under challenge as class discrimination. The courts had revised the definition of CO; ethical humanists received the same treatment as Quakers. A new movement promoting selective conscientious objection, rejecting only certain wars, gained ground. Selective Service struggled to find alternate service jobs for over 6,000 COs. And several hundred draftees fled to Canada to avoid induction.[1]

In the midst of the turmoil soldiers continued to fight in Vietnam and SS continued to provide replacements. Inductees used various ploys to obtain 4-F classification, and the rejection rate began to climb. Sympathetic physicians began offering supporting evidence for rejection. One psychiatrist even turned a nice profit at the task. The rejection rate for physical reasons jumped over 15 percentage points to almost half of all who appeared. Armed force recruiters on college campuses found themselves confronted with battle parodies, men doused with ketchup and shot with water pistols. ROTC units lost enrollment.[2] In the White House, Johnson took time from his peace initiatives to condemn the Communists that he believed were behind such actions and demand stronger prosecution by the Justice Department. The draft became an important issue in the unfolding presidential campaign.[3]

The draft had drawn attention from presidential candidates in the past, but without much effect. In 1956 Stevenson had called for ending the draft in a fruitless attempt to unseat Eisenhower. In 1964 Goldwater made the same pledge against what he called an "outmoded and unfair" system. During the 1968 campaign Senator Eugene McCarthy offered an unequivocal pledge to end the draft. Vice President Hubert Humphrey promised to remove General Hershey, institute a lottery, and offer more alternate service options. Governor Nelson Rockefeller also called for reform. Alabama's Governor George Wallace wanted more volunteers but wished to keep the draft. Richard Nixon, now reestablished as a leading Republican candidate, had been a supporter of the draft and in 1956 had denounced Stevenson for offering false hopes about ending something "indispensable to national security."[4]

No one was more adept at reversing his field because of political conditions than Nixon. After stumbling badly in the California governor's race in 1962, he had begun a remarkable political comeback which placed him in an attractive position for the 1968 nomination campaign.[5] His thinking on the draft had evolved accordingly. In theory the very idea of enlistment forced by the national government seemed inimical to the Republican emphasis on federalism. The classical liberalism embodied in such organizations as Young Republicans clubs rejected the draft on philosophical grounds. These points, combined with an elaborate defense of an all-volunteer military, had been cogently presented to Nixon by Martin Anderson, a young staff member. Anderson was influenced by Milton Friedman, the free market economist from the University of Chicago.

The political climate of 1968 also provided Nixon with ample justification for a new look at the draft. Here was a club begging to be used against the Democrats. Nixon first publicized his new line in an informal press conference in March 1968. He argued that the draft was an inappropriate device to use to man an antiguerilla war and spoke of the value of an all-volunteer force. Korea, according to Nixon, was the last war requiring conventional forces manned through conscription. Asked if he foresaw an early end to the draft, Nixon replied that he did but only after victory in Vietnam. A few weeks later he explained that changing SS in the midst of the war was a bad idea.[6]

Nixon's response to what was a burning issue for thousands of young men and their families was inadequate. Continued violent protest against the war, accusations by Rockefeller that Nixon favored continuing the present draft, and statements by Humphrey that an AVF was too costly forced an explanation from the Nixon organization. The draft became the focus for a major policy address by Nixon on CBS on 17 October 1968. According to Nixon a compulsory draft could not be accepted in a nation devoted to "liberty, justice and equality." There was no "fair" way to operate the draft. The evolution of military tactics and strategy from hand-to-hand combat to use of nuclear weapons made the necessity of the draft questionable and suggested the need for a professional, volunteer force.[7]

Nixon insisted that volunteers could be obtained if military manpower was considered a commodity in a market system. "There's no reason why our military should be exempt from peacetime competition for manpower." He also thought Americans could afford to pay for such a force. As for opponents of an all-volunteer system, Nixon called their arguments specious. The charge that such a force would be all black, "I regard . . . as sheer fantasy." The idea that a professional army of mercenaries posed a threat to the republic was equally dubious because the volunteers would be American citizens, proud to serve their flag. Nixon concluded by cautioning that the conversion from the draft to a volunteer system could not take place until the issue of Vietnam was resolved. But he did promise that something would be done if he were elected because the nation could not afford to continue with the "crisis of confidence" of young men in the draft. Under the new Nixon administration they could be assured of attention.[8]

The margin of victory in November 1968 which created the new Nixon administration was very narrow. Nixon obtained 302 electoral votes to 191 for Humphrey, but only 43.4 percent of the popular vote to 42.7 percent for Humphrey. Nixon owed his election to many things, but his call for replacing the draft with an AVF failed as a vote getter. Surveys in early 1969 showed that the American public favored continuing the draft rather than adopting a professional military of volunteers. In the first week of 1969 a Gallup poll found that 62 percent preferred continuing the draft to relying on volunteers; an AVF was supported by only 31 percent. A survey by the National Observer revealed little difference in attitude on the draft between those over 30 and those younger. Nixon's drive to replace the draft with an AVF was not based on a simple desire to cater to public demands, but politics was involved.[9]

To appreciate the motives behind Nixon's draft reforms one needs to recall the character of the armed forces in 1968 and the differential effect of the draft on American society. From a 1939 total of just 334,473 men, the armed forces had grown to 3,460,162 personnel on active duty by 1969. After World War II the strength of the armed forces had fluctuated with the various crises of the cold war. In 1949 the United States had reduced its armed strength to 1.4 million. By 1952, in response to the Korean War, the total had jumped to 3.7 million. Under Eisenhower a gradual shift in focus to strategic air defense had reduced the number to 2.5 million by 1961. But Vietnam had generated an increase to about 3.5 million by 1969. Army strength alone in 1968 reached about 1,570,000. From 1965 to 1972 some 6 million personnel passed through the military, with about half serving at some time in Vietnam. Replacement needs for enlisted men in 1969 stood at 818,000. And the enlisted men were the best educated and healthiest in the nation's history.[10]

The character of the armed forces had also evolved over time. As sociologists emphasized, the military had become "civilianized." While in the Civil War almost all military men were directly involved in combat, by 1943 only 29 percent had combat duties. By 1971 this number had declined to 14 percent. The number of personnel with technical or noncombat specialties had jumped from 50 percent in 1954 to 60 percent in 1965. There had been little change, however, in the ratio of officers to enlisted men. In 1935 officers made up 9.7 percent of the total; in 1967 9.9 percent. But it was a force with a very high turnover rate. In 1962 about 26 percent of all first timers decided to rejoin. By 1970 this number had dropped to 12 percent, and among draftees it dropped to less than 4 percent.[11]

Because of the insurance provided by the draft the DOD had raised its mental and educational standards for entry several times. In 1954 only 33.5 percent of new personnel scored in the two top levels of the AFQT. By 1966 some 39.6 ranked as high. In 1968 some 70 percent of new enlisted men were high school graduates, and the membership of the armed forces closely resembled the same cohort in civilian life. Officially, about 60 percent of enlisted men were draftees, but estimates on how many volunteers came in to avoid the draft ranged from 40 to 60 percent.[12]

During the Vietnam War SS had its largest draft pool in history. Reversing a downward trend in the birth rate, which had dropped to 20.3 in 1940, the total live births per 1,000 women aged 15 to 44 rose to 26.6

in 1947 and remained around this level until 1960 when it again declined. It reached 18.4 in 1970. By 1968 approximately 1,900,000 males were reaching age 19 each year. Since draft calls during the Johnson buildup had peaked at around 400,000 in 1966, and calls for fiscal year 1968 totaled only 340,000, the surplus manpower influenced debate on the draft. But the surplus, although real, was not as large as suggested at first glance. The SS reported in October 1968 that there were 33 million registrants. But 44.3 percent were overage, 14.8 percent were disqualified (4-F), 11 percent were deferred because of dependency (3-A), 18 percent were veterans or already in the service, and 7.7 percent were deferred as students. The system anticipated that of the 1,900,000 new draft-eligible 19 year olds, only about 669,000 would be available immediately. This figure emerged after factoring in a 40 percent rejection rate and the loss of 784,000 to student deferments.[13] Nevertheless, the huge total of new 18 year olds suggested that it would be possible to recruit an AVF.

The leaders of the armed forces, however, were reluctant to adopt the AVF idea. Critics said they were spoiled by the draft, and the charge was partially true. The draft provided men as both draftees and as volunteers. In the period after 1945, when the armed forces tried to create an all-volunteer, professional force, the draft ended in 1947 and volunteering ended in 1948. Each secretary of defense from Louis Johnson in 1950 to Robert McNamara in 1966 testified that without the draft there would be few volunteers.[14]

The exact number of volunteers entering the service because of the draft was hard to establish because it was influenced by many variables. The unemployment rate, the size of draft calls, the existence of combat possibilities, and the fringe benefits offered by the service all played a role. What seemed least important was the costly recruiting system operated by the armed forces. In fiscal year 1968 over 3,000 recruitment stations manned by 8,600 recruiters beat the bushes at the cost of over $100 million. Television, radio, and newspaper ads were all used to convince young men to volunteer. But two of three volunteers said they enlisted because of the draft. Most of those who volunteered had been notified of their impending induction by local boards and had already passed their preinduction exams.[15]

As Vietnam protest promoted the search for an alternative to the draft, various studies were conducted to try to establish the credibility of an AVF. Based on interviews of enlisted men, these studies concluded that about 40 percent of all volunteers were draft induced. But these estimates were undoubtedly very conservative because some men probably didn't want to admit their fear of the draft. In 1970 the army recruited 13,000 men each month, but only 6,000 were non-draft influenced, and of this smaller group only one in every 40 picked a combat arm as a specialty. Spokesmen for both the navy and the marines admitted that "the draft breathing down the necks of young men enable[s] us to keep our forces at the size they are."[16]

If the draft was important in recruiting enlisted men it was absolutely essential for obtaining officers and filling reserve and National Guard units. The percentage of new officers with college degrees increased from 55.5 percent in 1956 to 72.3 percent in 1965. Some 78 percent of all doctors entering the service in 1965 said the draft had influenced their decision. One college observer said that "enthusiasm for the ROTC is directly related to the quota of input into the draft at that time." Some 40 percent of all new officers on active duty in 1964 said the draft had pushed them into service.[17]

The picture for reserve units was similar. A DOD survey in 1964 found that fear of the draft accounted for 70.7 percent of all accessions to reserve and National Guard units. James Cantwell, president of the National Guard Association, admitted in January 1970 that up to 90 percent of his enlisted strength was draft induced. Vice Admiral William P. Mack reported that over 75 percent of naval reserve enlistments were draft related. And an Air Force survey found 43 percent of enlisted men, 39 percent of officers, and 80 percent of reserve enlistees had entered because of the draft. The draft not only drove men into the reserves but kept them honest about their commitment. Between June 1956 and 30 September 1968 local boards called up for induction some 10,159 reservists who were delinquent in attending reserve meetings.[18]

Despite the obvious importance of the draft to both the size and quality of the American military establishment in 1969, the new Nixon administration moved to end conscription. The move was prompted primarily by domestic political considerations. The bias of the draft had become a universal political cliché. During the campaign of 1968 all leading candidates had agreed that the draft lacked equity in its operation. But draft fairness was an issue of considerable complexity. Nixon simplified the issue by remarking that the draft was inherently unfair, but so was life. More realistic were sophisticated approaches of social scientists who tried to establish the class, racial, and educational bias of draft operations.[19]

But what most draft critics overlooked in 1969 was the original motive behind SS. Although distorted by the political need to appear egalitarian, the draft system created in World War I and resurrected in 1940 was supposed to be selective. It was planned to allow manpower management, so that the social priorities and biases of the culture and government influenced who went to war. The draft statute itself reflected a bias by offering escape routes to fathers and to certain specialists. Implemented by presidential order, these provisions had led to deferments for farmers and nuclear scientists and for parents and priests. Because the system provided that the officials of the armed forces had the final say about who was admitted, another bias emerged. When calls were low, the armed forces raised their mental and physical standards. This ability to regulate the quality of manpower and the flexibility of SS in responding to such shifts represented one of the virtues of the system and a manifestation of modern personnel management.[20]

Such management by the draft stood in contrast to total mobilization, to a "levee en masse." On an international scale the United States was no more militarized than other members of the Western alliance. In 1960, for example, the American armed forces represented 1.39 percent of the population, compared with 2.15 in France and 1.01 in Britain.[21]

American draft selectivity did lead to bias. It led to a geographic bias. Because of the physical standards and deferment policies in the 1960s, the highest rate of military service occurred in the north northeast, mid-Atlantic, and the Rocky Mountains to the Pacific coast regions, with the lowest rates in the south-Atlantic, eastern south-central and western south-central regions. Urban areas with populations of 100,000 or more provided a higher rate of military service than did farm and ranch or rural areas.[22]

Age provided another bias in draft operations. The experience of men moving through the 19 to 26 age cohort varied over the post–Korean War years. Military service had been close to universal through 1958. There were 1.1 million 26-year-old males in June 1958 and some 770,000 were in the service or were veterans. Since the disqualification rate had run about 22 percent of the total cohort, this meant that almost 90 percent of all qualified men had fulfilled military service. Even as late as June 1963 DOD insisted that "virtually no 1-A non-father who is qualified and available for service will be in a position to escape."[23]

As the size of the eligible male age cohort increased in the 1960s, however, the military participation rate (MPR) dropped dramatically. By 1968 only 46 percent of men reaching age 26 were serving or had served, and the projection was downward to 42 percent in 1974. Still, in 1968 veterans made up about 13 percent of the total population and 47 percent of the adult male population. A study in 1969 reported that half of all adult males had seen service, 90 percent as enlisted men. The direct and indirect effect of the draft had contributed to providing one of the few common experiences for American men in the nation's history.[24]

Inequity charges arose in the sixties because the MPR began declining as the Vietnam War began expanding. The draft's differential effect on social and economic groups became more noticeable. In 1966 a study of local boards in Wisconsin revealed that those in low income areas had a high rate of mental, physical, and dependency deferments and a low rate of student deferments and volunteer enlistments. Boards in high income areas showed a higher rate in volunteer enlistments and student deferments. Eligibles in high income areas often used reserve and National Guard enlistment to avoid the draft. But the study was misleading. More comprehensive investigations, using military service at all levels and in all forms, found a more egalitarian MPR. Controlling for father's educational level and occupation type, these studies found little difference in the MPR of fathers and sons. The only noticeable exception was that sons of farmers and sons of fathers with graduate education served less than the average. The class bias of the MPR was reduced further during the Vietnam era because the eligible age cohort grew in size and college attendance became less related to income. However, a survey in February 1970 found that "not one son or grandson of any U.S. Senator or Representative has ever been killed or missing in this Vietnam War."[25]

Another charge of inequity made during the late 1960s involved the apparent racial bias in the operation of the draft. In 1968 11 percent of all enlisted men in Vietnam were black, but 22.4 percent of all killed were black. Some 13 percent of the army and 8 percent of the marines were black. These figures hardly reflected a race-biased draft. Black inductions from 1964 to 1969 rose from 16,961 to 45,691, but as a percentage of the total inductions, they rose only from 15 to 16. The military experience of blacks in the Vietnam era had to be seen in a larger context. Blacks looked upon the armed forces as one of the few equal opportunity employers in America and reenlisted twice as often as whites. During the Vietnam War reenlistment rates dropped from 66 percent to 32 percent for blacks, while white rates dropped from 20 percent to 13 percent. Black military membership jumped in the 1960s because McNamara's ambitious rehabilitation plan, Project 100,000, was disproportionally black. ROTC and reserve duty was more open to whites. Physical and mental standards also operated to insure that the pool of draft eligibles was more black than the age cohort in the population.[26]

Besides bias against blacks, critics accused the draft of excusing the educated. Built into the system from the beginning, and elaborated in detail during the 1950s, the student deferment system during the 1960s incited visceral anger among draft critics. Education level did have a much stronger impact on MPR than race. The total number of young men classified as 1-S or 2-S, deferred for education, in 30 June 1960 was 178,871. On 30 June 1970 the total stood at 2,262,000, an incredible increase. The total enrollment of American students from grammar school through high school, both public and private, rose from 41,762,000 in 1960 to 50,742,000 in 1968, an increase of 22 percent, but during the same period, college male enrollment rose from 2,257,000 to 4,119,000, an increase of almost 82 percent. The male median school year finished rose from 10.7 years in 1959 to 12.1 in 1968, an increase of almost 20 percent.[27] Education deferments grew at a much faster rate than the increase in students and this affected MPR, but in unexpected ways.

Studies in 1964, 1969, and later all confirmed a positive correlation between education level and chances of entering the service. When the *entire male age cohort* was considered the figures came out as follows:

Education Level	Percentage Served in AF	
	1964	1969
Less than 8 years	30	
Some high school	50	
High school graduate only	70	74
Some college	56	60
College graduate	60	71
Some graduate work	27	

Note the increase in MPR for college types; their chances of serving increased rather than decreased despite the 2-S deferment.

When *only the males in the 1-A pool* were considered for the late 1960s the MPR revealed the following trend:

Education Level	MPR (in percent)
Not a high school graduate	85
High school graduate	75
Some college	74
College graduate	50

But this pool had already been lessened by men joining reserves and National Guard units and men who had failed the AFQT or the physical.[28]

The SS argued in vain that few escaped entirely from service through education. In 1966, 56 percent of men who attended college eventually served, while only 46 percent of noncollege men served. Of those who were rejected as 4-F, those with less than an eighth-grade education were turned down at a 41 percent rate while those with a high school diploma at an 8.5 percent rate. Men with some college were rejected at about a 13 percent rate. Education did have an effect on how one entered service. The group with less generated more volunteers:

Education Level	Volunteer MPR Percent (1964)	Draftee MPR Percent (1964)
Not a high school graduate	61	33
High school graduate	54	36
Some college	15.6	
College graduate	9	25
Graduate school	43	40

Education also influenced the level of entry into the service: For non–high school graduates, 94 percent entered as enlisted personnel; for college graduates, the figure was 33 percent.

Enlisted men constituted some 84 percent of all entries into the armed forces. Without the draft few college graduates would have entered the armed forces as enlisted men. In 1969 some 17,578 college graduates were drafted into the army and marines.[29] Overall, the draft seems to have contributed to an armed force which was proportionately mixed in educational level.

Besides ending an allegedly unfair system, however, Nixon and his advisers also believed that ending the draft would improve the quality of the armed forces. Advocates of an AVF were forever stressing the point that draftees made inferior fighters compared to professional volunteers. Comparing the effectiveness of draftees to volunteers is difficult because so many "volunteers" were really draft motivated, but there is data on draftee quality. Simply put, the draftee was brighter and better educated than the volunteer. The better educated the volunteer, the more likely that he entered the service to avoid the draft and was an indirect inductee. The supposed super patriotism and higher motivation of volunteers was always recognized as a myth by those on active duty. In the 1938 army, which consisted of only true volunteers, a college-educated man was seldom seen in the enlisted ranks. In fact, some 31 percent had less than an eighth-grade education. In all comparisons between enlistees and draftees during the Vietnam War, the latter had more years of education and scored higher on aptitude tests. In one survey the 8 percent who scored above 93 out of 100 on AFQT were all draftees. As draft calls went down in 1970, the number of category 4 men, who read at only a fifth-grade level, went up among those entering the service, and the two top categories showed a decline.[30]

Throughout history assignments in armies have correlated well with education and intelligence. The better educated usually found themselves behind the lines while the uneducated went to combat units at the front. The U.S. Army in World War II was no exception to this rule. But in Vietnam, surprisingly, the correlation was weaker. Since most draftees ended up in combat, it meant that the U.S. Army was, in an unprecedented fashion, using brain power on the front. By 1969 nine of every 10 draftees were in Vietnam. Some 70 percent of the combat slots in the army in 1970 were filled by draftees, compared to about 29 percent in 1963. Of every 100,000 combat assignments made by the army only 4 percent had selected such a military occupation specialty (MOS) as their first choice for duty, and because draftees had only two years of commitment, the military had to use them quickly.[31]

The effectiveness of the draftee as a soldier had become established long before the Vietnam buildup. Brig. Gen. S. L. A. Marshall reported that the Seventh Army got "its most adaptable, highest type soldier . . . via the draft boards." Maj. Gen. Ralph E. Haines, Jr., commander of the First Armored Division remarked that his draftees were "intelligent, enthusiastic," and highly motivated men. Col. Dan S. McMillin, commander of a training regiment at Fort Knox, Kentucky, said the draftees were "head and shoulders above the last generation of soldiers in education, desire, and sense of responsibility." Lt. Gen. James L. Richardson, G-1, Department of the Army, reported to Congress that draftees made fine soldiers. Reports from the Vietnam battlefield confirmed these impressions.[32] Draftees were less guilty than volunteers of violating military rules and regulations and had fewer problems with drugs. The draftees' higher level of education and intelligence, middle-class background, and maturity contributed to their superior performance as soldiers.[33]

But this competence was costly. Draftees made up over 80 percent of the infantry riflemen in Vietnam. A report issued in February 1970, covering the period from June 1965 to June 1969, indicated that one of every 104 draftees was killed in action. Some 33 percent of all Americans killed in combat were draftees. As of 30 June 1969 the army had lost 36,954 in action and 11,946 were draftees.[34]

In 1969 it was too simple to say that the draft had failed in its mission of providing men, or that it had seriously disrupted American society. It was equally difficult to argue that draftees had failed as soldiers or that military experience had seriously distorted the values of those who had been drafted. But Nixon wanted to believe that the draft should end. If one rationale failed, there were always others.

As a man who prided himself on his foresight in international relations and historical vision, Nixon particularly liked the argument that the draft was an anachronism. Theorists stressed that the modern draft had originated with the rise of mass armies in Europe in the nineteenth century. Victory in major wars for the previous 150 years had required mobilizing civilians through conscription. But because of a variety of changes in armaments, politics, and society, the concept of mass armies had become obsolete. Since the draft represented the instrument to achieve what was no longer required, it should be abolished.[35]

Equally persuasive to Nixon were advisers who attacked the draft by using free market theory. Economists such as Milton Friedman, Walter Oi, and others belabored this approach to an administration supposedly sympathetic to liberating the forces of capitalism from the burden of government regulation. At its crudest, this approach represented conscription as slavery, as involuntary servitude, as confiscation of labor. On a more sophisticated level, the argument represented forced military service as a tax. It was a hidden tax paid by the draftee and amounted to how much he had to forego in civilian earnings because of his military service. As liberal John Galbraith argued, it was a subsidy paid by young males to the military in lieu of increased taxes on the middle and upper classes for costly military manpower. Such a subsidy simply underwrote inefficiency in the use of manpower by the armed forces.[36] Although Galbraith appeared to be in strange company by taking such a Republican attitude, the draft made strange bedfellows.

The economic argument had an ideological angle which appealed to many conservative Republicans. On an ideological basis the draft represented a major intrusion by the state into the lives of its citizens. Those conservatives who lamented the manner in which the state had ceased to be a servant of the individual and become a burden pointed to the draft as a gross example of this trend. This approach provided a bond between conservatives and radicals in draft criticism; the New Left and the Young Republicans constituted a bizarre political partnership.[37]

Politics was always foremost in Nixon's consideration of any issue, including the draft. In 1969 the political context included demographic facts such as the growing number of 18-year-old males and an increased political activism by young Americans as a result of the civil rights protest. Most Americans were not young, not active, and not affected by the cultural revolt of youth, but were tiring of the war in Vietnam, and the draft was a symbol of the war. Boards existed in every local community, reminding everyone of the frustration in Asia. Reforming the draft offered breathing room for the administration to tackle the more challenging task of ending the war.

Based on the advice of several Republican theorists, Nixon assumed office with the goal of creating a new majority coalition. It would rest upon those Democrats and Republicans fed up with crime, with the rebellion of youth, with the pace and push of civil rights. At its heart the coalition rested upon silent resentment, and Nixon felt it represented a silent majority. Nixon's first instinct was to reject the protest against the draft and the war. As he wrote later, he considered the draft protesters merely cowards, but he also admitted that the protest influenced his approach to the war.[38] Publicly, he acted to reform and then end the draft. Privately, below the surface of rhetoric and reforms, the administration also acted to subvert the antidraft, antiwar movement.

During both the Johnson and the Nixon administrations the FBI, and for a time even the U.S. Army, spied on protesters. The FBI campaigned

Protest during Nixon's administration. Courtesy, Selective Service System National Headquarters.

to create chaos in the antiwar movement. Their tactics included issuing outrageous statements under phony names and exploiting and promoting racism in the movement. "To further the rift in the black-white movements," FBI undercover agents encouraged extortion by the Black Panthers of the Students for a Democratic Society (SDS). Agents planted stories with blacks that the white SDS sought to use blacks as "cannon fodder" in protests. Similar actions promoted black antisemitism, since Jews were prominent in the antiwar movement. Posters were manufactured calling for the "elimination of Jew boys." In the White House Jack Caulfield urged John Ehrlichman to set up undercover units on campuses to augment the FBI efforts. But when J. Edgar Hoover was approached about the units, he killed the idea.[39]

In public Nixon took only modest steps toward draft reform in his first several months in office. The American public supported continuation of the draft. A Gallup poll of 26 January 1969 showed that 62 percent felt the draft should go on, even if the Vietnam War ended. As for an AVF, only 32 percent favored the idea.[40] A survey of young people by the U.S. Youth Council found 61 percent in favor of the AVF, but only

More protests. Courtesy, Library of Congress.

42 percent said they would volunteer for it. Martin Anderson, a White House adviser, recognized the need to educate the public to a new view and urged Nixon to appoint a commission to plan for the AVF. Daniel Patrick Moynihan, a highly regarded liberal in the Nixon administration, supported Anderson. He observed that "if the Selective Service system did not exist, it would be impossible to invent it."[41]

Nixon finally instructed the DOD to begin a study on how to end the draft, and in March 1969 he appointed a committee under Thomas Gates, former secretary of defense, to study the feasibility of an AVF. Like Johnson before him, Nixon thought such studies would help defuse the issue while he worked on the more pressing matter of ending the war. But, as before, public-relations gestures failed. Protesters continued to burn draft cards, and Nixon had to "defuse" such protest or face the same fate as Lyndon Johnson. Unless Nixon acted, warned J. G. Larkin, a Massachusetts Republican, "in just a short time these young men (and women) and their faculty supporters will transfer their unreasonable hate to the new administration."[42]

Several members of the White House staff joined in a call for immediate action to end the draft. A group of manpower specialists, including

Thomas Schelling of Harvard and Stephen Canby of the Rand Corporation, pointed out that the system ignored changing social priorities. Peter Flanigan, a New York lawyer and Nixon staff member, argued that "some sort of cosmetic reform" of the current system should be achieved before an AVF became a reality. There were so many "inequities" in the system that any reform involved little political risk but could pay big dividends among younger people. Flanigan called specifically for delay in the induction of graduate students, replacing the members of the National Selective Service Appeal Board, the creation of a lottery calling the youngest first, and the removal of General Hershey.[43]

Drawing on these ideas, Nixon delivered a message to Congress on 13 May 1969 which established the draft priorities of the new administration. The president claimed that he wished to minimize the disruption caused by the draft as part of his campaign pledge to "bring us together again." He asked Congress for power to create a lottery system, to continue undergraduate deferments, and to delay the call of graduate students for a full academic year. Although this continued privileged protection, Nixon insisted that the nation had "a moral obligation to spread the risk of induction equally among those who are eligible." He promised that, with peace in Vietnam, he would end the draft entirely. But several politicians, seeking to avoid the issue, pointed out that, with the exception of the lottery, Nixon already had ample power to make the changes he wanted. The president had some selling to do. Fortunately, his staff was skilled in marketing and packaging.[44]

In the Nixon White House nothing was more important than selling an image. Any idea had to be packaged and polished and sold like so much lipstick or hair coloring.[45] The president had hardly finished addressing Congress before Bud Wilkinson, ex-Oklahoma football coach and White House staff member, began preparing what he and H. R. Haldeman called the "game plan" for selling draft reform to the public. The staff insisted that the reforms would "almost surely have an impact this fall on the anti-Vietnam demonstrations scheduled for Mid-October and mid-November." Arthur Burns, counselor to the president, argued that such reform was an effective response to campus unrest.[46]

Publicity was important. The Nixon team had to manipulate the press on the issue and feed favored reporters the right information. Soon favorable reaction began appearing. Jack Greene of the *New York News* said Nixon's plan was designed merely "to cool youthful unrest," but Fred Wallace of the Chicago Area Draft Resisters admitted that such changes would hurt recruiting for his group. The *New York Times* and *Wall Street Journal* praised the plan. But the publicity campaign could backfire and work against the AVF. Talk of ending the draft had an indirect effect on the armed forces. One month after Nixon offered his plan the army reported it had missed its volunteer enlistment goal by 9,000 men in the previous fiscal year. And the draft continued to send out induction notices.[47]

At SS, Nixon's message was taken with a grain of salt. Presidents had been promising for years to reform the system, but it continued rolling along like Old Man River. But even the jaded reserve officers who staffed the system had to admit that the level of protest was at an unprecedented high and having an impact on operations. Harassment of local boards forced them to meet at early morning sessions, and a few were forced to close down temporarily. Members even received threatening calls at home. The system stuttered because of the new antidraft counselors who appeared on college campuses and became masters of tying up the bureaucracy with paper work and appeals. The Justice Department seemed ineffective in prosecuting these draft counselors. In fiscal year 1950 only 1 appeal per 1,000 1-A types had appeared. In 1953 there were 47 per 1,000, and in 1969 there were 102 per 1,000.[48]

Nixon's first substantive change in the draft dealt with the appeals. Symbolically, his action had less to do with preventing abuse of the system than with insuring the success of appeals for political reasons. The president had no sooner taken office when Reverend Billy Graham, famous evangelist and Republican supporter, called to complain about the way the SS System was treating his followers among the Campus Crusade for Christ. This organization consisted mainly of athletes who became amateur evangelists and proselytized through the playing field. The issue prompting Reverend Graham's ire was the refusal of the draft to exempt these 4,000 young males as ministers, although they were not ordained.[49]

According to the law, ministerial exemption applied only to full-time, "regularly ordained" ministers. Thousands of Jehovah's Witnesses had gone to jail because of this definition. Graham wanted his crusaders deferred, and some local boards refused. Normally such an action could be overruled by Hershey or the president, but in 1947 Truman had created an independent National Selective Service Appeal Board (NSSAB). This board, which in 1969 consisted of three Democrats who had been appointed much earlier, refused to reverse the 1-A classification. Graham imagined that there was an anti-Christian conspiracy at work.[50]

More realistically, General Hershey explained the problem and offered a simple solution. He had been upset at the independence of the NSSAB since its inception and particularly resented rulings which contradicted his guidelines. He offered to protect Graham's crusaders if the president would abolish the appeal board by executive order. This approach found little support in the White House. Augmenting the power of an unpopular and ancient Hershey, whose removal was even then being planned, seemed dubious strategy. Presidential aides Harry Dent and Jonathan Rose recommended instead that, since the current members of the NSSAB were all Democrats, the president should replace them with loyal Republicans with orders to exempt the crusaders. After several weeks of debate, two of the members were replaced by Republicans. Graham's men then were deferred, but this action did little to relieve the pressure of protesters.[51]

Nixon followed with another cosmetic change aimed more directly at easing youth alienation. Ironically, the new scheme, to appoint youth advisory committees to the draft system in each state, had originated with the supposedly "out of touch" Hershey. After testing the system in five states and finding it innocuous, Nixon decided to make it national. At that point Haldeman decided such a move should redound to Nixon's credit. He thought the launching of the youth committees should be done by Nixon, and "although General Hershey would have to also be present, he will be kept in the background." On 6 June 1969 Nixon introduced a group of young advisers to the press. To improve the operation of the distasteful but necessary draft he insisted that local boards have the advice "from young people about young people." The young advisers were carefully selected, middle-class conservatives with rather narrow ideas. Eventually the 47 youth committees rendered a report that reflected the division of their peers. Some wanted college deferments to continue, others wanted them phased out. The committees had no effect on the course of draft reform, but they did win Nixon some air time to show his concern for youth.[52]

A less superficial reform idea from the White House centered on increasing the representative nature of the local board membership. This issue had been around for several years and had become embroiled in the civil rights movement. By June 1966, only 43 percent of those polled thought local boards were fair in their actions. Local board members served as volunteers; some had served since World War II. They were middle-class, white veterans. But as calls increased for Vietnam arguments arose that boards should represent the youth being called to service. Ted Kennedy in the Senate made an issue of this during hearings in May 1968. From only 267 in 1966, black representation had increased to 1,160 in late 1969, and over 500 Spanish-Americans and 169 women also began serving.[53] In 1966 only 1 percent of board members were black and 12.4 percent of all draftees were of that race. By 1970 almost 7 percent of board members were black but 15.8 percent of all draftees were also black.[54]

The problem involved the social and economic background of board members as well. Since the position paid nothing, only middle- and upper-class males could afford to serve. Nixon tried to solve this problem by revising the residence requirement of board members. The law recommended that a member reside in the county in which the board had jurisdiction. In September 1970 Nixon signed an executive order which *required* that local board members reside in the same county, that none be active or reserve members of the armed forces, and that they be at least 30 years old and need not be male. To supplement this bottom-level reform, Nixon also struck at the top.[55]

Although he had refrained from making threats in his election campaign, Nixon came into office convinced that General Hershey had to be relieved of duty. Hershey was like an embarrassing corpse in a murder mystery, which kept falling out of closets or appearing in bathtubs, to the general consternation of the host. The general was 75 years old, and his views had made him the bête noire of youth during the Johnson years. Although Hershey had strong support in Congress, Representative Donald Rumsfeld warned the president-elect that it would be "a terrible, terrible mistake if he were not replaced." But, although the president approved the removal as early as 17 February 1969, implementing the decision required, as Haldeman was wont to say, a "prep." Flanigan was put in charge of the task.[56]

Weeks passed and Hershey remained in office. Massive protest demonstrations were planned for October and November in Washington and Nixon grew impatient. "The President is anxious to move as quickly as possible on General Hershey," wrote Haldeman, "because of the significance this will have in the youth community." Flanigan, in charge of the removal, found Hershey "as engaging, intelligent and wily as ever," but his image was "a distinct liability," and his removal "of the utmost political importance." Such a "gesture" by Nixon was needed to deflate the predicted student riots in the fall.[57]

Hershey, unfortunately, refused to accept his assigned role in the Nixon play. Because he had relatives serving in Vietnam, the general refused to quit. For the 4,088 local boards and veterans' organizations, Hershey "is Selective Service." To fire him might lead conservatives to charge that Nixon had given in to the protesters. But the president had to act because something was needed to "lessen the steam behind student protest." Republican leaders in Congress also urged action. Since the general refused to retire voluntarily but promised to obey orders, Flanigan finally solved the problem by offering him a reassignment as special adviser on manpower to the president. Nixon agreed to award Hershey a fourth star and a medal. On 10 October 1969 the general slipped into the White House for a short talk with the president, after which the press secretary announced a reassignment effective mid-February 1970.[58]

The reassignment just created new problems. The demonstrations went on as planned. When Dan Rather reported that Hershey's reassignment had been prompted by attempts to defuse the protest, Nixon, consumed with his image, insisted that a correction be leaked to friendly sources. To complicate matters, Flanigan complained that he could not find a replacement for Hershey. Nixon wanted a civilian, someone familiar with the draft who was a good administrator. Several football coaches were suggested, and Nixon felt John Pont of Indiana was "excellent." But he and several others refused to play in the draft game. Finally, Jonathan Rose, a Flanigan aide, suggested Charles DiBona, a DOD weapons-system analyst. But when DiBona appeared before the Senate Armed Services Committee, as part of his confirmation, he made clear that he considered his task to bury rather than reform the draft. He wanted an AVF immediately. This so upset Chairman John Stennis and Senator Margaret Chase Smith that the administration hastily withdrew him. Not until April 1970 did Nixon dragoon Curtis Tarr, an Air Force Department official, into the job.[59]

The delay in removing Hershey had important implications for the crown piece in Nixon's draft reforms—adoption of a lottery or random selection system. Although the general was on record as opposing such

General Hershey with his fourth star. Courtesy, the Hershey family.

a system, he was a loyal bureaucrat, and the White House hoped to use him to sell the idea to a dubious Congress. The idea of a draft lottery was stale with age and had been offered by several leaders as a means of achieving equity. In the Vietnam era the lottery idea had reemerged in the protest over the unfairness of the draft, and the Johnson administration had made several studies of a lottery. Both the DOD and the Marshall commission had recommended using one by early 1967, and Johnson had urged the idea upon Congress, only to be rebuffed. Congress preferred the decentralized system of local boards, and the 1967 draft bill specifically prohibited the president from initiating a lottery system without congressional approval.[60]

In 1968 the idea was reborn. During the campaign Nelson Rockefeller suggested a lottery as a means to achieve equity. Senator Ted Kennedy continued to push the idea, and five separate bills for such a system were introduced in the Senate in early 1969. A poll of Congress by the *Christian Science Monitor* revealed that a majority supported the idea of a lottery, but they also wanted a continuation of college deferments. Under such a system a 19 year old would have only one short exposure to conscription. If he escaped the net, he could relax. In a speech of 13 May 1969 Nixon recommended a lottery aimed at calling first the youngest 1-A members.[61]

Nixon promoted the lottery as an interim cosmetic change. Flanigan, Haldeman, and Moynihan had convinced the president that the idea would help win over alienated youth, and even before his request to Congress, Nixon ordered planning for a lottery at a cabinet meeting on 30 April 1969.[62] The plan that emerged initially was a rehash of Johnson's random selection. A prime draft group for each year would consist of all men aged 19 to 20 who were available and qualified—that is, not including people who were deferred or exempt. An annual national lottery would then establish the sequence of induction by birth date. Such a system was designed to diminish the role of local boards and confront the problem of inconsistency in the draft.[63]

But the lottery had problems of implementation, because the draft was more complex than either Nixon or his staff realized. The president wanted a lottery before the end of the year because antiwar protesters remained active, and three different plans soon competed for adoption. As a quick fix SS officials urged Nixon to use an executive order to establish a prime group of eligibles and change the order of call to whatever age seemed desirable. The lottery would apply to a group born in a particular year, with the order of call established by random selection of birth numbers.[64] The DOD plan, as presented by Melvin Laird, also required that Nixon issue an executive order creating a prime age group. Laird preferred what he called a "conveyor belt" system, which meant a moving age group under which the oldest 19 year old was selected each month by local boards.[65]

Within the White House Stephen Enke, a manpower expert, had a third plan. He insisted that whatever the order of call, it had to be implemented on a national, rather than a local, basis. He said a national drawing of birth dates should be held in the Capitol Rotunda with Bob Hope presiding, but the order sequence of births established by the drawing had to be followed consistently by each local board. Although this approach violated the principle of decentralized control, which Congress supported, Enke assured Martin Anderson that the reform required no change in the law and could be "done fast and silent." Enke also warned that a lottery alone could not solve the problem of equity. The

1-A pool itself was built on the system of deferments, which, to some, was the basis of unfairness.[66]

With protesters all over Washington for a Moratorium Day in mid-October, Nixon had no time to work out quibbles over the lottery. On 15 November a massive March against Death demonstrated the continued strength of the antiwar lobby. Nixon had to persuade the public that he was making a sincere effort at draft reform while winding down the war. Congress passed an amendment permitting a lottery, and Nixon signed it on 26 November. The president announced that random selection would "end the agony of suspense over the draft." The same day he signed a proclamation creating the random selection system and scheduled a drawing for 1 December 1969 to establish a sequence of birthdays for each day of the year. This sequence was to be used to draft from a pool of all registrants who, before 1 January 1970, had reached the age of 19 but had not turned 26. Once a man had a sequence number he kept it as long as he was eligible. On first glance the system seemed to be fair and easily understood. Within weeks, however, the entire operation had become the focus of additional criticism and charges of corruption.[67]

On 1 December 1969 SS officials staged the lottery drawing, using the same fishbowls that had served in 1940. In 1969 the atmosphere was less celebratory. War planes did not fly over, and neither the president nor Bob Hope appeared. Members of the Youth Advisory Committees drew out the numbers. Reactions varied with sequence numbers. When James Fallows, then a Harvard student, heard his birth date called as number 45, he immediately began a diet to obtain a physical deferment. A University of Florida senior whose birth date, 8 June, was drawn last (365) announced he was satisfied with the soundness of the entire proceedings.[68]

The Pentagon predicted a requirement of 550,000 men for 1970 and expected 290,000 to volunteer. This left only 260,000 to be drafted. But, contrary to common sense, the White House estimated that volunteers would come equally from men with both high and low lottery numbers. Draft officials, more sensibly, argued that men with high priority numbers would immediately either volunteer, enter the reserve, or seek deferment, actions that would change the composition of the pool. Some local boards, left with only low priority numbers in the national sequence, would have to call them up to meet quotas. Draft officials predicted that no one was safe, regardless of sequence number.[69]

Nixon tries a lottery. Courtesy, Selective Service System National Headquarters.

Confusion reigned. Within weeks Henry Kissinger, the national security adviser, reported to the president that random selection was in trouble. Statisticians challenged the drawing of the numbers as not being truly random. A surprising number of high priority numbers came from birth dates late in the year. The capsules with the birth dates had been placed in the bowl in chronological order, with January dates going in first and December dates going in last. After a few perfunctory stirs with a paddle, the numbers had been drawn. The December dates remained largely at the top of the bowl. If this were not embarrassing enough, the action of local boards contributed to more chaos. Since each local board was responsible for its own 1-A pool, wide disparities existed in the number of unexamined, examined, and acceptable men in each pool. Some local boards began calling men with sequence numbers in the upper 200s, because there were no lower numbers in their 1-A pool. When the size of the annual call was announced with the sequence numbers, a wild scramble occurred among eligibles. Some men with deferments and low-priority numbers decided to give up their deferred status, gambling they would not be called.[70]

What had promised to be a public relations plus had turned out to be an embarrassment.[71] Nixon, preoccupied with plans to widen the war to force Hanoi to accept American terms, immediately ordered Kissinger and Flanigan to straighten out the mess. Senator Kennedy asked the National Academy of Science to investigate the randomness of the lottery results. Several statisticians denounced the drawing, and some inductees went to court, arguing that their call was illegal because the sequence had not been random. But despite these problems, Flanigan reassured the president that all was under control. Although the drawing had been conducted as described, it still generated enough randomness so that the Justice Department was confident of winning all court challenges.[72]

The randomness of the drawing might have been adequate, but a more serious problem involved the variations in calls by local boards. A national lottery failed to translate into a national draft call because of the inconsistency in local board action. Flanigan tried to make order of the chaos by asking SS to adopt a cutoff sequence number for all local boards. In January no board should call a sequence number higher than 30; or higher than 60 for February. Such a procedure made it impossible for some local boards to meet quotas, but the administration, in its commitment to achieving uniformity, was willing to accept the failure. Such a procedure also seemed in violation of the 1967 draft law. The law read that the president could "recommend criteria" for classifying draftees, and "recommend that such criteria be administered uniformly throughout the United States whenever practical; except that no local board . . . shall be required to postpone or defer any person . . . by reason" of any means or test prepared by the federal government. Draft quotas were levied upon states and subdivisions in proportion to the number of people local boards had in the 1-A pool. The final authority of local boards over classification remained, which meant a national sequence was illegal.[73]

Under pressure from Flanigan, SS ordered local boards, in filling the February call of 19,000 men, to call no man with a sequence number above 60. The state directors responded with dismay as it became clear that local boards lacked enough men to fill their calls. The White House was making the draft look ridiculous, according to acting director Dee

Ingold. The structure of decentralization was being dismantled by a president who made much of his commitment to federalism.[74]

With the lottery a mess, Nixon was even more intent on demolishing the draft. On 14 April staff members finally browbeat Curtis Tarr, an air force official, into accepting the directorship of SS. And at the end of the month Nixon authorized an armed excursion into Cambodia, hoping this last move would speed up withdrawal from the war.

For the president the draft was always an issue of public relations. Although he needed to fill the ranks of the armed forces to maintain credibility in his diplomacy, he was mainly concerned about the draft's cost in his popularity. The lottery had been created to solve that problem. When it failed, Tarr, Haldeman, and Flanigan worked mainly to "prevent further major public relations deterioration" and to get out "positive stories."[75]

Tarr had few illusions about his task as the new director of the draft. Until the AVF could be implemented, the lottery had to be made to work. All problems had to be resolved with "as little public fanfare as possible." Everyone forgot the original mission of the draft. By the end of March SS had failed to meet its quota by 11,700 men, and Tarr began urging a reduction in calls by the armed forces even as Nixon expanded the war. By the end of June Tarr had used up all sequence numbers to 170. At that rate everyone in the pot would be called, so a second lottery was conducted on 1 July 1970, overseen by an army of statisticians. By the end of the year a combination of reduced calls and improved controls had solved the public relations problem. Nixon still needed the draft, but it had ceased to be the main focus of protest.[76]

On 30 April 1970 American armed forces crossed into Cambodia to destroy Vietcong sanctuaries. Air force bombing raids had been hitting the area since 1969. News of the widening of the war sparked huge student protest all across the country. Law officers and National Guard troops killed several students at Kent State and Jackson State universities. Nixon referred to the student protesters as bums. On 9 May radicals conducted a massive protest in Washington and thousands were locked up without being charged. After all of his efforts to cultivate youth, Nixon faced the same chaotic domestic scene that had driven Johnson out of office.[77] Nixon, like Johnson, accused protesters of giving aid to the enemy, upsetting his negotiations, and engaging in senseless violence.

Kissinger remarked that the president had reached a point of exhaustion and psychological crisis.[78]

His anxiety was understandable. By 1970 the SS had referred some 210,000 cases of draft violators to the Department of Justice. In the academic year 1969–1970 the administration counted over 1,800 demonstrations, with over 200 deliberate fires and eight deaths. Bombings and bomb threats occurred by the hundreds. In certain areas of the country, such as Oakland, California, and Madison, Wisconsin, it became impossible to process draftees. When Tarr took office as SS director the mail room was on the lookout for a letter bomb.[79]

Yet most of the violations of draft laws had nothing to do with antiwar protest. About 250,000 eligible men during the Vietnam era never registered with the draft, but at least half of them were delinquent due to ignorance. The majority of those convicted for draft violations were Jehovah's Witnesses, Muslims, or others not active in the draft resistance or antiwar movement of the 1960s. Of the 210,000 cases SS referred to the Justice Department in 1970 only 3,275 led to jail terms. As of 1 March 1971 the FBI had only 3,000 arrest warrants out for draft evaders. While resistance was strong in some regions it hardly existed in most of the country. The vast majority of local boards continued to fill their calls. What eventually caused a slip in delivery was not the protest but Nixon's national lottery system.[80]

The protest outburst in the spring of 1970 was a temporary deviation in a downward trend. Protest declined because troop withdrawals accelerated and draft calls declined. Nixon announced another cut in calls on 14 September 1970. The lottery, for all its confusion, was still in place. Thomas Gates's report calling for an AVF was issued on 20 February 1970, and Nixon seemed committed to its implementation. Counteractions by the FBI and army personnel helped split and discredit the civil rights movement, and the protest ebbed as many young men found it easy to avoid the draft through manipulation of rules and appeals. The courts were also more sympathetic, despite the new tough line on law and order adopted by Nixon.[81]

In late 1969 Attorney General John Mitchell had promised to get tough against draft evaders, to speed up prosecution. "If we find any of these radical, revolutionary, narcissistic kids violate the law, we'll prosecute." But in early 1970 the Supreme Court handed the administration a setback. In the case of *Gutknecht v. U.S.* it found that a protester who burned his draft card or violated the draft law could not be ordered for induction as punishment. Draft officials remained sanguine about their power because Gutknecht was already 1-A and was appealing the refusal to grant him CO status when he destroyed his card. The court did not rule specifically on the power of local boards to remove deferments from those who burned their cards. Justice White restricted his comment to the case before the court, and Justice Harlan said the existing delinquency rules, providing for reclassification, were acceptable provided the registrants' rights were protected.[82]

Although Nixon felt that the draft was more trouble than it was worth, his diplomatic and military actions had not produced the opportunity to withdraw completely from Vietnam. General Giap's Communist forces continued to endure heavy punishment without any weakening of their will, and the North Vietnamese were unmovable at the Paris negotiation table. Given such problems, Nixon accepted the discomforting fact that the draft would have to remain. Even more distasteful, he had to ask Congress to renew the power of induction, which expired 30 June 1971. Despite his desire for an AVF, the president found himself once again grappling with draft reform.

In October 1969 Kissinger informed the director of SS and the DOD that the president wanted a full review of all guidelines for deferments and exemptions. Above all, Nixon wanted new standards adopted that would end inconsistency, something Eisenhower had called for in 1953.[83]

What Nixon really wanted was a plan providing political breathing space so he could continue temporarily the draft, end the war, and then establish an AVF. Enke, in offering a report in late January 1970, tried to meet these needs.[84] He called for an executive order ending all non-student deferments. The class 2-A (occupation deferment) and class 2-C (farm deferment) could be ended easily. In 1970 only 32,000 men were in 2-A, only 1,700 in 2-C, but 150,000 had dependency deferments (3-A), including about 63,000 19 year olds. But if 3-A remained while other deferments were ended, it would create pressure for early marriage and conception.[85]

Equally troublesome were the student deferments (2-S), which since 1967 required congressional approval to end. There were over 1.7 million men at that time holding 2-S classification, and no other deferment generated more charges of class bias in the draft. College officials objected to running draft havens, but if 2-S were ended suddenly, it meant a loss of about 7 percent of undergraduate enrollment for about two years. To ease the shock, if Congress cooperated, the president could permit a drafted student to finish out his academic year before being called. Enke predicted that ending such deferments would enhance the integrity of the lottery.[86]

Despite the logic of Enke's report, it met opposition. The Department of Commerce; Health, Education, and Welfare; and the Bureau of the Budget all had reservations about ending student deferments,[87] and the DOD had major objections. Laird protested the blatantly political tone of the document. It was bad form to argue that the motive for revising deferments was to enhance the prospects for an AVF. Enke also erred in assuming that the draft pool consisted only of 19 year olds. If all student deferments were ended, something would have to be done to ensure that medical doctors retained their liability to age 35, because the armed forces could not get these people without the pressure of a draft. Laird also felt that the age of liability should remain at 19 rather than be dropped to 18.5 as Enke recommended. Finally, Laird and Enke had different ideas on the timing of an AVF.[88]

The optimist in the White House and on the Gates Committee favored creating such a force within one year.[89] Laird and others at the DOD were not so sanguine. The secretary explained on "Meet the Press" that he doubted the armed forces could be reduced to 2.5 million in 1971. Draft calls had been 290,000 in the last fiscal year, and he expected them to be 210,000 in the next fiscal year. But even with these cuts in calls it was clear that the draft was essential. Rather than rush into an AVF, Laird preferred to reduce the inequity of the draft by ending deferments.[90]

Nixon wish to end the draft, not merely deferments, but he had to delay taking a public stand while some agreement was reached between the DOD and the Enke and Gates committees. The point of contention revolved around the timing of ending the draft. Enke and Anderson felt strongly that Nixon should come out for an early end of the draft and take the steps, mainly grant raises, needed to achieve the AVF. Laird and DOD insisted that Anderson and Gates were too optimistic about the number of men who would volunteer and that American military commitments required a continuation and even extension of the draft beyond the deadline. The generals feared losing officers as well as enlisted men if the draft suddenly ended. Laird wanted to end deferments and revise the law to permit a national draft call, but he insisted that the draft be maintained and extended for perhaps two years. In the meantime, the DOD would continue to push volunteering.[91]

At a meeting of the National Security Council on 25 March 1970 the president reluctantly accepted Laird's arguments. The hopes of the ad hoc committee, that the president could end the draft in 1972 just before the election, were dashed. On 23 April 1970 Nixon issued an executive order and sent a message to Congress. He endorsed the Gates report and called for pay increases to make the AVF feasible. But he admitted that he could not end the draft in one year. Instead, his executive order ended occupational, agricultural, and all future paternity deferments. He also asked Congress to pass legislation which would restore his authority to control undergraduate student deferments and establish a national draft call. If Congress acted, he promised to prohibit all new student defer-ments and to insure that the lottery sequence operated consistently in every state. With a rhetorical and hyperbolic flourish, Nixon insisted that his actions demonstrated "our continuing commitment to the maximum freedom for the individual . . . , demonstrated in one more area the superiority of a society based upon belief in the dignity of man over a society based on the supremacy of the state."[92]

Although disappointed at having to renew the draft, the president drew some satisfaction from having replaced Hershey and put his own man in charge of SS. Curtis Tarr, a former college president and assistant secre-tary of the air force for manpower, was a very reluctant appointee to the Nixon administration. Nixon, who knew nothing of Tarr but knew that Congress had rejected DiBona, adopted his most dissimulating manner to sell the appointment. Tarr, Nixon insisted, was an ideal choice because of his youth and his college experience. As for the job itself, Flanigan prompted Nixon to insist that "no other single governmental activity is more important in convincing youth that the establishment is worthy of their support." Unless he changed the image of the draft and created consistent guidelines to local boards, Solicitor General Erwin Griswold warned Tarr, the administration would find it impossible to enforce the law in court.[93]

Tarr rose to these blandishments but was always a reluctant bride.[94] When he first arrived at SS headquarters Tarr found the place "squalid." The people were ancient, the building was collapsing, and the office system was something out of a Dickens novel. Yet the system had suc-ceeded in its primary task for 20 years. Tarr introduced the beauty of modern management, of youth, of computers, all in pursuit, not of im-proving the delivery of men to the service, but of improving Nixon's image and preparing the burial of the draft. Tarr destroyed old draft records and replaced many of the older officials with young management experts. He had more detailed instructions sent to local boards. But when Tarr threatened to close one-third of the boards, he was prevented by Congress. A resolution in the House, signed by such leaders as John Stennis and Strom Thurmond, insisted that Tarr maintain the "present system of operation . . . within local boards within the states." Stennis threatened to fight any draft extension if local boards were closed.[95]

Although discouraged by the opposition and the intractable problems offered by conscientious objectors and court decisions, Tarr labored on. In his final report to Nixon in April 1972 the director tallied up his accomplishments: random selection was working, headquarters had improved its management techniques, the lottery was more random, local boards provided more information to draftees, over half of all draft regulations had been rewritten, and the dream of consistent national calls had been largely realized. Much of what Tarr claimed was true, but most of the changes had come not because of management experts but as a result of the new draft extension law of September 1971.[96]

The president called for the September 1971 extension with a decided lack of enthusiasm. The AVF remained a paper plan, negotiations with both Hanoi and Saigon were mired down, and volunteers were scarce. Congressional leaders feared that if they opened up debate on the draft bill they could expect many radical amendments, some to deny Vietnam service to draftees, and some to end the draft entirely. Enke felt any extension hurt the credibility of the AVF and preferred to draft only a certain number of men. Gates wanted to end the draft, not extend it. Only the DOD insisted on renewal.[97]

Since Nixon's election to office the DOD had been working to end reliance on the draft through Project Volunteer. The goal was zero draft calls, but it remained a dream. In 1970 the DOD estimated a need of 550,000 men. Only 290,000 were projected as volunteers, so 250,000 had to come from the draft. During the year the draft total was scaled down to 204,000 and monthly calls to only 10,000 by September. In March 1970 Laird advised Nixon to call for a two-year draft extension beyond June 1971, although a one-year extension might be acceptable. DOD still projected a need of 750,000 for fiscal year 1971, which would require about 200,000 draftees. Even if fighting ended in Vietnam, Laird

Curtis Tarr stirs the last capsules. Courtesy, Library of Congress.

estimated a need of 200,000 draftees to maintain an armed force of 2.5 million.[98]

In his message to Congress of 23 April 1970 Nixon endorsed the Gates report calling for an AVF but also admitted that the draft would have to be extended beyond 1 July 1971. Both the White House and the DOD announced that even when no draft calls were needed, and no one could predict precisely when that would happen, a standby draft would be needed in the event of total mobilization. Nixon urged renewal in 1970, but Congress refused to act. In January 1971 he again called for action. Accepting Laird's ideas, Nixon called for a two-year extension of induction authority, rather than the four years which had been usual. He also called for several reforms: a phasing out of undergraduate deferments and

exemptions for divinity students, and a reduction of local board autonomy to make possible a consistent national call under the lottery.[99]

Congress received the call with mixed feelings. Congressional attitudes
to the draft had changed dramatically in the previous two years. For most
of its history the draft had enjoyed bipartisan, overwhelming support in
Congress. The Vietnam War cracked the consensus. Although at first
skeptical of all reform, Congress had reversed its ideas. When the Gates
report emerged in February 1970 a bizarre new coalition for ending the
draft also emerged. It included liberals such as George McGovern and
conservatives such as Barry Goldwater. A bill to end the draft in 1971,
sponsored by Mark Hatfield and Goldwater had been defeated in August
1970 by opposition from the White House and Senator Ted Kennedy.
But by the end of the year even old-line supporters of the draft, such as
Stennis in the Senate and Hebert in the House, had come to accept the
need to make radical changes. The continued antiwar protest by college
students had eroded sympathy for college deferments in Congress. Stennis admitted that Nixon's actions and proposals had helped defuse the
issue, and he promised hearings on the administration proposal for a
two-year extension.[100]

The administration bill sent to Congress in early 1971 contained several new features. The authority to induct men was extended for two
years only and the measure also included pay raises for the enlisted ranks.
The raises were designed to make the AVF feasible. The major change
included ending the requirement that national calls be prorated among
the states in terms of the varying pool of 1-As. In the new bill a national
call was established to permit sequences in the lottery to be followed in
all states. Exemptions for divinity students were ended. The president
again received the discretionary power to defer college students, something Nixon had promised to phase out. The liability to the draft for
health personnel was extended to age 35, and special calls for such men
were again authorized. The statute of limitations on prosecuting draft
evaders was extended until they became 32.[101]

As anticipated, the bill drew opposition from both liberal and conservative factions in Congress. On the Senate floor McGovern and Hatfield
again offered a proposal to end all drafting by December 1971. Senator
Kennedy wanted to cut out a $3,000 cash bonus for combat infantrymen,
and Senator Peter Dominici wanted an end to the draft in 18 months.
In response the White House mobilized SS officials, veterans' organizations, and members of the DOD. Wavering senators were offered new

Nixon renews the last draft (1971). Courtesy, U.S. News and World Report.

power projects in their states. But there was much sympathy for an extension of only 18 months.[102]

The president used his powers of persuasion in meetings with senators Stennis and Smith, who were in charge of the floor management of the bill. Both senators preferred a four-year draft extension and had no faith in the AVF, but they vowed to fight for Nixon's proposal. Stennis kept the package off the floor until after the May Day antiwar demonstrations in Washington. The Senate approved a version of the bill which then went to conference. In the House the bill had smooth sailing. A final motion to table the bill in the Senate was fought off in September. Nixon met with senators Mansfield and Scott and explained that the failure of Congress to pass the bill would totally undermine all peace efforts. Presidential reasoning prevailed, and the bill was finally passed into law on 28 September 1971.[103]

As soon as the new law passed Nixon began phasing out all educational deferments. Tarr used the new law to insure that the lottery sequences were followed rigidly by local boards. The general reductions in forces in Vietnam helped smooth the actions. In late 1971 the DOD announced there was a zero draft call for January 1972. Secretary Laird felt he might be able to avoid calls in February as well. These actions dovetailed nicely with Nixon's reelection campaign. [104]

Nixon's reelection enterprise, involving both covert and overt and legal and illegal actions, had been under way for months. Nixon had insisted that all those who had criticized his Vietnam policy be assaulted by Charles Colson's special group. Painting his opponents, especially the Democrats, as comforters of the enemy was Nixon's way of garnering votes from his new majority. George McGovern, the Democratic candidate, was particularly vulnerable because he supported selective conscientious objection, something that both the draft law and the courts had declared illegal. [105]

Killing the draft was again part of the campaign for the president. After having resisted a similar amendment in 1971, on 28 June 1972 Nixon announced that no more draftees would be sent to Vietnam. By July he had cut American forces to only 45,000 (the last combat troops left in August). Nixon and Haldeman considered announcing the end of the draft right before the election. Nixon yearned for such a gesture but Laird refused to cooperate. Instead the president had to settle for an announcement on 28 August that the draft would definitely end in July 1973. He made the announcement because, as he informed Haldeman, such a promise might not be credible if made by Laird. "I think," however, "that if I say that the draft is going to end . . . it would be both credible and very, very effective." The lottery scheduled for 1973 was canceled. On 26 October Kissinger told the press that "peace is at hand" in Vietnam. The draft was effectively dead by spring 1973. Celebrations were aborted, however, because the Watergate scandal was spreading. The AVF came on line but Nixon, on 8 August 1974, resigned. Gerald Ford inherited the new military manpower policy of the United States. For the first time since 1947 the country defended its interests with true volunteers alone. [106]

10

The AVF and the Future

Once again politics triumphed over all. The demise of the draft and the rise of an All Volunteer Force (AVF) illustrate the defeat of theory by context in modern American history. Nixon ended the draft in 1973, but thoretical opposition began earlier. Hanson Baldwin argued in 1941 that the German blitzkrieg had made obsolete the mass army and the draft upon which it rested. A year later the war in Europe returned to the tradition of mass formations, especially on the eastern front. In 1944 the U.S. Army, despite its technology, lacked manpower when fighting in Europe. Eisenhower had had great need for draftees. But after World War II the United States had built up an arsenal of nuclear missiles, and with war becoming more and more technical, the drafting of masses of untrained men seemed ridiculous. Like Baldwin earlier, scholars such as Samuel Huntington wrote that the draft was an anachronism resting on the obsolete idea of massed armies fighting conventional battles. Nuclear deterrence was designed to prevent a nuclear exchange, but, ironically, it enhanced the prospect of conflict assuming traditional mass formations, as in the Korean War.[1]

Other theories predicted the end of the draft because of the general weakening of nationalism in industrial society after World War II. With the advent of the United Nations and hopes for international law, the patriotic enthusiasm needed to call a nation to arms waned. Sociologists, writing under the spell of the antiwar protest, saw the rise in antimilitarism in America demolishing the draft. With the growth of pacifism, augmented by fear of a nuclear exchange, men pointed to the draft as the cause of needless war. B. H. Liddell Hart, the British military authority,

259

had made such a case much earlier with the blunt statement: "Conscription serves to precipitate war, but not to accelerate it."[2]

Economists explained that the fading of the draft was owing to changes in the American economy. By the late 1960s several theorists, led by Milton Friedman of Chicago, argued that the manpower needs of the armed forces could be satisfied on a voluntary basis if the DOD used traditional market incentives. In this argument, the draft was seen as a tax on a small group of American males. But, if a money tax rather than a physical tax was spread throughout the population, enough money was available to raise military pay to a level competitive with the private sector. Attempts to raise military pay had consistently fallen short of needs in the period after World War II, but by the 1970s there were additional incentives to try the market system. Political scientists and sociologists offered a theory explaining the end of the draft which focused on the inefficient administration of SS. The root of the problem, according to some critics, came from the decentralized authority of local boards and the attempt to sustain an increasingly unrealistic myth that men were chosen by "little groups of neighbors." As the entire trend of modernity was toward centralization of authority, such local boards seemed an anachronism. How could a local board in New York City pretend to be familiar with the thousands of men on its rolls? Decentralization had originally been erected to ensure political credibility but now placed too much responsibility on local boards. The evolution of the system after World War II into a manpower management agency, through the erection of myriad deferments, seemed inappropriate by 1970. SS assumed the duty of channeling men into desirable academic fields after World War II because of a temporary shortage of scientific personnel. Such a duty remained in place even as the enrollment of colleges expanded and specialized manpower shortages disappeared by the 1960s.[3]

All of the theories have merit, but none of them alone could have insured the demise of the draft without the political context of the Vietnam War and a leadership keenly attentive to public image and political risk. Context upset theory. For example, cultural critics in the 1960s called into question the benefits of modernization and centralization of authority and spoke of the beauty of local, small operating agencies. The local board principle should have fit nicely in such a climate. But the local draft boards functioned to send men away from home to fight a foreign war perceived as imperialistic by the proponents of the cultural revolution. The political and cultural context favored volunteers over draftees. An anonymous wit once wrote that "if the rich could hire the poor to die for them, what a living the poor would make." Throughout history the rich have hired the poor to die; the hiring of American volunteers in the 1970s was just a variation on this old theme.

Richard Nixon ended the draft, not because of the inevitability of strategic or economic changes or theories of modernization, but because an all-volunteer force made his reelection more likely. Nixon had pledged an AVF in the 1968 campaign despite historical precedent. The all-volunteer army before World War II had been filled with ill-educated, undisciplined men seeking relief from the economic depression. After the war the armed forces began a massive campaign to promote volunteers. The Armed Forces Voluntary Recruiting Act, passed in October 1945, offered enlistments for 12, 18, 24, or 36 months; age eligibility was dropped to 17; and liberal bonuses were offered for enlistment and reenlistment.[4] Some $20 million was spent on posters, pamphlets, promotions, but the army still fell 38,000 below its six-month quota of 180,000 for July–December 1947.[5]

During the 1950s, after the Korean War, Eisenhower made another modest effort at achieving an all-volunteer force. The issue took on political overtones in the 1956 campaign when Adlai Stevenson criticized Eisenhower because of the draft. The Cordiner report called for increased pay and promised an end to the draft if Congress cooperated. Congress did raise military pay levels and reenlistments jumped to 30 percent in fiscal year 1959, but they had dropped back to 21 percent by 1960. Pay was not the most important variable in inducing enlistments or reenlistments. The typical volunteer attracted by the services in the 1950s looked very much like the dropout and disciplinary problem of the 1930s.[6]

When the Democrats regained control of the White House in 1961, the Republicans took the occasion to promote an AVF and denounce the draft. Johnson, aware of the political liability of the draft, studied the feasibility of an AVF, but the DOD reported in July 1966 that, without the draft, deficits in enlistment personnel would range up to 88 percent and officer recruits would drop by 37 percent. The reserve forces could be expected to drop 36 percent in strength. Such figures convinced the Marshall commission studying the draft that an AVF was impossible. Cost estimates for such a force ranged from $4 billion to $17 billion more in defense spending.[7] Such precedents offered Nixon little encouragement for AVF in 1968.

Equally discouraging was the clear superiority of new theories of military manpower procurement. The basic theory for an AVF included disputed ideas. Promoters of the AVF argued that the nature of warfare had shifted since World War II. With strategic atomic weapons the day of the mass armies had come to an end. Also, the skills needed in the new military were more refined than those under the old mass armies.[8] Third, an all-volunteer force was more consistent with American ideals of equity.

But defenders of the draft also had valid theories. The old theory used in 1917—that the draft provided for scientific manpower management—fell in the 1960s before the enthusiasm for egalitarianism. Instead, defenders of the draft insisted that it offered a means of national social integration, while the AVF contributed to alienation of the military from civil life. John D. Rockefeller IV announced on "Meet the Press" that he had changed his mind on the draft. He considered it "one of the truly democratic experiences in this country." It was a "leavening, equalizing, democratic experience." Aristotle had written, "The citizens of a free state ought to consist of those only who bear arms." Secretary McNamara in November 1966 rejected the AVF because it would be too separate from "the life of a nation." Draftees, a scholar wrote, "in a sense civilianize the military . . . and thereby tie it more closely to the fundamental elements of our national life." To attract recruits an AVF had to replicate the benefits of civilian life, but too much replication contributed to military inefficiency. Yet, if the AVF offered a totally alien lifestyle it would attract only alienated misfits, who might use their power for a military coup.[9]

Critics argued that the draft made possible military adventurism, but draft defenders insisted that the presence of large numbers of draftees in the armed forces insured that adventures needed wide public and congressional support. As casualties mounted among the civilians in uniform, or draftees, the impact of the political decision was brought home to the entire home front. The draft meant that the wounded and dead came from all areas of the country, not just from the Midwest, a traditional source of volunteers. The correlation of protest with the decision to expand the draft in the 1960s lent support to this argument.[10]

The theoretical debate could go on endlessly, but Nixon had to act and he did. Although often critcized for catering to mass opinion, in the case of the AVF he was truly an event-making leader. The AVF went against the grain of precedent and opinion. The British adoption of an AVF several years earlier had been disastrous for their armed forces. Despite a pay scale that was higher than in the civilian economy, massive recruiting drives, and a high unemployment rate, the British failed repeatedly to meet their goals for volunteers. Public opinion in England favored a return of the draft. Australia also had tried the AVF but had been forced to return to the draft in the mid-1960s.[11]

American public opinion should have discouraged Nixon. In 1967 a poll of young people found 61 percent favoring an AVF but 58 percent voting not to volunteer. If the government offered to pay all college tuition before military service, only 31 percent of those who said they wanted an AVF offered to volunteer. If the scholarship came after military service, only 12 percent offered to enlist. In 1968 a poll of college freshmen found only 37 percent in favor of an AVF; in 1969 the figure was only 40 percent, and a national poll preferred the draft over an AVF by two to one. By 1970 national opinion had become split on the issue, and college freshman favored the AVF by 65 percent. But this change just meant the college students wanted to avoid service. A 1971 poll among males 16 to 21 found 65 percent opposed to volunteering.[12] Columnists were divided, and Michael Harrington, the socialist writer, felt the AVF was just a scheme to hire working-class people to die for the upper class. With such disagreement, Nixon had his work cut out for him in winning approval for an AVF.[13]

The president himself had come rather late to the AVF camp. In the 1960 election campaign he was still insisting upon the need for the draft, but AVF was a natural in the politics of 1968. The protest around the country focused on the coercion of conscription, and the fact that Republicans should offer a remedy to what they labeled a Democratic draft was as predictable as repeaters in Chicago elections.[14] After the election victory Martin Anderson continued to prod Nixon, explaining that AVF was an issue that Nixon could "use to establish a rapport with the youth of the country." Because Anderson and others on the staff doubted the Pentagon's commitment to ending the draft, Nixon decided to appoint a special blue ribbon panel to generate an AVF plan.[15]

On 27 March 1969 Nixon announced the formation of a Presidential Committee on an All-Volunteer Force (PCAVF) chaired by Thomas Gates, former Republican secretary of defense. Gates had earlier denounced the draft for "warping the whole national attitude toward civic responsibility." It was well known that Nixon was committed to the success of the AVF concept for political reasons, and the membership and staff of the PCAVF were heavily weighted with individuals who agreed with him. Reverend Theodore Hesburgh, president of Notre Dame and committee member, explained to a correspondent that "many of us on the commission are determined to do all in our power to eliminate conscription." Crawford Greenewalt complained that the entire commission staff was engaged in lobbying for AVF. Yet when the commission was first formed, Gates reassured the committee members that, despite Nixon's hopes for the AVF, they were free to support or reject the idea.[16]

The commission began its work with a pessimistic briefing from Secretary Laird. He explained that DOD was already involved in Project Volunteer, designed to expand the number of true volunteers and reduce dependency on the draft. But the armed forces needed 700,000 men each year, and by the most optimistic reading only 350,000 true volunteers had appeared the previous year. Particularly worrisome for defense officials was the way in which ending the draft would alter enlistments in reserve units. Veterans remembered that in June through December 1941, when a draft lottery started, the total strength of reserve components dropped some 45,000 below statutory minimums. Finally, Laird's officials disagreed with assumptions by Gates's staff about the cost of the AVF.[17]

More discouraging opinion emerged after the Gates committee had conducted several surveys. Veterans' organizations disputed the percentage of "true volunteers," putting a much lower estimate on them than the DOD. National Guard officials insisted that without the draft they would be ruined. The Executive Council of the AFL-CIO also preferred the draft and local boards, but wanted an end to educational deferments. Several critics agreed with DOD that an AVF was too costly and would bankrupt the country.[18]

But estimates on the cost of ending the draft always varied wildly. In 1966 Thomas D. Morris informed Congress that it would cost over $17 billion, plus a pay raise of 280 percent, to achieve an active force at preexpansion levels. Several studies done in 1966 and 1967 came to the same conclusion. If there was a 4 percent unemployment rate in the civilian economy, it would still cost $8 billion a year to obtain enough volunteers. And this expense did not cover providing recruits for the reserves, ROTC, or the National Guard.[19]

Rather than studying seriously such criticisms, the Gates commission labored at length to rebut them. To the charge that the AVF would be manned by lower-class blacks, Anderson and the commission responded that this was demographically impossible. But if blacks found the AVF a promising opportunity, to deny it to them was racism. To the charge that an AVF would draw disproportionately from the lower class, the commission answered that AVF meant that no income group "would bear an unjust proportion of coercion." The AVF would be like a new plant opening in the neighborhood with open employment rules. To counter charges that the AVF might lead to dictatorships, several commission studies showed that draft armies also led to coups and that the small size of the volunteer force would inhibit presidential rashness in diplomacy.[20]

Weathering all criticisms, Gates and the commission kept their course, propelled by an antidraft protest which grew stronger and more bizarre. The desire to end the draft, rather than the virtues of AVF, created an unexpected political coalition. Into this group fell left-wing groups such as SANE, Women's International League for Peace and Freedom, and the Americans for Democratic Action, as well as conservative groups such as the Young Americans for Freedom. Jim Sutton of the U.S. National Student Association wrote to Gates, "Our views are quite simple: conscription is immoral." This antidraft movement provided solid support for AVF.[21]

The commission rebutted charges that volunteers would be too costly and relied on the wisdom of the true intellectual father of the AVF. No one played a more important role in selling the idea to members of the government and the public than Milton Friedman, Chicago economist, free-market advocate, and commission member. As early as April 1967 Friedman had insisted that the draft was un-American and wasteful. The deferment system "jams colleges, raises the birth rate and fuels the divorce courts." He estimated that an additional $4 billion in the budget would buy an AVF of 2.7 million men. To those worried about hiring the underclass, he insisted that "equal opportunity" was important.[22]

Through a combination of obsequious questioning and arrogant blandishment of numbers, Friedman swept his foes from the field. He argued over and over that three-fourths of the opposition to the war was because of the draft. AVF could end most of the protest, and Nixon could then conduct his foreign policy without such distractions. Using the work of Walter Oi and Bruce Chapman, Friedman contended that the draft was a tax in kind. A raise in combat pay of only $1,000 a year, costing only half a billion dollars, would generate a sufficient number of volunteers. In his mind, this was a small price to pay for ending a system which eroded patriotism, and "thwarts the natural desire of youths to commit themselves to society." To complaints by Secretary of the Navy John H. Chafee that there would be a shortage of officers without the draft, Friedman repeated that the draft hurt the image of the military and generated the protest.[23]

Friedman was a persuasive advocate, but not all commission members were convinced. Gates supported AVF not for economic reasons but because he found the use of draftees for combat in Vietnam particularly unfair and a source of the war's unpopularity. But General Lauris Norstad, General Al Gruenther, and Crawford Greenwalt had serious reservations. Norstad argued that the AVF would lead to inferior enlisted men. Gruenther worried about the creation of a military elite. And Greenwalt thought the AVF impractical and feared a lack of volunteers. A minority felt that the AVF was not as feasible as the draft report indicated. The majority obtained a unanimous final document only after inserting the recommendation that SS be kept on a standby basis. Gates presented the report to the president on 21 February 1970.[24]

In substance the report reflected the ideas of Milton Friedman and Adam Smith. The preamble expressed the principles of classical liberalism and fears of government domination of individual freedom. Ending the draft would "limit the military's influence on the setting of social priorities in America." An AVF would return to the American tradition of free choice, restore the dignity of the armed forces, and offer an honest outlet for the natural patriotism of youth. The report also assumed that the United States had to maintain an armed force of between 2 million and 3 million because the role of world policeman remained. But since half of all volunteers were true volunteers, the military needed to recruit only 325,000 men a year. These numbers could be had without any pay increase, if the force level were reduced to 2 million men. The report did call for pay raises because of equity needs, but only a modest increase of $2.7 billion in defense appropriation. As for the reserves, a raise in pay would provide adequate staffing. The document assured the president that all could be achieved by mid-1971.[25]

As well he might, since it followed his lead, Nixon applauded the commission's work. But he urged members to participate in a campaign of education to sell the AVF proposal to the "movers and shakers" of mass opinion, and the selling began the same day the report appeared.[26]

Gates insisted to the press that the AVF was consistent with maintaining a strong military establishment for many years to come. He described as realistic the recommendation that the AVF be implemented by June 1971. Reverend Hesburgh, with a particularly pollyanna-like vision, insisted that if the draft were ended college kids would again support the government.[27] Friedman scolded Secretary of Defense Laird who expressed doubts about AVF in an appearance on "Meet the Press." The professor argued that there were only two viable options facing the administration: either extend the draft after 30 June 1971, which would be a disaster, or follow the Gates report recommendation and implement AVF in 1971. Friedman insisted that upon reflection he felt the report had been too high in estimating the cost of the AVF, because "I underestimated the inefficiency of conscription." Friedman urged Laird to get on the bandwagon.[28]

The AVF bandwagon soon carried an unusual collection of political figures. Friedman was driving, but in the backseat were a group of radicals, liberals, and conservatives. The National Council to Repeal the Draft, headed by Thomas C. Reeves, included antiwar activists such as Benjamin Spock and Gordon Zahn, as well as Mrs. Martin Luther King, senators Ernest Gruening and George McGovern, theologian Harvey Cox, and Ralph Abernathy. The council applauded the Gates report and urged a quick end to the draft, no later than 1 July 1971. Dr. Spock found himself embarrassed to agree with Nixon. Initially skeptical about the president's promise to end the draft, Spock, with sophomoric enthusiasm, embraced the Gates report. The draft had to be ended, the pediatrician felt, because it offered a "blank check authorization to the White House and Pentagon to prosecute any war they choose."[29]

Those critics trying to sidetrack the AVF express labored in vain. L. James Binder, editor of *Army Magazine*, set a recurring theme by denouncing the translation of military service into a marketable commodity by the Gates commission. Raising the price or wage insured a higher number of recruits in this scheme. Binder also felt the report's assumption about the idealism of youth was sheer hogwash. Joseph Califano, one-time adviser to President Johnson, insisted that adopting a volunteer system would remove the "greatest inhibition on a President's decision to wage war." Without the draftees in Vietnam, little protest would have emerged according to these critics, who saw things from the reverse side of Dr. Spock's mirror. Columnist Stewart Alsop wrote that only the draft could raise enough men for combat. The *New York Times* editorialized that it would be impossible to keep an army in Vietnam with volunteers alone. Curtis Tarr, on a tour of Vietnam, reported that all the enlisted men he interviewed said the same thing.[30]

Such sentiments drew public attention, but Nixon was more bothered by the dissenting views of the military establishment. The Gates group called for an AVF in 1971. But the president could not ignore the virtually unanimous military opinion in favor of draft extension in 1971. DOD analysis of foreign manpower systems revealed that there was no substitute for the draft if the United States wished to remain a world power. In April 1969 Laird had launched Project Volunteer, headed by Roger Kelley, with the goal of ending the need for draftees. Yet Lt. General Albert Connor, head of army personnel, predicted to Congress a drop in quality without the draft and more disciplinary problems. Connor told the House Appropriation subcommittee, "I cannot see an all-professional Army doing much more than separating away from the people."[31]

The official report by Project Volunteer, like the Gates report, followed Nixon's guidelines about ending the draft, but was less enthusiastic about meeting the president's goal. Drawing upon studies by each service branch, by academics, and by foreign governments, defense officials announced that there were too many variables operating to determine the feasibility of an AVF. Size of the armed forces was one major variable, but another difficulty was the motivation for volunteering and the number of true volunteers. Various studies seemed to demonstrate that more pay alone had little impact on recruitment. In surveys done in the United States, young males responded most positively to the offer of a four-year college scholarship in exchange for four years of active duty. But this method was expensive and hardly provided the type of career man that Gates projected. Spending another half billion per year for housing improvements might help with retention, but not with recruitment of new men. Defense officials concluded that such uncertainties required renewal of the draft. Nixon kept this pessimistic appraisal confidential, so as not to undermine Gates's rosy estimate, but the press soon discovered it.[32]

When Laird sat before the panel of "Meet the Press," headed by the ageless curmudgeon, Lawrence E. Spivak, the secretary tried to follow the White House line. He emphasized that the United States was winning in Vietnam. Under the Nixon doctrine the nation had no plans to provide massive ground forces for wars in the third world. But then he threw cold water on the AVF idea by saying that defense studies recommended that no date be set for an end to the draft and that the United States should concentrate on reforming the procedure rather than rushing into an AVF. He agreed that the draft should eventually be phased out, but he could not specify a particular date and felt that 1971 was certainly too early.[33]

In a private letter to Nixon, Laird made his objections stronger and more detailed. He said Gates was wrong in asserting that zero draft calls could be achieved by July 1971. DOD estimates were that draft calls could be cut to 5,000 a month only in early fiscal 1973. Gates's report also exaggerated the idea of the influence of pay on recruitment and its influence on retention. Laird recommended that Nixon phase out draft deferments and call for legislation to allow a national call in the lottery. In other words, clean up the draft and forget the AVF for the next few years.[34]

The Pentagon officials then began to praise the draft. An army general insisted that the draft provided outstanding quality in military manpower. "We have come to rely upon them [draftees]," he insisted, "to perform the technical jobs for the modern Army." Another officer commented, "I do not know of a single Army officer who favors returning to an all-volunteer force." He thought quality would drop too drastically and the force would be all black. He also believed it impossible to man an armed force of 2.5 million with volunteers. An air force general added that the draft insured high quality for his branch and that he "would be amazed if the . . . all-volunteer force works."[35]

Before Nixon could resolve this division in his selling campaign, Congress began assuming the initiative on the AVF. Polls of congressional sentiment in 1969 had shown that while a clear majority favored an AVF, an even larger majority insisted that it be adopted only after the Vietnam War was over. Senator Stennis, a key player in any manpower reform, was growing increasingly disenchanted because the administration had issued a report on the AVF which the DOD had rejected. Stennis insisted that most of the pro-AVF sentiment in Congress really represented antiwar sentiment. Personally, he preferred draft reform but wanted the administration to make a firm decision to go for either draft renewal or an AVF.[36]

Soon bills were introduced in both houses to implement Gates's recommendation. Senate bill 503 had as bipartisan co-sponsors Mark Hatfield, Barry Goldwater, Robert Dole, Gaylord Nelson, and George McGovern. The House bill was sponsored by William A. Steiger (R-Wis.) and Allard K. Lowenstein (D-N.Y.). Hatfield wrote Nixon that the bill was general and provided considerable presidential discretion. The senator was anxious to "learn if you approve." But Nixon was boxed in. To endorse the bill offered a victory to the "peaceniks" and a slap in the face to the president's own military advisers. But to reject the bill meant rejecting the recommendations of his own AVF commission. To make the political scene even messier, Senator Kennedy opposed the Gates recommendation and the Hatfield bill and had recommended ending all deferments but retaining the draft.[37]

For the next several weeks the White House debated the pros and cons of various tactics for a message to Congress. There was political allure in ending the draft before the 1972 election, but too many obstacles were raised. From Kelley at DOD came assertions that X amount of money could not guarantee Y amount of recruits. Kelley also doubted Gates's assumption of youth patriotism. No one could be sure of how much the antiwar movement had jaundiced youth about volunteering for a military career. Gates had also not taken world events and employment rates into consideration.[38]

Before Nixon's draft message was sent to Congress, it passed through the hands of Ehrlichman, Kissinger, Laird, and, most decisively, Robert P. Mayo, director of the budget. After pointing out that the Gates recommendations meant more spending, Mayo concluded that there was no flexibility in the budget unless Nixon approved "unacceptable cuts in the Defense program." Larry Lynn of the National Security Council also insisted that the Gates commission had seriously miscalculated cost. The AVP was impossible without causing a big deficit or higher taxes. Given this information, Nixon decided to ask Congress for draft reform and extension in 1971, still hoping for political credit. The administration worked to defeat the Hatfield bill, and Nixon issued his message in April 1970.[39]

After derailing congressional radicals, the president began his own campaign for an AVF. Confident of his Vietnam strategy, even as he called for draft renewal, Nixon ordered the DOD to put an AVF into effect by June 1973. The projected size of the armed forces under such a plan remained vague. Gates had insisted that 2.4 million was a possible figure, but Laird insisted that 2 million was the maximum strength obtainable by volunteer methods alone. To win the Pentagon over, Nixon recommended that the draft be extended for at least two years after July 1971. In addition, the administration bill offered a major increase in pay for first termers, promised to spend much more on education and training, and ROTC scholarships. It also promised to build 400,000 new quarters for the troops and to expand recruiting by buying more television and radio time.[40]

Nixon went along with these concessions because he was firm in his commitment to replace the draft in 1973, whatever adjustments had to be made. The army created 16,000 new ROTC scholarships and in 1971 spent an average of $2,585 recruiting dollars per man. Projected strength levels for the armed forces dropped, and Gates's idea of 2.5 million men was soon forgotten. By 1972 Laird had cut the figure to 2.3 million, and, in his January 1973 budget message, Nixon spoke of 2.2 millon. Manpower costs as a percentage of the total defense budget rose from 34 percent in 1964 to 40 percent in 1973. Large raises went into effect in 1972, and the combination of more spending and fewer personnel permitted Nixon to end the draft in June 1973, after which the DOD immediately announced the success of the AVF.[41]

The AVF represented Nixon's triumph of will in military manpower, but the checkered history of the institution over the following decade offers an opportunity to compare it with what America had gained and lost by relying on conscription from 1940 to 1973. For AVF the most basic problem was simply finding volunteers. The rhetoric of the Gates report about the patriotism of American youth turned out to be more wishful than prophetic. In 1973 army recruiters in Fall River, Massachusetts, a location with a 7.2 percent unemployment rate, offered a $1,500 enlistment bonus. The local paper misprinted the bonus figure as $15,000. Despite this inflated figure, no one turned out. The army missed its recruiting goal so consistently and by such a large margin up to 1975 that one defender of the AVF charged deliberate sabotage.[42]

After 1975 the situation seemed to improve briefly. One reason was the continued reduction of armed force strength to 2 million by 1980. Another factor involved fraud by recruiters. In 1979, 393 recruiters accepted 12,720 fraudulent enlistments by faking high school diplomas and other means. In 1979 the army said that 47 percent of the nation's high schools refused to provide student names to recruiters, and that year all of the services failed to meet their quotas for the first time. Demographers predicted that the male cohort of 18 year olds would shrink until the mid-1990s, and in 1984 recruiters had to sign up one of every two male, noncollege men. Retention rates also declined. The navy, one of the most attractive service options, reported that its retention rate dropped from 90 percent in 1971 to 62 percent in 1979. The army Ready Reserve virtually collapsed, with a shortage of over 300,000 in 1980. Some 60 percent of reservists failed to finish their initial term. By 1980 problems of cost and quality also appeared.[43]

The cost of the AVF was affected by many variables in the civilian economy and the political orientation of the White House. But certain overall trends became clear. In 1971 the army offered a bonus of $2,585 for special enlistments. In 1985 the navy offered its fighter pilots lump sum bonuses of $36,000 for reenlisting. In 1968, under the draft and with a 3.5-million-man armed force, personnel costs had stood at $32 billion, or 42 percent of the defense budget. By 1974 the total strength had declined to 2.2 million but personnel costs stood at $43.9 billion, or 56 percent of the budget. Strength had declined by 37 percent, but costs had risen 30 percent. Yet the increase in cost reflected much more than just recruitment of enlisted men. More money was going into increased retirement benefits, higher officer pay, and covering the cost of more dependents. The AVF had more married personnel and more women who had children at government expense. In estimating cost, the General Accounting Office (GAO) seemed at a loss. In 1978 GAO reported that the AVF cost $18 billion more than the draft would have for the same force. Yet under President Reagan the same office reported that the AVF cost $2.6 billion less than a drafted force.[44]

Another apparent failing of the AVF was easier to document. Critics from both the left and the right in the 1960s had denounced the draft because it forced the poor to die for the rich and was antiegalitarian. Yet by the 1980s Richard A. Gabriel wrote that "an examination of the social composition of the AVF reveals it to be one of the most unrepresentative social institutions in American history." Several sources documented the same problem. These objections remained ineffective because, unlike service in the 1960s, no one in the armed forces was dying in battle.[45]

The AVF consisted largely of the lower class and poorly educated minorities. Yet both critics and defenders of the AVF insisted that intelligence was closely correlated with performance, discipline, and retention rates. Defenders of the system constantly pointed to the rise in years of formal education by first-time enlistees. Although the number of first timers who had some college education dropped from 13.9 percent in the draft-influenced class of 1964, to only 3.2 percent in 1979, the percentage of recruits with high school diplomas continued to climb until it reached almost 90 percent in 1984. In 1964 only 71 percent of all draftees had diplomas.[46]

But this apparently encouraging sign ignored the general degradation in value of a high school diploma. Evidence of the degradation appeared when the services tested the new graduates with a battery of exams. In the four categories of performance in the battery, category 1 represented the highest score, and category 4 the lowest. In 1964, under the draft, some 42 percent of all new men tested in categories 1 and 2. In 1971 draft calls dropped and the percentage of category 4 climbed from 26.7 percent to 40 percent. In 1979 only 27 percent reached category 1 and 2 levels. In 1978 the army reported that 57 percent of all its recruits were in category 4. More disturbing, the Pentagon admitted in 1979 that its test had flaws which inflated grades, so that perhaps one-quarter of all testing in category 2 were really in category 4. Congress became so upset that in 1981 it mandated that only 25 percent of category 4 types were to be permitted in any recruiting class.[47]

If performance correlated to intelligence, several rather frightening reports become more understandable. A survey in 1976 found that 53 percent of all infantrymen at Fort Benning read at only a fifth-grade level. An army survey of automotive repairmen in 1978 discovered that less than half could perform their specialty. In 1983 the navy found that 48 percent of its new recruits had recently used drugs and that there were 23,000 cases of alcoholism among active duty personnel. In 1985 a massive survey of recruits from 1983 and 1984 found that 20 percent were unable to read at a ninth-grade level, yet 88 percent of them had high school diplomas.[48]

Taking so many men with low test scores translated into a wide variety of other problems besides functional ability. Like the pre–World War II army, the AVF faced serious morale, disciplinary, and retention problems. Part of the cause of the problems was the outlandish methods used by recruiters to reach their quotas. Television ads suggested that recruits spent all of their time learning to operate sophisticated electronics or expensive hardware. None of the men apparently had to kill anyone; there was no waiting around; there was no boredom. KP ended, short-order menus arrived in the mess hall, beer was dispensed in the barracks, and go-go dancers performed in the service clubs. It was simply impossible for service life to live up to the expectations generated by recruiting campaigns.

Disillusionment meant at worst desertion, the rate of which doubled under the AVF from the pre-Vietnam period. At best, it meant quitting, which was permitted under the new enlistment contract. The Gates commission had stressed the savings that would accrue from the longer four-year term of volunteers rather than the two-year term of draftees. But by the late 1970s service records showed that over 40 percent of all volunteers had failed to finish their first year. The draftee army had lost an average of 20 percent in the first year. From 1973 to the early 1980s there were over 600,000 discharges for misconduct, personality conflicts, and other reasons. The army admitted that 20 percent of its personnel were using drugs once a month, and they still dropped out.[49]

By the late 1970s the AVF had become a sensitive issue, not because of the presence of illiterates, nor because of the declining retention rate, nor the morale problem. The big problem was the large number of black soldiers. Here was an issue that had provoked consternation in the 1960s, led civil rights leaders to join the antiwar crusade, and provoked a major internal reform of SS. Critics had warned of the danger of an all-black volunteer force. The rejoinder was always that it could not happen and that equal employment opportunity was a blessing for blacks. In 1978 Clifford L. Alexander, Jr., secretary of the army, insisted that color made no difference in soldierly competence, and columnist George Will dismissed figures on blacks with a "so what?"[50]

Defenders of the AVF justified their position by pointing to military service as a means of social uplift, an argument that had also been used by draft advocates. After all, the draft forced the alleged uplift upon even the lazy, while the AVF helped only those who volunteered. But proving the benefits of military service stretched the imagination. Various studies showed various results. Felons who were paroled into the armed forces during World War II had had a much lower recidivism rate than men who had been paroled directly to civilian life. Undoubtedly, military life in World War II and later provided opportunities for lower-class men to gain more self-esteem. Many were put in the rare position of directing individuals with higher social and economic standing. But how long did such effects last in civilian life? The gain in esteem by lower-class individuals may have been balanced by the loss in esteem by highly educated men forced into demeaning tasks.[51]

Equally nebulous were claims about military duty leading to unique attitudes later in life. Such a question raised concern in 1968 because some 13 percent of the total population—23 percent of the adult population, and 47 percent of the adult male population—were veterans. The old canards about military duty inculcating authoritarian tendencies in youth were farfetched. Studies of authoritarian tendencies were rather tendentious, but a sociologist who studied such cases concluded that nonveterans were more belligerent than veterans. Authoritarianism apparently decreased with the level of military training. Margaret Mead reported that her veteran students after World War II showed an increased dislike of authority and no evidence of military brainwashing.[52]

Some surveys showed that veterans, even after Vietnam, were more likely to favor military service for their sons than nonveterans. After Vietnam there seemed to be a slight rise in feelings of guilt among nonveterans for not having served.[53] Yet surveys conducted in the 1960s by Gallup, Roper, and the National Opinion Research Center found it difficult to isolate veteran status from other variables, such as occupation and education, in determining opinions. The surveys also failed to distinguish between the length of service of veterans, officer veterans from enlisted veterans, and draftees from enlistee veterans.[54]

Several studies in the 1970s questioned the value of military training once an individual left the service. More than twice as many volunteers as draftees served in their preferred activity. Naturally, combat-related training had the least convertability; health care–related training the most. The Veterans Administration might insist that millions of enlisted men left the service with some civilian skill, but the more important question was whether the skill level acquired was higher than would have been obtained in civilian life. In 1968 the College Entrance Board of New York reported the results of a College Level Exam Program (CLEP) test given to 43,877 servicemen from July 1965 to December 1966. Only 4,200 of the men had attended college, but over 18,000 scored at a level above that expected from someone who had completed one year of college. Such results supported those who insisted that a tour of military duty was worth a year of college. Unfortunately, the military tour was two years and, especially in the 1960s, more perilous than a year on campus.[55]

AVP advocates applauded because black enlistees benefited from miliary service. As one scholar put it, the more disadvantaged a youth, the more he gains from military service. This was proven in studies of income.[56] But because variables affecting income over an adult life span are many and complex, only very raw associations can be established for large populations. One study in 1967 found that of the 47.8 million males 25 and older in the civilian, noninstitutionalized population, the median income was $5,500. The 20.7 million who were veterans, however, had a median income of $6,600. A comparison between mean annual earnings for veterans and nonveterans by race between 1958 and 1964 found that veterans earned more in both races. Yet these figures did not prove that military service alone led to increased income. And none of the studies seemed to substantiate the claims by veterans that military service had been decisive in their later success.[57]

As the least discriminating service with the greatest needs, the army depended more and more on black enlistees to fill quotas. In 1955 blacks had represented only 8 percent of all service personnel. In 1964, with the draft, some 12 percent of army enlisted men were black. From 1972 to 1979, under the AVF, black enlisted strength rose by 103,000 and white strength dropped by 400,000. In fall 1978, 40 percent of all new recruits were black, and in combat units the percentage was higher. The 197th Combat Brigade was 33 percent black and its combat units over 50 percent black. The First Armored Division was 38 percent black. Generally, black recruits had graduated from high school and had more education than the average white recruit. Black enlistees were more representative of black society than white recruits were representative of white society. This trend seemed healthy because it did provide employment opportunities, without discrimination, to a segment of the population with a high unemployment tradition.[58]

As Secretary Alexander said, the issue was competence not color. Such nice words, along with the economic attractiveness of the AVF, glossed over a potential political problem. As Stokely Carmichael and Rap Brown had demonstrated in the 1960s, throwing so many blacks into combat could provoke charges of genocide. Joseph Marshariki, the head of a group called Black Veterans for Social Justice, predicted problems if black soldiers were ever sent to fight in Africa. The army insisted that the line soldier would do his duty, but black politicians would also do their duty for their constituents. The social composition of the AVF might provide a check on how and where it could be used.[59]

Given the problems with the AVF—before the Soviet invasion of Afghanistan in January 1980—several public figures began agitating for a return of the draft. Senator Stennis had reassured everyone in a report issued 31 December 1978 that the AVF was working well and it had "quality equal to or superior to that achieved under the draft." But other leaders knew better. Senators Sam Nunn of Georgia, Sonny Montgomery of Mississippi, David Boren of Oklahoma, Ernest Hollings of South Carolina, and Representative Robin Beard of Tennessee began questioning publicly the capability and social composition of the AVF. Evaluation seemed necessary because in late 1979 the DOD admitted that for the first time every service had missed recruiting quotas.[60]

The Joint Chiefs were calling for three additional divisions for West Germany. In January 1979 President Jimmy Carter called for a Rapid Deployment Force and Secretary of Defense Harold Brown urged full staffing of the reserves. General Edward C. Meyer, army chief of staff, told Congress he had only "a hollow Army." Chief of Naval Operations Admiral Thomas B. Hayward spoke of "a hemorrhage of talent." On 13 and 14 December 1979 the Hoover Institution sponsored a conference on the viability of the AVF and the advisability of renewing the draft.[61]

It was ironic that critics of the AVF accused the system of inequity and lack of representativeness, the same accusations that had once been used to lash the draft. Without doubt the AVF was much less representative than the drafted military had been. But, except for a few high-placed critics, the public remained indifferent, probably because the United States was at peace.[62]

In January 1980, however, President Jimmy Carter was dealing with several problems on foreign soil. A year earlier Shah Mohammed Reza Pahlevi, occupant of the Peacock Throne in Iran, had fled the country before a raging mob led by the religious leader Ayatollah Khomeini. In November 1979 Iranians had stormed the American embassy and had taken hostage 53 Americans in protest of the United States offering medical assistance to the cancer-stricken shah. The man every American president since Eisenhower had counted on to stem communism in the Middle East lay drugged in the Western Hemisphere, while America's position in the Fertile Crescent lay in tatters. And on 27 December 1979 Soviet troops entered Afghanistan to support a coup and install a puppet government. In June 1980 a faulty computer in the American defense command sent a signal that Soviet missiles were flying toward the United States.

In a reversal that makes history the bane of the determinist, Carter, who in 1977 had extended a presidential pardon to all men convicted of violating the draft act during the Vietnam War, began considering a return to conscription. Secretary of Defense Brown and Director of the Budget James McIntyre called for upgrading the registration capability of a standby SS System. In April 1979 a Gallup poll reported that 76 percent of all those questioned and 73 percent of the men in the draft-eligible cohort favored registration. But an unneeded bill in the House to reinstate registration was defeated 259 to 155. On 31 July 1979 Carter announced that the administration was reconsidering registration as a "precautionary measure." Although draft calls and authority to induct had ended in 1973 and registration in 1975, the SS law remained on the books. Under it the president had the power to renew registration without a new law, but he had to obtain the money from Congress.[63]

Faced with the crises in diplomacy, Carter requested money from Congress for registration on 23 January 1980. His bill called for registering both men and women turning 19 and 20 in the summer. Thereafter each person would register upon reaching age 18. Congress replied with the rhetoric of the Vietnam era. Senator Mark Hatfield opposed the return to the draft, but even defenders of the draft, such as Senator Nunn, objected to the registration of females, because it confused a message sent to Russia with "sociological issues." The administration, however, won votes by pointing to the importance of the Persian Gulf to America's economy and arguing that registration did not mean conscription. Having the information in SS computers would save several months in mobilizing for an emergency. Congress finally authorized the money, but prohibited female registration, and on 27 June registration returned to America. But about 9 percent of those eligible failed to register.[64]

This failure was partially the consequence of the political rhetoric of the 1980 presidential campaign. In the Democratic camp, candidates Edward Kennedy and Edmund (Jerry) Brown opposed registration. Independent candidate John Anderson also opposed it. In the Republican camp, Ronald Reagan opposed it, but George Bush supported it. When Reagan won the nomination, the Republican platform called for a repeal of this new burden on individual rights. During the campaign Carter tried unsuccessfully to paint Reagan as a warmonger, but the Republican's theme of returning America to greatness struck sympathy in many a patriotic breast, even among those who rejected registration. Reagan pledged to end the registration and replace it with better pay and benefits for the AVF. He defeated Carter in a landslide, taking 489 electoral votes, 43.9 million popular votes, and 43 states to Carter's 49 electoral votes, 35.5 million votes, and 6 states.

Reagan won mainly because of rampant inflation in the economy, the hostage situation in Iran, and Carter's general failure in dealing with Congress. In one of his first addresses as president, at West Point in May, Reagan repeated his distaste for the draft. Unlike other nations, he insisted, the United States held to the sacred tradition of a "military always composed of citizen volunteers." West Pointers applauded this dubious rendering of the American military tradition even as international events forced a reconsideration.[65]

At the White House on 7 January 1982, Edwin Meese, presidential counsel, read a statement by President Reagan. Despite campaign pledges and repeated reassurances, Reagan announced that he planned to continue registration of young males under SS. "We live in a dangerous world," wrote the chief executive, and "in the event of a future threat to national safety, registration could save . . . as much as six weeks in mobilizing emergency manpower." But, he reassured young males, there would be no return to the draft except in a "severe national emergency."[66]

Once committed to registration, Reagan acted to insure compliance with the law. An ad campaign aired on radio and television saying that registration was the law. Men who had failed to register during the first year faced prosecution. Beginning in June 1982 the Justice Department proceeded with selective action against 160 men. The Supreme Court upheld the action, and Congress cooperated by tying registration to federal education benefits. Protest disappeared, and registration became a regular part of maturation for male adolescents. Even as he made registration work, Reagan also provided incentives to overcome the recruitment crisis for the AVF. Carter had raised military pay by 11.7 percent, but Reagan got another 14.3 percent increase. More important, Reagan's general economic policy created a 10 percent unemployment rate, mak-

Now machines do it all. Courtesy, Selective Service System National Headquarters.

ing the AVF much more attractive. By 1981 all services were meeting their recruiting goals and retention rates were up.[67]

Reagan's solution to the AVF recruiting problem failed to satisfy those critics who looked beyond cost and numbers. In July 1982 General Andrew Goodpaster and former Secretary of Defense Robert McNamara joined Nunn and others in calling for a return to the draft to insure a socially representative military. Even Senator Gary Hart of Colorado, a former antiwar activist, began urging a draft for national service. All the old arguments were rehashed. Draft supporters spoke of reenforcing concepts of citizenship, insuring popular concern with foreign policy actions, overcoming military isolation from society, creating better socioeconomic representation, easing high youth unemployment, and strengthening character and health. Opponents of the draft also repeated the same litany: draftees were short term, expensive, and unprofessional. A draft was an unequitable burden in a democracy. During Reagan's term the General Accounting Office issued two studies, both of which insisted that the AVF was much cheaper than a drafted force. As the 1988 election rolled around the prospects of a new draft remained dim.[68]

Both of the main candidates in the presidential race, George Bush and Michael Dukakis, endorsed the AVF. The Pentagon released information in October showing that 90 percent of all new recruits had a high school education, compared to only 75 percent of the civilian population. Black enrollment leveled off at about 20 percent. The GAO announced that the AVF cost $2.6 billion less than a drafted force of the same size and ability, whatever that meant. Senator Nunn continued to utter complaints, but no one was listening. After Bush won the election, he and the departing Reagan agreed on a 3.6 percent pay raise for all military personnel, because the army had failed to meet its recruiting quota for the first quarter of the fiscal year. Problems obviously still existed.[69]

In late summer 1989 the Pentagon provided information on recruiting obstacles. The unemployed rate had declined, but more important, the age cohort was shrinking. Males and females between 18 and 24 were a diminishing portion of the population. Some relief came from the reduction of the total strength of the armed forces, from 2,174,000 in 1987 to 2,129,000 in 1989. But the army and marines continued to miss recruiting goals. David J. Berteau of the Pentagon complained that the proportion of recruits who signed enlistment contracts a year in advance of reporting was down to 42 percent of the goal, and continued to decline. The percentage of recruits in all services who had a high school education began to drop again.[70]

Within months, however, the armed forces seemed too large and recruiting goals of little interest. Bonuses had been used to retain men; now bonuses were used to retire men. Mikhail Gorbachev's new leadership in the Soviet Union revised the Communist system. The Warsaw Pact collapsed, and the Berlin Wall fell. Congress began demanding a peace dividend. The growing federal deficit led politicians to sharpen their knives for the defense budget. Peace had broken out, and the West had won the cold war. The AVF performed indifferently in two Gilbert and Sullivan adventures in Grenada and Panama. But in early 1991 American electronic air power made a shambles of Saddam Hussein's Iraqi forces in Kuwait. Ground forces met little resistance, concerns raised by critics of the AVF remained untested, and the draft remained distrusted.

The basic problem of drafting scientifically in a democracy was unresolved. The tensions conscription generated between the myth of efficient, centralized manpower utilization and the myth of equality of sacrifice in a democratic polity remained unrelieved. Such tensions had evaporated in a popular World War II with its massive mobilization and in peacetime when few were drafted. But in limited war conflicts, with marginal public support, the draft could not sustain itself for long. But neither had the all-professional volunteer force proved itself in anything beyond very quick and clean action against minor opposition. What would happen if the United States again required a mass army for a lengthy tour is anyone's guess in the 1990s.

Notes

Chapter 1. Introduction

1. For Marwick's ideas see Keith L. Nelson, *The Impact of War on American Life* (New York: Holt, Rinehart, Winston, 1971), p. 3n; Richard H. Kohn, "The Social History of the American Soldier: A Review and Prospectus for Research," *American Historical Review* 86 (June 1981):566; Walter E. Kaegi, "The Crisis in Military Historiography," *Armed Forces and Society* 7 (Winter 1981):310; and John W. Chambers II, "The New Military History: Myth and Reality," *Journal of Military History* 55 (July 1991):395–406.

2. Russell F. Weigley to author, 9 July 1991. See also Weigley, *History of the United States Army*, enl. ed. (Bloomington: Indiana University Press, 1984), and William L. Hauser, *America's Army in Crisis: A Study in Civil-Military Relations* (Baltimore, Md.: Johns Hopkins, 1973), p. 154.

3. Herman Beukema, "The Social and Political Aspects of Conscription: Europe's Experience," in Jesse B. Clarkson and T. C. Cochran, eds., *War as a Social Institution: The Historian's Perspective* (New York: Columbia, 1941), pp. 114–18, and Louis Morton, "The Origins of American Military Policy," in Martin Anderson, ed., *The Military Draft* (Stanford, Calif.: Hoover Institution, 1982), p. 47.

4. Quoted in Walter Millis, *Arms and Men: A Study of American Military Experience* (New York: Putnam, 1956), p. 54.

5. William H. McNeill, "The Draft in the Light of History," in Anderson, *The Military Draft*, p. 62; Jacques Van Doorn, *The Soldier and Social Change* (Beverly Hills, Calif.: Sage, 1975), p. 56, writes: "The size of the army is an inverse function of the volunteer/conscript ratio."

6. Eliot A. Cohen, *Citizens and Soldiers: The Dilemma of Military Service* (Ithaca, N.Y.: Cornell, 1985), p. 37.

7. Engels quote in Morris Janowitz, *Military Conflict* (Beverly Hills, Calif.: Sage, 1975), p. 71; Roosevelt quote in Robert P. Friedman and Charles Leistner, eds., *Compulsory Service Systems* (Columbia, Mo.: Artcraft, 1968), p. 300; Johnson quote in *Selective Service Newsletter* (hereafter cited as *SSN*), April 1967, p. 6. In the United States the draft during the 1960s played a role in the adoption of a constitutional amendment reducing the voting age to the draft age of 18.

8. For the tie between voting rights and compulsory military service see Stanislav Andreski, *Military Organization and Society*, 2d ed. (London: Routledge & Kegan Paul, 1954), pp. 116, 145, and Janowitz, *Military Conflict*, pp. 71, 74–77.

9. Huntington argues that more professionalism in the armed forces means more political neutralization. But see Van Doorn, *Soldier*, pp. 59 and 99, who argues that

the key to preventing coups may be the level of political maturity of the state. The refusal of draftees to obey regular officers in the attempted French army coup against de Gaulle in 1960 is cited by people favoring a conscript army, but the debate goes on; see Steven L. Canby, *Military Manpower Procurement* (Lexington, Mass.: Heath, 1972), p. 43; Hauser, *America's Army*, p. 213; and Janowitz, *Military Conflict*, p. 76.

10. For discussion of the issue see McNeill, "The Draft," p. 64; George E. Reedy, *Who Will Do Our Fighting for Us?* (New York: World, 1969), p. 124; and I. B. Holley, Jr., *General John M. Palmer: Citizen Soldiers and the Army of a Democracy* (Westport, Conn.: Greenwood, 1982), pp. 525, 607. Quote in H. Scott, "Comments on Compulsory Military Service," in Anderson, *The Military Draft*, p. 519.

11. Quote in Robert Cuff, "American Mobilization for War, 1917–1945: Political Culture vs Bureaucratic Administration," in N. F. Dreisziger, ed., *Mobilization for Total War* (Waterloo, Ont.: Laurier University, 1981), p. 84. Such advocacy of the citizen-soldier myth has met with strong objections in recent years, and the association of conscription with a broadening of the franchise has been dismissed. First and foremost the nineteenth-century states sought to enhance the size of their armies, and although the world wars of this century, with their high military participation rate, may have contributed to a leveling effect, they also enhanced the power of the state. Therefore, the draft can also be seen as a manifestation of a trend toward totalitarianism, even in parliamentary democracies. The argument that the army acts as a school for citizens has also been turned on its head, with critics now arguing that military life generates despotic, drug-addicted individuals.

12. See Arthur Marwick, *The Home Front: The British and the Second World War* (London: Thames & Hudson, 1976), p. 182.

13. Quoted in Adam Yarmolinsky, *The Military Establishment: Its Impact on American Society* (New York: Harper & Row, 1971), p. 131.

14. Donald D. Stewart, "Local Boards: A Study of the Place of Volunteer Participation in Bureaucratic Organization" (Ph.D. dissertation, Columbia University, 1950), p. 3; Cuff, "American Mobilization," pp. 73, 86. Morris Janowitz sees the army in the 1950s as moving "from an organization ruled by 'domination' to one of managerial philosophy." Yet we should note that even with centralization the various military branches continued to fight their own bureaucratic wars after World War II. Indeed, the unification of the armed forces in the United States just insured that three, rather than one, military lobbies would confront Congress. See Charles C. Moskos, *The American Enlisted Man: The Rank and File in Today's Military* (New York: Sage, 1970), pp. 14–15; Morris Janowitz, *The Professional Soldier: A Social and Political Portrait* (New York: Free Press, 1960), a classic study; and Samuel Huntington, *The Common Defense: Strategic Programs in National Politics* (New York: Columbia, 1961), p. 371.

15. Johnson quote in *SSN*, April 1967, p. 6; other quote in Cuff, "American Mobilization," pp. 85, 73–74; Arthur Marwick, "Problems and Consequences of Organizing Society for Total War," in Dreisziger, *Mobilization*, p. 12, and Gary L. Wamsley, *Selective Service and a Changing America* (Columbus, Ohio: Merrill, 1969), pp. 212–13.

16. Van Doorn, *Soldier*, p. 51.

17. Van Doorn (ibid., p. 55) argues that the military mobilization of mass armies schooled leaders in methods of mobilizing society for domestic purposes, but there is little evidence of such a trend in the United States. Nor can we expect a surge of individualism in society as mass armies disappear.

18. Andreski, *Military Organization*, p. 102.

19. Ibid., p. 136.

20. Michael Useem, *Conscription, Protest, and Social Conflict: The Life and Death of a Draft Resistance Movement* (New York: John Wiley & Sons, 1973), p. 81, and Moskos, *American Enlisted Man*, p. 180.

21. Jack Rafuse to director, 27 June 1969, President's Commission on All Volunteer Force, Box 9, RG 220, National Archives, Washington, D.C. (hereafter cited as PCAVF); James A. Barber, "The Military Services and American Society: Relationships and Attitudes," in Stephen Ambrose and James Barber, *The Military and American Society* (New York: Free Press, 1972), p. 300; and Millis, *Arms and Men*, pp. 104, 97, 133, 25, 31, 135. See also Albert B. Moore, *Conscription and Conflict* (New York: McMillan, 1924); James McCague, *Second Rebellion* (New York: Dial Press, 1968); and Adrian Cook, *The Armies of the Street: The New York Draft Riots of 1863* (Lexington: University of Kentucky, 1974).

22. Millis, *Arms and Men*, pp. 173, 198; Holley, *Palmer*, pp. 715–16.

23. See John W. Chambers II, *To Raise an Army: The Draft Comes to Modern America* (New York: Free Press, 1987), for a detailed discussion of the origins and operation of the World War I draft.

24. Kohn, "Social History of the American Soldier," pp. 562–63.

25. See Beukema, "Social and Political Aspects of Conscription," p. 480, and Kohn, "Social History of the American Soldier," p. 564. My thanks to an anonymous critic at the University Press of Kansas for the distinctions in types of politics.

26. M. R. D. Foot, *Men in Uniform: Military Manpower in Modern Industrial Societies* (New York: Praeger, 1961), p. 108.

27. The issue of appropriate criteria to evaluate the draft has drawn attention from a highly respected group of authors. See especially Canby, *Military Manpower*, pp. xviii, 53–54, 62; Kenneth E. Boulding, "The Impact of the Draft on the Legitimacy of the National State," in Sol Tax, ed., *The Draft: A Handbook of Facts and Alternatives* (Chicago: University of Chicago, 1967), p. 191; Wamsley, *Selective Service*, p. 15; Reedy, *Who Will Do Our Fighting for Us?* pp. 44, 55; Huntington, *The Common Defense*, p. 1; Stewart, "Local Boards," p. 203; Foot, *Men in Uniform*, pp. 108, 154–55; and Roger W. Little, "Compulsion: Implications for Change," in Little, *Selective Service and American Society* (New York: Russell Sage, 1969), p. 3.

Chapter 2. Creating Conscription, 1940–1941

1. Quote in Walter Millis, *Arms and Men* (New York: Putnam, 1956), p. 268.

2. See Wayne S. Cole, *Roosevelt and the Isolationist, 1932–1945* (Lincoln: University of Nebraska, 1982), and Robert Dallek, *Franklin Roosevelt and American Foreign Policy, 1932–1945* (New York: Oxford, 1979), for a general discussion of this diplomacy. On mobilization steps see Millis, *Arms and Men*, pp. 266–74, and Robert K. Griffith, Jr., *Men Wanted for the U.S. Army* (Westport, Conn.: Greenwood, 1982), pp. 175, 177, 180–83.

3. Griffith, *Men Wanted*, pp. 175, 177, 180–81; Marvin A. Kreidberg and M. G. Henry, *History of Military Mobilization in the United States Army, 1775–1945* (Washington, D.C.: USGPO, 1955), pp. 425, 463; and Millis, *Arms and Men*, pp. 271, 274.

4. J. Garry Clifford and Samuel R. Spencer, Jr., *The First Peacetime Draft* (Lawrence: University Press of Kansas, 1986), p. 120.

5. Millis, *Arms and Men*, pp. 271–74; Griffith, *Men Wanted*, 175, 177, 180–83.

6. Clifford and Spencer, *First Peacetime Draft*, tell this story in detail; for information on sponsorship of the bill see chapters 5 and 6.

7. John W. Chambers II, *To Raise an Army: The Draft Comes to Modern America* (New York: Free Press, 1987), p. 164, discusses motives for the World War I lobby which was resurrected in 1940. Clifford and Spencer, *First Peacetime Draft*, p. 27.

8. Clifford and Spencer, *First Peacetime Draft*, chapters 10 and 11; I. B. Holley, Jr., *General John M. Palmer: Citizen Soldiers and the Army of a Democracy* (Westport, Conn.: Greenwood, 1982), pp. 590, 593, 602–4; and Griffith, *Men Wanted*, pp. 186–87.

9. Quotes in Clifford and Spencer, *First Peacetime Draft*, p. 13.

10. Clifford and Spencer, ibid., establish the decisive importance of the Clark group in initiating and promoting the passage of the first draft. They imply that Clark's ideas were also realized in the law, but the War Department and the JANSSC plans were ratified in the law.

11. Ibid., p. 109.

12. Ibid., pp. 112–13.

13. For problems in World War I mobilization see Chambers, *To Raise an Army*, chapter 7; for British volunteer problems see Peter Dennis, *Decision by Default: Peacetime Conscription and British Defense 1919–39* (Durham, N.C.: Duke University, 1972).

14. Albert A. Blum and J. D. Smyth, "Who Should Serve: Pre–World War II Planning for Selective Service," *Journal of Economic History* 30 (February 1970):385, 387, 388, 391, 395–99; Col. H. C. Kramer, "Selective Service," lecture, 11 October 1934, Box 1, RG 147-97, NA; Statement by Douglas MacArthur, 13 May 1931, Box 2, ibid.; and Hugh S. Johnson lecture, 20 October 1939, ibid.

15. Kramer, "Selective Service Lecture," 11 October 1934; Johnson lecture, 20 Oct. 1939; see also file VF 330.2S13, Lewis B. Hershey Papers, Military History Institute, Carlisle, Pa. (hereafter cited as LBH).

16. See George Q. Flynn, "Selective Service and the Conscientious Objector," in Michael F. Noone, ed., *Selective Conscientious Objection* (Boulder, Colo.: Westview Press, 1989), pp. 35–55.

17. Ibid. For the evolution of attitudes of COs see Charles C. Moskos and John W. Chambers, eds., *The New Conscientious Objection: The Secularization of Objection to Military Service* (forthcoming, 1992).

18. Neal M. Wherry, "Ministerial Exemptions, 1940–45," file E97, Box 59, RG 147, NA.

19. Ready to Woodring, 21, 25 November 1939, and Woodring to Ready, 1 December 1939, both in file 345, Box 24, RG 147-97, NA; E. Raymond Wilson, "Evolution of the C.O. Provisions in the 1940 Conscription Bill," *Quaker History* 64 (1975):8; Patricia McNeal, "Catholic Conscientious Objection during World War II, *Catholic Historical Review* 61 (1975):223–34; R. R. Russell, "Development of Conscientious Objector Recognition in the United States," *George Washington Law Review* 20 (1951–52):430–31; Selective Service System, *Conscientious Objection*, Special Monograph no. 11, 2 vols. (Washington, D.C.: USGPO, 1950), 1:1, 75, 141; Mulford Q. Sibley and Philip Jacob, *Conscription of Conscience: The American State and the Conscientious Objector, 1940–1947* (Ithaca, N.Y.: Cornell, 1952), p. 48; and Wherry paper, file E97, Box 59, RG 147, NA. Deferments for divinity students did not require school accreditation, only recognition by a denomination.

20. Ulysses Lee, "The Draft and the Negro," *Current History* 55 (July 1968):30; Col. John Langston to Hershey, 11 April 1938, file 171.81, Box 48, RG 147-97,

NA; U.S. Department of Commerce, *Historical Statistics of the United States: Colonial Times to 1970*, 2 pts. (Washington, D.C.: USGPO, 1975), 2:15–18.

21. Richard M. Dalfiume, *Desegregation of the U.S. Armed Forces* (Columbia: University of Missouri, 1969), p. 31; Lee, "The Draft," p. 31; and Selective Service, *Special Groups*, Special Monograph no. 10, 2 vols. (Washington, D.C.: USGPO, 1953), 1:29, 46.

22. See John O'Sullivan and A. M. Meckler, eds., *The Draft and Its Enemies: A Documentary History* (Urbana: University of Illinois, 1974) for a history of opposition to conscription.

23. Quote in Holley, *Palmer*, p. 596; Kreidberg and Henry, *History*, p. 577; Denis S. Philipps, "American People and Compulsory Military Service" (Ph.D. diss., New York University, 1955), p. 407; Griffith, *Men Wanted*, pp. 188–191; Sullivan and Meckler, *The Draft*, pp. 174–75; E. T. Katzoff and A. R. Gilliland, "Student Attitudes on the World Conflict," *Journal of Psychology* 12 (October 1941):228.

24. Clifford and Spencer, *First Peacetime Draft*, pp. 167, 205–8.

25. Ibid., pp. 210–21.

26. Griffith, *Men Wanted*, pp. 191–92; Clifford and Spencer, *First Peacetime Draft*, pp. 186, 218, 220–21; 231; Philipps, "American People," p. 404; Philip A. Grant, Jr., "The Kansas Congressional Delegation and the Selective Service Act of 1940," *Kansas History* 2 (March 1979):196, 198–99, 202, 204; and Glenn H. Smith, "Senator William Langer and Military Conscription, 1945–1959," *North Dakota Quarterly* 37 (Autumn 1969):15.

27. Quote in FDR to L. B. Sheley, 26 August 1940, Box 103, War Department, PSF, Franklin D. Roosevelt Papers, Roosevelt Library, Hyde Park, N.Y. (hereafter cited as FDR); Griffith, *Men Wanted*, p. 191; Grant, "Kansas," p. 196; Clifford and Spencer, *First Peacetime Draft*, pp. 191, 194, 201, 203, 204.

28. U.S., *Statutes at Large*, vol. 54 (13 and 16 September 1940), pp. 885–97.

29. Ibid.

30. Ibid.

31. Ibid.

32. Ibid.

33. Ibid.

34. Walker S. Edwards, "The Administration of Selective Service in the United States" (M.A. thesis, Stanford University, 1948), p. 38.

35. Gary L. Wamsley, *Selective Service and a Changing America* (Columbus, Ohio: Merrill, 1969), p. 155.

36. *New York Times*, 10 November 1940, 7:9.

37. Victor A. Rapport, "Sociological Implications of Selective Service," *American Sociological Review* 6 (April 1941):227–29.

38. Stephen Early memo to Forster, 13 October 1940, Box 1, OF 1413, FDR, for quote; Early memo for James Rowe, 21 September 1940, ibid; President statement, 19 September 1940, Box 8, OF 1413C, ibid.

39. *New York Times*, 18 October 1940, p. 8; ibid., 17 October 1940, p. 1; FDR memo for Director of Budget, 3 September 1940, Box 5, OF 1413, FDR; Clifford and Spencer, *First Peacetime Draft*, p. 223.

40. See p. 117 in this book for draft categories.

41. EMW to President, 8 October 1940, Box 103, War Dept. file, PSF, FDR; Rowe to President, 7 October 1940, Box 1, OF 1413; and Harold Smith and James Rowe to President, 14 October 1940, War Dept. file, Box 103, PSF, FDR.

42. *New York Times*, 23 October 1940, p. 12; 27 October 1940, p. 2.

43. Clifford and Spencer, *First Peacetime Draft*, p. 1; Presidential press release, 29 October 1940, PPF 4404, FDR; *New York Times*, 23 October 1940, p. 12; 30 October 1940, p. 1; 31 October 1940, p. 8.

44. FDR memo for Secretary of War, 19 September 1940, Box 103, PSF War Dept., FDR; Minutes of Harold Smith conference with President, 24 September 1940, Smith Papers, presidential conferences, vol. 12, FDR; Harry A. Marmion, *Selective Service: Conflict and Compromise* (New York: Wiley, 1968), pp. 8–10; Robert H. Jackson to President, 28 September 1940, Reel 116, item 2711, George C. Marshall Papers, VMI, Lexington, Va. (hereafter cited as GCM); *New York Times*, 16 October 1940, p. 10.

45. Donald D. Stewart, "Local Boards: A Study of the Place of Volunteer Participation in Bureaucratic Organization" (Ph.D. diss., Columbia University, 1950), pp. 5, 67, 70, 72, 119; Wamsley, *Selective Service*, p. 86; FDR to Governor George D. Aiken, 21 September 1940, Box 1, OF 1413, FDR; Dykstra to Susan M. Kingsbury, 23 October 1940, Box 7, misc., OF 1413, ibid.

46. *New York Times*, 3 November 1940, p. 1; Science Research Association, Inc., *Unfit for Service: A Review of the Draft and Basic Education in the Army* (Chicago: SRA, Inc., 1966), p. 17, and Chief of Staff memo for Gen. Watson, 4 October 1940, Box 1, OF 1413, FDR.

47. *New York Times*, 1 November 1940, pp. 11–13; 7 November 1940, p. 52; and 16 April 1941, p. 20; Hershey memo to Major Gen. Watson, 2 October 1940, Box 1, OF 1413, FDR; and Minute book for LB 104, Franklin County, Mass., 14 August 1941, File E61, Box 3, RG 147, NA.

48. Langston for Col. O'Kelliher, 28 February 1941, Box 69, RG 147, NA.

49. *New York Times*, 27 November 1940, p. 22; 24 November p. 37; 3 December 1940, p. 19; 6 December 1940, p. 25; and 28 December 1940, p. 8; Lee Kennett, *GI: The American Soldier in World War II* (New York: Scribners, 1987), p. 6; *Unfit*, p. 196.

50. *New York Times*, 17 October 1940, p. 13; 24 December 1940, p. 6; 2 February 1941, p. 25; 3 April 1941, p. 18; 17 April 1941, p. 22; 4 May 1941, p. 2; 8 March 1941, p. 6; 18 July 1941, p. 9; 3 August 1941, p. 28; 15 September 1941, p. 10.

51. Ibid., 18 October 1940, p. 29; 23 December 1940, p. 26; 14 April 1941, p. 19; 25 January 1941, p. 18; 12 December 1940, p. 38.

52. Ibid., 16 January 1941, p. 28; 21 February 1941, p. 24; 25 February 1941, p. 29; 26 February 1941, p. 25; 8 May 1941, p. 28; 6 December 1941, p. 21; 21 June 1941, p. 12; 14 June 1941, p. 12; 13 June 1941, p. 23; 12 June 1941, p. 30; 11 Jan. 1941, p. 9; 30 March 1940, 5:6; 6 August 1941, p. 23; 22 November 1941, p. 17; 10 September 1941, p. 31; 18 October 1941, p. 14; 1 February 1941, p. 12; 20 October 1940, p. 19.

53. Ibid., 23 February 1941, 5:1; Griffith to Watson, 12 April 1941, Box 9, OF 1413, FDR; Digest of Significant Memos, Selective Service, 1941, file E37A, vol. 1, RG 147, NA; *New York Times*, 25 February 1941, p. 28; and Kennett, *GI*, p. 15.

54. Patti M. Peterson, "Student Organizations and the Antiwar Movement in America, 1900–1960," *American Studies* 13 (Spring 1972):141; *New York Times*, 17 October 1940, p. 14; 15 November 1940, p. 1; 29 December 1940, p. 20; 31 December 1940, p. 16; and 8 February 1941, p. 8.

55. *New York Times*, 3 June 1941, p. 15; 11 November 1941, p. 46; and Lewis B. Hershey, *Legal Aspects of Selective Service* (Washington, D.C.: USGPO, 1969), pp. 6–7.

56. *New York Times*, 20 October 1940, p. 20; 1 November 1940, p. 10; 12 July 1941, p. 11.

57. Ibid., 9 April 1941, p. 29; 26 June 1941, p. 24; 24 January 1941, p. 10; and Digest of Significant Memos, Selective Service System, 1941, file E37A, vol. 1, RG 147, NA.

58. *New York Times*, 2 February 1941, p. 25; 5 March 1941, p. 23; 4 September 1941, p. 13; 16 September 1941, p. 13; 27 November 1941, p. 5.

59. Donald D. Stewart, "Selective Service Appeal Boards," *Southwestern Social Science Quarterly* 31 (June 1950):30–31, 33; *New York Times*; 10 November 1940, 4:10; 18 December 1940, p. 51; 22 March 1941, p. 7; 5 May 1941, p. 10; and 16 June 1941, p. 8.

60. U.S., *Statutes at Large*, vol. 54 (13 and 16 September 1940), p. 888.

61. Quote from *New York Times*, 22 January 1941, p. 13.

62. Ibid., 13 December 1940, p. 20; 9 December 1940, p. 22; 14 January 1941, p. 27; 22 January 1941, p. 13; 22 February 1941, p. 8; 29 June 1941, p. 31; 4 May 1941, p. 1; 15 November 1941, p. 13. Hershey to Rep. A. Leonard Allen, 20 May 1941, File E15, Box 68, RG 147, NA; Kennett, *GI*, p. 13; Local Board minute book, 4 March 1941, E61, Box 3, RG 147, NA; idem, 30 July 1941, ibid.; *Historical Statistics*, 1:20.

63. George Q. Flynn, *Lewis B. Hershey: Mr. Selective Service* (Chapel Hill: University of North Carolina, 1985), pp. 110, 116–17; *New York Times*, 20 October 1940, 2:4; 24 October 1940, p. 28; 17 December 1940, p. 20; and 9 February 1941, p. 38.

64. See Daniel S. Hirshfield, *The Lost Reform: The Campaign for Compulsory Health Insurance in the United States from 1932 to 1943* (Cambridge, Mass.: Harvard, 1970), for this story.

65. Hershey memo to state directors, 6 October 1941, Box 31, RG 147–97, NA; *New York Times*, 13 November 1940, p. 15; Eanes file, 20 May 1941, VF 434E125, Lewis B. Hershey Papers, Military History Institute, Carlisle, Pa.; George Q. Flynn, "American Medicine and Selective Service in World War II," *Journal of the History of Medicine and Allied Sciences* 42 (July 1987):311–12, 314; *New York Times*, 27 Nov. 1940, p.1; 1 December 1940, p. 48; 6 April 1941, p. 43; 15 April 1941, p. 7; 1 May 1941, p. 22; 18 June 1941, p. 20; and 19 October 1941, 4:8; Kennett, *GI*, p. 27; Memo, May 1941, Box 50, RG 147–97, NA; "Medical Division History, 1941," p. 7, Box 50, ibid.

66. Flynn, "American Medicine"; West quoted in *New York Times*, 31 May 1941, p. 13; Mrs. Roosevelt quoted in ibid., 17 December 1940, p. 20; Lee quoted in ibid., 21 April 1941, p. 3; also ibid., 16 November 1941, p. 14; 28 May 1941, p. 12; 27 May 1941, p. 20.

67. *New York Times*, 1 April 1941, p. 12; 6 September 1941, p. 17; 8 June 1941, p. 39; 17 April 1941, p. 14; 24 February 1941, p. 9; 28 November 1940, p. 26; and "Medical Division History, 1941," Box 50, RG 147–97, NA.

68. See Flynn, "American Medicine."

69. *New York Times*, 30 May 1941, p. 10; 16 November 1941, p. 40; and Flynn, *Hershey*, p. 96.

70. Hershey to Charles Poletti, 27 May 1941, Box 31, RG 147–97, NA; Dargusch to Rowntree, 3 July 1941, "Medical Division History," Box 50, ibid.; *New York Times*, 18 June 1941, p. 14; 22 July 1941, p. 21; 16 August 1941, p. 7; and 21 August 1941, p. 9.

71. *New York Times*, 4 October 1941, p. 8; Hershey to Mrs. Roosevelt, 23 Sep-

tember 1941, Box 8, OF 1413–misc., FDR; Hershey to President, 10 October 1941, Box 1, OF 1413, ibid.

72. *New York Times*, 11 October 1941, p. 1; Smith conference with President, H. Smith conferences, vol. 12, 14 October 1941, FDR.

73. *New York Times*, 18 October 1941, p. 10; Hershey to President, 27 October 1941, Box 8, OF 1413–misc., FDR; Smith memo for FDR, 11 December 1941, Box 8, OF 1413, ibid.

74. Keith L. Nelson, comp., *The Impact of War on American Life* (New York: Holt, Rinehart, Winston, 1971) p. 101, and *New York Times*, 26 October 1940, p. 35.

75. See George Q. Flynn, *The Mess in Washington: Manpower Mobilizaton in World War II* (Westport, Conn.: Greenwood, 1979), chap. 1, for discussion of planning; Ford quoted in *New York Times*, 21 November 1940, p. 20; ibid., 24 November 1940, 3:7; 20 October 1940, 3:1; 25 November 1941, p. 46; and 28 October 1940, p. 1.

76. *New York Times*, 23 February 1941, p. 26; 2 March 1941, p. 12; 12 March 1941, p. 42; 19 April 1941, p. 8; 3 May 1941, p. 1; 17 May 1941, p. 8; 18 May 1941, p. 38; 26 May 1941, p. 8; 26 July 1941, p. 13; and Jack F. Leach, *Conscription in the United States: Historical Background* (Rutland, Vt.: Tuttle, 1952), ii.

77. *New York Times*, 2 January 1941, p. 8; 20 November 1940, p. 8; 8 November 1940, p. 8; 20 October 1941, p. 7; 12 October 1941, p. 36; 4 September 1941, p. 14; 2 September 1941, p. 28; 25 August 1941, p. 1.

78. Chambers, *To Raise an Army*, p. 159; Clifford and Spencer, *First Peacetime Draft*, p. 211.

79. Flynn, *Hershey*, p. 72.

80. Diary of Harold Ickes, 7 October 1940, p. 4883, Manuscript Room, Library of Congress, Washington; Dykstra quote in *New York Times*, 2 December 1940, p. 16; and Albert A. Blum, *Drafted or Deferred: Practices Past and Present* (Ann Arbor: University of Michigan, 1967), p. 31n. For labor protest over draft appointments see OF 1413–misc., Box 7, 30 September 1940, FDR.

81. Quote in *New York Times*, 17 January 1941, p. 10.

82. Ibid., 27 April 1941, p. 34; 8 June 1941, p. 34; Kennett, *GI*, p. 15; Omer to Parker, 10 June 1941, Box 30–31, RG 147, NA.

83. *New York Times*, 3 April 1941, p. 15; 26 March 1941, p. 1; 28 March 1941, p. 1; 6 June 1941, p. 14; and 8 June 1941, p. 37.

84. Ibid., 10 June 1941, p. 1; 11 June 1941, pp. 11, 13; Omer to Shattuck, 10 June 1941, Box 30–31, RG 147, NA. In World War I President Wilson had used a similar threat to end strikes in New York and Bridgeport, Connecticut. See *New York Times*, 10 June 1941, p. 17, and Chambers, *To Raise an Army*, p. 192.

85. *New York Times*, 13 July 1941, 4:8; 5 July 1941, p. 15; 24 July 1941, p. 18; and 26 July 1941, p. 17.

86. Flynn, *Hershey*, p. 105; *New York Times*, 9 August 1941, p. 6; 10 August 1941, p. 34; and 12 August 1941, p. 12.

87. *New York Times*, 16 August 1941, p. 8; 19 November 1941, p. 17; 15 November 1941, p. 8.

88. U.S., *Statutes at Large*, vol. 54 (13, and 16 September 1940), pp. 888–89.

89. Clifford and Spencer, *First Peacetime Draft*, pp. 141–44.

90. George F. Zook, "How the Colleges Went to War," American Academy of Political and Social Science, *Annals* 231 (January 1944):1.

91. Seymour quoted in *New York Times*, 8 November 1940, p. 10; 6 December

1940, p. 18; 10 November 1940, p. 25 for NASU quote; 25 January 1941, p. 8; 16 February 1941, p. 31; and 23 February 1941, 1:31, 2:6.

92. Charles Sawyer to President, 7 April 1941, Box 5, OF 1413, FDR; *New York Times*, 7 April 1941, p. 19; 7 April 1941, p. 19; 16 April 1941, p. 19; Press release by ACE, 16 April 1941, Box 5, OF 1413, FDR; Fox to Patterson, 17 April 1941, Box 173, Patterson Papers, Manuscript Room, Library of Congress. The strategic assumption that machines would be more important than manpower in winning the war was widely accepted in the scientific community; See *New York Times*, 26 April 1941, p. 16, and 30 April 1941, p. 18.

93. Frederick Osborn to Patterson, 4 March 1941, Box 173, Patterson Papers, Library of Congress; *New York Times*, 30 March 1941, p. 31; Roosevelt to Charles Sawyer, 14 April 1941, Box 5, OF 1413, FDR; *New York Times*, 16 April 1941, p. 1; Patterson to Fox, 24 April 1941, Box 173, Patterson Papers; Patterson to Hiram C. Todd, 28 April 1941, ibid.

94. Selective Service, *Selective Service in Peacetime, First Report of Director of Selective Service, 1940–41* (Washington, D.C.: USGPO, 1942), pp. 191–92.

95. *New York Times*, 4 May 1941, p. 49; Elbert D. Thomas to Gen. Watson, 21 July 1941, Box 1, OF 1413, FDR; Patterson to Senator Robert R. Reynolds, 20 May 41, Box 174, Selective Service file, Patterson Papers; K. C. Leebrick to Senator Elbert D. Thomas, 8 July 1941, Box 1, OF 1413, FDR; *New York Times*, 25 May 1941, p. 7; and 22 May 1941, p. 1.

96. Memo I-99, 12 May 1941, Box 50–medical division, RG 147–97, NA; Hershey memo for President, 15 July 1941, Box 5, OF 1413, FDR.

97. Digest of Significant Memos and Correspondence, 1941, file E37a, vols. 1 and 2, RG 147, NA; *New York Times*, 31 July 1941, p. 15; and Hershey to Gen. Watson, 11 August 1941, Box 1, OF 1413, FDR.

98. *New York Times*, 28 October 1941, p. 28; 28 August 1941, p. 16; 8 October 1941, p. 19; 14 September 1941, p. 37; 13 September 1941, p. 8; and 16 November 1941, II, 6.

99. Selective Service memo to State Directors, 16 September 1941, VF 314B36, LBH; *New York Times*, 21 September 1941, p. 32; 23 September 1941, p. 25; Patterson to Sen. Styles Bridges, 22 October 1941, Box 174, SS file, Patterson Papers; S. Early memo for Hershey, 13 December 1941, Box 1, OF 1413, FDR.

100. Selective Service, *Special Groups*, 1:10.

101. Phillip McGuire, "Judge William H. Hastie and Army Recruitment, 1940–42," *Military Affairs* 42 (April 1978): 75–76; *Special Groups*, 1:31.

102. Unsigned memo on participation of Negroes in Selective Service, 8 January 1941, file 070, Box 31, RG 147–97, NA; *Special Groups*, 1:33; Johnson news release, 7 February 1941, file 171.1, Box 48, RG 147–97, NA; Johnson to Rep. Vito Marcantonio, 6 September 1941, Box 31, ibid.; Johnson to A. W. Dent, 22 October 1941, ibid.; and Johnson news release, 10 November 1941, file 171.1, Box 48, RG 147–97, NA.

103. *Special Groups*, 1:26, 47, 71; *New York Times*, 4 January 1941, p. 6; 13 December 1940, p. 20; and 24 January 1941, p. 10.

104. Selective Service news release, 7 February 1941 and 11 March 1941, file 171.1, Box 48, RG 147–97, NA; Dykstra to Secretary of War, 14 February 1941, Box 4, OF 93, FDR.

105. *New York Times*, 17 March 1941, p. 19; *Times-Star* (Bridgeport, Conn.), 25 March 1941; C. S. Dargusch to Gen. Metts, 25 March 1941, Box 31, RG 147–97, NA; C. Johnson to Dargusch, 5 September 1941, ibid.; and *Special Groups*, 1:71–73.

106. Hershey to Secretary of War, 18 September 1941, Box 4, OF 93, FDR; Hershey to President, 4 October 1941, ibid.; P. L. Prattis to President, 25 September 1941, ibid.; Roosevelt to Prattis, 7 October 1941, ibid. See also *Special Groups*, 1:92.

107. Quoted in Chambers, *To Raise an Army*, p. 158.

108. Clifford and Spencer, *First Peacetime Draft*, pp. 140–42; George Q. Flynn, *Roosevelt and Romanism: Catholics and American Diplomacy, 1937–1945* (Westport, Conn.: Greenwood, 1976), pp. 73–74.

109. First quote in *New York Times*, 6 February 1941, p. 11; Spellman quoted in Clifford and Spencer, *First Peacetime Draft*, p. 1; Williams quote in *New York Times*, 25 November 1940, p. 13; 20 September 1941, p. 15; 1 November 1941, p. 17; and 20 October 1940, p. 24.

110. *New York Times*, 17 September 1941, p. 15; quote in Digest of Significant Memos, file E37A, vol. 1, RG 147, NA; Major Edward S. Shattuck, 24 January 1941, National HQ Opinions, vol. 3, file E42, ibid.; *New York Times*, 27 June 1941, p. 10; Lewis B. Hershey, National HQ opinion, 14 October 1941, vol. 3, file E42, RG 147, NA; and Hershey to Armstrong, 7 July 1941, Box 31, ibid.

111. Sibley and Jacob, *Conscription*, p. 54; Selective Service System, *Conscientious Objection*, 1:141, 255; John D. Langston to Major Morgan, 7 April 1941, file 323.5, Box 31, RG 147–97, NA; and Linton M. Collins to Maj. Edward S. Shattuck, 22 March 1941, ibid.

112. Kennett, *GI*, p. 12; Sibley and Jacob, *Conscription*, p. 110; quote from Digest of Significant Memos, 1941, vol. 1, E37A, RG 147, NA; quote from *New York Times*, 7 May 1941, p. 13.

113. Selective Service System, *Conscientious Objection*, 1:1, 7; *New York Times*, 22 December 1940, p. 27; 8 February 1941, p. 8; 12 April 1941, p.13; 15 May 1941, p. 14; A. S. Imirie to Fred Morrel, 30 January 1941, file 323.5, Box 31, RG 147–97, NA; Hershey to S. L. Van Akin, 23 April 1941, ibid.; and *New York Times*, 15 January 1941, p. 12.

114. *New York Times*, 26 June 1941, p. 13; Major Franklin A. McLean to Paul C. French, 13 October 1941, file 323.5, Box 31, RG 147–97, NA; Kosch to Hershey, 29 October 1941, ibid.

115. *New York Times*, 19 November 1940, p. 12; 29 November 1940, p. 12; and Griffith, *Men Wanted*, p. 209.

116. *New York Times*, 29 November 1940, p. 13; 1 December 1940, p. 48; 18 January 1941, p. 8; 2 February 1941, 4:10; 7 March 1941, p. 1; and Knox to President, 18 June 1941, Box 1, OF 1413, FDR.

117. *New York Times*, 24 March 1941, p. 20; 19 April 1941, p. 7; 20 April 1941, p. 35; 27 May 1941, p. 1; 30 June 1941, p. 1; 1 July 1941, p. 14; 17 July 1941, p. 10.

118. Ibid., 20 April, 1941, IV, 6; 9 May 1941, p. 17; and Kreidberg and Henry, *History*, p. 589. Griffith, *Men Wanted*, pp. 192, 194, concludes that the peacetime draft probably did not make the nation any better prepared for war. Not until October 1941 did the army have a new division ready for combat. See also Eliot A. Cohen, *Citizens and Soldiers: The Dilemmas of Military Service* (Ithaca, N.Y.: Cornell, 1985), p. 79.

119. Dykstra to President, 8 January 1941, Box 1, OF 1413, FDR; FDR to Dykstra, 11 January 1941, ibid.; HM memo for Forster, 6 March 1941, Box 1, OF 1413, FDR; *New York Times*, 5 May 1941, p. 1; 6 May 1941, p. 4; and 5 January 1941, p. 20.

120. *New York Times*, 11 May 1941, p. 37; 17 April 1941, p. 14; 13 May 1941, p. 14; 7 June 1941, p. 8; 10 June 1941, p. 19; and 2 July 1941, p. 1.

121. Ibid., 22 December 1940, p. 27; 23 April 1941, p. 11; 22 June 1941, p. 19; 24 June 1941, p. 12; and 29 June 1941, 4:10.

122. Ibid., 4 July 1941, pp. 1, 5; 8 July 1941, p. 2; 9 July 1941, p. 1; 11 July 1941, p. 1; 15 July 1941, p. 1; 16 July 1941, p. 1; and Patterson memo for Chief of Staff, Reserve Files, xerox 1763, 18 July 1941, GCM.

123. *New York Times*, 20 July 1941, p. 18; 21 July 1941, p. 1; 22 July 1941, p. 1; and 22 July 1941, p. 7.

124. Ibid., 4 July 1941, p. 1; 5 July 1941, p. 24; 6 July 1941, p. 16; 12 July 1941, p. 5; 11 July 1941, p. 14; 10 July 1941, p. 13; 13 July 1941, 4:3; 15 July 1941, p. 18; 25 July 1941, p. 1; 14 July 1941, p. 7; 18 July 1941, p. 1.

125. Ibid., 21 July 1941, p. 3; 22 July 1941, p. 8; 24 July 1941, p. 10; and MG Virgil L. Peterson to Chief of Staff, 23 July 1941, Reel 272, item 4230, GCM.

126. Division of Press Intelligence summary, 8 August 1941, Box 3, OF 788, FDR; George H. Gallup, ed., *The Gallup Poll: Public Opinion, 1935–1971*, 3 vols. (New York: Random House, 1972), 1:291–92.

127. See unsigned memo on draft extension, 21 July 1941, and 12 August 1941, file 245, Box 844, OF, Harry S. Truman Papers, Truman Library, Independence, Mo (hereafter cited as HST); *New York Times*, 9 August 1941. Rep. Lyndon Johnson of Texas played a major role in rounding up support for the extension. See Carl Vinson interview, 24 May 1970, Lyndon B. Johnson Library, Austin, Texas (hereafter cited as LBJ).

128. Flynn, *Hershey*, p. 83.

129. *New York Times*, 19 August 1941, p. 1.

130. Ibid., 20 August 1941, pp. 1, 10; 30 August 1941, p. 1; 1 September 1941, p. 1; and 7 November 1941, p. 11.

Chapter 3. From Pearl Harbor to D-Day

1. Hershey quoted in George Q. Flynn, *Lewis B. Hershey: Mr. Selective Service* (Chapel Hill: University of North Carolina, 1985) p. 84; Hoover quoted in Frank Freidel, *Franklin D. Roosevelt: A Rendezvous with Destiny* (Boston: Little, Brown, 1990), p. 407.

2. Walter Millis, *Arms and Men: A Study of American Military History* (New York: Putnam, 1950), p. 297. For a recent revision of the Millis view see Mark H. Leff, "The Politics of Sacrifice on the American Home Front in World War II," *Journal of American History* 77 (March 1991):1296–1318, who shows the endurance of interest-group politics.

3. FDR to L. B. School, 26 August 1940, Box 103, War Dept., PSF, Franklin D. Roosevelt Papers, Roosevelt Library, Hyde Park, N.Y. (hereafter cited as FDR).

4. *New York Times*, 6 January 1942, p. 10, and 10 January 1942, p. 8.

5. Quote in ibid., 12 September 1942, p. 1, and Marvin A. Kreidberg and M. G. Henry, *A History of Military Mobilization in the United States Army, 1775–1945* (Washington, D.C.: USGPO, 1955), p. 696.

6. *New York Times*, 24 February 1942, p. 20; Robert R. Palmer, B. I. Wiley, and W. R. Keast, *The Procurement and Training of Ground Combat Troops* (Washington, D.C.: Department of Army, 1948), p. 10.

7. *New York Times*, 14 December 1941, p. 57, and 20 January 1942, p. 21.

8. Ibid., 22 February 1942, p. 20; 26 February 1942, p. 11; Patterson to Stimson, 28 March 1942, item 2715, reel 116, GCM; Stimson to Clark, 7 April 1942, ibid.; and *New York Times*, 20 March 1943, p. 1.

9. Stimson for President, 16 February 1942, OF 1413, Box 2, FDR; *New York Times*, 28 June 1942, p. 22; 27 June 1942, p. 1; 6 November 1942, p. 19; Albert A. Blum and J. D. Smyth, "Who Should Serve: Pre–World War II Planning for Selective Service," *Journal of Economic History* 30 (February 1970):401.

10. See George Q. Flynn, *The Mess in Washington: Manpower Mobilization in World War II* (Westport, Conn.: Greenwood, 1979), pp. 11–20.

11. *New York Times*, 3 November 1942, p. 1; 24 November 1942, p. 16; 6 December 1942, p. 1; Flynn, *Mess in Washington*, pp. 30–35.

12. Flynn, *Mess in Washington*, chap. 10.

13. See Donald D. Stewart, "Local Boards: A Study of the Place of Volunteer Participation in a Bureaucratic Organization" (Ph.D. diss., Columbia University, 1950), p. 15.

14. Stewart, "Local Boards," p. 197; Carl B. Swisher, "Enhancement of the Executive," in Keith L. Nelson, ed., *The Impact of War on American Life* (New York: Holt, Rinehart & Winston, 1971), pp. 116–17.

15. Stewart, "Local Boards," pp. 25, 148, 152, 196.

16. Phillip Selznick quoted in Gary L. Wamsley, "Decision Making in Local Boards: A Case Study," in Roger W. Little, ed., *Selective Service and American Society* (New York: Sage, 1969), p. 105n.

17. Hershey to BG L. V. Regan, 1 August 1940, and Hershey to John Sawczyn, 4 August 1940, Box 26, RG 147, National Archives (NA); Holmes B. Springs, *Selective Service in South Carolina* (Columbia, S.C.: Selective Service Headquarters, 1948), p. 1; Gary L. Wamsley, *Selective Service and a Changing America* (Columbus, Ohio: Merrill, 1969), p. 128; and Science Research Associates, Inc., *Unfit for Service: A Review of the Draft and Basic Education in the Army* (Chicago: SRA, 1966), p. 10. For another view, which argues that the system had "no institutional roots in the various local community," see Stewart, "Local Boards," pp. 64, 200.

18. Stewart, "Local Boards," p. 100.

19. Minute book for LB 104, 21 July 1943, and 1 March 1944, file E61, Box 3, RG 147; Stewart, "Local Boards," pp. 5, 100; and Survey of Local Boards, 1947, Box 62, RG 147.

20. *New York Times*, 30 October 1942, p. 15, and Stewart, "Local Boards," pp. 127, 132, 141, 152.

21. Survey of Local Boards, 1947, chap. 2, Box 62, RG 147. See also VF 131.1s1, rl54, Lewis B. Hershey Papers, Military History Institute, Carlisle, Pa. (hereafter cited as LBH).

22. During the 1960s critics of the draft insisted that everyone be treated alike, but in World War II the emphasis was on individuality; Stewart, "Local Boards," p. 138.

23. Ibid., p. 88. However, they were loyal to Selective Service, and many continued to serve the system into the 1960s.

24. Harry A. Marmion, *Selective Service: Conflict and Compromise* (New York: Wiley, 1968), p. 13; Donald D. Stewart, "Selective Service Appeal Boards," *Southwestern Social Science Quarterly* 31 (June 1950):33, 35; Survey of Local Boards, 1947, chap. 3, Box 62, RG 147–97; and Stewart, "Local Boards," pp. 54, 57.

25. Saltonstall to Roosevelt, 10 November 1942, Box 6, OF 1413, FDR; Stewart, "Appeal Boards," pp. 36–37; *New York Times*, 23 July 1943, p. 19. Roosevelt refused

to intervene even when the state system was controlled by outspoken political enemies; see A. P. Ardourel to F. Walker, 24 February 1943, misc., Box 7, OF 1413, FDR.

26. *New York Times,* 1 May 1942, p. 11; 10 May 1942, IV, 7. See also Lee Kennett, *G.I.: The American Soldier in World War II* (New York: Scribners, 1987), p. 31.

27. Quote from Office of War Information survey, 9 January 1943, file E15, Box 67, RG 147.

28. *New York Times,* 18 December 1941, p. 13, and 11 January 1942, p. 20.

29. Quote in ibid., 26 September 1942, p. 6; 16 August 1943, p. 12; 10 November 1942, p. 26; 6 September 1942, IV, 5; Survey of Local Board Members, 1947, VF 131.1s1rl53, LBH; and "Public Reaction to the Draft," 9 January 1943, OWI file, E15, Box 67, RG 147.

30. Walker S. Edwards, "The Administration of Selective Service in the United States" (M.A. thesis, Stanford University, 1948), pp. 80, 115.

31. Stewart, "Local Boards," pp. 20, 46–47, and *New York Times,* 19 December 1941, p. 21.

32. *New York Times,* 9 February 1942, p. 1; 15 February 1942, 8:5; 4 March 1942, p. 1; 28 September 1943, p. 30; and 3 February 1943, p. 24.

33. John S. Brown, "Draftee Division: A Study of the 88th Infantry Division, First All Selective Service Division into Combat in World War II" (Ph.D. diss., Indiana University, 1983), p. 19.

34. *New York Times,* 31 December 1941, p. 3; 6 June 1942, p.1; 16 June 1942, p. 42; 13 December 1942, p. 69; 14 February 1943, p. 1; 2 May 1943, p. 3; and Leonard G. Rowntree, "The Medical Needs of the War and the Selective Service System," *Journal of the American Medical Association* (12 December 1942):1–10.

35. *New York Times,* 17 September 1943, p. 16, and 29 November 1943, p. 1.

36. FDR to McNutt and Hershey, 26 February 1944, Box 3, OF 1413, FDR, and Marshall to Byrnes, 6 April 1944, item 2715, reel 116, GCM.

37. See George Q. Flynn, "Drafting Farmers in World War II," in John Wunder, ed., *At Home on the Range: Essays on the History of Western Social and Domestic Life* (Westport, Conn.: Greenwood, 1985), pp. 157–74 for more on this problem.

38. *New York Times,* 19 March 1943, p. 11; Flynn, "Drafting Farmers," pp. 158–59; Mapheus Smith, "The Differential Impact of Selective Service Inductions on Occupations in the United States," *American Sociological Review* 11 (October 1946):572.

39. Flynn, "Drafting Farmers," p. 159.

40. Ibid., p. 160; Louis J. Ducoff, Margaret J. Hagood, and Conrad Taeuber, "Effects of the War on the Agricultural Working Force and on the Rural-Farm Population," *Social Forces* 21 (May 1943):407.

41. *New York Times,* 1 February 1942, IV, 8, and 8 February 1942, p. 38.

42. John Moses to FDR, 17 February 1942, Box 2, OF 1413, FDR.

43. *New York Times,* 5 March 1942, p. 18; 8 March 1942, IV, 7; 24 February 1942, p. 1; and Moses to FDR, 3 July 1942, Box 6, OF 1413, FDR.

44. *New York Times,* 1 April 1942, p. 16; 5 September 1942, p. 13; and FDR to Moses, 15 July 1942, Box 6, OF 1413, FDR.

45. Flynn, "Drafting Farmers," p. 162; *New York Times,* 10 October 1942, p. 1; 4 November 1942, p. 35; 7 October 1942, p. 15; and Garner Jackson to President, 16 December 1942, Box 6, OF 1413-misc., FDR.

46. Flynn, "Drafting Farmers," pp. 162–63; *New York Times,* 19 October 1942, p. 12; 19 November 1942, p. 1; and 6 December 1942, p. 62.

47. Stimson to President, 13 November 1942, Box 2, OF 1413, FDR; Murray to President, 13 November 1942, Box 6, misc., ibid; Marshall to McNutt, 23 October 1942, SS, Reel 116, item 2679, GCM; and *New York Times*, 30 October 1942, p. 21.

48. *New York Times*, 7 January 1943, p. 13; 4 February 1943, p. 17; 19 February 1943, p. 12; 18 March 1943, p. 1; 26 March 1943, pp. 1, 26; Flynn, "Drafting Farmers," p. 163; and "Public Reaction to the Draft," OWI Survey, 9 January 1943, file E15, Box 67, RG 147.

49. *New York Times*, 20 February 1943, p. 8; 20 January 1943, p. 33; 2 March 1943, p. 12; 27 March 1943, p. 1; 1 May 1943, p. 10; and 8 April 1943, p. 22.

50. Ibid., 26 September 1943, p. 15; "Hearings of President's Commission on Induction Standards," 7 January 1944, pp. 15, 26, Box 3, OF 1413, FDR; Keesling to Rosenman, February 1944, ibid.; Minutes of Manpower Hearing, 3 March 1944, Book 7, Box 324, Harry Hopkins Papers, FDR; Hershey to William D. Hassett, 13 January 1944, misc., Box 7, OF 1413, FDR; and Flynn, "Drafting Farmers," pp. 164–66.

51. Selective Service System, *Selective Service in Peacetime: First Report of the Director of Selective Service, 1940–41* (Washington, D.C.: USGPO, 1942), p. 17; Selective Service memo, 1942, VF 330.2S13, LBH; and *New York Times*, 13 January 1942, p. 20.

52. *Selective Service in Peacetime*, p. 17; U.S. Department of Commerce, *Historical Statistics of the United States: Colonial Times to 1970*, 2 pts. (Washington, D.C.: USGPO, 1975), 1:49, 64; *New York Times*, 27 November 1942, p. 15. In New York City the marriage trend in one local board area jumped from less than 10 each month to almost 40 a month after the draft bill passed. *Selective Service in Wartime: Second Report of the Director of Selective Service, 1941–42* (Washington, D.C.: USGPO, 1943), p. 128.

53. *New York Times*, 14 July 1942, p. 1, and 26 April 1942, p. 38.

54. *Selective Service in Wartime*, p. 135.

55. *New York Times*, 19 August 1942, p. 21, and *Selective Service in Wartime*, pp. 134–36.

56. *New York Times*, 6 February 1942, p. 1; 22 March 1942, p. 22; 2 September 1942, p. 12; and George H. Gallup, ed., *The Gallup Poll: Public Opinion, 1935–1971*, 3 vols. (New York: Random House, 1972), 1:326.

57. Quote in *New York Times*, 10 July 1942, p. 4.

58. Press release, 18 June 1942, Selective Service folder, Box 791, Robert Taft Papers, Manuscript Room, Library of Congress, Washington (hereafter cited as LC); *New York Times*, 6 May 1942, p. 11; 12 June 1942, p. 11; 13 June 1942, p. 1; 16 June 1942, p. 10; 17 June 1942, p. 9; 31 August 1942, p. 19; 30 December 1942, p. 13; and *Selective Service in Wartime*, pp. 141–43, 145. In January 1942 some 10,102,000 men were in class 3-A out of 16,640,212 classified. By November there were 26,767,364 classified, 13,214,536 in 3-A, and 1,653,100 in 3-B. *Selective Service in Wartime*, p. 145.

59. FDR to Andrew J. May, 16 December 1941, Box 1, OF 1413, FDR, and E.M.W. memo for President, 12 December 1941, ibid.

60. Quote in Hershey to President, 25 June 1942, Box 2, OF 1413, FDR; *Gallup Poll*, 1:347, 352, 353; and Cox to Hopkins, 6 November 1942, cont. 302, military training file, Hopkins Papers, FDR.

61. *New York Times*, 16 September 1942, p. 48; 13 October 1942, p. 1; and 8 November 1942, p. 31.

62. H. Smith to President, 10 October 1942, Box 2, OF 1413, FDR; *New York Times*, 19 October 1942, p. 21; and 16 October 1942, p. 18.

63. Selective Service, Local Board memo, 30 January 1943, VF 330.2S13, LBH; *New York Times*, 18 February 1943, p. 8; and 27 April 1943, p. 10.

64. *New York Times*, 13 April 1943, p. 1.

65. Ibid., 9 January 1943, p. 11; 12 February 1943, p. 21; 18 May 1943, p. 25; and 13 April 1943, p. 13.

66. Quotes in ibid., 28 August 1943, p. 9, and 7 September 1943, p. 25; 12 September 1943, p. 9; 5 June 1943, p. 11; 6 August 1943, p. 7; 15 September 1943, p. 15.

67. Ibid., 14 October 1943, p. 13; 15 August 1943, p. 34; 18 August 1943, p. 40; 22 September 1943, p. 9; and 15 September 1943, p. 17.

68. Flynn, *Mess in Washington*, pp. 204–6.

69. Quote in *New York Times*, 16 September 1943, p. 1; 23 September 1943, p. 1.

70. Ibid., 17 November 1943, p. 1.

71. Flynn, *Mess in Washington*, pp. 207–8, and quote in *New York Times*, 18 December 1943, p. 3.

72. Richard Polenberg, *War and Society: The United States, 1941–1945* (New York: Lippincott, 1972), pp. 145–49. See also Flynn, *Mess in Washington*, chapter 8 for information on women workers, and for a contemporary view see Ernest W. Burgess, "The Family," in William F. Ogburn, ed., *American Society in Wartime* (Chicago: University of Chicago, 1943), pp. 17–39.

73. G. J. Dudycha, "Attitude of College Students Toward War," *Journal of Social Psychology* 15 (February 1942):75, 86–88.

74. George F. Zook, "How the Colleges Went to War," American Academy of Political and Social Sciences, *Annals* 231 (January 1944):2.

75. Undergraduate enrollment declined from 1,388,000 to 1,319,000 from 1940 to 1942, and graduate enrollment dropped from 106,000 to 85,000. See U.S. Department of Commerce, *Historical Statistics of the United States* (Washington, D.C.: Department of Commerce, 1975), 1:383; Raymond Walters, "Facts and Figures of Colleges at War," *Annals* 231 (January 1944):11–12.

76. Selective Service, Research and Statistics Division Survey (hereafter cited as R. and S.), 18 February 1942, VF 314s, LBH; idem., 20 March 1942, VF 314, misc., ibid.

77. Ibid.

78. Paper by Philip Schaffner, 18 February 1942, VF 314s, LBH; SS, R. and S. memo, 16 March 1942, VF 314 misc., ibid., and *New York Times*, 17 February 1942, p. 8.

79. *New York Times*, 22 January 1942, p. 15; 13 February 1942, p. 34; 7 June 1942, p. 38; 31 July 1942, p. 13; Conant to President, 28 March 1942, Box 6, OF, 1413 misc., FDR; FDR to Conant, 27 April 1942, ibid.

80. *New York Times*, 18 October 1942, p. 45; La Guardia speech, 21 October 1942, WMC file, Box 183, Robert Patterson Papers, Manuscript Room, LC; and Harold Smith to President, 10 October 1942, Box 2 OF 1413, FDR.

81. Smith to President, 10 October 1942, Box 2, OF 1413, FDR, and Patterson to Felix Frankfurter, 3 November 1942, WMC file, Box 183, Patterson Papers.

82. *New York Times*, 29 November 1942, pp. 8, 10; 12 December 1942, p. 8; 5 December 1942, p. 17; Minutes of meeting of Engineering College Deans, 1 December 1942, VF 314F55, LBH; *New York Times*, 6 November 1942, p. 19; and 8 November 1942, IV, 9.

83. FDR memo to Stimson and Knox, 15 October 1942, Box 2, OF 1413, FDR.

84. Patterson to Frankfurter, 3 November 1942, WMC file, Box 183, Patterson Papers; quote in Palmer, Wiley, and Keast, *Procurement and Training of Ground Combat Forces*, pp. 28–29.

85. *Selective Service in Wartime*, p. 236, and Brown, "Draftees Division," p. 32.

86. Twaddle to Chief of Military History, 5 August 1953, Box 669, RG 319, NA.

87. Walter, "Facts and Figures," pp. 8–9; *New York Times*, 28 April 1943, p. 44; and 3 January 1943, IV, 7.

88. *New York Times*, 22 December 1942, p. 18; McNutt to Stimson, 8 February 1943, reel 116, item 2715, SS, GCM; "McNutt Testimony before House Armed Services Committee," 2 February 1943, ibid.; *Washington Star*, 2 February 1943; Stimson to Knox, 13 February 1943, reel 116, item 2715, GCM; and Patterson to McNutt, 19 February 1943, ibid.

89. *New York Times*, 5 March 1943, p. 19, and Zook, "Colleges," pp. 6–7.

90. Col. Francis V. Keesling, Jr., to Sam Rosenman, 7 February 1944, Box 8, OF 1413D, FDR; Selective Service, *Selective Service as the Tide of War Turns: 3rd Report of the Director of Selective Service, 1943–1944* (Washington, D.C.: USGPO, 1945), pp. 79–80.

91. Patterson to Hershey, 12 February 1944, WMC file, Box 183, Patterson Papers, LC, and Stimson to President, 4 March 1944, Box 3, OF 1413, FDR.

92. Charles L. Parsons to President, 14 March 1944, Box 7, OF 1413, FDR; Frank B. Jewett to President, 22 March 1944, ibid.; FDR to Parsons, 18 March 1944, ibid.

93. Local Board Survey, 1947, VF 131.1s1, LBH; Smith, "Differential Impact of Selective Service," p. 372.

94. George A. Lincoln, William Y. Smith, and Jay B. Durst, "The Industrial Achievement," in Nelson, *Impact*, p. 100.

95. EMB memo to Major Hershey, 14 May 1940, Box 23, E.97, RG 147, NA.

96. Smith, "Differential Impact of Selective Service," p. 569.

97. W. J. Rorabaugh, "Who Fought for the North in the Civil War," *Journal of American History* 73 (December 1986):699. For creation of the modern draft see John W. Chambers II, *To Raise an Army: The Draft Comes to Modern America* (New York: Free Press, 1987).

98. Smith, "The Differential Impact of Selective Service," pp. 568–72.

99. Battley speech, 13 April 1940, E97, Box 13, RG 147.

100. *New York Times*, 22 December 1941, p. 10 for quote; 19 February 1942, p. 32; 22 March 1942, p. 44; and 23 March 1942, p. 6.

101. Ibid., 6 May 1942, p. 11; Hershey to Patterson, 23 January 1942, Selective Service file, Box 174, Patterson Papers, LC.

102. *New York Times*, 25 January 1942, p. 10; 12 May 1942, p. 20; 5 June 1942, p. 38; 4 September 1942, p. 25; and 3 September 1942, p. 1.

103. Ibid., 10 January 1942, p. 6; 3 September 1942, p. 30; 24 October 1942, p. 8; 29 November 1942, p. 49; and Hershey to M. C. Thompson, correspondence file, Box 836, Eleanor Roosevelt Papers, FDR. A Selective Service investigation of the Ford plant at Willow Run failed to show that the draft had hurt production.

104. *New York Times*, 15 February 1943, p. 22.

105. Ibid., 19 May 1943, p. 11.

106. Ibid., 5 August 1943, p. 8.

107. See Richard Polenberg, *War and Society: The United States, 1941–1945* (New York: Lippincott, 1972), chap. 8 for a discussion of the OWM.

108. The New York Shipbuilding Company said the draft was "torpedoing" the task of supplying the front. See *New York Times*, 22 October 1943, p. 12.

109. See item 5317, Reel 360, April 1944, GCM for this affair.

110. *Gallup Polls*, 1:234, 251, 363, 407, 431, 448, 486, and *New York Times*, 18 April 1943, p. 40. See also Flynn, *Mess in Washington*, chap. 4.

111. Blum and Smyth, "Who Should Serve," p. 402; John Green to President, 27 January 1942, misc., Box 6, OF 1413, FDR; *New York Times*, 17 February 1942, p. 1; 18 February 1942, pp. 1, 15; and 22 February 1942, p. 20.

112. The National War Labor Board was created in January 1942 to force arbitration to prevent a strike. At its request, the president was empowered to take over plants.

113. *New York Times*, 13 August 1942, p. 38; Patterson, Knox, and Wayne Morse to President, 20 August 1942, Box 2, OF 1413, FDR; *New York Times*, 13 September 1942, p. 29; 15 September 1942, p. 1; 25 September 1942, p. 42; and Merrill C. Meigs to Patterson, 26 October 1942, WMC file, Box 183, Patterson Papers, LC.

114. *New York Times*, 3 February 1943, p. 1, and 9 February 1943, p. 1.

115. Ibid., 4 June 1943, p. 1 for quote; 20 March 1943, p. 7; 11 April 1943, p. 38; and 20 June 1943, p. 19.

116. Ibid., 5 June 1943, p. 4, and unsigned, undated memo from Solicitor General's office to President, Book 7, F-3, Box 324, Harry Hopkins Papers, FDR.

117. Marshall note, meeting with Stimson, 21 June 1943, item 937, reel 55, SS, GCM; *New York Times*, 14 June 1943, p. 1; 26 June 1943, p. 2; 15 August 1943, pp. 1, 35; and 19 August 1943, p. 1. See also Joel Seidman, *American Labor from Defense to Reconversion* (Chicago: University of Chicago, 1953).

118. Local Board Survey, 1947, VF 131.1s1, LBH.

119. See Mapheus Smith, "Population Characteristics of American Servicemen in World War II," *The Scientific Monthly* 65 (September 1947): 246–52.

120. Ibid.

121. Ibid.

Chapter 4. Truman, UMT, and the Draft

1. Willard Waller, "A Sociologist Looks at Conscription," American Academy of Political and Social Sciences, *Annals* 241 (September 1945):97; Norman Thomas to President, 21 January 1945, Box 4, OF 1413, Franklin D. Roosevelt Papers, Hyde Park, New York (hereafter cited as FDR).

2. Truman statement, 9 May 1945, Zimmerman files, Box 9, Harry S. Truman Library, Independence, Mo. (hereafter cited as HST); Marshall to Rep. Andrew J. May, 2 May 1945, item 5317, reel 360, George C. Marshall Papers, Marshall Research Center, Lexington, Virginia (hereafter cited as GCM); Stimson to Senator Brian McMahon, 15 May 1945, ibid.

3. Rocco M. Paone, "The Last Volunteer Army, 1946–1948," *Military Review* 49 (December 1969):9.

4. Philip B. Fleming to Matthew J. Connelly, 18 August 1945, Connelly Papers, Box 1, Cabinet Minutes, HST.

5. James M. Gerhardt, *The Draft and Public Policy* (Columbus: Ohio State University, 1971), pp. 38–39; *New York Times*, 15 August 1945, p. 13; and 27 August 1945, p. 12.

6. Quote in Hershey to President, 5 December 1946, Clifford Papers, HST; Her-

shey to Director of War Mobilization and Reconversion, 11 August 1945, White House file, Lewis B. Hershey Papers, Military History Institute, Carlisle, Pa. (hereafter cited as LBH); *New York Times*, 27 August 1945, p. 1. See also George Q. Flynn, *Lewis B. Hershey: Mr. Selective Service* (Chapel Hill: University of North Carolina, 1985), chap. 6, for Hershey's attempt to preserve a permanent place for his agency in the postwar world.

7. Forrestal to President, 23 August 1945, file 245, Box 844, OF, HST; Paone, "Volunteer," pp. 11–12. See also Michael S. Sherry, *Preparing for the Next War* (New Haven, Conn.: Yale University Press, 1977) for an analysis of War Department plans for the postwar world.

8. Stimson to Fred Vinson, 30 May 1945, item 5317, reel 360, GCM; Stimson to President, 11 August 1945, ibid.

9. Quote in Notes of Cabinet Meeting, 17 August 1945, Connelly Papers, Box 1, HST; Truman to Governor Olin D. Johnston, 20 August 1945, Box 844, OF 245, ibid.

10. Paone, "Volunteer," p. 9; Marshall to President, 16 August 1945, reel 360, item 5317, GCM; and Minutes of Cabinet Meeting, 17 August 1945, Connelly Papers, Box 1, HST.

11. Truman to Johnston, 20 August 1945, OF 245, Box 844, HST; Truman to Andrew J. May, 27 August 1945, Frank V. Keesling Papers, privately held, San Francisco, Calif.; and Patterson to President, 5 October 1945, OF 419, Box 1258, HST.

12. Marshall to President, 23 August 1945, Selective Service, reel 360, item 5317, GCM; John M. Kendall, "An Inflexible Response: United States Army Manpower Mobilization Policies, 1945–1957" (Ph.D. diss., Duke University Press, 1982), p. 56; and Patterson to Charles A. Lee, 30 December 1945, Selective Service, reel 360, item 5317, GCM.

13. OWMR Report on Demobilization, 2 November 1945, SS, reel 659, item 6106, GCM; John Snyder to Secretary of War, 10 November 1945, ibid.; Marshall to Snyder, 3 December 1945, ibid.; Patterson to Snyder, 3 December 1945, reel 360, item 5317, ibid.

14. *New York Times*, 1 January 1946, p. 1; 5 January 1946, p. 26; 10 January 1946, p. 22; 16 January 1946, p. 15; and 18 January 1946, p. 6.

15. Selective Service, *Selective Service and Victory, The 4th Report of the Director of Selective Service, 1944–1947* (Washington, D.C.: USGPO, 1948), pp. 51, 75–76; *New York Times*, 18 January 1946, p. 6; and 17 January 1946, p. 6.

16. Senate Military Affairs subcommittee hearings, 18 January 1946, pp. 403–6; and *New York Times*, 17 January 1946, p. 6.

17. U.S. Congress, Senate, Military Affairs Committee, *Hearings on Demobilization*, 79th Cong., 1st and 2d sess., 18 January 1946, p. 408; Hershey to Kenneth C. Royall, 25 January 1946, Op-war file, LBH, MHI; *New York Times*, 21 January 1946, p. 22; 29 January 1946, p. 8; 15 February 1946, p. 11; 1 April 1946, p. 14; 2 May 1946, p. 8; *SS Newsletter*, 1 April 1946, p. 1; Hershey to Attorney General, 30 January 1946, legal file, LBH, MHI; Patterson report, 1 February 1946, Cabinet minutes, Connelly Papers, Box 1, HST; and Gerhardt, *Draft and Public Policy*, p. 42. Despite these gestures the army informed Hershey that he had to draft 125,000 men in April, but in the first two weeks of that month only 17,000 were inducted.

18. *Hearings on Demobilization*, pp. 421–22; Gerhardt, *Draft and Public Policy*, pp. 42, 50; *New York Times*, 19 January 1946, p. 7; 22 January 1946, p. 16; Eisenhower to Hershey, 21 January 1946, OP-War, LBH, MHI.

19. See George H. Gallup, ed., *The Gallup Polls, Public Opinion, 1935–1971*, 3 vols. (New York: Random House, 1972), 1:523; 527, 529, 539, 546, 566–67.

20. U.S. Congress, House, Military Affairs Committee, *Hearings on Selective Service Extension*, 79th Cong., 2d sess., 21 March 1946, pp. 2–10; U.S. Congress, Senate, Military Affairs Committee, *Hearings on Selective Service Extension*, 79th Cong., 2d sess., 28 March 1946, pp. 2, 42; *New York Times*, 1 March 1946, p. 10; 6 March 1946, p. 12; 7 March 1946, p. 24; 14 March 1946, p. 1; 18 March 1946, p. 2; 19 March 1946, p. 1; 22 March 1946, p. 1; and 7 April 1946, p. 1; Truman speech, 5 April 1946, PPF 200, Box 277, HST.

21. *New York Times*, 6 April 1946, p. 1; 12 April 1946, p. 13; 16 April 1946, p. 1; 18 April 1946, p. 1; 4 May 1946, p. 8; 10 May 1946, p. 4; memo for Eisenhower, 10 May 1946, Diary, Box 12, Dwight D. Eisenhower Papers, Eisenhower Library, Abilene, Kansas (hereafter cited as DDE).

22. Truman statement, 16 May 1946, OF 242, A-245, Box 44, HST, and Hershey to President, 16 May 1946, White House file, LBH, MHI.

23. *New York Times*, 30 May 1946, p. 4; 28 May 1946, p. 1; 1 June 1946, p. 12; 3 June 1946, p. 1; and 15 June 1946, p. 6.

24. Ibid., 8 June 1946, p. 6; 11 June 1946, p. 5; 18 June 1946, p. 27; and 24 June 1946, p. 33.

25. Ibid., 25 May 1946, p. 17; 27 May 1946, p. 5; 21 June 1946, p. 2; and 31 May 1946, p. 22.

26. Hershey to President, 26 June 1946, OF 245, Box 844, HST.

27. *New York Times*, 16 May 1946, p. 20; 5 June 1946, p. 1; and 26 June 1946, p. 1.

28. One scholar has described the phases of manpower policy: from 1945 to September 1946 represented phase one, reliance upon the draft. Phase two, from September 1946 to April 1947, saw a serious attempt to create a volunteer recruitment system to fill all needs. But by April 1947, in the final phase, the army admitted failure with recruiting and again sought the solace of the SS. See Paone, "Volunteer," pp. 10–12.

29. Ibid., p. 10ff.

30. Kenneth McGill, interview with author, Abilene, Kans., 17 August 1978; Hedvig Ylvisaker, "Public Opinion toward Compulsory Military Training, American Academy of Political and Social Sciences, *Annals* 242 (1 September 1945):86–87. In the postwar period public support for the draft never fell below 63 percent. In 1938 the same idea had had only a 37 percent approval rating.

31. Karl T. Compton memo, 30 January 1947, UMT Advisory Commission, Box 3, HST; Truman to Compton, 17 January 1947, PSF-Agencies, Box 146, ibid.

32. John J. McCloy, "The Plan of Armed Services for Universal Military Training," *Annals* 241 (1 September 1945):26; Kendall, "Inflexible Response," pp. 55, 62, 70, 86; J. Lawton Collins testimony at *Hearings on Universal Military Training*, pp. 112–13, 28 December 1946, in Box 89, Joseph Davies Papers, Manuscript Room, Library of Congress (hereafter cited as LC); Eisenhower quoted in memo by Compton of conference with Patterson and Eisenhower, 10 February 1947, Minutes of President's Advisory Committee on UMT, Box 6, HST.

33. Copy of *Hearings on UMT*, 28 February 1947, in Box 90, Davies Papers, LC. A War Department study, "Soldier Attitudes Toward Required Military Training," 11 February 1947, copy in Box 91, ibid., found rapid erosion of enlisted men's support for UMT.

34. The historiography on Truman's response to the USSR is represented by John

L. Gaddis, *The United States and Origins of the Cold War, 1941–1947* (New York: Columbia University Press,1972) and *Strategies of Containment* (New York: Oxford University Press, 1982), who argues for Truman's flexibility toward Russia, and Walter LaFeber, *America, Russia and the Cold War, 1945–1990*, 6th ed. (New York: McGraw-Hill, 1991), who is more critical.

35. As a senator Truman had been inundated with requests that he interfere with the draft to obtain occupational deferments for farmers and others. Hershey to President, 25 March 1946, OF 245, Box 852, HST; President to Lemke, 27 March 1946, ibid; Lemke to President, 28 March and 9 April 1946; Truman to Lemke, 15 April 1946, ibid.

36. *New York Times*, 15 April 1946, p. 13.

37. Selective Service, Research and Statistics Memo, "Labor Turnover," 18 April 1945, VF 320S18, LBH.

38. *New York Times*, 26 May 1946, p. 1; Patterson to President, 24 May 1946, OF 419–F, Box 1261, HST.

39. *New York Times*, 26 May 1946, pp. 1, 26.

40. Ibid., 27 May 1946, p. 1; 28 May 1946, pp. 1, 3, 20; 29 May 1946, pp. 1, 2, 4; and 30 May 1946, pp. 1, 3.

41. Selective Service, *Special Groups*, Special Monograph No. 10, 2 vols. (Washington, D.C.: USGPO, 1953), 1:51–52.

42. Wilkins to President, 5 January 1945, UMT Advisory Commission file, Box 3, HST, and Richard M. Dalfiume, *Desegregation of the United States Armed Forces* (Columbia: University of Missouri, 1969), p. 103.

43. Selective Service, Memos on Pertinent Data on Blacks in Various States, 1 March 1945, Boxes 138, 142, RG 147. These reports were submitted by state headquarters at various times in 1945 at the request of national headquarters. The reports are filled with statistical data on African Americans across the nation. For example, in Virginia blacks made up 24.7 percent or 661,449 of the total population. Some 27.5 percent of all registrants were black, and 25.9 percent of all inductees through 1 March 1945, were black. In Alabama blacks made up 34.7 percent of the population. They constituted 34.7 percent of all registrants and 31.6 percent of all inductees by 1 March 1945. In Texas blacks made up 14.4 percent of the population, 15.5 percent of all registrants, and 12.4 percent of those who served.

44. *Special Groups*, 2:112; Campbell Johnson, Report to State Director's Conference, 21 March 1947, Box 34, file 120.2, RG 147–97, NA. Blacks served in separate units in the army and marines. The navy would not allow them on ships at first, but in February 1946 became the first service to end segregation, although few blacks were recruited; see Ulysses Lee, "The Draft and the Negro," *Current History* 55 (July 1968):32.

45. For a description of this scene see George Q. Flynn, "Selective Service and American Blacks during World War II," *Journal of Negro History* 69 (Winter 1984):14–25, and Campbell Johnson, Report to State Director's Conference, 21 March 1947, Box 34, file 120.2, RG 147–97.

46. Gallup poll of 1 June 1945, in VF 100S11a, LBH.

47. Campbell Johnson, report to State Directors conference, 21 March 1947, LBH; *New York Times*, 30 May 1946, p. 3; and 31 May 1946, p. 38.

48. For a general discussion of Truman and blacks see David McCullough, *Truman* (New York: Simon & Shuster, 1992), pp. 587, 651; William C. Berman, *The Politics of Civil Rights in the Truman Administration* (Columbus: Ohio State University Press,

1970); Morris MacGregor, *Integration in the Armed Forces* (Washington, D.C.: Office of Chief of Military History, 1981); Dalfiume, *Desegregation*, p. 155.

49. Edward A. Fitzpatrick, "The Volunteer and the Conscript in American Military History," *Current History* 38 (April 1960):212.

50. Stephen E. Ambrose, *Rise to Globalism*, 4th ed., rev. (New York: Penguin, 1985), pp. 96–99; *Historical Statistics of the United States*, 2 pts. (Washington, D.C.: Department of Commerce, 1975), 2:1116; U.S., Department of Defense, *Selected Manpower Statistics, Fiscal Year 1989* (Washington, D.C.: Directorate for Information Operations and Reports, 1989), p. 58.

51. Clair Blair, *The Forgotten War: America in Korea, 1950–1953* (New York: Times Books, 1987), pp. 4–29.

52. Gerhardt, *Draft and Public Policy*, p. 87, and Blair, *Forgotten*, pp. 9–10.

53. See Randolph and Taft correspondence, 12 December 1947 to 5 February 1948, in Box 891, SS Act file and Box 895, Compulsory Military Training file, Robert Taft Papers, Manuscript Room, LC, and Stephen M. Kohn, *Jailed for Peace: The History of American Draft Law Violators, 1658–1985* (Westport, Conn.: Greenwood, 1986), p. 69.

54. Press release by Committee Against Jim Crow in Military Service and Training, 5 February 1948, in Box 894, Compulsory Military Training file, staff papers, Robert Taft Papers, Manuscript Room, Library of Congress, Washington, D.C. (hereafter cited as Taft Papers, LC).

55. Dalfiume, *Desegregation*, pp. 163–64.

56. Grant Reynolds and Randolph to Taft, 31 May 1948, Compulsory Military Training file, Box 894, Taft Papers, LC; *New York Times*, 18 July 1948, p. 1; Dalfiume, *Desegregation*, p. 166; Gerhardt, *Draft*, p. 117; Bernard Franck, interview with author, 1 September 1977, Arlington, Va.; and Lee, "The Draft," p. 32.

57. Dalfiume, *Desegregation*, pp. 167–69; Royall press conference, 28 June 1948, VF 100x12, Lewis B. Hershey Papers, Military History Institute, Carlisle, Pa. (hereafter cited as LBH); and Bradley to President, 30 July 1948, PSF-Agencies, Box 146, HST.

58. Gerhardt, *Draft*, p. 125; *New York Times*, 20 July 1948, p. 1; Hershey speech to Industrial Conference of Armed Forces, 13 September 1948, Carton 65, RG 147, National Archives, Washington, D.C. (hereafter cited as NA); and Flynn, *Hershey*, p. 255; quote in Hershey to Joint Chiefs of Staff, 4 February 1949, Army file, LBH; quote in Hershey to Secretary of Defense, 20 May 1949, xerox file, LBH.

59. Hershey address, 9 April 1949, misc., LBH, MHI; Raoul A. Cortez to President, 31 July 1948, OF 440, Box 1288, HST.

60. Dalfiume, *Desegregation*, pp. 202, 210–11. The army issued no racial draft calls but did keep a lid on black enlistments until the Korean War. See Paone, "Volunteer," p. 17.

61. Edgar F. Puryear to Edward D. McKim, 11 June 1945, OF 245, Box 852, HST; Alfred Schindler to President, 25 May 1945, ibid.; Edward D. McKin to Alfred Schindler, 1 June 1945, ibid.

62. Vannevar Bush, *Science: the Endless Frontier: Report for the President on a Program for Postwar Science Research* (Washington, D.C.: USGPO, 1945), p. 25; Senator Alex S. Smith to G. H. Dorr, 8 August 1945, Science folder, Box 173, Patterson Papers, LC; quote in John Q. Stewart to Senator H. Alexander Smith, 7 August 1945, ibid.; Bradley Dewey to James R. Newman, 11 September 1945, ibid.; Bush to President, 16 August 1945, OF 53, Box 266, HST.

63. Patterson memo for Secretary of War, 9 August 1945, Science file, Box 173, Patterson papers, LC.

64. Selective Service memo, 17 September 1945, E15, Box 68, RG 147; Hershey to Vaughan, 28 September 1945, White House file, LBH; Patterson to Hershey, 10 October 1945, OF 245, Box 844, HST; Snyder to Secretary of War, 16 October 1945, item 5317, SS, reel 360, GCM; Patterson to Snyder, 24 November 1945, ibid; and Hershey to Matthew J. Connelly, White House file, LBH.

65. Statement by George Zook, ACE, 1946, in E15, Box 68, RG 147; Walter V. Bingham, "Inequalities in Adult Capacity—From Military Data," *Science* 104 (16 August 1946):152; Howard A. Meyerhoff to President, 4 January 1946, Box 845, OF 245, HST; *New York Times*, 26 January 1946, p. 28; and Lloyd W. Taylor to Robert Taft, 24 April 1946, SS folder, Box 880, Taft Papers, LC.

66. *New York Times*, 5 August 1946, p. 11; 5 June 1946, p. 17; 5 October 1946, p. 18; and draft letter, M. H. Trytten to Zimmerman, 20 June 1946, Ray R. Zimmerman file, HST.

67. Patterson to Hershey, 10 October 1945, Box 844, OF 245, HST; John R. Steelman to Hershey, 29 July 1946, OP, MHI; quote in Hershey to Senator Elbert D. Thomas, 22 March 1946, conf. file, MHI; William D. Hassett to Meyerhoff, 28 January 1946, Box 845, OF 245, HST; and Hershey to Taft, 7 October 1946, SS folder, Box 880, Taft Papers, LC.

68. *New York Times*, 8 March 1947, p. 11; 4 August 1947, p. 3; and 18 August 1947, p. 16. The American Chemical Society (ACS) published the results of a poll of its members on utilization during the war. From over 31,000 responses almost 60 percent of chemists and chemical engineers reported that their principal jobs were in industry. They had been deferred from combat or active duty, but the report ignored this salient fact, concentrating instead on the perception of those 21 percent who had served in the armed forces as a result of the draft. The people polled felt they had been underutilized by the military, and probably they had. But SS seems to have functioned well by deferring so many specialists. American Chemical Society, "Utilization of Chemists and Chemical Engineers in World War II," *Chemical and Engineering News* 25 (4 August 1947):2206–8; President's Commission on Higher Education, *Report, Higher Education for Democracy*, 6 vols. (Washington, D.C.: USGPO, 1947), 1:80.

69. The DOD came into existence as a result of the National Security Act of 26 July 1947. The act merged the army, navy, and air force under a Secretary of Defense and created the Central Intelligence Agency and the National Security Council.

70. See George Q. Flynn, "The Draft and College Deferments during the Korean War," *The Historian* 50 (May 1988):369–85, for a detailed discussion of the creation of this system. The plan remained dormant because the 1948 draft law acted merely as a stimulant to recruitment of volunteers for the armed forces. Draft calls withered away by 1949. The new law also provided for deferment of all students to the end of their academic year. The administration and the nation seemed content with the situation, and even the education and science lobby fell silent. The contradictions between a democratic ethos and a selective draft remained unresolved but untroubling during a period of manpower surplus.

71. Gerhardt, *Draft*, pp. 87, 112; Presidential speech file, 17 March 1948, Clifford file, HST.

72. Flynn, *Hershey*, pp. 168–69; Gerhardt, *Draft*, p. 93; Selective Service, *Selective Service under the 1948 Act* (Washington, D.C.: USGPO, 1951), pp. 7–8.

73. Harry A. Marmion, "Historical Background of Selective Service in the United

States," in Roger Little, ed., *Selective Service and American Society* (New York: Sage, 1969), p. 42; *Selective Service under 1948 Act*, p. 26.

74. Gary L. Wamsley, *Selective Service and a Changing America* (Columbus, Ohio: Merrill, 1969), p. 199; *Selective Service under 1948 Act*, p. 90; Richard Gillam, "The Peacetime Draft: Voluntarism to Coercion," in Martin Anderson, ed., *The Military Draft: Selected Readings on Conscription* (Stanford, Calif.: Hoover Institution, 1982), pp. 106, 108; Gerhardt, *Draft*, p. 126.

75. Samuel P. Huntington, *The Common Defense: Strategic Programs in National Politics* (New York: Columbia, 1961), p. 278; Gerhardt, *Draft*, p. 126; John M. Kendall, "An Inflexible Response: United States Army Manpower Mobilization Policies, 1945–1957" (Ph.D. diss., Duke University, 1982), pp. 142, 274.

Chapter 5. Korea

1. Selective Service, *Selective Service under 1948 Act Extended* (Washington, D.C.: USGPO, 1953), p. 3; Roger W. Gerhardt, *The Draft and Public Policy*, (Columbus, Ohio University, 1971) p. 128; John M. Kendall, "An Inflexible Response: United States Army Manpower Mobilization Policies, 1945–1957" (Ph.D. diss., Duke University Press, 1982), p. 152; C. Joseph Bernardo and E. H. Bacon, *American Military Policy* (Westport, Conn.: Greenwood, 1957, rep., 1977), p. 476.

2. Stephen E. Ambrose, *Rise to Globalism: American Foreign Policy Since 1938*, 4th ed. (New York: Penguin, 1985), pp. 113–15.

3. Patterson to Arthur Schlesinger, Jr., 1 June 1950, Box 45, Robert Patterson Papers, Manuscript Room, Library of Congress (hereafter LC).

4. Gerhardt, *Draft*, p. 129; Louis Johnson to Carl Vinson, 24 January 1950, OF 440, Box 1288, Harry S. Truman Library (hereafter HST); and George M. Elsey for Murphy, 11 January 1950, Elsey Papers, ibid.

5. For a discussion of how the war came about see Clay Blair, *The Forgotten War: America in Korea* (New York: Times Books, 1987); Joseph C. Goulden, *Korea: The Untold Story of the War* (New York: McGraw-Hill, 1983); and Bruce Cumings, *The Origins of the Korean War* (Princeton, N.J.: Princeton University Press, 1987).

6. Gerhardt, *Draft*, pp. 110, 128; Richard Gillam, "The Peacetime Draft, Voluntarism to Coercion," in Martin Anderson, ed., *The Military Draft: Selected Readings on Conscription* (Stanford, Calif.: Hoover Institution, 1982), p. 111; *Selective Service under 1948 Act* (Washington, D.C.: USGPO, 1951), p. 136; and *Selective Service under 1948 Act Extended*, p. 5.

7. Robert K. Griffith, Jr., "About Face? The U.S. Army and the Draft," *Armed Forces and Society* 12 (Fall 1985):114.

8. Connelly notes on Cabinet meeting, 8 July 1950, Connelly Papers, Box 1, HST.

9. Kendall, "Inflexible," pp. 2, 158, 179.

10. Ibid., pp. 2, 158, 179, 195, 274, 275. Johnson quote in *Selective Service under 1948 Act Extended*, p. 7.

11. Kendall, "Inflexible," pp. 167, 170, 172, 180, 183, 201; and Gerhardt, *Draft*, p. 148.

12. Robert J. Donovan, *Tumultuous Years: The Presidency of Harry S. Truman, 1949–1953* (New York: Norton, 1982), p. 254, and Samuel P. Huntington, *The Common Defense: Strategic Programs in National Politics* (New York: Columbia, 1961), p. 279.

13. Kendall, "Inflexible," p. 190, and Hershey to Fulbright, 3 November 1950,

xerox 2606/SD370.01, B595, George C. Marshall Papers, Marshall Research Center, Lexington, Va. (hereafter GCM).

14. Kendall, "Inflexible," pp. 185–86; U.S., Dept. of Commerce, *Historical Statistics of the United States*, 2 pts. (Washington, D.C.: USGPO, 1975), 2:1143.

15. Kendall, "Inflexible," p. 193, and J. D. Small to Hershey, 12 December 1950, xerox 2606/SD370.01, B595, GCM.

16. Rosenberg, Memo for Record, 1 March 1951, Ent 56, Box 11, RG 330; idem, 16 April 1951, ent 57, Box 2, ibid.; idem., 1 May 1951, ent 56, Box 12, ibid.

17. Rosenberg to Hershey, n.d., ent 56, Box 11, ibid.; and *Selective Service under 1948 Act Extended*, p. 12.

18. Rosenberg for President, 18 October 1952, WHCF, DOD, Box 15, HST; *Selective Service under 1948 Act Extended*, p. 65; *Selective Service Annual Report, 1952* (Washington, D.C.: USGPO, 1953), p. 17; *Selective Service Annual Report, 1953* (Washington, D.C.: USGPO, 1954), pp. 1, 11–12, 26; A 1 percent sample inventory of all registrants in 1953 found the following distribution: Unclassified, 6.2 percent; Classified, 93.8 percent; 1-A, 10.4 percent; 1-S, 2.0 percent; 1-C ind., 10.5 percent; 1-C enl., 16.2 percent; 2-C agr., 1.1 percent; 2-A ind., 0.3 percent; 2-S, 2.0 percent; 3-A dep., 12.6 percent; 4-A vet., 10.1 percent; 4-F, 18.5 percent; see "Selective Service Sample Inventory," 30 April 1953, Lewis B. Hershey Papers (hereafter cited as LBH).

19. *Selective Service Newsletter*, November 1951, p. 4 (hereafter cited as *SSN*).

20. Martin V. Coffey to President, 10 February 1950, OF 440, Box 1288, HST.

21. Research and Statistics Memo, 12 September 1951, VF 200S5, LBH.

22. Selective Service, Research and Statistics Memo, VF 351S1, 31 January 1950, LBH. This study estimated that in 1949 the result of Selective Service was an additional 20,000 volunteers each month. Harold Wool, "Military Manpower Procurement and Supply," in Roger Little, ed., *A Survey of Military Institutions* (Chicago: InterUniversity Seminar, 1969), p. 65.

23. U.S., *Statutes at Large*, 62 Stat. 624 (24 June 1948). The 1948 law had included an agreement between the Department of Defense and SS. Section 15(d) provided that voluntary enlistments could continue alongside the draft, but that "no person shall be accepted for enlistment after he has received orders to report for induction." Through an interservice agreement, the enlistment deadline had been extended to the date a man received notice of his preinduction physical.

24. John T. Gibson to T. S. Repplier, 29 June 1950, Gibson Papers, HST. In the six months before the Korean invasion no branch of the service had averaged better than 80 percent of its recruiting quota.

25. Ford to Marshall, 18 January 1951, ent 66, file 327.02, RG 330, and Marshall to Representative E. P. Scrivner, 4 September 1951, xerox 2607/SD341.01, SS, B639, GCM.

26. Robert A. Lovett to Rep. Gerald Ford, 23 February 1951, ent 66, 327.02, RG 330; Marshall to Rep. Ford, 3 April 1951, ent 56, Box 12, ibid.; idem to Rep. Errett P. Scrivner, 4 September 1951, SS, xerox 2607/SD 341.01, B639, GCM; Rosenberg for Col. K. R. Kreps, 4 September 1951, ibid.

27. Roger Little, "Procurement of Manpower," in Roger Little, ed., *Selective Service and American Society* (New York: Sage, 1969) p. 27; Samuel H. Hays, "A Military View of Selective Service," in Sol Tax, ed., *The Draft: A Handbook of Facts and Alternatives* (Chicago: University of Chicago, 1967), p. 12; Samuel H. Hays, *Defense Manpower: The Management of Military Conscription* (Washington, D.C.: ICAF,

1968), p. 7; Victory Hicken, *The American Fighting Man* (New York: Macmillan, 1969), p. 191.

28. Hershey to Secretary of Defense, 27 February 1951, xerox 2607/ SD321.B586, GCM, and Marshall to Secretaries of Army, Navy, AF, 4 April 1951, ibid.

29. One source of controversy was the prohibition of legal representation at the local board appearance, but the boards could allow witnesses to appear.

30. *Selective Service under the 1948 Act Extended*, p. 60; *Selective Service Annual Report, 1952*, pp. 36–37; *Selective Service Annual Report, 1954*, p. 29.

31. SSN, October 1952, p. 3; Science Research Associates, *Unfit for Service: A Review of the Draft and Basic Education in the Army* (Chicago: SRA, 1966), p. 200; SSN, April 1953, p. 1; George H. Gallup, *The Gallup Poll: Public Opinion, 1935–1971*, 3 vols. (New York: Random House, 1972) 2: 1124–25.

32. Huntington, *Common Defense*, p. 181; George Q. Flynn, *Lewis B. Hershey: Mr. Selective Service* (Chapel Hill: University of North Carolina, 1985), p. 190.

33. *Selective Service under 1948 Act Extended*, p. 10; and Lovett quoted in SSN, September 1952, p. 1;

34. Conant to Eisenhower, 22 September 1950, Pre-president, Pres. file, Box 27, Dwight D. Eisenhower Papers, Eisenhower Library, Abilene, Kansas (hereafter cited as DDE); Resolution for Association of American Universities, 30 November 1950, PP, Box 164, ibid.; James A. Barber, Jr., "The Social Effects of Military Service," in Stephen Ambrose and James Barber, eds., *The Military and American Society* (New York: Free Press, 1972), p. 152.

35. Report by DOD on Manpower Mobilization, 28 December 1950, xerox 2606/SD370.01, B595, GCM; Notes of Meeting, General Marshall, Rosenberg, et al., 20 December 1950, ent 56, RG 330; Marshall to Secretaries of Army, Navy, Air Force, etc., 28 December 1950, ibid.

36. Report by DOD on Manpower Mobilization, 28 December 1950, Xerox 2606/SD370.01, B595, GCM, and Rosenberg statement to Johnson Committee, 9 January 1951, ibid.

37. Kendall, "Inflexible," p. 216; Gen. William O. Quirey to Paul Wollstadt, 20 October 1969, Box 9, RG 220.

38. Kendall, "Inflexible," p. 205; Pvt. Doug Brown to Taft, Selective Service Act file, Box 1061, Robert Taft Papers, LC.

39. Rosenberg to Daniel F. Curran, 27 April 1951, ent 56, Box 12, RG 330; Marshall quote, to Senator Theodore F. Green, 17 May 1951, ibid.; Marshall to Rep. George P. Miller, 22 May 1951, ibid.; Rosenberg to Rep. A. B. Kelley, 31 May 1951, ibid. For the voluminous correspondence by complaining veterans see the entire ent 66, ibid.

40. Denis S. Phillipps, "The American People and Compulsory Military Service" (Ph.D. diss., New York University, 1955), p. 471; and Marshall to Senator _____ , 6 March 1951, ent 56, Box 11, RG 330.

41. Alfred O'Gara to Taft, 13 January 1951, draft folder, Box 962, Taft Papers; Taft to Rev. Archibald G. Adams, 3 April 1951, ibid.; Roswell B. Perkins to Taft, 9 February 1951, ibid.; James G. Patton to Taft, 9 February 1951, ibid.; Mark Leva and R. Lovett to Chief of Staff, 27 February 1951, ent 56, Box 11, RG 330; Cabinet Meeting Notes, 9 February 1951, M. Connelly Papers, Box 1, HST; and Patterson to Rosenberg, 23 January 1951, Box 45, Robert Patterson Papers, LC.

42. Harry A. Marmion, "Historical Background of Selective Service in the United

States," in Little, *Selective Service in American Society*, p. 43; Wool, "Military Manpower Procurement," p. 39; *Selective Service under 1948 Act Extended*, p. 13.

43. Joe P. Dunn, "UMT: A Historical Perspective," *Military Review* 61 (January 1981):16–17, and Kendall, "Inflexible," p. 223.

44. *SSN*, January 1952, p. 2; June 1952, p. 3; *Selective Service under 1948 Act Extended*, pp. 69, 86; *Selective Service Annual Report, 1952*, p. 37; *Selective Service Annual Report, 1953*, p. 27; *Selective Service Annual Report, 1954* (Washington, D.C.: USGPO, 1955), p. 30; and *Historical Statistics*, 2:1144.

45. "The Silent Generation," in Keith L. Nelson, ed., *The Impact of War on American Life* (New York: Holt, Rinehart and Winston, 1971), p. 229; *SSN*, June 1952, p. 3; and October 1951, p. 3.

46. Quotes from Albert J. Mayer and Thomas F. Hoult, "Social Stratification and Combat Survival," *Social Forces* 34 (December 1955): 155–58; Morris Janowitz, "The Logic of National Service," in Tax, *The Draft*, pp. 75–76; Morris Janowitz memo, n.d., Box 39, NACSS, RG 220.

47. Michael Useem, *Conscription, Protest, and Social Conflict: The Life and Death of a Draft Resistance Movement* (New York: John Wiley and Sons, 1973), pp. 82–83; Charles C. Moskos, Jr., *The American Enlisted Man* (New York: Sage, 1970), p. 9. Mayer and Hoult also found that nonwhite casualty rates were almost 50 percent higher than white rates when average value of homes, the class variable, was controlled. But once again we find that nonwhites rushed to enlist in the army when race barriers were lifted in early 1950. Albert J. Mayer and Thomas F. Hoult, "Social Stratification and Combat Survival," *Social Forces* 34 (1 December 1955):158. See also Richard M. Dalfiume, *Desegregation of the United States Armed Forces* (Columbia: University of Missouri, 1969), pp. 210–11.

48. Bill Boyd, memo for files, 3 November 1950, OF 440, Box 1288, HST; A. Rosenberg to Lee Clark, 8 May 1951, ent 56, Box 12, RG 330; Rosenberg to Mrs. Douglas Horton, 2 May 1951, ibid.; and Science Research Associates, *Unfit for Service*, p. 207.

49. *Selective Service under 1948 Act Extended*, p. 56, and *Selective Service Annual Report, 1953*, p. 16.

50. *Selective Service Annual Report, 1953*, pp. 16–18, and Hershey to Taft, 26 November 1951, SS Act file, Box 1061, Taft Papers.

51. George H. Gallup, *The Gallup Poll: Public Opinion, 1935–1971*, 3 vols. (New York: Random House, 1972), 2:1067; *New York Times*, 12 October 1951, p. 1; Rosenberg for President, 18 October 1952, WHCF, DOD, Box 15, HST; and Connelly cabinet meeting notes, 12 September 1952, Connelly Papers, Box 1, HST.

52. For a discussion of Selective Service treatment of COs see George Q. Flynn, "Lewis Hershey and the Conscientious Objector: World War II," *Military Affairs* 47 (February 1983):1–6, and George Q. Flynn, "Selective Service and the Conscientious Objector," in Michael Noone, ed., *Selective Conscientious Objection* (Boulder, Colo.: Westview, 1989), pp. 35–55.

53. *Selective Service under the 1948 Act*, pp. 31, 78; U.S. Department of Commerce *Historical Statistics of the United States: Colonial Times to 1970*, 2 pts. (Washington, D.C.: USGPO, 1975) 2:1143; Clip from *War Resister*, Spring 1953, in VF 345.84W25, LBH; *Selective Service Annual Report, 1951*, p. 3; *Selective Service Annual Report, 1954*, p. 28; Roger W. Jones to Hopkins, 19 February 1952, OF 245, Box 845, HST; and SS, Research and Statistics memo, 14 March 1952, Study of IV-D, VF 344S3, LBH.

54. Ulysses Lee, "The Draft and the Negro," *Current History* 55 (July 1968):32;

Selective Service under 1948 Act Extended, p. 4 for quote; Campbell C. Johnson mss., 1 October 1951, Box 47, 171J66N, RG 147–97; Bernard Franck interview with author, 1 September 1977, Arlington, Va.; Dalfiume, *Desegregation*, pp. 202, 210–11.

55. J. F. Cassidy memo for Adm. McCrea, 9 August 1950, ent 66,327.02, RG 330; and *SSN*, June 1952, p. 3.

56. *Historical Statistics*, 1:501.

57. Selective Service, Research and Statistics memo on 2-C, 26 December 1951, VF 321S11, LBH; *Selective Service Annual Report, 1952*, pp. 9, 26; Selective Service, Research and Statistics Sample Survey, 25 November 1953, LBH; and *Selective Service Annual Report, 1954*, p. 20.

58. Gerhardt, *Draft*, p. 107; James G. Patton to President, 12 February 1952, OF 245, Box 845, HST; Patton to President, 28 April 1953, CF, OF 133-K-1, Box 664, DDE; Rep. James T. Patterson to Hershey, 21 April 1953, ibid.; Hershey to Sherman Adams, 3 July 1953, ibid.; J. E. Carroll to Gen. Vaughan, 15 September 1950, OF 440, Box 1288, HST; and Loren B. Lewis to Sen. Taft, 8 November 1951, SS Act, Box 1061, Taft Papers, LC.

59. Science Research Associates, *Unfit for Service*, p. 206.

60. Hershey to President, 18 February 1952, OF 245, Box 852, HST.

61. Office of Defense Mobilization, Policy Statement, 27 June 1952, OF 440, Box 1288, HST; Truman to Hershey, 26 June 1952, ibid.; Truman on EO, ibid.; and Hershey to President, 27 June 1952, ibid.

62. Ambrose and Barber, *Military and American Society*, p. 46; Selective Service, Research and Statistics Memo, 6 August 1952, VF 320.651, LBH; and *Selective Service Annual Report, 1952*, p. 29.

63. EO amending SS Regs., 31 March 1951, OF 245, Box 845, HST; News release by Charles Sawyer, 8 April 1951, ent 66, 327.02, RG 330; News release by Department of Labor, 7 May 1951, ibid.

64. *SSN*, September 1951, p. 1; *National Manpower Council, Student Deferments and National Manpower Policy* (New York: Columbia, 1952), p. 4; EO, 26 June 1952, OF 440, Box 1288, HST; White House News Release, 27 June 1952, ibid.; *SSN*, August, 1952, p. 1; W. M. Flowers to John R. Steelman, 19 September 1952, OF 245, Box 852, HST; and Carl A. Frische to Hershey, 26 June 1953, OASD, 327.22, RG 330.

65. Report of National Security Resource Board, 1951, PSF-NSRB, Box 146, HST; President to Heads of Ex. Depts. and Agencies, 17 January 1951, OF 2855, Box 1731, ibid.; Hugh L. Dryden to Alexander Wetmore, 25 January 1952, OF 245, Box 852, ibid.; and Betty M. Vetter to *Washington Post*, 14 October 1969, Alpha file, LBH.

66. W. Albert Noyes, Jr., to President, 21 August 1950, OF 2855, Box 1731, HST, and Report by Alex C. Monteith, 18 December 1950, Trytten file, LBH.

67. This discussion relies mainly on George Q. Flynn, "The Draft and College Deferments," pp. 369–85.

Chapter 6. The 1950s and Military Manpower

1. See especially William L. O'Neill, *American High: The Years of Confidence, 1945–1960* (New York: Free Press, 1986) and Stephen E. Ambrose, *Eisenhower: The President* (New York: Simon and Schuster, 1984).

2. Eisenhower Diary, 10 May 1946, Box 12, Dwight David Eisenhower Papers, Eisenhower Library, Abilene, Kansas (hereafter cited as DDE); ibid., 15 May 1946; and Rocco M. Paone, "The Last Volunteer Army, 1946–1948," *Military Review* 49 (December 1969):9; John M. Kendall, "Inflexible Response: United States Army Manpower Mobilization Policies, 1945–1957" (Ph.D. diss., Duke University, 1982), pp. 56, 58, 86; and DDE Diary, 10 May 1946, Box 12, DDE. James M. Gerhardt, *The Draft and Public Policy* (Columbus: Ohio State, 1971), pp. 38–39, speaks of Eisenhower's desire for an army of 1.5 million in summer 1946.

3. Quote in memo of conference by Karl T. Compton with Robert Patterson and Eisenhower, 10 February 1947, President's Advisory Commission on UMT, Box 6, Harry S. Truman Papers, Truman Library, Independence, Mo. (hereafter cited as HST); and Major General F. L. Parks to Hershey, 19 February 1947, Op. War file, Lewis B. Hershey Papers, Military History Institute, Carlisle, Pa. (hereafter cited as LBH).

4. Statement before Armed Services Committee, April 1948, copy in CF OP, Box 663, DDE; Eisenhower to Johnson, 31 July 1950, PSF Cabinet, Box 156, HST; James B. Conant to Eisenhower, 22 September 1950, Pre-presidential file, Box 27, DDE; Kendall, "Inflexible," p. 216; and *New York Times*, 8 December 1950, p. 22.

5. Leon Bramson, "The High School Student, the Draft, and Voluntary National Service Alternatives: Some Survey Data," in Sol Tax, ed., *The Draft: A Handbook of Facts and Alternatives* (Chicago: University of Chicago, 1967), p. 185.

6. Eisenhower to Cole and Johnson, 3 March 1952, Central file, OF, Box 663, DDE; Press conference, 7 June 1952, ibid.

7. Memo from National Security Training Commission to General Eisenhower, 29 December 1952, Central file, OF, Box 663, DDE.

8. Stephen E. Ambrose, *Eisenhower: The President* (New York: Simon and Schuster, 1984) pp. 51–52.

9. Notes by B.N.H. for General Persons, 10 February 1953, Central file, OF, Box 663, DDE.

10. Minutes of meeting on legislation, 9 February 1953, WHO: Staff Sec, Leg. Mt., 1, DDE; and Persons Memo for Shanley, 10 February 1953, Central file, OF, Box 663, ibid.

11. Harlow to Person, 2 March 1953, CF, OF, Box 664, DDE; *New York Times*, 28 January 1953, p. 13; Hershey to Persons, 6 March 1953, 1950s misc. file, LBH; and Joe C. Stewart to Charles Wilson, 29 July 1953, OASD, 327.22, RG 330, NA.

12. Minutes of meeting on legislation, 24 June 1953, WHO: Staff sec., Leg. Mt., 4, DDE.

13. Minutes of meeting on legislation, 24 June 1953, WHO: Staff sec., leg. Mt., 4, DDE; Arthur S. Flemming to Jones, 29 June 1953, CF, OF, Box 664, DDE; and *Newsweek*, 5 October 1953, p. 24.

14. Minutes of ODM Manpower Policy meeting, 3 June 1953, OASD, 327.22, RG 330, NA; Flemming to Jones, 29 June 1953, CF, OF, Box 664, DDE; Roger W. Jones to AG, 30 June 1953, ibid; Albert Kay, memo for record, 4 June 1953, OASD, 327.22, RG 330, National Archives, Washington, D.C.; and John A. Hannah to Rep. Gerald R. Ford, 5 June 1953, OASD 327.02, ibid.

15. Press release, 11 July 1953, CF, OF, Box 664, DDE, and Wilton B. Persons to Rep. Bob Wilson, 13 August 1953, ibid.

16. Dee Ingold, "Selective Service, 1953–1965," mss. in Dee Ingold file, author's possession; Selective Service, *Selective Service Annual Report, 1953* (Washington, D.C.: USGPO, 1954), pp. 1, 11.

17. U.S., Dept. of Commerce, *Historical Statistics of the United States*, 2 pts. (Washington, D.C.: USGPO, 1975), 2:1143.

18. *New York Times*, 19 September 1953, p. 3; 10 November 1953, p. 34; and 15 March 1954, p. 11.

19. *Historical Statistics*, 2:1141, and Dargusch to Flemming, 20 December 1955, CF, OF, Box 664, DDE.

20. Staff Sec. notes, Cabinet meeting, 19 July 1957, WHO, Box 4, DDE; *Washington Star*, 12 August 1957; Toner Notes, 21 April 1958, Box 32, DDE Diary, DDE; and Selective Service, Research and Statistics memo, 29 March 1960, LBH.

21. Memo from Charles F. Willis to Arthur S. Flemming, 8 September 1954, CF, Box 231, DDE. Originally this appeal board had operated from the director's office, but Truman had made it independent. By the 1950s the three members on the board had established a reputation for bipartisanship and integrity. In early 1954, however, a dispute arose between the board and the director. Hershey resented the independence of the board because some of its appeal decisions had gone against agency policy, and he sought to resume control of all appeals. The board learned of his effort and immediately mobilized its considerable constituency. Eventually the White House entered the picture, and the board remained independent. See Roger W. Jones to Gen. Wilton B. Persons, 25 February 1954, CF, Box 231, DDE, and VF 140S5, 31 December 1955, LBH.

22. Selective Service, Research and Statistics memo, 26 November 1956, VF 100S13, LBH.

23. Hershey speech, State Directors Conference, 16 May 1960, LBH.

24. Publicity release, Selective Service, Public Information Office, 9 April 1958, VF 100S7, LBH; Hershey to Congress, copy in *Selective Service Newsletter*, March 1958, p. 1 (hereafter cited as *SSN*); Ingold Mss., p. 18; and Briefing note for PB Mtg gW/11w, 21 June 1960, Gray Papers, DDE.

25. Memo for NSC, 8 June 1960, Gray Papers, DDE; Briefing note for PB MTG gW/11w, 21 June 1960, ibid.; quote in U.S. Congress, House, Committee on Appropriations, *Hearings, Independent Office Appropriation*, 87th Cong., 1st sess. 18 January 1960, p. 9 (hereafter cited as HSAC).

26. George Q. Flynn, "The Draft and College Deferments during the Korean War," *The Historian* 50 (May 1988):375–77; HSAC, 1 September 1953, p. 9.

27. Conant to Eisenhower, 27 November 1948, Prepres, 1916–1952, PF, Box 27, DDE; Minutes of Science Adv. Com., 9 December 1948, VF 324s2, LBH.

28. HSAC, 1 September 1953, p. 11, and Flynn, "College Deferments," p. 377.

29. Research and Statistics report, 31 March 1958, "Selective Service and the College Student," Statistics, vol. 3, Box 3, RG 147; HSAC, p. 13. Freshmen originally had to score 70 or be in the upper half of their class; sophomores 70 or upper two-thirds of their class; juniors 70 or upper three-fourths; seniors entering graduate school 75 or upper half; entering professional schools 70 or upper half of their class.

30. "The College Student and Selective Service," 1 July 1953, brochures in VF 314T2g, LBH. Before the program began to operate effectively several principles were compromised at national headquarters. Reluctantly, Selective Service agreed to accept the eligibility of part-time instructors who were pursuing graduate degrees, if teaching was part of their training. Hershey also, in early 1951, accepted a temporary delay in the call of graduating seniors, giving them a chance to find jobs in a defense industry.

31. Flynn, "College Deferments," p. 380–81; Donald D. Stewart, "The Dilemma of Deferment," *Journal of Higher Education* 24 (April 1953):187; and HSAC, p. 14.

32. George H. Gallup, *The Gallup Poll: Public Opinion, 1935–1971*, 3 vols. (New York: Random House, 1972), 2:966, 985, 1067; Flynn, "College Deferments," pp. 381, 384; and *Selective Service Annual Report, 1953*, p. 18.

33. E. Suchman, R. M. Williams, and R. K. Goldsen, "Student Reaction to Impending Military Service," *American Sociological Review* 18 (June 1953):296–302, and Patti M. Peterson, "Student Organizations and the Antiwar Movement in America, 1900–1960," *American Studies* 13 (Spring 1972):142.

34. Selective Service, Research and Statistics memo, 15 October 1956, LBH, and *Historical Statistics*, 1:380.

35. Selective Service, Research and Statistics memo, 15 October 1956, LBH.

36. Ibid., 1 February 1955, LBH.

37. Selective Service, SAC memo "Does a Military Interruption Decrease Chances of Obtaining a Degree?" 1 April 1953, VF 314s41, LBH. A recent study suggests that, for black Americans, military service had a generally beneficial effect upon social mobility. See John Modell, Marc Goulden, and Sigurdur Magnusson, "World War II in the Lives of Black Americans," *Journal of American History* 76 (December 1989):838. A similar experience occurred in World War II with American Indians, who had initially resisted Selective Service intrusion onto the reservation. Eventually American Indians were drafted and the service time proved assimilating; see Alison R. Bernstein, *Ameican Indians and World War II: Toward a New Era in Indian Affairs* (Norman: University of Oklahoma Press, 1991).

38. Editorial, "The College Eye," 17 July 1953, Cedar Falls, Iowa; Vernon R. Loucks to John A. Hannah, 17 February 1953, OASD, 327.22, RG 330; Gerald Ford to President, 1 June 1953, ibid., 327.02; Stewart, "Dilemma," pp. 188–90; Kenny S. Kaminski to Hannah, 5 March 1953, OASC, ent. 66, 327.22, RG 330; Hannah to Kutner, ? February 1953, ibid.; and Joe C. Stewart to Charles Wilson, 29 July 1953, ibid.

39. HSAC, pp. 19–24; Albert Kay memo, 4 June 1953, OASD, 327.22, RG 330; Minutes, ODM committee on manpower policy, 19 March 1953, OASD, 327.22, ibid.; Wilton B. Persons memo for Hershey, 3 March 1953, CF, OF, Box 664, DDE; and Defense Manpower Administration, Dept. of Labor, memo, 8 April 1953, ent 66, OASD, 327.22, RG 330.

40. Blake R. Van Leer to Renfrow, 22 June 1954, Renfrow staybacks, LBH, and *Selective Service Annual Report, 1954* (Washington, D.C.: USGPO, 1955), p. 20.

41. Meeting of National Selective Service Scientific Advisory Group (SSSAG), 25 May 1955, LBH.

42. Selective Service, Research and Statistics study, sample survey, 8 February 1955, LBH, and *Historical Statistics*, 1:371.

43. "Campus to Chaos," pp. 33–40; SSN, 28 April 1960, p. 1; Selective Service, Research and Statistics report, 31 March 1960, Box 3, RG 147; and idem., vol. 3, 31 March 1958, Box 3, ibid.

44. Hershey to Carl Vinson, 29 June 1959, Congressional file, LBH; news clipping, 15 November 1959, VF 357, LBH; U.S. Congress, Senate, Committee On Appropriations, *Hearings on Independent Office Appropriations*, 86th Cong., 1st sess., 26 May 1959, p. 9; and Selective Service, Research and Statistics, vol. 3, 31 March 1958, Box 3, RG 147.

45. Selective Service, minutes of State Director's Conference, 16–20 May 1960, LBH.

46. Hershey quote in *Chemical and Engineering News*, 7 April 1955, p. 702; and Minutes of National SSS Advisory Group, 16 February 1956, LBH.

47. Howard A. Meyerhoff, "Arms and Manpower," mss. copy in VF 324.1M61, LBH; Carmichael quoted in mss. "Whittemore Symposium Sponsored by American Psychology Association," 1 March 1953, in VF 324W62mv, ibid.; Lohr in *Chemical and Engineering News*, 7 April 1955, p. 700; and Fletcher, ibid.

48. Dargusch speech, 15 May 1956, VF 324D21, LBH, and *Chemical and Engineering News*, 7 April 1955, p. 700.

49. Killian to Senator Paul Douglas, 12 May 1958, CF, OF 133-k-1, Box 665, DDE; *Chemical and Engineering News*, 7 April 1955, pp. 702, 704; and Selective Service, Research and Statistics memo, 31 March 1960, LBH.

50. Selective Service, Research and Statistics report, 31 March 1960, pp. 6-7, Box 3, RG 147.

51. Meyerhoff, "Arms and Manpower," 1954, in VF 324.1m61, LBH, and Donald S. Clark to Hershey, 13 October 1953, OASD file, 327.22, RG 330.

52. Clark to Hershey, 13 October 1953, OASD file, 327.22, RG 330; John A. Hannah to Donald S. Clark, 12 November 1953, ibid.; Meyerhoff, "Arms and Manpower," 1954, in VF 324.1m61, LBH; Flemming to Rowland R. Hughes, 26 August 1954, CF, Box 664, DDE; and Haggerty on EO, 20 September 1954, ibid.

53. Lawrence H. O'Neill to Senator Javits, 7 May 1954, CF, OF 133-k-1, Box 665, DDE; Javits to Gerald D. Morgan, 24 August 1954, ibid; Morgan to Javits, 13 July 1954 and 17 November 1954, ibid.

54. Cited in George Q. Flynn, *Lewis B. Hershey: Mr. Selective Service* (Chapel Hill: University of North Carolina, 1985), pp. 207-8.

55. Meyerhoff to Arthur S. Flemming, 14 March 1955, CF, OF 133-k-1, Box 665, DDE; Selective Service, Research and Statistics memo, sample survey, 8 February 1955, LBH. Additional deferments for specialized personnel became available under the 1955 Reserve Forces Act. The act offered an opportunity for men with critical skills over age 18.5 to enlist in a six-month training program, after which they were allowed to return to their jobs. See Gerhardt, *Draft*, p. 208.

Ideally, the six-month program would offer help to those scientists who had used up their 2-A deferments. But the easing of eligibility for other deferments worked against the pressure to enlist for six months. Enlistment in the reserves did rise after the act passed, but not only from the actions of specialized personnel. From 1956 through 1958 some 10,611 men applied for the program, but actual enlistments totalled only 5,897. By fall 1960 there were 11,975 individuals serving. The group included chemists (641), engineer draftsmen (1,403), engineer professionals (7,381), mathematicians (206), physicists (174), orthopedic appliance technicians (4), and a variety of other specialists. See MG Harry L. Twaddle, memo to Chief of Military History, 5 August 1953, Army staff, Box 669, RG 319; NSS Science Advisory Group minutes, 25 May 1955, LBH; Proceedings of Engineers Joint Council, 26 January 1956, VF 100H26, LBH; NSS Science Advisory Group minutes, 16 February 1956, LBH; ibid, 18 December 1958, LBH; and Report on Part 1680 of Selective Service regulations, 30 September 1960, CF, OF, Box 664, DDE.

56. Carl A. Frische to Hershey, 26 June 1953, OASD, 327.22, RG 330, and Howard A. Meyerhoff, "Arms and Manpower," 1954, in VF 324.1M61, LBH.

57. Hershey to Flemming, 6 August 1954, CF, Box 664, DDE; NSS Science Advisory Group minutes, 25 May 1955, LBH; and Michigan Survey, 1955, VF 324.s12, LBH.

58. Hershey speech, Proceedings of Engineers Joint Council assembly, 26 January 1956, VF 100H26, LBH.

59. Minutes of NSS, Science Advisory Group, 18 December 1958, LBH.

60. Selective Service, Research and Statistics report, 31 March 1960, pp. 10–11, Box 3, RG 147–97. Yet as deferments were soon offered to all students, Selective Service's claim to be channeling men into special areas of shortage seems dubious.

61. Report on Physical Fitness on Selective Service Registrants, 12 September 1955, CF, OF, Box 664, DDE; Selective Service, *Selective Service Annual Report, 1957* (Washington, D.C.: USGPO, 1958), p. 32; and Selective Service, Research and Statistics memo, 3 February 1955, p. 3, LBH.

62. Report on Physical Fitness on Selective Service Registrants, 12 September 1955, CF, OF, Box 664, DDE; Bernard D. Karpinos, "Evaluation of the Physical Fitness of Present-Day Inductees," *Armed Forces Medical Journal* 4 (1 March 1953):232; Bernard D. Karpinos, "Statistics on Men Disqualified for Military Service Because of Cancer," *Journal of the National Cancer Institute* 24 (1960):755.

63. Karpinos, "Fitness," pp. 222, 239–40.

64. Dee Ingold, Selective Service, 1953–1965 mss., ca. 1970, Ingold file; *Selective Service Annual Report, 1954*, p. 31; J. F. C. Hyde to A. J. Goodpaster, 15 July 1957, CF, OF, Box 664, DDE; Secretary of Defense to Hon. Sam Rayburn, 15 July 1957, ibid.; Press release, 28 July 1958, ibid.; and Briefing note for PB Mtg GW/11w, 21 June 1960, Gray Papers, ibid.

65. Lewis Hershey, "The Inside Story on Rejection Rates," *Journal of the American Association for Health, Physical Education and Recreation*, 1 January 1953, pp. 9, 26; Whittemore symposium, 1 March 1953, p. 119, VF 324W62mv, LBH; Eanes to Hershey, 20 September 1955, Box 60, file 630e12, RG 147; and Minutes of Selective Service Science Advisory Group, 18 December 1958, LBH.

66. See Flynn, "American Medicine and Selective Service in World War II," *Journal of the History of Medicine and Allied Sciences* 42 (July 1987):325–26; William D. Tribble, *Doctor Draft Justified?* (San Antonio: National Biomedical Laboratories, 1968), p. 35; and Roma K. McNickle, "Medical Manpower," *Editorial Research Reports* 1 (14 February 1951):103, 112.

67. Local board memo no. 7, Healing Arts Educational Advisory Committee, 2 November 1948, VF 324.6s11, LBH; Selective Service, Research and Statistics Report, 20 April 1949, VF 324.6s11, ibid.; *Proceedings of Engineering Joint Council*, 24 April 1951, p. 4; and Eanes speech, 11 June 1952, VF 314E12, LBH.

68. Quote from Selective Service Research and Statistics memo, 22 March 1955, LBH, and Tribble, *Doctor Draft*, pp. 30, 35.

69. Roma K. McNickle, "Medical Manpower," pp. 109–10, 112.

70. Extract from House Armed Services Committee, Hearings on HR 9554, 28 August 1950, in xerox 2606/sd370.01,b795, George C. Marshall Papers, Marshall Research Center, Lexington, Va. (hereafter cited as GCM).

71. McNickle, "Medical Manpower," p. 110.

72. Truman to Secretary of Defense, 9 September 1950, OF 145, Box 845, HST.

73. *Selective Service under 1948 Act Extended* (Washington, D.C.: USGPO, 1953), p. 9; Frank Pace, Jr., to Sec. of Defense, 23 September 1950, xerox 2606/sd370.01,b595, GCM; Marshall to President, 5 October 1950, ibid; McNickle, "Medical Manpower," pp. 110, 111; and Rosenberg to Homburger, 24 May 1951, ent 56, ASD, Box 12, RG 330.

74. Rusk quoted in *New York Times*, 4 October 1950. See OF 440, Box 1288, HST.

75. Quote in Harry J. McGregor to Bert Wheeler, 5 October 1950, OF 440, Box 1288, HST; Martin L. Friedman memo for Donald S. Dawson, 25 October 1950,

ibid.; Memo Secretary of Defense to Secretaries of Army, Navy, Air Force, 1951, ent 56, Box 11, RG 330, NA; and McNickle, "Medical Manpower," pp. 113-14.

76. McNickle, "Medical Manpower," p. 103; and Omer speech, 22 February 1953, LBH file. Dr. Rusk announced that if the military rose to 5 million there would be a shortage of 22,000 doctors in the nation by 1954.

77. Harold W. Glattly, "Problems of the Armed Forces," *Journal of the Student American Medical Association* 2 (November 1953):44-45.

78. Omer speech, 22 February 1953, LBH, and *Journal of the American Medical Association*, editorial, 7 February 1953 (hereafter cited as *JAMA*) in Selective Service Gen. file, Box 1270, Robert Taft Papers, Manuscript Room, Library of Congress, Washington, D.C.

79. Selective Service, Research and Statistics memo, 27 April 1953, LBH; and idem., 3 May 1955, ibid.

80. C. Joseph Stetler, "The Doctor Draft and You," *Journal of the Student American Medical Association* 2 (November 1953):70, and Whitman, Press, Conf. box 1, 25 February 1953, DDE.

81. Stetler, "Doctor Draft," pp. 44, 70, 74; JAMA editorial, 7 February 1953, in Selective Service Gen. file, Box 1270, Taft Papers, LC.

82. C. R. Lulenski, MD, to Taft, 26 March 1953, Selective Service Gen. file, Box 1270, Taft Papers; J. Harry Hayes to Taft, 10 March 1953, ibid.; Robert Gorman to Taft, 25 May 1953, ibid.; G. Richard Hardin to Taft, 16 January 1953, ibid.; Hershey to Taft, 4 March 1953, ibid.; A. A. Weech to National Advisory Commission to SSS, 8 January 1953, ibid.; Senator Edward Martin to President, 22 September 1953, OF 133-k-1, Box 664, DDE; Stetler, "Doctor Draft," 1 November 1953, p. 74; and Paul G. Armstrong, "Selective Service System," *Journal of the Student American Medical Association* 2 (November 1953):45.

83. *Selective Service Annual Report, 1954*, p. 41; Glattly, "Problems," p. 45; Presidential Executive Order, 11 December 1953, CF, OF, Box 664, DDE.

84. See Nelson v. Peckham, 4 Cir. 210 F. 2d 574, 9 February 1954 and Orloff v. Willoughby, 345 US. 83, 73 S. Ct. 534. Charles Wilson statement, 18 March 1954, CF, OF, Box 664, DDE; Omer speech, 22 February 1953, LBH; Lewis B. Hershey, *Legal Aspects of Selective Service*, rev. ed. (Washington, D.C.: USGPO, 1969), p. 44. Even without this minor adjustment, the law had worked very effectively. By the end of fiscal year 1954 over 90 percent of those men in priorities 1, 2, and 3 had been classified, with 23 percent in the service, 46 percent exempted or deferred, and another 31 percent in 1-A. Through 30 June 1953 there had been only 18 cases of delinquency involving doctors and dentists; see *Selective Service Annual Report, 1954*, pp. 41-42.

85. Selective Service, Research and Statistics memo, 2 May 1955, p. 1, LBH, and Gerhardt, *Draft*, p. 224.

86. Selective Service, Research and Statistics memo, 2 May 1955, p. 1, LBH; Gerhardt, *Draft*, p. 224; Tribble, *Doctor Draft*, pp. 104-5; and Legislative meeting minutes, 28 June 1955, WHO: staff sec., legmt, 3, DDE.

87. SSN, February 1956, p. 4; ibid., June 1956, p. 2; Hershey to President, 7 September 1956, CF, OF, Box 664, DDE; Eisenhower to Hershey, 28 September 1956, ibid.; and statement by Berry to AMA, 1 October 1956, ibid.

88. Dr. Howard A. Rusk resigned in May 1957. Rusk admitted that administering a special draft was a difficult chore but the great cooperation from the government and the various professional societies had made it work with "equity." Dr. Elmer Hess, who replaced Rusk, spent most of his time insuring that his commission was

entirely Republican in character. Rusk to President, 15 May 1957, CF, Box 231, DDE, and Mary B. Kedick memo for Robert Gray, 20 September 1957, CF, Box 231, ibid.

89. *SSN*, August 1957, p. 1; Presidential press release, 18 October 1957, CF, OF, Box 664, DDE; Wilber M. Burcker to Percival F. Brundage, 19 September 1957, ibid.; *SSN*, July 1957, pp. 1, 3. Under the Berry plan medical students were offered an opportunity to accept a reserve commission in the Medical Corps while remaining in school. Although members of the reserve, they had no training obligation and could agree to enter active duty after internship or residency. They were then obligated to serve for only 24 months with no further reserve duty.

90. *SSN*, October 1959, p. 1; Tribble, *Doctor Draft*, p. 106; Capt. Thomas speech, 18 May 1960, minutes of State Directors Conference, LBH; and Toner notes, 16 September 1958, Diary, Box 36, DDE.

91. U.S. Congress, House, Committee on Appropriations, *Hearings*, 87th Cong., 1st sess., 17 January 1962, p. 48; SS National Advisory Committee to all LB chairmen, 27 March 1963, VF 324, LBH; Hershey to Busby, 24 September 1965, WHCF, ND 9–4, ct. 148, Lyndon B. Johnson Papers, Johnson Library, Austin, Texas (hereafter cited as LBJ). Vietnam soon destroyed the crust of complacency in this special manpower area as well as others. In 1964 DOD issued a special draft call for 1,175 doctors, the first such call since Korea and since the doctors' draft had officially ended. The Berry plan had failed to satisfy the new needs as the strength of the armed forces rose from 2,476,000 in 1960 to 3,094,000 in 1966. In January 1965 another special call went out for 1,085 doctors. In September the same year another 1,529 doctors and 350 dentists were called. See James C. Cain to Lyndon and Bird, 20 September 1965, WHCF, nd 9–4, ct. 148, LBJ; Califano to Jack Valenti, 11 October 1965, ibid.; Valenti to Califano, 22 September 1965, EXFG 282, cont. 303, LBJ; Report T, AMA, 7 November 1966, WHCF ND 9–4, ct. 148, LBJ; and Ralph L. Ireland, Am. Assoc. of Dental Schools, to Marshall, 29 November 1966, Box 46, NACSS, RG 220, NA.

Many residents had ignored their obligations and the Berry plan, and hospitals had ignored SS's warning to appoint residents only from those interns who were not classified 1-A. Medical schools again insisted upon special deferment treatment, and the AMA insisted upon taking over the entire task of mobilizing physicians. As Report T of the AMA stated in November 1966, a national roster of medical manpower was needed, and calls should be made on a national basis without reference to local boards.

92. Report to NSC by NSC Planning Board, 13 November 1953, OSANSA-NSC Ser., Box 8, DDE.

93. Wilton B. Persons for Adams, 6 May 1953, CF, OF, Box 663, DDE, and Minutes of Leg. Meeting, 27 November 1953, WHO: Staff Sec, Leg. Mt., 6, ibid.

94. John A. Hannah memo, 9 November 1953, CF, OF, Box 664, DDE; quotes in Minutes of leg. meeting, 27 November 1953, WHO: staff sec., lef. mt. 6, DDE; idem., 17 December 1953, ibid. In 1955 the Reserve Forces Act extended the draft for four years but also created a five-year reserve obligation for all enlistees and inductees. In addition a special six-month active-duty training program was created for up to 250,000 enlistees a year between the ages of 17 and 18.5. These six-months soldiers also had a 7.5-year reserve obligation of required drill. Selective Service announced that DOD calls were running some 200,000 below the total of draft eligibles, so the program also provided a means of soaking up surpluses. After the act of 1955, little more was heard of UMT.

95. Samuel P. Huntington, "Men at Arms?" *Air Force Magazine* 43 (March 1960):46, 50; Art to Bern, 11 August 1954, Central file, Box 664, DDE; and Eisenhower Diary, 23 January 1956, Box 12, ibid.

96. Copy of Stevenson speech, 18 October 1956, in WHCF, Martin Anderson file, Box 11, Richard M. Nixon Papers, Nixon Presidential Papers Project, National Archives, Arlington, Va.; Stephen E. Ambrose, *Nixon: The Education of a Politician, 1913–1962* (New York: Simon and Schuster, 1987), p. 418.

97. Ambrose, *Nixon: Education*, p. 418, and Ambrose, *Eisenhower*, pp. 348–49; quotes in presidential statement, 7 October 1956, in CF, OF, Box 664, DDE.

98. *U.S. News and World Report*, 8 February 1957, pp. 25–29.

99. Huntington, "Men at Arms?" p. 50, and *Washington Star*, 12 August 1957.

100. Ambrose, *Eisenhower*, p. 394; Gerhardt, *Draft*, pp. 246–47; and Huntington, "Men at Arms?" p. 53.

101. Toner notes, 16 September 1958, Eisenhower Diary, Box 36, DDE; quotes in "The Draft—Campus to Chaos," *Newsweek*, 4 April 1960, pp. 33–40.

102. Staff study paper, OCDM, 16 October 1958, CF, OF, Box 664, DDE, and J. Roy Price to Roger Jones, 21 October 1958, ibid.

103. Staff Study, OCDM, 16 October 1958, CF, OF, Box 664, DDE.

104. Quote from "Campus to Chaos," pp. 33–40.

105. *Newsweek*, 4 April 1960, p. 40.

106. Quote in Denis S. Philipps, "American People and Compulsory Military Service" (Ph.D. diss., New York University, 1955), p. 472; Robert K. Griffith, Jr., "About Face? The United States Army and the Draft," *Armed Forces & Society* 12 (Fall 1985):114; Joan M. Jensen, "The Army and Domestic Surveillance on Campus," in Gary D. Ryan and T. K. Nenninger, eds., *Soldiers and Civilians: The U.S. Army and the American People* (Washington, D.C.: National Archives, 1987), p. 171; and Huntington, "Men at Arms?" p. 53.

107. Quote in Ambrose, *Eisenhower*, p. 661; Joe P. Dunn, "UMT: A Historical Perspective," *Military Review* 61 (January 1981):18; and Huntington, "Men at Arms?" p. 46.

Chapter 7. LBJ and Vietnam

1. The best one-volume treatment of U.S. involvement in Vietnam is George C. Herring, *America's Longest War: The United States and Vietnam, 1950–1975*, 2d ed. (New York: Knopf, 1986). For additional works see John C. Pratt, ed., *Reading the Wind: Literature of the Vietnam War* (Durham, N.C.: Duke University Press, 1987); David Halberstam, *The Best and the Brightest* (New York: Random House, 1972); and Larry Berman, *Lyndon Johnson's War* (New York: Norton, 1989).

2. James M. Gerhardt, *The Draft and Public Policy* (Columbus: Ohio State University, 1971), p. 284.

3. "Vietnam Buildup: Expanding without Strain," *Business Week*, 7 August 1965, p. 25; Harry A. Marmion, *Selective Service: Conflict and Compromise* (New York: Wiley, 1968), p. 59; Earl G. Wheeler interviews, August 1969 and March 1970, Lyndon B. Johnson Papers, Johnson Library, Austin, Texas (hereafter cited as LBJ), p. 18; quote from Stephen E. Ambrose, *Eisenhower: The President* (New York: Simon and Schuster, 1984), p. 661; and Marmion, *Selective Service*, p. 59; See also William W. Berg to Rep. Julia B. Hansen, 26 September 1966, whcf, gen nd 9-4, ct. 150, LBJ; Zeb B. Bradford, Jr., and F. J. Brown, *The United States Army in Transition*

(Beverly Hills, Calif.: Sage, 1973), p. 39; and Eliot A. Cohen, *Citizens and Soldiers: The Dilemmas of Military Service* (Ithaca, N.Y.: Cornell, 1985), p. 115, who argues that the French gave up in the area precisely because they faced the need to use draftees to continue and refused to accept the political risk involved.

4. George E. Reedy, *Who Will Do Our Fighting for Us?* (New York: World Publishing Company, 1969), p. 33, is under the mistaken impression that the mobilization of World War II defused criticism of those who avoided the draft.

5. "Who Goes to War," *The Economist* 220 (9 July 1966):142; and John C. Esty, Jr., "The Future of the Draft," *The Nation*, 12 September 1966, p. 209, who says the percentage of men reaching 26 with military experience was 70 in 1958, 58 in 1962, and 46 in 1966.

6. Quoted in Marmion, *Selective Service*, p. 19. Daniel Yankelovich, *Generations Apart, 1969* (Ann Arbor, Mich.: IUCPR, 1975) found a significant correlation. As parents' income goes up a higher percentage of the sample were willing to obey their conscience and protest the draft.

7. See John W. Chambers II, *To Raise an Army: The Draft Comes to Modern America* (New York: Free Press, 1987) for a discussion of how progressive elites promoted the draft from efficiency motives.

8. Gary L. Wamsley, *Selective Service and a Changing America* (Columbus, Ohio: Merrill, 1969), p. 28.

9. Michael Useem, *Conscription, Protest, and Social Conflict* (New York: Wiley, 1973) pp. 8, 10-14. See also Stephen M. Kohn, *Jailed for Peace: The History of American Draft Law Violators, 1658-1985* (Westport, Conn.: Greenwood, 1986), and Staughton Lynd and Michael Ferber, *The Resistance* (Boston: Beacon, 1971), but both should be used with caution because of the bias of the authors in favor of resistance.

10. In 1951 the Universal Military Training and Service Act had established Selective Service on a permanent basis but required that draft induction authority be renewed every four years.

11. Paul Conkin, *Big Daddy from the Pedernales: Lyndon B. Johnson* (Boston: Twayne, 1987), p. 269; Herring, *Longest War*, pp. 139-40; U.S., Bureau of the Census, *Historical Statistics of the United States*, 2 pts. (Washington, D.C.: USGPO, 1975), 2:1141.

12. George Q. Flynn, *Lewis B. Hershey: Mr. Selective Service* (Chapel Hill: University of North Carolina, 1985), pp. 208-9, 211-13, 221-22.

13. "How Fair is the Draft? As High School Students See It," *Senior Scholastics* 87 (2 December 1965):16, and Jerome Johnston and Jerald G. Bachman, *Young Men Look at Military Service: A Preliminary Report* (Ann Arbor, Mich.: Institute for Social Research, 1970), p. 12.

14. Robert K. Griffith, Jr., *Men Wanted for the U.S. Army* (Westport, Conn.: Greenwood, 1982), p. 219, and *Historical Statistics*, 1:10; 2:1143.

15. *Historical Statistics*, 2:1143.

16. *Selective Service Newsletter*, February 1965, p. 1 (hereafter cited as *SSN*); speech by Fitt, 11 November 1967, Fitt Papers, cont. 5, LBJ; and Griffith, *Men Wanted*, p. 219.

17. Herring, *Longest War*, pp. 139-41.

18. Gerhardt, *Draft*, pp. 273-74; John Graham, "Historical Survey," National Advisory Committee on Selective Service (hereafter cited as NACSS), Box 37, RG 220, National Archives, Washington, D.C. (hereafter cited as NA); Bernard D. Karpinos, "Examination of Youths for Military Service," 10 October 1966, in Box 50,

ibid.; and Elinor Langer, "Vietnam: Growing War and Campus Protest Threatens Student Deferments," *Science* 150 (17 December 1965):1568.

19. Flynn, *Hershey*, p. 234; Gerhardt, *Draft*, p. 273; President's Commission on an All-Volunteer Armed Forces, *Report* (Washington, D.C.: USGPO, 1970), p. 166 (hereafter cited as Gates report); Fitt speech, 11 November 1967, Fitt papers, cont. 5, LBJ; Edward B. Glick, "The Draft and Nonmilitary National Service," *Military Review* 49 (December 1969):86; and David S. Surrey, *Choice of Conscience: Vietnam Era Military and Draft Resisters in Canada* (New York: Praeger, 1982), p. 37.

20. Gerhardt, *Draft*, pp. 277–78; *SSN*, November 1967, p. 1; U.S. Congress, Senate, Subcommittee on Employment, Manpower, and Poverty of Committee on Labor and Public Welfare, *Hearings on Manpower Implications of Selective Service*, 90th Cong. 1st sess., 20–23 March, 4–6 April 1967, p. 55; Griffith, *Men Wanted*, p. 219 says 50 percent of combat deaths; Cohen, *Citizens*, p. 107 says 70 percent; Robert K. Griffith, Jr., "About Face? The U.S. Army and the Draft," *Armed Forces and Society* 12 (Fall 1985):117. Reenlistment rates for draftees increased from 8.4 percent in FY 1965 to 20.8 percent in FY 1967. In this same period the reenlistment rate for volunteers declined.

21. Quote from Johnston and Bachman, *Young Men*, pp. 19, 22; Stuart Altman and R. J. Barro, "Model of Officer Supply under Draft and No Draft Conditions," *Studies*, with Gates Report (Washington, D.C.: USGPO, 1970), 2:649, 661; Fitt speech on Manpower Procurement, 11 November 1967, Fitt Papers, Cont. 5, LBJ; and William A. Knowlton to James Jones, 1 April 1966, WHCF, and 9-4, ct. 148, LBJ, reported that the six-month reserve program was being oversubscribed by men seeking haven from the draft.

22. "Who Goes to War," p. 143; Useem, *Conscription*, p. 164; Hershey to Mendel Rivers, 28 April 1966, Cong. file, Lewis B. Hershey Papers, Military History Institute, Carlisle, Pa. (hereafter cited as LBH); U.S. Congress, Senate, Committee on Appropriations, *Hearings on Independent Offices Appropriations*, 89th Cong., 1st sess., 25 May 1965, p. 653; and *Business Week*, 26 February 1966, p. 44.

23. Senate, *Hearings on Independent Appropriations*, 25 May 1965, p. 653; *New York Times*, 1 September 1965, p. 17; 18 November 1965, p. 6; and *Washington Sunday Star*, 16 December 1965.

24. *U.S. News and World Report*, 10 January 1966, p. 41; *SSN* February 1966, p. 3; Dan Omer, "The Selective Service Today," in June A. Willenz, ed., *Dialogue on the Draft* (Washington, D.C.: American Veterans' Commission, 1967), p 16; *SSN*, September 1966, p. 1; *New York Times*, 4 October 1966, p. 1; and Summary of Responses to LB questionnaires, n.d., NACSS, Box 44, RG 220, NA. The existence of the draft also had an effect on the military strategy used in Vietnam. Because of this proven means of obtaining men the military could use a twelve-month tour of duty, and commanders could more easily adopt a policy of attrition because of a constant stream of replacements; see Roger Little, "For Choice, Not Chance," *Society* 18 (1981):50.

25. *Newsweek*, 28 February 1966, p. 21; Dee Ingold, "Discussion: The Present System of Selective Service," in Sol Tax, ed., *The Draft: A Handbook of Facts and Alternatives* (Chicago: University of Chicago, 1967), p. 303; Bruce Chapman, "Selective Service and National Needs," *The Reporter*, 16 June 1966, p. 16; and Albert A. Blum, *Drafted or Deferred: Practices Past and Present* (Ann Arbor: University of Michigan, 1967), p. 225.

26. Responses to Local Board opinion questions, n.d., Box 1, NACSS, RG 220,

and Minutes of meeting of National Selective Service Scientific Advisory Group (NSSSAG), 16 February 1966, Science adv. Folder, MHI.

27. Chambers, *To Raise an Army*, pp. 210–15, has the best discussion of these conflicting figures, but see also Donald D. Stewart, "Local Boards: A Study of the Place of Volunteer Participation in a Bureaucratic Organization" (Ph.D. diss., Columbia University, 1950), p. 36; Mark Sullivan, "Submission to Autocracy," in Keith L. Nelson, ed., *The Impact of War on Amerian Life: The Twentieth-Century Experience* (New York: Holt, Rinehart and Winston, 1971), p. 36; Victory Hicken, *The American Fighting Man* (New York: Macmillan, 1969), p. 37; and *Studies* with Gates Report, 2:1–22.

28. Richard H. Kohn, "The Social History of the American Soldier: A Review and Prospectus for Research," *American Historical Review* 86 (June 1981):558; Stewart, "Local Boards," p. 203; Walker S. Edwards, "The Administration of Selective Service in the United States" (M.A. thesis, Stanford, 1948), p. 57; M. J. Pescor, "A Study of Selective Service Law Violators," *American Journal of Psychiatry* 105 (March 1949):643; and Report of President's Amnesty Board (n.d.), Box 844, OF 245, Harry S. Truman Papers, Truman Library, Independence, Mo. (hereafter cited as HST).

29. *SSN*, December 1969, p. 3, and Selective Service, Research and Statistics Digest, 30 April 1961, LBH.

30. Useem, *Conscription*, pp. 3–4, 54, 61–63; *New York Times*, 30 December 1967, p. 2; and Library of Congress, Congressional Research Services, *United States Draft Policy* (Washington, D.C.: Library of Congress, July 1968), p. 13.

31. Lewis Hershey oral history interview, 15 December 1970, LBJ, p. 45; *New York Times*, 22 March 1967, p. 13; Richard M. Dalfiume, *Desegregation of the U.S. Armed Forces* (Columbia: University of Missouri, 1969), p. 225; *New York Times*, 9 March 1968, p. 3; J. Edgar Hoover to Hershey, 5 April 1968, Private files of Gilbert Hershey, Jacksonville, N.C. (hereafter cited as Gilbert files); and *New York Times*, 16 May 1968, p. 51.

32. *Time*, 20 May 1966, p. 72; Herbert M., D. F., and D. Engel, "Belling the Berrigans," *The Catholic World* 213 (August 1971):228; Charles E. Rice, "Conscientious Objection: A Conservative View," *Modern Age* 13 (Winter, 1968–1969):67; Kohn, *Jailed for Peace*, p. 82; Steve Hamilton to President, telegram, 9 October 1967, WHCF, gen. (n.d.), 9–4, ct. 151, LBJ; Useem, *Conscription*, p. 267; Joseph E. Mulligan, "Reform or Resistance," *The Catholic World* 212 (December 1970):131; Gaetano Marino, "Protest and Procurement," *The Marine Corps Gazette* 53 (1969):42.

33. See James Burke, "Debating the Draft in America," *Armed Forces and Society* 15 (Spring 1989):431–48, and Charles DeBenedetti, "On the Significance of the Citizens' Peace Activism: America, 1961–1975," *Peace and Change* 9 (Summer 1983):11.

34. DeBenedetti, "Significance," pp. 6, 9; Patti Peterson, "Student Organizations and the Antiwar Movement in America, 1900–1960," *American Studies* 13 (Spring 1972):142; Kohn, *Jailed for Peace*, p. 75. See also Charles DeBenedetti and C. Chatfield, *An American Ordeal: the Antiwar Movement of the Vietnam Era* (Syracuse, N.Y.: Syracuse University, 1990) for a comprehensive and sympathetic treatment of the movement.

35. Useem, *Conscription*, pp. 49–51, 55–56, and Edward Hoagland, "The Draft Card Gesture," *Commentary* 45 (1 February 1968): 77–79.

36. Irwin Unger, *The Movement: A History of the New Left* (New York: Harper and Row, 1974), pp. 91–92; Peterson, "Student Organizations," pp. 131, 144; Useem,

Conscription, pp. 6, 16; Allen J. Matusow, *The Unraveling of America: A History of Liberalism in the 1960s* (New York: Harper and Row, 1984), p. 324; DeBenedetti, "Significance," pp. 11, 13; Robert P. Friedman and Charles Leistner, *Compulsory Service Systems* (Columbia, Mo.: Artcraft Press, 1968), p. 463; John Lovell, "Military Service, Nationalism and the Global Community," in Michael L. Martin and E. S. McCrate, eds., *The Military, Militarism and the Polity: Essays in Honor of Morris Janowitz* (New York: Free Press, 1984), p. 69.

37. Joe P. Dunn, "UMT: A Historical Perspective," *Military Review* 61 (January 1981):18; Wilson quoted in Friedman and Leisther, p. 466; second quote in Useem, *Conscription*, pp. 36, 183; and Harriet E. Gross, "Micro and Macro Level Implications for a Sociology of Virtue: The Case of Draft Protesters to the Vietnam War," *Sociological Quarterly* 18 (Summer 1977):328.

38. Johnston and Bachman, *Young Men*, p. 5; "Draft Riots on College Campuses, *School and Society*, 13 November 1965, p. 420, and Useem, *Conscription*, pp. 53, 165–66, 173–74; quote in Friedman and Leistner, *Compulsory Service Systems*, p. 464.

39. Ramsey Clark interview, Oral History Project, 3 June 1969, LBJ, and "Resistance to Military Service," *Congressional Quarterly*, 20 March 1968, p. 11.

40. Boyer memo, 22 November 1966, National Advisory Committee on Selective Service, Box 3, RG 220, National Archives, Washington, D.C. (hereafter cited as NACSS); *New York Times* clip, Box 11, ibid.; Keith L. Nelson, comp., *The Impact of War on American Life* (New York: Holt, Rinehart and Winston, 1971), p. 239; and Useem, *Conscription*, p. 202.

41. Quote from Gross, "Micro," p. 321; Useem, *Conscription*, p. 177; Allan Brotsky, "Trial of a Conscientious Objector," in Ann F. Ginger, ed., *The Relevant Lawyers* (New York: Simon and Schuster, 1972), p. 102; Spock quote in Rice, "Conscientious Objection," pp. 69, 71; DeBenedetti, "Significance," p. 11.

42. For a general survey of the draft and CO status see George Q. Flynn, "Selective Service and the Conscientious Objector," in Michael Noone, ed., *Selective Conscientious Objection* (Boulder, Colo.: Westview, 1989), pp. 39–55.

43. Kohn, *Jailed for Peace*, p. 126; Lawrence M. Baskir and William A. Strauss, *Chance and Circumstance: The Draft, the War, and the Vietnam Generation* (New York: Knopf, 1978), p. 40; quote in Walter S. Griggs, Jr., "The Selective Conscientious Objector: A Vietnam Legacy," *Journal of Church and State* 21 (January 1979):100; Surrey, *Choice of Conscience*, p. 39; but see Baskir and Strauss, p. 41, who write of 172,000 Vietnam era COs and Useem, *Conscription*, p. 57, who writes that resisters made "little headway" in obtaining such status.

44. Richard J. Niebanck, *Conscience, War, and the Selective Objector* (New York: Lutheran Church in America, 1968), p. 39; Peter J. Riga, "Selective Conscientious Objection: A Progress Report," *Catholic World* 211 (1970):162; Griggs, "Selective Conscientious Objector," p. 97; and Rice, "Conscientious Objection," p. 75. Obtaining a CO classification proved easier than in earlier wars. In World War II local boards granted only 4 CO classifications for every 10,000 registrants classified; during the Korean War the rate ran from 13 per 10,000 at the beginning to 5 per 10,000 at the end. In fiscal year 1969 local boards granted about 8 CO classifications per 10,000 classified registrants; see Robert B. Smith, "Disaffection, Delegitimation, and Consequences: Aggregate Trends for World War II, Korea and Vietnam," in Charles C. Moskos, Jr., *Public Opinion and the Military Establishment* (Beverly Hills, Calif.: Sage, 1971), p. 233.

45. Some studies distinguish between draft avoiders and draft resisters, using a continuum. One might start out by trying to avoid induction by a variety of legal

means, but as these tactics failed, one eventually became a draft resister. It seems clear that very few young Americans either started or ended as resisters; see Surrey, *Choice of Conscience,* p. 52, and Gross, "Micro," p. 323.

46. Saul V. Levine, "Draft Dodgers: Coping with Stress, Adapting to Exile," *American Journal of Orthopsychiatry* 42 (1 April 1972):432, and Langer, "Vietnam," pp. 1567–69.

47. Useem, *Conscription,* p. 64; James Fallows, "What Did You Do in the Class War, Daddy?" *Washington Monthly* 7 (October 1975):7, 11. Only two members of Fallow's Harvard class were drafted.

48. Bashir and Strauss, *Chance and Circumstance,* p. 33; Fallows, "What Did You Do?" pp. 5–6; and Henry E. Anderson, "The Folklore of Draft Resistance," *New York Folklore Quarterly* 28 (1972):135, 137, 141, 142, 146.

49. Smith, "Disaffection," pp. 229, 233, 235.

50. David Shichor and Dr. R. Ranish, "President Carter's Vietnam Amnesty: An Analysis of a Public Policy Decision," *Presidential Studies Quarterly* 10 (1980):446, 448, writes of draft evasion becoming legitimate, but this seems impossible to measure.

51. For government infiltration of protest see Kenneth O'Reilly, "The FBI and the Politics of the Riots, 1964–1968," *Journal of American History* 75 (June 1988):91–114.

52. Hershey speech, 21 November 1951, State Director's Conference, LBH; Hershey to Dargusch, 20 December 1965, alpha file, ibid.; Langer, "Vietnam," p. 1568; Elizabeth Denny, interview with author, 16, 22 August 1977, Vienna, Va.; SSN, 1 March 1968, p. 1; and quote in Hershey speech to State Directors Conference, 22 April 1968, MHI.

53. *The Atlanta Constitution,* 20 June 1968; S. Bruce Scidmore to President, 24 June 1968, whcf, fg 282, ct. 304, LBJ; and Report of Subcommittee, State Directors Conference, 9 May 1969, LBH.

54. Joint Army Navy Selective Service Committee, *American Selective Service: A Brief Historical Account* (Washington, D.C.: USGPO, 1939), p. 24; Hershey to State Directors, 8 October 1941, Legal Div. File, Box 30, RG 147–97, NA; See George Q. Flynn, "The Draft and College Deferments during the Korean War," *Historian* 50 (May 1988):369–85.

55. Andrew O. Shapiro and John M. Striker, *Mastering the Draft* (Boston: Little, Brown, 1970), p. 103; Press release by Murray Snyder, 16 February 1956, Cent. file, OF, Box 664, Dwight D. Eisenhower Papers, Eisenhower Library, Abilene, Kans. (hereafter cited as DDE); Science Research Association, *Unfit for Service: A Review of the Draft and Basic Education in the Army* (Chicago: SRA, Inc., 1966), p. 14.

56. Dee Ingold, interview with author, Alamagordo, N.M., 15 August 1978.

57. William Averill, interview with author, Tupelo, Miss., 27 July 1978; *U.S. News and World Report,* 10 January 1966, p. 43; *New York Times,* 5 December 1965, p. 70; and Richard A. Merrill, "Deficiencies in the Selective Service System: The Samuel Friedman Case," in Willenz, *Dialogue,* pp. 30–33, 38.

58. Hershey to Rep. Emanuel Celler, 15 December 1965, in *U.S. News and World Report,* 10 January 1966, p. 39; SSN, February 1966, p. 4; Transcript of program "From the Capital," 27 December 1965, copy in NACSS, Box 48, RG 220.

59. See Fallows, "What Did You Do?" and John M. Swomley, Jr., "Why the Draft Should Go," in Martin Anderson, ed, *The Military Draft* (Stanford, Calif.: Hoover Institution, 1982), pp. 578–79.

60. Peter Karsten, *Soldiers and Society: The Effects of Military Service and War on*

American Life (Westport, Conn.: Greenwood, 1978), pp. 118, 127; Useem, *Conscription*, pp. 58–60, 104; James W. Davis, Jr., and Kenneth M. Dolbeare, *Little Groups of Neighbors: The Selective Service System* (Chicago: Markham, 1968), p. 98; Hershey editorial, 14 August 1968, alpha file, LBH, MHI. Kohn, *Jailed*, p. 116, writes that in one year 537 students who turned in their draft cards lost their student deferments, but such a figure is impossible to determine with accuracy as reclassification could be disguised by local boards for a variety of reasons.

61. Johnston and Bachman, "Draft Riots on Campuses," p. 420; *New York Times*, 17 December 1965, p. 4; Marino, "Protest and Procurement," p. 44; Melvin Small, "The Impact of the Antiwar Movement on Lyndon Johnson, 1965–1968," *Peace and Change* 10 (Spring 1984):9; David Ment to President, 6 January 1966, whcf, nd 9–4, ct. 149, LBJ; Marmion, *Selective Service*, p. 19; Peter W. Martin, "Trial by Hershey: The Draft as Punishment," *The Nation* 206 (January 1968):141; Vinson to John S. Stillman, 1 February 1966, NACSS, Box 48, RG 220, NA.

62. *New York Times*, 12 January 1966, p. 8.

63. Reedy to President, 16 December 1965, whcf nd 9–4, ct. 148, LBJ. See also marginal notation by Johnson.

64. On veteran support see responses to survey by NACSS, Box 28, RG 220. Quote from Charles C. Moskos, Jr., *The American Enlisted Man: The Rank and File in Today's Military* (New York: Sage, 1970), p. 163; Hayes Redmon to Bill Moyers, 27 November 1965, whcf nd 9–4, ct. 148, LBJ; *US Draft Policy*, July 1968, p. 28; DeBenedetti, "Significance," p. 14; Johnston and Bachman, *Young Men*, pp. 6, 16–17; and John Helmer, *Bringing the War Home: The American Soldier in Vietnam and After* (New York: Free Press, 1974), p. 11. Richard M. Nixon, *No More Vietnams* (New York: Arbor House, 1985), p. 127, says he split the youth vote evenly with McGovern in 1972.

65. *New York Times*, 1 September 1965, p. 17; 21 October 1965, p. 1; and Kohn, *Jailed*, p. 73.

66. Frank M. Slatinshek, interview with author, Alexandria, Va., 31 August 1977; F. Edward Hebert, interview with author, New Orleans, La., 19 July 1978; Clark to Charles L. Schultze, 25 July 1966, cong. file, MHI; and Hershey to L. Mendel Rivers, 27 January 1966, ibid.

67. Gerhardt, *Draft*, p. 286, and Chapman, "Selective Service," p. 15.

68. *New York Times*, 22 December 1965, p. 3, and *Washington Post*, 13 March 1966.

Chapter 8. Protest and Reform

1. George Q. Flynn, *Lewis B. Hershey: Mr. Selective Servic* (Chapel Hill: University of North Carolina, 1985), pp. 225–26, and King Carr to Director, 30 October 1962, National Advisory Committee on Selective Service, Box 44, RG 220, National Archives, Washington, D.C. (hereafter cited as NACSS).

2. James M. Gerhardt, *The Draft and Public Policy* (Columbus: Ohio State University, 1971), p. 286, and Flynn, *Hershey*, pp. 225–26.

3. Flynn, *Hershey*, 226; News conference, whcf, gen nd. 9–4, cont. 150, Lyndon B. Johnson Papers, Johnson Library, Austin, Texas (hereafter cited as LBJ); Gerhardt, *Draft*, p. 286; Myer Feldman to James G. Patton, 11 March 1964, whcf nd 4–1, map. fold., LBJ; and quote in Hayes Redmon to Bill Moyers, 20 November 1965, whcf, nd 9–4, ct. 148, LBJ.

4. McNamara for President, 5 April 1965, whcf nd 9–4, ct. 148, LBJ.

5. Goldman Report, 7 February 1966, p. 142, and Robert E. Kintner memo for President, 21 May 1966, whcf nd 9–4, ct 148, LBJ.

6. Eric Goldman, *The Tragedy of Lyndon Johnson* (New York: Knopf, 1969), pp. 492–95.

7. Califano for President, 20 June 1966, whcf nd 9–4, ct. 148, LBJ; *Selective Service News Letter*, August 1966, p. 3 (hereafter cited as *SSN*).

8. Goldman, *Tragedy*, 495; LBJ speech, 18 August 1966, NACSS, Box 24, RG 220; and Lewis B. Hershey interview, 15 December 1970, Oral History Project, LBJ.

9. Humphrey memo for President, 7 July 1966, whcf nd 9–4, ct 148, LBJ; Flynn, *Hershey*, p. 242; U.S. National Advisory Committee on Selective Service, *In Pursuit of Equity: Who Serves When Not All Serve* (Washington, D.C.: USGPO, 1967), v. Among the 20 committee members were academics such as Kingman Brewster of Yale and Luther L. Terry of the University of Pennsylvania. Thomas S. Gates, Jr., and Anna Rosenberg Hoffman were both former DOD officials. John H. Johnson of *Ebony-Jet* magazine represented the black community. George E. Reedy, Jr., was a former Johnson aide; John Courtney Murray, a Jesuit theologian. General David M. Shoup of the Marines represented the military point of view. Other prominent members included John A. McCone, Oveta Culp Hobby, Paul J. Jennings, Vernon E. Jordan, James H. McCrocklin, Jeanne L. Noble, Fiorindo A. Simeone, James A. Suffridge, Frank S. Szymanski, and Warren G. Woodward.

10. Flynn, *Hershey*, p. 242; Minutes of NACSS, 30 July 1966, Califano statement, Box 87, NACSS, RG 220.

11. John K. Folger paper, 16 August 1966, Box 46, NACSS, RG 220.

12. Minutes, NACSS, 30 July 1966, Box 87, ibid. See also file c.10.2, Box 39, ibid., for the advocacy of staff members.

13. See Box 88, NACSS, RG 220.

14. Neil Boyer to Harry Middleton, 1 January 1967, Box 7, NACSS, RG 220; NACSS, minutes, 1 November 1966, Box 89, RG 220; 30 July 1966, Box 87, ibid; 2 December 1966, Box 89, ibid; 18 December 1966, Box 90, ibid; and Proceedings, n.d., Box 89, ibid. See Box 97, file 6, ibid., for press clippings.

15. John J. Pemberton, Jr., to Patterson, 21 December 1966, Box 29, NACSS, RG 220.

16. "Who Goes to War," *Economist* 220 (6 July 1966):143; and Keenan to Patterson, 28 October 1966, Box 24, NACSS, RG 220.

17. Roger W. Little, "Selective Service in Illinois," in June A. Willenz, ed., *Dialogue on the Draft* (Washington, D.C.: American Veterans Commission, 1967), p. 26; National Advisory Committee on Selective Service, *In Pursuit of Equity*, p. 29; and Student Opinion Report, Forrest O. Beaty, Box 36, NACSS, RG 220. James W. Davis, Jr., and Kenneth M. Dolbeare, *Little Groups of Neighbors: The Selective Service System* (Chicago: Markham, 1968) is the best study of the structure of local boards.

18. David S. Surrey, *Choice of Conscience: Vietnam Era Military and Draft Resisters in Canada* (New York: Praeger, 1982), p. 35; Little, "Selective Service," pp. 25–26; and NACSS, Proceedings, n.d., Box 89, RG 220.

19. Quote in Little, "Selective Service," p. 27; Jacques Feuillen to Patterson, 2 November 1966, Box 1–3, NACSS, RG 220; Record of action, 17–18 November 1966, Box 89, ibid.; and Record of action, 18–19 December 1966, Box 88, ibid.

20. See James W. Davis, Jr., and Kenneth M. Dolbeare, "Selective Service and Military Manpower Procurement," in Austin Ramsey, ed., *Political Science and Public Policy* (Chicago: Markham, 1968), p. 103; James Fallows, "What Did You Do in the

Class War, Daddy?" *Washington Monthly* 7 (October 1975):8; Surrey, *Choice*, pp. 3, 37, 45–46; and Michael Useem, "Conscription and Class," *Society* 18 (1981):28–31.

Draft critics such as Michael Harrington, Senators Robert and Ted Kennedy, Gaylord Nelson, and most leaders of the Students for a Democratic Society and civil rights groups insisted that the draft forced the poor to fight in Vietnam. Government officials never really succeeded in rebutting this charge, and it was still being made years later. Indeed, it became part of the folklore of the war. Bruce Chapman, "Selective Service and National Needs," *The Reporters*, 16 June 1966, p. 15.

Duane E. Leigh and R. E. Berney, "The Distribution of Hostile Casualties on Draft Eligible Males with Differing Socioeconomic Characteristics," *Social Science Quarterly* 51 (March 1971):933–34, 939–40, write, "The empirical evidence suggested that hostile causalities tended to be disproportionally concentrated among those draftees and reluctant volunteers with relatively low civilian income potentials."

21. Roger Little, "For Choice, Not Chance," *Society* 18 (1981):49.

Samuel H. Hays, "A Military View of Selective Service," in Sol Tax, ed., *The Draft: A Handbook of Facts and Alternatives* (Chicago: University of Chicago, 1967), p. 12, writes, "The differences in sacrifice between those who are called to the service and those excused are less drastic than the differences which result from different assignments in the services."

See Neil D. Fligstein, "Who Served in the Military, 1940–1973," *Armed Forces and Society* 6 (Winter 1979):297–312, who finds a good cross section of all classes serving, and Patricia M. Shields, "The Burden of the Draft: The Vietnam Years," *Journal of Political and Military Sociology* 9 (February 1981):215–28, who writes that Selective Service did not achieve equity during Vietnam, but her figures reveal that no social indicator was significant in predicting draftability and that "the fortunes of war or the luck of the draw was an important factor in determining who served." See also p. 226.

22. Chapman, "Selective Service," p. 15; John Helmer, *Bringing the War Home: The American Soldier in Vietnam and After* (New York: Free Press, 1974), p. 7; and Fitt speech, 11 November 1967, cont. 5, Fitt Papers, LBJ.

23. Quote from Little, "For Choice," p. 49; Kurt Lang, "Service Inequality," *Society* 18 (1981):41.

24. Quote in David R. Segal, "How Equal Is 'Equity'?" *Society* 18 (1981):31–33; Little, "For Choice," p. 50; Zeb B. Bradford, Jr., and F. J. Brown, *The United States Army in Transition* (Beverly Hills, Calif.: Sage, 1973), p. 40. See also Shields, "Burden of the Draft," 226.

25. Segal, "How Equal," pp. 31–33, and quote from Fligstein, "Who Served," pp. 43–44.

26. Robert P. Friedman and Charles Leistner, eds., *Compulsory Service Systems* (Columbia, Mo.: Artcraft Press, 1968), pp. 340–45; James A. Barber, Jr., "The Draft and Alternatives of the Draft," in Stephen Ambrose and James Barber, eds., *The Military and American Society* (New York: Free Press, 1972), p. 218. The American Legion and the Jewish War Veterans, as well as other veteran groups, gave SS ringing endorsements, particularly its decentralization.

27. Interview with Dwight D. Eisenhower, 11 October 1966, by Marshall, Hobby, Gates, and Patterson, Box 37, NACSS, RG 220; Little, "Selective Service," p. 28; "Let Every Young Man Serve," *Farm Journal* 90 (October 1966):110. For support of UNS see Chapman, "Selective Service," p. 17; Donald J. Eberly, "Service Experience and Educational Growth," *Educational Record* 49 (Spring 1968):197; Minutes of NACSS, 7 October 1966, Box 88, NACSS, RG 220; Reed Martin to Marshall,

30 November 1966, Box 33, ibid.; and Lawrence R. Velvel, "Economic Service Abroad and the Draft," *Midwest Quarterly* 8 (February 1967):120.

28. United States Youth Council, "Youth Opinion on the Selective Service," in Willenz, *Dialogue*, p. 68; Eliot A. Cohen, *Citizens and Soldiers: The Dilemmas of Military Service* (Ithaca, N.Y.: Cornell, 1985), pp. 33–34.

29. T. Roland Berner to President, 27 June 1967, whcf, fg 282, ct. 304, LBJ; "Draft Riots on College Campuses," *School and Society* 93 (13 November 1965):420; Harvard Draft Study Group report, 25 May 1967, whcf, nd. 9–4, ct. 148, LBJ. For Oi's argument see Walter Y. Oi, "The Economic Cost of the Draft," in Martin Anderson, *The Military Draft* (Stanford, Calif.: Hoover Institution, 1982), pp. 318–46 and Oi and Brian E. Forst, "Manpower and Budgetary Implications of Ending Conscription," in *Studies Prepared for the President's Commission on an All-Volunteer Force (PCAVF)*, (Washington, D.C.: GPO, 1970), 1:63; and Paul Weinstein, "Comments on papers by Altman, Fechter, and Oi," *American Economic Review: Papers and Proceedings*, 1 May 1967, p. 65.

30. James B. Jacobs, "Punishment or Obligation," *Society* 18 (1981):56; and Weinstein, "Comments," p. 67.

31. Chapman, "Selective Service," p. 18, and Weinstein, "Comments," pp. 63, 69–70.

32. Quote from Weinstein, "Comments," p. 67; "Youth Opinion on Selective Service," p. 67; "Who Goes to War," p. 142; and John C. Esty, Jr., "The Future of the Draft," *The Nation*, 12 September 1966, p. 210.

33. Carl Kaysen for Califano, 25 June 66, whcf, n.d. 9–4, ct. 148, LBJ, and Harry A. Marmion, *Selective Service: Conflict and Compromise* (New York: Wiley, 1968), p. 77.

34. NACSS minutes, 2 December 1966, Box 89, NACSS, RG 220.

35. Hays, "A Military View," p. 17; Morris Janowitz, "The Logic of National Service," in Tax, *The Draft*, p. 74; and Chapman, "Selective Service," p. 17.

36. Marmion, *Selective Service*, p. 86; Chapman, "Selective Service," p. 16; Gerhardt, *Draft*, p. 288; and Willenz, *Dialogue*, p. 3.

37. National Advisory Committee on Selective Service, *In Pursuit of Equity*, pp. 4–8; Comparison of Clark Report, memo, NACSS, Box 5, RG 220; SSN, May 1967, pp. 2–3; and Hershey interview, LBJ, p. 10.

38. See George Q. Flynn, "The Draft and College Deferments during the Korean War," *The Historian* 50 (May 1988):369–85.

39. Elinor Langer, "Vietnam: Growing War and Campus Protest Threatens Student Deferments," *Science* 150 (17 December 1965), pp. 1567–68.

40. SSN, June 1966, p. 1; *New York Times*, 4 January 1966, p. 10; *Washington Sunday Star*, 16 December 1965; Selective Service Statistics, vol. 4, pt. 3, Research and Statistics report, 18 January 1966, Box 4, RG 147–106; Michael Useem, *Conscription, Protest and Social Conflict* (New York: Wiley, 1973), p. 92; and *The Washington Post*, 24 January 1966.

41. Jean Carper, *Bitter Greetings: The Scandal of the Military Draft* (New York: Grossman, 1967), p. 60; Dan Omer, "The Selective Service System Today," in Willenz, *Dialogue*, p. 17; M. Janowitz memo, n.d., Box 39, NACSS, RG 220; U.S. Congress, House, Armed Services Committee, *Review of Selective Service Administration*, 89th Cong. 2d sess., 22 June 1966, p. 9624; Hershey to Dr. Leonard Carmichael, 20 January 1966, Science Advisory file, LBH; and SSN, March 1966, p. 1.

42. U.S. Congress, Senate, Committee on Appropriations, *Hearings on Independent Office Appropriations*, 89th Cong., 2d sess., 25 May 1966, p. 1205; "Students and

Their Deferment," *The Saturday Review* 49 (19 November 1966):92; Hershey to Meyerhoff, 19 December 1966, alpha file, LBH; and local board opinions, Box 1, NACSS, RG 220.

43. U.S. Congress, Senate, Subcommittee on Employment, Manpower, and Poverty, *Hearings, Manpower Implications of Selective Service*, 90th Cong., 1st sess., 20 March 1967, p. 16; *Review of Selective Service Administration*, 24 June 1966, p. 9718; *SSN*, March, 1968, p. 1; *Rocky Mountain News*, 16 Feburary 1966; *SSN*, September 1969, p. 2; and Fitt to Califano, 14 November 1967, Califano Papers, SS, LBJ.

44. Beaty report, NACSS proceedings, n.d., Box 89, NACSS, RG 220.

45. Hershey to W. H. Rommel, 22 November 1966, Cong. file, LBH; *New York Times*, 6 May 1967; Melvin Small, *Johnson, Nixon, and the Doves* (New Brunswick, N.J.: Rutgers University, 1988), p. 84; Hershey to Meyerhoff, 8 December 1968, alpha file, LBH; Esty, "Future," p. 209; and "Students and Their Deferment," p. 92.

46. Stuart H. Altman and R. J. Barro, "Model of Officer Supply under Draft and No Draft Conditions," in *Studies*, PCAVF, p. 661; Mordechai Lando, "Health Services in the All-Volunteer Armed Force," ibid., p. 41. See also Albert D. Klassen, Jr., *Military Service in American Life since World War II*, NORC report 117 (Chicago: NORC/University of Chicago, 1966), pp. 54–55.

47. Lando, "Health Services," p. 41; quote from Useem, *Conscription*, p. 95; Dee Ingold, "Discussion: The Present System of Selective Service," in Tax, *The Draft*, pp. 302–5; and Edward B. Glick, "The Draft and Non-military National Service," *Military Review* 49 (December 1969):87. Surrey, *Choice*, p. 42, says reforms led to the great educational cross section, but he is wrong. Compare these figures of military participation rate by education with the AVF which in early 1980 had only 3 percent of enlistees with some college education.

48. Harry C. McPherson for President, 28 January 1967, whcf, nd 9-4, ct. 148, LBJ, and White House press release, 30 January 1967, ibid.

49. Califano for President, 26 February 1967, whcf, nd 9-4, ct. 148, LBJ.

50. Hershey interview, Oral History, 15 December 1970, LBJ.

51. Ibid.

52. Flynn, *Hershey*, p. 248.

53. Congressional Reference Service, *United States Draft Policy* (Washington, D.C.: Library of Congress, July 1968), p. 1; Marmion, *Selective Service*, pp. 33–34; Chapman, "Selective Service," p. 16; Califano for President, 20 June 1966, whcf, nd 9-4, ct. 148, LBJ; and "Who Goes to War," p. 142.

54. *United States Draft Policy*, pp. 7, 9; Tax, *Draft*, p. 345; Flynn, *Hershey*, p. 249; *Hearings on Manpower Implications of S.S.*, pp. 1–4.

55. John O'Sullivan questionnaires, 13 November 1974, Papers of Gilbert Hershey, Jacksonville, N.C. (private); *Hearings, Manpower Implications of Selective Service*, 23 March 1967, pp. 117, 119, 153–54, 180, 228; and *United States Draft Policy*, p. 7.

56. Report of Task Force to Review National Advisory Committee Recommendations on Draft, 14 April 1967, I-1, Box 59, RG 247-97, NA (hereafter cited as Task Force Report).

57. Flynn, *Hershey*, p. 253; quote in Task Force Report, 14 April 1967, Box 59, RG 147-97, NA. See also Task Force on Status of Selective Service System, 16 October 1967, Task Force 1, LBJ (hereafter cited as Status of SSS). Only in the classification of a few occupations, especially teachers, did the task force find much lack of uniformity. A study of 5,000 classification actions by local boards failed to substantiate charges of exceeding authority.

58. Hebert quoted in Marmion, *Selective Service*, p. 121; Davis and Dolbeare, *Little*

Groups, p. 11; Emmett G. Lenihan to House Armed Services Committee, 4 May 1967, Box 4, RG 220, NA.

59. Marmion, *Selective Service*, pp. 129–30; Califano for President, 22 May 1967, Ex le/ma, cont. 140, LBJ; Mike Manatos for Barefoot Sanders, 25 May 1967, ibid; and Reedy to President, 16 May 1967, whcf nd 9–4, ct. 148, ibid.

60. *United States Draft Policy*, July 1968, p. 26, and Marmion, *Selective Service*, p. 128.

61. Califano for President, 29 June 1967, Ex le/ma, ct. 140, LBJ; Gary L. Wamsley, *Selective Service and a Changing America* (Columbus, Ohio: Merrill, 1969), pp. 231–32; and *United States Draft Policy*, July 1968, p. 1.

62. Cyrus Vance to Califano, 24 May 1967, Ex le/ma, ct. 140, LBJ; LBJ quoted in margin, Califano for President, 12 June 1967, ibid.; and Califano for President, 28 June 1967, whcf, nd 9–4, ct. 148, ibid.

63. *United States Draft Policy*, July 1968, p. 2.

64. William Brink and Louis Harris, *Black and White: A Study of U.S. Racial Attitudes Today* (New York: Simon and Schuster, 1966), pp. 164, 167.

65. Richard M. Dalfiume, *Desegregation of the U.S. Armed Forces* (Columbia: University of Missouri, 1969), pp. 223–24; Paul T. Murray, "Local Draft Board Composition and Institutional Racism," *Social Problems* 19 (1971):129; Stephen M. Kohn, *Jailed for Peace: The History of American Draft Law Violators* (Westport, Conn.: Greenwood, 1986), p. 80; and quotes from Ulysses Lee, "The Draft and the Negro," *Current History* 55 (July 1968):47.

66. McGill to Hershey, 22 March 1966, file 171.1, Box 48, RG 147-97; SS, 1 August 1966, p. 1; Lee, "The Draft and the Negro," pp. 33, 47.

67. Dalfiume, *Desegregation*, pp. 224–25; Lee, "The Draft and the Negro," p. 33; and Murray, "Local Draft Board," p. 131.

68. *Review of Selective Service Administration*, 23 June 1966, pp. 9649, 9665; Senate, *Hearings on Independent Office Appropriations*, 26 May 1966, pp. 1233–34; Lewis B. Hershey, "Selective Service," *Current History* 55 (1 July 1968):3; Lee, "The Draft and the Negro," p. 44; and quote from Murray, "Local Draft Board," p. 131.

69. During World War II blacks in Harlem were often suspected of draft dodging because so many failed to report when called. An investigation by Campbell Johnson of national headquarters found there was no deliberate conspiracy involved. The principle causes of delinquency were the housing conditions in Harlem, which made permanent addresses a joke, and the "don't give a damn" attitude of many of the men who lived there; see Campbell Johnson, Notes on Trip to New York City, 28 July 1942, Box 140, RG 147.

70. Brink and Harris, *Black and White*, p. 167; Langer, "Vietnam," p. 1568.

71. Bernard D. Karpinos, "The Mental Qualification of American Youth for Military Service and Its Relationship to Educational Attainment," *Proceedings* of Social Statistics Section, American Statistics Association, 1 January 1966, p. 95; and Murray, "Local Draft Board," p. 132. Little, "For Choice," p. 50, says the second highest cause was hypertension.

72. Bernard D. Karpinos, "Profiles of 'Military Chargable Accessions,'" Medical Statistics Agency, Office of Surgeon General, Department of the Army, 1967, p. 11, in LBH; Glick, "The Draft," p. 87; Surrey, *Choice*, p. 36; and *New York Times*, 24 June 1966, p. 2. The disparity in performance on preinduction and induction exams contributed to charges of a racist draft. If a local board operated in an area with a high percentage of blacks, because over half the blacks called were not qualified the board had to call twice as many men to meet its quota as a board in a white suburb.

In 1966 out of every 10,000 men called some 8,831 were white and 1,169 were black.

73. Flynn, *Hershey*, pp. 229-31; Selective Service, Research and Statistics memo, 1 March 1966, LBH.

74. Albert A. Blum, *Drafted or Deferred: Practices Past and Present* (Ann Arbor: University of Michigan, 1967), p. 213, and Flynn, *Hershey*, p. 230.

75. Helmer, *Bringing the War Home*, pp. 8-9; Surrey, *Choice*, p. 41; McNamara quoted in Murray, "Local Draft Board," p. 135; Kohn, *Jailed*, p. 55.

76. William Averill, interview with author, Tupelo, Miss., 27 July 1978; Carper, *Bitter Greetings*, p. 107; U.S. Congress, House, Committee on Post Office and Civil Service, Subcommittee on Civil Service, *Hearings on Compensation for Selective Service System Employees*, 89th Cong., 2d sess., 18 April 1966, p. 13.

77. Andrew O. Shapiro and John M. Striker, *Mastering the Draft* (Boston: Little, Brown, 1970), pp. 12-13. The 1967 draft law required that local board membership be restricted to persons 30 to 75 years old who were civilian citizens of the United States and living within the county of jurisdiction. No race or sex qualification was allowed.

78. Curtis M. Graves to Rep. Jack Jackson, 13 September 1966, whcf, fg 282, ct. 304, LBJ; Hershey to Califano, 14 April 1967, WH Corresp., LBH; Clark to President, 2 June 1967, Califano file, ct. 55, LBJ; and Jim Gaither to Califano, 3 June 1967, ibid.

79. *New York Times*, 14 January 1968, p. 1, and Hershey to Califano, 14 April 1967, WH Corresp., LBH.

80. Levinson to President, 1 September 1967, EX, FG 282, cont. 303, LBJ; *New York Times*, 14 January 1968, p. 1; Hershey to Nixon, 1 December 1969, Gilbert file; Murray, "Local Draft Board," p. 130. Not surprisingly, Mississippi proved slowest to act. George Wallace had vowed to cooperate, but his wife, who replaced him as governor, refused to appoint blacks; see *New York Times*, 14 January 1968, p. 1, and 3 February 1968, p. 10.

81. Murray, "Local Draft Board," pp. 130-31.

82. Quoted in John W. Chambers II, *To Raise an Army: The Draft Comes to Modern America* (New York: Free Press, 1987), p. 56.

83. *U.S. Draft Policy*, July 1968, p. 22; Hershey quote in Hershey interview, 15 December 1970, Oral History Project, p. 18, LBJ; Ramsey Clark oral history, 3 June 1969, ibid.; Larry Temple to President, 16 January 1968, whcf, nd 9-4, ct. 149, ibid.; and *Washington Evening Star*, 6 December 1967. Clark later admitted that the department was probably "soft" on draft prosecutions; Clark to author, 14 July 1980.

84. Clark to President, 6 November 1967, whcf, nd 9-4, ct. 148, LBJ. The table shows that the percentage of men who failed to report actually went down during the Vietnam period and the percentage of cases prosecuted went up. The failure-to-report group as a percentage of the draft call declined from 0.07 percent in 1955 to 0.02 percent in 1967. Apparently a larger draft call produces a higher percentage willing to report. The prosecutions as a percentage of those who failed to report went up from 0.05 percent in 1954 to 0.08 percent in 1966 and 0.18 percent in 1967. As Clark reminded Johnson, in fiscal year 1967 some 2.5 percent of all men called failed to report. This compared favorably with the 7 percent who failed to report in 1954 and the 8 percent in 1955 and 1956. In 1961 some 11 percent failed to report. Although nearly twice as many men were called in 1953 as in 1967, more than three times as many failed to report in 1953. See Clark memo for President, 16 November 1967, ex fg 282, cont. 303, LBJ; Clark for President, 6 November 1967, whcf nd

9–4, ct. 148, ibid.; Califano to President, 18 November 1967, ibid.; and *Selective Service Annual Report, 1954* (Washington, D.C.: USGPO, 1955), p. 30.

85. Useem, *Conscription*, pp. 126, 169; Peter W. Martin, "Trial by Hershey: The Draft as Punishment," *The Nation* 206 (29 January 1968):141; Surrey, *Choice*, p. 51. See also Lawrence M. Baskir and William A. Strauss, *Chance and Circumstance: The Draft, the War, and the Vietnam Generation* (New York: Knopf, 1978), chap. 3, who make much over 209,517 accused, 25,279 indicted, 8,750 convicted, and 4,000 jailed. But see Charles E. Silberman, *Criminal Violence, Criminal Justice* (New York: Random House, 1978), who argues that such a pattern is normal.

86. Kohn, *Jailed*, p. 87; Lawrence M. Baskir and William A. Strauss, *Reconciliation After Vietnam* (Notre Dame, Ind.: Notre Dame University, 1977), pp. 3, 15; Surrey, *Choice*, p. 51; *SSN*, March 1967, p. 3; February 1968, p. 3; April 1968, p. 2; *Washington Daily News*, 6 May 1967; Warren Christopher to Larry Temple, whcf nd 9–4, ct. 149, LBJ; and Report by Inspection Team of Amnesty International, 20 June 1969, VF 270, LBH.

87. For Johnson quote, see Lyndon B. Johnson, *Public Papers of the President of the United States: Lyndon B. Johnson*, 10 vols. (Washington, D.C.: USGPO, 1965–1970), 1:513.

88. Small, "The Impact of the Antiwar Movement," pp. 8, 9, 12, 15; Paul M. Popple to S/5 Van B. Manning, 29 May 1967, whcf gen. n.d. 9–4, ct. 151, LBJ. Johnson became very emotional about draft protesters, questioning their sanity and vowing swift justice for them. See Ramsey Clark interview, 3 June 1969, oral history, LBJ, and George C. Herring, *America's Longest War: The United States and Vietnam, 1950–1975*, 2d ed. (New York: Knopf, 1986), p. 181.

89. Small, "Impact of Antiwar Movement," pp. 14, 16, 21 n. 58; Joan M. Jensen, "The Army and Domestic Surveillance," in Garry D. Ryan and T. K. Nenninger, eds., *Soldiers and Civilians: The U.S. Army and the American People* (Washington, D.C.: National Archives, 1987), p. 171; and Johnson memo for Ramsey Clark, 20 October 1967, whcf, nd 9–4, ct. 148, LBJ.

90. Bernard Franck, interview with author, Arlington, Va., 24 October 1967; Hershey interview, oral history, 15 December 1970, LBJ.

91. Hershey to all members of Selective Service System, 26 October 1967, Letter file, LBH.

92. *SSN*, January 1968, p. 3; quote from *New York Times*, 9 November 1967, p. 3; Larry Temple to President, 16 November 1967, whcf, nd 9–4, ct. 148, LBJ; and Matt Nimetz for Califano, 16 November 1967, ibid.

93. Joseph A. Scerra to President, 30 November 1967, whcf fg 282, ct. 304, LBJ; Martin G. Riley to President, 11 December 1967, whcf nd 9–4, ct. 151, ibid.; Robert B. Cochran to President, 23 January 1968, whcf gen nd, 9–4, ct. 152, ibid.; Lewis B. Hershey, "The Ephemeral Criticism of the October Letter," *Forensic Quarterly* 42 (May 1968), copy in Box 4a, RG 147 NA; Hershey interview, oral history, LBJ.

94. See Box 151, gen nd 9–4, whcf, LBJ, for opposition letters; Flynn, *Hershey*, p. 261; Martin, "Trial," p. 141; quote from *New York Times*, 9 November 1967, p. 3; and *SSN*, January 1968, p. 1.

95. Rivers quote in *SSN*, 1 December 1967, pp. 1–2; Califano for President, 18 November 1967, whcf, nd 9–4, ct. 148, LBJ.

96. President Sterling to President, 13 December 1967, whcf nd 9–4, ct. 151, LBJ; Douglas Cater for President, 16 November 1967, ibid, ct. 148; and Jim Gaither for Califano, 29 November 1967, ibid.

97. Martin, "Trial," p. 143; Brewster quoted in *New York Times*, 4 December 1967, p. 26; and Small, "The Impact of Antiwar," p. 9.

98. *New York Times*, 9 December 1967, p. 1, and 10 December 1967, p. 1.

99. Califano to Brewster, 26 December 1967, whcf nd 9-4, ct. 149, LBJ; Hershey to Neumaier, 9 January 1968, Gilbert Papers. But other officials continued to lobby college presidents to support the war; see Small, "The Impact of Antiwar," p. 9.

100. Califano to President, 11 December 1967, EX nd 9-4, LBJ; also found in whcf, nd 9-4, ct. 149, LBJ; and Hershey interview, oral history, LBJ.

101. Flynn, *Hershey*, p. 262; Martin, "Trial," p. 140; Hershey to Moss, 19 March 1968, cong. file, LBH; *New Republic*, editorial, 23 December 1967, p. 9; *New York Times*, 2 January 1968, p. 74; Christopher to Califano, 29 December 1967, ex fg 282, cont. 303, LBJ; and Small, *Johnson*, p. 156.

102. Robert B. Smith, "Disaffection, Delegitimation and Consequence: Aggregate Trends for World War II, Korea and Vietnam," in Charles C. Moskos, Jr., ed., *Public Opinion and the Military Establishment* (Beverly Hills, Calif.: Sage, 1971), p. 235, and Harold E. Klein, "Attitudes Toward Military Service and Career Patterns of Youth," in Willenz, *Dialogue*, p. 64.

103. *Washington Daily News*, 6 June 1968; SSN, February 1968, p. 4; ibid., November 1968, p. 2; Dan Vernards to President, 6 February 1968, whcf, gen nd 9-4, ct. 152, LBJ; and George H. Gallup, ed., *The Gallup Poll: Public Opinion, 1935–1971*, 3 vols. (New York: Random House, 1972), 3:2180, 2105.

104. George Reedy for President, 7 October 1968, whcf nd 9-4, ct. 149, LBJ; Jerome Johnston and Jerald G. Bachman, *Young Men Look at Military Service* (Ann Arbor, Mich.: Institute for Social Research, 1970), pp. 13, 34;

105. Johnston and Bachman, *Young Men*, pp. 13, 34; Fallows, "What Did You Do?" p. 14; U.S. Youth Council, "Youth Opinion Survey," 30 November 1966, NACSS, Box 33, RG 220; Charles C. Moskos, Jr., *The American Enlisted Man: The Rank and File in Today's Military* (New York: Sage, 1970), p. 35.

106. Gerald F. Linderman, "Commentary on 'Roots of American Military Policy,'" in Ryan and Nenninger, *Soldiers and Civilians*, p. 41; and Smith, "Disaffection," pp. 221, 223, 225, 227.

107. Friedman and Leistner, *Compulsory Service*, p. 408; Local board opinion poll, NACSS, Box 44, RG 220; Hershey, "Selective Service," p. 2; and quotes in Hershey memo for Clark, 1967, LBJ xerox. tech.

108. Connell to Califano, 7 March 1968, whcf nd 9-4, ct. 149; Doris Kearns to Levinson, 5 August 1968, ibid; Surrey, *Choice*, p. 37; *United States Draft Policy*, July 1968, p. 10; Gerhardt, *Draft*, p. 322; and Richard A. Laing to Patterson, 25 April 1967, NACSS, Box 36, RG 220.

109. SSN, May 1968, p. 4, and August 1968, p. 3.

110. Minutes of National Selective Service Scientific Advisory Group, 16 February 1966, LBH.

111. Minutes of SSN Science Advisory Committee, 29 June 1967, LBH; Hershey to State Directors, 14 July 1967, Official Papers, Science, ibid.; Hershey to National Security Council, 8 September 1967, ibid.

112. Fitt to Califano, 14 November 1967, Califano Papers, cont. 55, LBJ; A. Wolff, "Nobody Likes the Draft," *Look*, 2 April 1968, p. 34; Bromley Smith to Harry D. Feltenstein, Jr., 15 November 1967, whcf gen nd 9-4, ct. 151, LBJ; and Califano for President, 18 November 1967, ibid, ct. 148, LBJ.

113. *New York Times*, 8 December 1967, p. 13, and 10 February 1968, p. 1;

Califano for President, 13 February 1968, whcf, nd 9-4, ct. 153, LBJ; and 16 February 1968, ibid.

114. *New York Times*, 17 February 1968, p. 1, and 18 February 1968, p. 2; quote in *United States Draft Policy*, July 1968, p. 2; Califano for President, 16 February 1968, whcf nd 9-4, ct. 153, LBJ; and Hershey to Douglas Cater, 17 May 1968, EX FG 282, ct. 304, LBJ.

115. Quote in Hershey speech, 12 March 1968, speech file, LBH; newspaper file, 1968, ibid.; Hershey to Douglas Cater, 17 May 1968, EX FG 282, ct. 304, LBJ; and *New York Times*, 2 March 1968, p. 3.

116. Lawrence E. Levinson to Califano, 25 April 1968, EX FG 282, ct. 304, LBJ, and Emery F. Bacon to Secretary, HEW, 24 May 1968, whcf nd 9-4, ct. 153, ibid.

117. Hershey speech, 12 March 1968, speech file, LBH; *New York Times*, 13 March 1968, p. 15; *SSN*, March 1968, p. 1; *New York Times*, 18 February 1968, p. 2; Hershey to Phil C. Neal, 30 October 1968, White House Correspondence, LBH; quotes from Minutes of State Directors Conference, 22-26 April 1968, LBH; and Hershey to Meyerhoff, 8 December 1968, alpha file, ibid.

118. Carmichael to Col. Robert H. Rankin, 29 August 1969, Science Advisory file, LBH, and Meyerhoff to Hershey, 29 April 1969, alpha file, ibid.

119. De Vier Pierson for President, 7 September 1968, whcf nd 9-4, ct. 153, LBJ; clipping from *Time*, 6 September 1968, ibid; *SSN*, October 1968, p. 2; and *Washington Evening Star*, 17 July 1969. A report in the *Stanford Research Institute Journal* in 1969 concluded that threats to graduate enrollment were overblown. Surveys showed only 10.3 percent of responding universities had any change in male graduate enrollment affected by the draft. There could be some short-term falloff, said the report, but no need for major concern. See clipping, 1 April 1969, Anderson file, Box 27, WHCF, RMN, and SMC report, 1 January 1969, ibid., Box 38.

Chapter 9. Nixon and the Draft

1. On the class dimension of deferments see James Fallows, "What Did You Do in the Class War, Daddy?" *Washington Monthly* 7 (October 1975):10, 11, 14. For the evolution of CO status see George Q. Flynn, "Selective Service and the Conscientious Objector" in Michael Noone, ed., *Selective Conscientious Objection* (Boulder, Colo.: Westview, 1989); Patricia McNeal, "Catholic Conscientious Objection during World War II," *Catholic Historical Review* 61 (1975):222; Richard J. Niebanck, *Conscience, War, and the Selective Objector* (New York: Lutheran Church of America, 1968), pp. 39, 45; Charles E. Rice, "Conscientious Objection: A Conservative View," *Modern Age* 13 (Winter 1968-1969):73; *New York Times*, 19 November 1968; and J. Harold Sherk, "The Position of the Conscientious Objector," *Current History* 55 (1968):18, 21-22.

2. See clippings, Martin Anderson file, WHCF, Box 39, Richard M. Nixon Presidential Materials Project, N.A., Alexandria, Va. (hereafter cited as RMN), and Gaetano Marino, "Protest and Procurement," *Marine Corps Gazette* 53 (1969):42, 44.

3. See Melvin Small, *Johnson, Nixon, and the Doves* (New Brunswick, N.J.: Rutgers University, 1988), pp. 3, 21, and Irvin and Debbi Unger, *The Turning Point: 1968* (New York: Scribner's, 1988), for attempts to prove the impact of protest on Johnson. Louis Hershey interview, Oral History Project, LBJ, 15 December 1970.

4. See clippings, Martin Anderson file, WHCF, Boxes 11, 14, RMN; Stephen E.

Ambrose, *Nixon: The Education of a Politician 1913-1962* (New York: Simon and Schuster, 1987), pp. 409, 418; "The Draft: Campus to Chaos," *Newsweek*, 4 April 1960, p. 40; and Robert K. Griffith, Jr., "About Face? The U.S. Army and the Draft," *Armed Forces and Society* 12 (Fall 1985):119. As a member of the House Un-American Activities Committee, young Nixon had passed on to Selective Service the names of men suspected of being Communists who had been drafted into the armed forces; see Marx Leva to Hershey, 7 August 1950, Denny file, Lewis B. Hershey Papers, Military History Institute, Carlisle, Pa. (hereafter cited as LBH).

5. See Herbert Parmet, *Richard Nixon and His America* (Boston: Little, Brown, 1990), pp. 489-509.

6. Press conference, 6 March 1968, Anderson file, WHCF, Box 14, RMN, and Herb Klein to Anderson, 27 June 1968, ibid., Box 11.

7. Herb Klein to Anderson, 27 June 1968, Anderson file, WHCF, Box 11, RMN, and Nixon speech, 17 October 1968, Box 25, ibid.

8. Griffith, "About Face," p. 120.

9. George H. Gallup, ed., *The Gallup Poll: Public Opinion, 1935-1971*, 3 vols. (New York: Random House, 1972), 3:2180, and *The National Observer*, 10 March 1969, in Anderson file, WHCF, Box 11, RMN. James Burk, "Debating the Draft in America," *Armed Forces and Society* 15 (Spring 1989):437, is misleading in writing "public opinion never perceived the Vietnam conflict as a threat sufficient to justify compulsory military service."

10. Zeb B. Bradford, Jr., and F. J. Brown, *The United States Army in Transition* (Beverly Hills, Calif.: Sage, 1970), p. 74; Charles C. Moskos, Jr., *The American Enlisted Man: The Rank and File in Today's Military* (New York: Sage, 1970), pp. 13, 169-70; Stephen E. Ambrose, "The Military and American Society: An Overview," in Ambrose and James A. Barber, eds., *The Military and American Society* (New York: Free Press, 1972), p. 4; statement by Roger T. Kelley to Senate Armed Services Committee, 2 February 1971, copy in Anderson file, WHCF, Box 39, RMN; and John Helmer, *Bringing the War Home: The American Soldier in Vietnam and After* (New York: Free Press, 1974), p. 2.

11. On turnover see Harold Wool, "Military Manpower Procurement and Supply," in Roger Little, ed., *A Survey of Military Institutions* (Chicago: Interuniversity Seminar, 1969), p. 50; *Selective Service Newsletter*, November 1968, p. 3 (hereafter cited as *SSN*); Kelley to Anderson, 10 August 1970, Anderson file, WHCF, Box 37, RMN; and on civilianization see Morris Janowitz, *The Professional Soldier: A Social and Political Portrait* (New York: Free Press, 1960), p. 65; Eliot A. Cohen, *Citizen and Soldier* (Ithaca, N.Y.: Cornell, 1985), pp. 63-65; and Samuel H. Hays, "A Military View of Selective Service," in Sol Tax, ed., *The Draft* (Chicago: University of Chicago, 1967), p. 9. On the ratio of officers to enlisted men see William L. Hauser, *America's Army in Crisis: A Study in Civil-Military Relations* (Baltimore, Md.: Johns Hopkins, 1973), p. 177.

12. Moskos, *Enlisted Man*, p. 40. On percent of force drafted or draft influenced see James W. Davis and K. M. Dolbeare, "Selective Service and Military Manpower Procurement," in Austin Ranney, ed., *Political Science and Public Policy* (Chicago: Markam, 1968), p. 83; Harold Wool, "Military Manpower: Procurement and Supply," in Roger Little, ed., *A Survey of Military Institutions* (Chicago: Interuniversity Seminar, 1969), p. 37; Moskos, *Enlisted Man*, pp. 49, 169-70; Sam C. Sarkesian, "Who Serves?" *Society* 18 (1981):57-59; Stuart H. Altman, "Is the Draft Needed?" paper in NACSS, Box 7, RG 220, National Archives, Washington, D.C. (hereafter cited as NA).

13. Dee Ingold, "Countdown on the Draft," 30 August 1968, Ingold files, author's possession, and ibid., 28 March 1969; DOD Study of Draft, July 1966, in NACSS, Box 23, RG 220, NA; Davis and Dolbeare, "Selective Service," p. 86fn; Gary L. Wamsley, *Selective Service and a Changing America* (Columbus, Ohio: Merrill, 1969), p. 197. From 1965 to 1969 the draft took in 2,347,325 men, and 10,487,352 volunteered. But Lt. Gen. A. O. Connor, deputy chief of staff for personnel, estimated that some 45 percent of the volunteers joined only because of the draft; see *U.S. News and World Report*, 9 March 1970.

14. *SSN*, August 1969, p. 2, and McNamara testimony before NACSS, 30 July 1966, minutes, Box 87, RG 220, NA.

15. Thomas D. Morris, "Department of Defense Report on Study of the Draft," in Martin Anderson, ed., *The Military Draft* (Stanford, Calif.: Hoover Institution, 1982), p. 555, and Wool, "Military Manpower," p. 40.

16. Quote from *SSN*, August 1965, p. 4, for testimony of CNP B. J. Semmes, Jr., to House Committee on Appropriations. On the various surveys to determine the percentage of draft-induced volunteers see the following: Wamsley, *Selective Service*, p. 92; *SSN*, October 1959, p. 4; Tax, *The Draft*, p. 364; Hauser, *America's Army*, p. 139; Davis and Dolbeare, "Selective Service," p. 91; James M. Gerhardt, *The Draft and Public Policy* (Columbus: Ohio State, 1971), p. 291; and news conference by Roger T. Kelley, 14 October 1970, Anderson file, WHCF, Box 40, RMN. The studies also suggest that educational and training opportunities carried more weight than higher pay in generating volunteers. See Kelley press conference, 14 October 1970, Anderson file, Box 40, RMN, and Wool, "Military Manpower," p. 61.

17. Quote from Dr. McCrocklin in NACSS proceedings, n.d., Box 89, RG 220, NA; Science Research Associates, Inc., *Unfit for Service: A Review of the Draft and Basic Education in the Army* (Chicago: SRA, 1966), p. 73; Wool, "Military Manpower," p. 48; and *New York Times*, 2 March 1970, clip in President's Commission on an All-Volunteer Armed Force, RG 220, NA (hereafter cited as PCAVF).

18. McNamara testimony, 30 July 1966, minutes of NACSS, Box 87, RG 220, NA; *SSN*, April 1969, p. 2; Moskos, *Enlisted Man*, p. 177; U.S. President, Commission on an All-Volunteer Force, *Report* (Washington, D.C.: USGPO, 1970), p. 113–15 (hereafter cited as Gates report); and Gerhardt, *The Draft*, p. 282; DOD, "Career Motivation in the Ready Reserve," June 1969, PCAVF, Box 1, RG 220, NA. Johnson had learned from the mistakes of Truman and Kennedy that the political cost of activating reserve units for combat was too high. Officially, he refused to use them in Vietnam because it would disrupt the economy and lives of many families; see Earle G. Wheeler interview, August 1969, May 1970, Oral History Project, p. 21, LBJ.

19. Nixon press conference, 1968, WHCF, Anderson file, Box 14, RMN.

20. Albert D. Klassen, Jr., *Military Service in American Life since World War II* (Chicago: National Opinion Research Center, 1966), pp. 9–10, and *SSN*, April 1966, p. 1.

21. M. R. D. Foot, *Men In Uniform: Military Manpower in Modern Industrial Societies* (New York: Praeger, 1961), p. 162. Interestingly enough, the United States had a higher ratio of servicemen to population in 1981, after the AVF, than did France in 1789; see Cohen, *Citizen*, p. 47.

22. Klassen, *Military Service*, pp. 68, 72, found that about 70 percent served in urban areas and about 55–57 percent in rural areas. Rejection rates in the South accounted for a lower military participation rate.

23. Quote from Gerhardt, *The Draft*, p. 244; Wool, "Military Manpower," p. 54.

24. Harry A. Marmion, *Selective Service: Conflict and Compromise* (New York: Wiley, 1968), p. 29; PCAVF, 2:7–1, RG 220, NA; Moskos, *Enlisted Man*, p. 1; DOD Study, July 1966, in Box 23, NACSS, RG 220, NA; and Helmer, *Bringing the War Home*, p. 4.

25. Davis and Dolbeare, "Selective Service," pp. 99, 102; Klassen, *Military Service*, pp. 29–34; David R. Segal, "How Equal Is Equity?" *Society* 18 (1981):31–33; Neil D. Fligstein, "Military Service," ibid., p. 44. For a survey of Congress see Dick Shoup to J. Edgar Hoover, 1 June 1971, DR/Prot/105170160, FBI files, J. Edgar Hoover Building, Washington, D.C.

26. Ulysses Lee, "The Draft and the Negro," *Current History* 55 (July 1968):33; Lewis B. Hershey, "Selective Service," ibid., p. 3; Edward B. Glick, "The Draft and Non-military National Service," *Military Review* 49 (December 1969):87; Paul T. Murray, "Local Draft Board Composition and Institutional Racism," *Social Problems* 19 (1971):131–32, 134–35; David S. Surrey, *Choice of Conscience: Vietnam Era Military and Draft Resisters in Canada* (New York: Praeger, 1982), p. 40; Morris Janowitz, *Military Conflict: Essays in the Institutional Analysis of War and Peace* (Beverly Hills, Calif.: Sage, 1975), p. 274; and Dee Ingold, "Countdown on the Draft," 14 June 1968, Ingold file. In the period from 1950 to 1966 whites were physically disqualified at twice the rate of blacks, but blacks were five times more likely to fail the mental qualifications, which meant that only one-third of all blacks eligible were found acceptable.

27. U.S., Bureau of the Census, *Historical Statistics of the United States: Colonial Times to 1970*, 2 pts. (Washington, D.C.: USGPO, 1975), 1:368, 380, 383; SS, *Annual Report, 1960* (Washington, D.C.: USGPO, 1961), p. 88; SS, *Semi-Annual Report, 1970* (Washington, D.C.: USGPO, 1971), p. 32.

28. For the first chart see any of the following sources: Sam C. Sarkesian, "Who Serves?" pp. 43, 72; Klassen, *Military Service*, pp. 15, 48; Wool statement to NACSSC, 2 December 1966, Box 89, RG 220, NA; Marmion, *Selective Service*, p. 30; Davis and Dolbeare, "Selective Service," p. 93; Wool, "Military Manpower," pp. 57, 59; SSN, October 1962, p. 1; ibid., May 1969, p. 1; and ibid., July 1969, p. 3. For the second chart see Moskos, *Enlisted Man*, p. 50.

29. Peter Karsten, *Soldiers and Society: The Effect of Military Service and War on American Life* (Westport, Conn.: Greenwood, 1978), p. 121; Klassen, *Military Service*, p. 22; George H. Walton, "Sole Source Procurement through Selective Service," *Army* 14 (1 September 1968):33; Sarkesian, "Who Serves?" p. 72; Irvin G. Katenbrink, Jr., "Military Service and Occupational Mobility," in Roger W. Little, ed., *Selective Service and American Society* (Beverly Hills, Calif.: Sage, 1969), p. 169; Thomas B. Curtis, "Conscription and Commitment," copy in Anderson file, WHCF, Box 14, RMN.

30. Robert K. Griffith, Jr., *Men Wanted for the U.S. Army* (Westport, Conn.: Greenwood, 1982), p. 213; SSN, April 1963, p. 3, and November 1963, p. 1; James A. Barber, Jr., "The Draft and Alternatives of the Draft," in Ambrose and Barber, eds., *The Military and American Society*, p. 212; Moskos, *Enlisted Man*, p. 49; Samuel H. Hays, *Defense Manpower: The Management of Military Conscription* (Washington, D.C.: ICAF, 1968), p. 9; Curtis W. Tarr, *By the Numbers: The Reform of the Selective Service System, 1970–1972* (Washington, D.C.: National Defense University Press, 1981), p. 130; Foot, *Men in Uniform*, p. 97; and Roger Little, "Procurement of Manpower," in Little, *Selective Service*, pp. 17, 20, 26.

31. Karsten, *Soldiers and Society*, p. 120; Moskos, *Enlisted Man*, pp. 51–52; Congressional Reference Service, *United States Draft Policy*, July 1968, p. 25; Roger T.

Kelley, press conference, 14 October 1970, in Anderson file, WHCF, Box 40, RMN; *Christian Science Monitor*, 9 December 1969, clip in WHCF, Box 27; *SSN*, July 1969, p. 4; and Michael Useem, *Conscription, Protest, and Social Conflict: The Life and Death of a Draft Resistance Movement* (New York: John Wiley and Sons, 1973), p. 106.

32. First quote, *SSN*, March 1958, p. 2; second quote, ibid., March 1963, p. 4; third quote, ibid., January 1962, p. 3; ibid., August 1965, p. 3; ibid., December 1966, p. 1; and Hays, "Military View," p. 14.

33. Kurt Lang, "The Dissolution of Armies in the Vietnam Pespective," in Michael L. Martin and E. S. McCrate, eds., *The Military, Militarism, and the Polity: Essays in Honor of Morris Janowitz* (New York: Free Press, 1984), pp. 117, 125, 128–129, 135n, and Moskos, *Enlisted Man*, pp. 140, 163. Moskos also reports that total desertion rates for the Vietnam period 1967–1968 were lower than those for World War II and only slightly higher than those for the Korean War; see p. 160.

34. Albert D. Biderman, "What Is Military?" in Tax, *The Draft*, p. 132; Surrey, *Choice*, p. 47; and *New York Times*, 11 February 1970, clip in PCAVF, Box 11, RG220, NA. Duane E. Leigh, "The Distribution of Hostile Casualties on Draft Eligible Males with Differing Socioeconomic Characteristics," *Social Science Quarterly* 51 (March 1971):934, 939–40, tries to establish a correlation between battle death and education and income, with those at the low end of the latter suffering the highest rate of loss. Such a correlation offers a partial explanation for the relative immunity of the draftee over the enlistee, who was less well educated.

35. Jacques Van Doorn, *The Soldier and Social Change* (Beverly Hills, Calif.: Sage, 1975), pp. 19, 51, 53, 56; Cohen, *Citizen*, pp. 37, 58; and Janowitz, *Military Conflict*, pp. 243–44.

36. Robert Evans, Jr., "The Military Draft as a Slave System: An Economic View," *Social Science Quarterly* 50 (1969):543; Cohen, *Citizen*, pp. 20, 27; Burk, "Debating," p. 441; Anthony C. Fisher, "The Cost of Draft and the Cost of Ending the Draft," *American Economics Review* 59 (1969):239–40; Leigh, "Distribution," p. 940; Blair Clark, "The Question Is What Kind of Army?" *Harpers*, 1 September 1969, p. 82; and Memo, n.d., quote of Galbraith, Anderson file, Box 14, WHCF, RMN.

37. Burk, "Debating," pp. 433, 442; Cohen, *Citizen*, 33–34; and Clark, "Question," p. 82.

38. Richard M. Nixon, *No More Vietnams* (New York: Arbor House, 1985), pp. 102, 125.

39. First quote, SAC, Chicago to Director, 1 May 1969, DR/Prot/100449698, FBI files, Washington, D.C.; second quote, SAC, NYC, to Director, 2 April 1969, ibid. See also SAC, WFO, to Director, 9 August 1969, ibid. Director to SAC, San Francisco, 10 November 1969, ibid.; SAC, San Francisco, to Director, 26 June 1969, ibid.; Director to SAC, major cities, 21 August 1969, DR/Prot/100449698-50, ibid.; Boston, SAC to Director, 17 November 1970; ibid.; SAC, Chicago to Director, 1 May 1969, ibid.; Ehrlichman to Mitchell, Burns, Moynihan, Finch, 5 May 1969, Krogh file, WHSF, Box 66, RMN; Jack Caulfield for Ehrlichman, 20 June 1969, ibid.; and Krogh for Ehrlichman, 26 June 1969, ibid.

40. George Q. Flynn, *Lewis B. Hershey: Mr. Selective Service* (Chapel Hill: University of North Carolina Press, 1985), p. 273.

41. Anderson memo for Nixon, 3 January 1969, Anderson file, WHCF, Box 11, RMN; Moynihan quote in *Newsday* clipping, 6 February 1969, ibid.; and minutes of Haldeman staff meeting, 8 April 1969, Haldeman file, WHSF, Box 373, ibid.

42. J. G. Larkin to Cong. F. Bradford Morse, 3 April 1969, Anderson file, WHCF, Box 27, RMN.

43. Jack W. Carlson to Arthur Burns, 21 April 1969, Anderson file, WHCF, Box 27, RMN; Flanigan to Burns, Ehrlichman, 26 April 1969, Subject file: CF, WHCF, Box 43, ibid.; Dean to Richard Kleindienst, 12 May 1969, Dean file, WHSF, Box 16, ibid.

44. Nixon message to Congress, 13 May 1969, Anderson file, Box 27, WHCF, RMN.

45. See Stephen E. Ambrose, *Nixon: The Triumph of a Politician, 1962–1972* (New York: Simon and Schuster, 1989), pp. 248–51; Herbert Parmet, *Richard Nixon*, pp. 4–5; and Jonathan Schell, *The Time of Illusion* (New York: Knopf, 1976), for this aspect of the Nixon presidency.

46. Summary of staff meeting, 15 May 1969, Haldeman file, WHSF, Box 373, RMN; idem., 19 May 1969, ibid.; Arthur Burns for President, 19 July 1969, Krogh file, WHSF, Box 66, RMN; quote in staff paper for draft reform, 21 August 1969, FG 216, SS, EXFG, Box 3, RMN; Bud Wilkinson to Haldeman, 25 August 1969, Haldeman file, WHSF, Box 52, RMN; Haldeman for Flanigan, 1 September 1969, ibid.; and Haldeman for Wilkinson, ibid.

47. News Analysis of Press Commentary, 28 May 1969, Anderson file, WHCF, Box 11, RMN; clip from *Christian Science Monitor*, 27 February 1969, ibid.; Staff paper on draft meeting, 21 August 1969, FG 216, SS, EXFG, Box 3, ibid.; and *New York Times*, 24 July 1969, clip in Box 11, PCAVF, RG 220, NA.

48. Ingold, "Countdown," 10 January 1969, Ingold file; Selective Service memo on protest, 9 May 1969, pp. 6–7, LBH; Robert B. Smith, "Disaffection, Delegitimation, and Consequence: Aggregate Trends for World War II, Korea and Vietnam," in Charles C. Moskos, Jr., ed., *Public Opinion and the Military Establishment* (Beverly Hills, Calif.: Sage, 1971), p. 229.

49. Dwight L. Chapin to Haldeman and Ehrlichman, 15 February 1969, RM, Religion file, WHCF, RMN, and J. Rose notes on meeting, 26 April 1969, Subject File: CF, Box 43, WHCF, RMN.

50. Robert Ellsworth for Jay Wilkinson, 22 February 1969, FG 216, SS, Box 1, RMN, and Rose for Harry Dent, 26 February 1969, ibid, Box 3. Graham's opinion in Dwight L. Chapin to Haldeman, 15 February 1969, WHCF, Relig., RMN.

51. Rose for Harry Dent, 26 February 1969, FG 216, SS, EXFG, Box 3, RMN; Dent for Ehrlichman, 27 February 1969, ibid.; EO draft, 5 June 1969, ibid., Box 1; Robert Ellsworth to Ehrlichman, 20 March 1969, ibid., Box 3; Flanigan to Dent, 31 March 1969, ibid.; Rose to Flanigan, 26 April 1969, Subject File: CF, Box 43, WHCF, RMN; and Rose to Flanigan, 6 May 1969, FG 216, SS, EXFG, Box 3, ibid.

52. First quote, minutes of Haldeman staff meeting, 15 May 1969, Haldeman file, WHSF, Box 373, RMN; second quote, Nixon press statement, 6 June 1969, Anderson file, WHCF, Box 27, ibid.; Report of 47 Youth Advisory Committees, 3 April 1970, VF 110x3, LBH; and Flynn, *Hershey*, p. 275.

53. Murray, "Local Draft Board," pp. 129–30; Smith, "Disaffection," p. 235; U.S., Senate, Judiciary Committee, Subcommittee on Administration, *Hearing*, 16 May 1968, p. 25; Hershey to Nixon, 1 December 1969, Gilbert Hershey File (private), Jacksonville, N.C.; and Ingold, "Countdown," 9 June 1969.

54. Murray, "Local Draft Board," pp. 130–31. See Pranad Chatterjee and B. F. Chatterjee, "Some Structural Dilemmas of Selective Service," *Human Organization* 29 (1970):288, 292, for composition of boards in 1968 in Cleveland.

55. B. V. Pepitone to Shultz, 5 August 1970, FG 216, SS, Box 1, RMN; EO file,

25 August 1970, ibid.; EO, 2 September 1970, ibid.; and Curtis Tarr final report to President, 30 April 1972, FG 216, SS, EXFG, Box 2, ibid.

56. First quote, Don Rumsfeld to Flanigan, 25 November 1968, FG 216, SS, Box 1, RMN; John W. Macy, Jr., for William J. Hopkins, 30 December 1968, WHCF, FG 282, ct. 304, LBJ; Haldeman to Flanigan, 17 February 1969, FG 216, SS, Box 1, RMN; and Flanigan to B. Harlow, 20 February 1969, ibid.

57. Haldeman to Flanigan, 28 April 1969, FG 216, SS, Box 1, RMN; Flanigan for President, 30 April 1969, WHCF, Subject file: CF, Box 43, ibid.; Houston for Haldeman, 8 August 1969, Haldeman file, WHSF, Box 52, ibid.; and Flynn, *Hershey*, pp. 279–80.

58. Quote in staff paper, 21 August 1969, FG 216, SS, EXFG, Box 3, RMN; Haldeman to Ehrlichman, 16 September 1969, ibid., Box 24; Rose for Flanigan, 17 September 1969, ibid.; President for Ehrlichman, 19 September 1969, WHSF, Subject file: CF, Box 24, RMN; Flanigan to Chapin, 7 October 1969, WHSF, FG 216, Box 24, ibid.; Flanigan memo for President, 9 October 1969, ibid.; and Memo for President's file, 14 October 1969, WHSF, Subject file: CF, Box 24, ibid.

59. Flynn, *Hershey*, p. 284; Ken Cole for Flanigan, 13 October 1969, FG 216, SS, Box 1, RMN; Staff secretary to Flanigan, 17 October 1969, ibid.; Flanigan for staff secretary, 18 October 1969, ibid.; Flanigan to Harlow, et al., 4 November 1969, ibid.; Nixon quote on margin, Flanigan to Haldeman, 10 December 1969, POF, President's handwriting, Box 4, ibid.; Ken Belleu for Harlow, 27 January 1970, ibid., Box 1; Goldwater, Tower, Thurmond, and Byrd also opposed DiBona, ibid., 28 January 1970; and Rose to Flanigan, 29 January 1970, ibid. The White House kept a close watch on Senator Smith by stealing letters from her office; see Rose to Harlow, 9 Feb. 1970, FG 216, SS, Box 1, RMN.

60. Harold Wool to Anderson, 13 March 1969, Martin Anderson file, WHCF, Box 11 RMN; Thomas B. Curtis, "Conscription and Commitment," clip in Anderson file, Box 14, ibid.; Hershey speech, 1 March 1968, speech file, Lewis B. Hershey Papers, Military History Institute, Carlisle, Pa. (hereafter cited as LBH); Carter B. Magruder to Dee Ingold, 9 January 1969, Dee Ingold Papers, author's possession.

61. Wool to Anderson, 13 March 1969, Anderson file, WHCF, Box 11, and *Christian Science Monitor*, 27 February 1969.

62. Dee Ingold, "Countdown on the Draft," 18 April 1969, Ingold Papers; Rose to Flanigan, 16 April 1969, Subject file: CF, Box 43, WHCF, ibid; Flanigan to Burns, Ehrlichman, 26 April 1969, Subject File: CF, Box 43, WHCF, RMN; minutes of Haldeman staff meeting, 29 April 1969, Haldeman file, Box 373, WHSF, ibid.; and Rose to Bud, 30 April 1969, Subject file: CF, Box 43, WHCF, ibid.

63. Flanigan for President, 30 April 1969, Subject file: CF, Box 43, WHCF, RMN; News analysis of press commentary, 28 May 1969, Anderson file, Box 11, WHCF, ibid.; Ingold, "Countdown," 16 May 1969; and SSN, December 1969, p. 2.

64. Bernard T. Franck to J. Rose, 20 June 1969, Anderson file, Box 25, WHCF, RMN; Flanigan memo for B. Harlow et al., 9 August 1969, Subject File: CF, Box 43, WHCF, ibid.; Hershey to President, 3 September 1969, FG 216, SS, EXFG, Box 3, ibid.; Hershey to Flanigan, 24 October 1969, Ingold file; also 4 November 1969, WHCF, Subject file, EXFE, Box 6, RMN; and Ingold, "Countdown," 7 November 1969.

65. Laird to President, 29 August 1969, FG 216, SS, EXFG, Box 3, RMN, and staff paper on draft, 21 August 1969, ibid.

66. Stephen Enke to Anderson, 12 November 1969, Anderson file, Box 25,

WHCF, RMN, and quote in Enke staff paper on draft reform, 17 November 1969, ibid.

67. Nixon remarks, 26 November 1969, Anderson file, Box 27, WHCF, RMN, and presidential proclamation, 26 November 1969, ibid.

68. Flynn, *Hershey*, p. 283; James Fallows, "What Did You Do in the Class War, Daddy?" *Washington Monthly* 7 (October 1975):5; Zick Rubin and Anne Peplau, "Belief in a Just World and Reactions to Another's Lot," *Journal of Social Issues* 29 (1973):73.

69. Joseph E. Mulligan, "Reform or Resistance," *Catholic World* 212 (December 1970):133, and *Baltimore Sun*, 14 December 1969.

70. Kissinger to President, 26 December 1969, CF, ND21–Cons, Box 65, WHSF, RMN.

71. John R. Brown for President to Flanigan, 29 December 1969, Subject file: CF, Box 43, WHCF, RMN. David R. Segal, "The All Volunteer Force in a Multidisciplinary Perspective," in Michael L. Martin and E. S. McCrate, eds., *The Military, Militarism, and the Polity: Essays in Honor of Morris Janowitz* (New York: Free Press, 1984), p. 177, points out that public opinion followed Nixon's actions. Polls preferred the draft that existed before the lottery was created, then showed approval by three-fourths to the lottery over the AVF, but approved the latter once Gates and Nixon began pushing it in 1970.

72. *New York Times*, 4 January 1970; Flanigan to staff secretary, 9 January 1970, Subject file: CF, Box 43, WHCF, RMN.

73. Flanigan to staff secretary, 9 January 1970, Subject file: CF, Box 43, WHCF, RMN; Enke to Rose, 11 December 1969, FG 216, SS, Box 1, RMN; Melvin Laird to Kissinger, 10 January 1970, Anderson file, Box 38, WHCF, ibid.; NSC staff study on draft reform, 22 January 1970, ibid.; and U.S. *Statutes at Large* 81 Stat. 103. Both Laird and Enke recognized that the law had to be amended to allow a direct national call by sequence number, but not until the draft act of 1971 was a national call authorized.

74. *Washington Post*, 24 January 1970, and Ingold to Hershey, 29 January 1970, Ingold Papers.

75. First quote, Flanigan to Haldeman, 20 February 1970, Haldeman file, Box 209, WHSF, RMN; second quote, Haldeman for Flanigan, 23 February 1970, ibid.; Hershey to Nixon, 11 March 1970, WHCF, Subject file: CF, Box 43, ibid., and 2 June 1970, FG 216, SS, Box 1, ibid.

76. Quote from Flanigan to Tarr, 4 May 1970, FG 216, SS, Box 1, RMN; Tarr to Flanigan, 14 April 1970, ibid., and 8 May 1970, ibid., and Tarr for President, 23 October 1970, ibid.

77. George C. Herring, *America's Longest War: The United States and Vietnam, 1950–1975*, 2d ed. (New York: Knopf, 1986), pp. 234–35, and Parmet, *Richard Nixon*, p. 588. See Irwin Unger, *The Movement: A History of the New Left* (New York: Harper and Row, 1974), for discussion of antiwar actions.

78. For the most detailed discussion of the antiwar movement see Charles DeBenedetti and C. Chatfield, *An American Ordeal: The Antiwar Movement of the Vietnam Era* (Syracuse, N.Y.: Syracuse University, 1990), esp. pp. 279–80, for reaction to the Cambodia event. Nixon, *No More*, p. 126, says the protest "prolonged the war." Kissinger quote in Henry Kissinger, *White House Years* (Boston: Little, Brown, 1979) p. 514.

79. Tarr, *By the Numbers*, p. 9; Nixon, *No More*, pp. 126–27; Lawrence M. Baskir and William A. Strauss, *Reconciliation after Vietnam* (Notre Dame, Ind.: Notre Dame

University, 1977), pp. 3, 15; Robert B. Smith, "Disaffection," p. 223; News survey, 11 May 1970, Anderson file, Box 39, WHCF, RMN; and ibid., 5 December 1970.

80. Nancy Zaroulis and G. Sullivan, *Who Spoke Up? American Protest against the War in Vietnam* (New York: Doubleday, 1984), p. 311; Baskir, *Reconciliation*, pp. viii, 15; John Dean to Jon Huntsman, 26 March 1971, Dean file, Box 26, WHSF, RMN; Smith, "Disaffection," pp. 221, 225; Anderson for Ehrlichman, 13 July 1970, Anderson file, Box 37, WHCF, RMN; Tarr, *By the Numbers*, p. 51; Robert G. Dixon to John Dean, 25 September 1970, WHSF, Dean file, Box 16, RMN; and Jack C. Lane, "Ideology and the American Military Experience," in Garry D. Ryan and T. K. Nenninger, eds., *Soldiers and Civilians: The U.S. Army and the Amerian People* (Washington, D.C.: National Archives, 1987), p. 15. For a passion-filled critique of the unfairness of the draft and prosecution see Lawrence M. Baskir and William A. Strauss, *Chance and Circumstance: The Draft, the War, and the Vietnam Generation* (New York: Knopf, 1978). For an overview of the uneven hand of justice in the United States see Charles E. Silberman, *Criminal Violence, Criminal Justice* (New York: Random House, 1978).

Politicians debated endlessly over the motives and causes of the student protest movement. Suggestions ranged from the narrow notion offered by Nixon, that the protesters were under Communist influence and out to save their skins, to the vague social theory that youth was responding to a shift in national ethos away from collective responsibility and toward individual satisfaction. But by 1970 protest was directed not only against the war itself but also against the failure to win it. Public dissatisfaction grew at about the same rate for the limited war in Korea. Increasingly, the very idea of protest became legitimized among a widening social group, and the courts had ensured that protest was protected, even considered acceptable. Cambodia sparked a new burst of the same phenomenon. George E. Reedy, *Who Will Do Our Fighting for Us?* (New York: World Publishing Company, 1969), p. 115, and Nixon, *No More*, adopt the selfish explanation; James Burk, "Debating the Draft in America," *Armed Forces and Society* 15 (Spring 1989):443, and Harriet E. Gross, "Micro and Macro Level Implications for a Sociology of Virtue: The Case of Draft Protesters to the Vietnam War," *Sociological Quarterly* 18 (Summer 1977):323, use social theory jargon.

81. Melvin Small, *Johnson, Nixon, and the Doves* (New Brunswick, N.J.: Rutgers University, 1988), p. 219; *New York Times*, 20 September 1969, p. 1, and 30 November 1969, p. 1; *Wall Street Journal*, 28 January 1971; Saul V. Levine, "Draft Dodgers: Coping with Stress, Adapting to Exile," *American Journal of Orthopsychiatry* 42 (1 April 1972):438; DeBenedetti, *Ordeal*, p. 397; Joan M. Jensen, "The Army and Domestic Surveillance," in Garry D. Ryan and T. K. Nenninger, eds., *Soldiers and Civilians: The U.S. Army and the Amerian People* (Washington, D.C.: National Archives, 1987), p. 172.

82. Quote in *SSN*, November 1969, p. 2; *Chicago Tribune*, 20 January 1970; *New York Times*, 20 January 1970; and James M. Gerhardt, *The Draft and Public Policy* (Columbus: Ohio State University, 1971), p. 343. The Justice Department next worried that some lower courts might deny to local boards all authority to order men for induction. The regulations required that a registrant had to report for induction only after he had passed a preinduction physical. If he refused to take the physical, regulations provided that he was declared delinquent and given 1-A status. The lower courts could question such actions. Mitchell and Kissinger proposed a presidential executive order to circumvent such a danger, and on 16 June 1970 Nixon signed an

order stating that when a registrant in 1-A refused to comply with a local board order to report for a physical, "he may be selected and ordered to report for induction even though he has not been found acceptable . . . and in such a case physical examination shall be performed after he has reported for induction." But he was not officially inducted until after he had passed the examination. See Arthur B. Focke to Mitchell, 26 February 1970, Subject file: ND 21, Box 43, WHSF, RMN; Kissinger to President, 16 June 1970, Subject file: CF, Box 43, ibid.; Press release, E.O, 16 June 1970, Subject file: CF, Box 43, WHCF, ibid.; and Tarr, *By the Numbers*, p. 59.

83. Kissinger to Director, SS, et al., 8 October 1969, National Security Study Memo 78, 8 October 1969, Anderson file, Box 39, WHCF, RMN. The special group that would prepare the report included Anderson, John Court, and Jonathan Rose, with special technical advice provided by Stephen Enke. Indeed, Enke, a manpower specialist, provided most of the input for the White House, since he was the only one familiar with the law; see Enke to Anderson, et al., 6 October 1969, Box 25, ibid.

84. NSC staff study on draft reform, 22 January 1970, Anderson file, Box 38, WHCF, RMN.

85. NSC staff study on draft reform, 22 January 1970, Anderson file, Box 38, WHCF, RMN.

86. Hershey to President, 1 December 1969, Ingold Papers, and NSC staff study on draft reform, 22 January 1970, Anderson file, Box 38, WHCF, RMN.

87. Enke to Anderson, 15 January 1970, Anderson file, Box 38, WHCF, RMN.

88. Melvin Laird to Kissinger, 10 January 1970, Anderson file, Box 38, WHCF, RMN.

89. See chapter 10 in this book for discussion of AVF.

90. SSN, February 1970, p. 4, and transcript, "Meet the Press," 22 February 1970, Anderson file, Box 37, WHCF, RMN.

91. Enke to Anderson, 10 February 1970, Anderson file, Box 37, WHCF, RMN; Laird to President, 11 March 1970, Subject file: CF, Box 43, WHCF, ibid.; *Washington Daily News*, 30 March 1970.

92. Kissinger for Nixon, 25 March 1970, Anderson file, Box 39, WHCF, RMN; unsigned chart in file, VAF, 16 March 1970, ibid., Box 37; Nixon to Congress, 23 April 1970, ibid., Box 39. As a result of Nixon's action as of 23 April 1970 deferments ended for occupational, agricultural, and paternity reasons. The men holding the deferments were safe as long as they continued to be qualified. The order also extended 2-A deferment status to students in approved junior or community colleges or apprentice schools. At the time of the order there were about 450,000 men in 2-A, 22,000 in 2-C, and 4.5 million in 3-A; see Local Board memo, 105, 23 April 1970, Lyndon B. Johnson Papers, Johnson Library, Austin, Texas (hereafter cited as LBJ), and Press conference, Curtis Tarr, 23 April 1970, Anderson file, Box 40, WHCF, RMN.

93. Flanigan for President, 3 March 1970, FG 216, SS, Box 1, RMN, and Tarr, *By the Numbers*, p. 57.

94. Rose for Ehrlichman, 31 March 1970, FG 216, SS, EXFG, Box 3, RMN, and *Washington Evening Star*, 19 March 1970.

95. Quote in Tarr, *By the Numbers*, p. 14; Flanigan for Tarr, 4 May 1970, FG 216, SS, Box 1, RMN; Tarr to Flanigan, 8 May 1970, ibid.; Rose to Tarr, 8 May 1970, ibid.; Tarr to Flanigan, 23 October 1970, ibid.; Tarr to President, 23 October 1970, ibid.; and quote in Tarr to Flanigan, 18 March 1971, ibid.

96. Flanigan to President, 25 November 1970, FG 216, SS, Box 1, RMN, and Tarr report to President, 30 September 1972, ibid., Box 2.

97. Haldeman staff meeting minutes, 8 May 1969, Haldeman file, Box 373, WHSF, RMN; Enke to Anderson, 26 February 1970, Anderson file, Box 37, WHCF, ibid.; Rose to Flanigan, 18 November 1970, FG 216, SS, Box 1, ibid.; Hershey to President, 11 March 1970, Subject file: CF, Box 43, WHCF, ibid.; and Tarr to President, 23 October 1970, FG 216, SS, Box 1, ibid. Theoretically, draftable men remained even if there were no renewal of induction authority. Several hundred thousand men who had held deferments remained draftable, but since most were college graduates they represented an ultrasensitive pool.

98. White House fact sheet on random selection, 26 November 1969, Anderson file, Box 27, WHCF, RMN; Laird to President, 11 March 1970, Subject file: CF, Box 43, WHCF, ibid.; *Washington Evening Star*, 23 July 1970; and Coli to Anderson, 10 August 1970, Anderson file, Box 37, WHCF, RMN.

99. Nixon to Congress, 23 April 1970, in Anderson file, Box 39, WHCF, RMN; News conference by Roger T. Coli, 14 October 1970, ibid., Box 40; Laird to President, 28 December 1970, ibid., Box 39; and Nixon to Congress, 28 January 1971, ibid.

100. News release by Sen. Charles E. Goodell, 7 May 1969, Anderson file, Box 27, WHCF, RMN; News analysis on President's draft reform message, 28 May 1969, ibid., Box 11; *New York Times*, 19 August 1970; Wire service reports, 26 August 1970, Anderson file, Box 39, WHCF, RMN; News survey, 1 July 1970, ibid.; and Laird to Stennis, 14 August 1970, ibid., Box 37.

101. Samuel R. Shaw to Anderson, 27 January 1971, Anderson file, Box 39, WHCF, RMN.

102. Ken Belieu for President, 4 May 1971, Subject file: CF, ND 21, Box 43, WHSF, RMN; 21 May 1971, President's Handwriting, POF, Box 11, ibid.; and 25 May 1971, ibid.

103. Ken Belieu for President, 23 April 1971, POF, President's handwriting, Box 10, RMN; Memo for file, Clark MacGregor, 14 April 1971, Flanigan file, Box 10, WHSF, ibid.; Dick Cook memo for Haig, 16 July 1971, CF, ND21–Cons, Box 65, ibid.; Kissinger for President, 13 September 1971, ibid.; Clark MacGregor for President, 13 September 1971, Box 43, ibid.; Nixon to Stennis and Smith, 21 September 1971, POF, President's hand, Box 13, ibid.; and U.S. *Statues at Large*, 85 stat (28 September 1971), 348–63.

104. Tarr, *By the Numbers*, p. 133.

105. The sordid story of the 1972 campaign has been told in detail by Anthony J. Lukas, *Nightmare: The Underside of the Nixon Years* (New York: Viking, 1976); Schell, *Illusion*; and others. See also Nixon to Haldeman, 30 April 1972, Haldeman file, Box 162, WHSF, RMN; Ken Khachigian for P. Buchanan, 10 May 1972, Buchanan file, Box 11, WHSF, ibid.; and Nixon to Haldeman, 18 May 1972, Haldeman file, Box 162, ibid.

106. Quote in Nixon memo for Haldeman, 14 August 1972, Haldeman file, Box 162, WHSF, RMN; Rose to Ehrlichman, 11 January 1973, FG 216, SS, EXFG, Box 2, ibid.; Hershey to President, 2 January 1973, Ingold Papers; and Rose to staff secretary, 23 January 1973, FG 216, SS, EXFG, Box 2, RMN.

Chapter 10. The AVF and the Future

1. Jacques Van Doorn, *The Soldier and Social Change* (Beverly Hills, Calif.: Sage, 1975), p. 53; Morris Janowitz, *Military Conflict: Essays in the Institutional Analysis of War and Peace* (Beverly Hills, Calif.: Sage, 1975), p. 241; Samuel P. Huntington, *The Common Defense: Strategic Programs in National Politics* (New York: Columbia University, 1961), pp. 436–37; Steven L. Canby, *Military Manpower Procurement* (Lexington, Mass.: Heath, 1971), p. 3; I. B. Holley, Jr., *General John M. Palmer, Citizen Soldiers and the Army of a Democracy* (Westport, Conn.: Greenwood, 1982), p. 616; and Russell F. Weigley, *Eisenhower's Lieutenants* (Bloomington: Indiana University, 1981), pp. 728–30.

2. Janowitz, *Military Conflict*, pp. 85, 244, 259, 243, and B. H. Liddell Hart, "Why Don't We Learn from History," in Martin Anderson, ed., *The Military Draft* (Stanford, Calif.: Hoover Institution, 1982), pp. 36–37. J. F. C. Fuller argued that the draft made soldiers cheap when they had been expensive before, causing generals to seek battle rather than to avoid it.

3. Walker S. Edwards, "The Administration of the Selective Service System in the United States," (M.A. thesis, Stanford University, 1948), p. 24; Canby, *Military Manpower*, pp. 13, 55; and George E. Reedy, *Who Will Do Our Fighting for Us?* (New York: World Publishing Company, 1969), p. 89.

4. See Edward M. Coffman, *The Old Army: A Portrait of the American Army in Peacetime, 1784–1898* (New York: Oxford, 1986); Robert K. Griffith, Jr., *Men Wanted for the U.S. Army* (Westport, Conn.: Greenwood, 1982), xiv; and Rocco M. Paone, "The Last Volunteer Army, 1946–1948," *Military Review* 49 (December 1969):11–12.

5. See chapter 5 in this book.

6. James M. Gerhardt, *The Draft and Public Policy* (Columbus: Ohio State University, 1971), p. 215; Stevenson speech, October 1956, copy in Martin Anderson file, Box 11, WHCF, Richard M. Nixon Presidential Materials Project, N.A., Alexandria, Va. (hereafter cited as RMN); and Samuel H. Hays, *Defense Manpower: The Management of Military Conscription* (Washington, D.C.: ICAF, 1968), p. 8.

7. Copy of Republican platform, 14 July 1964, in Anderson file, Box 11, WHCF, RMN; Speech by Alfred B. Fitt, 11 November 1967, Fitt Papers, cont. 5, Lyndon B. Johnson Papers, Johnson Library, Austin, Texas (hereafter cited as LBJ); DOD draft study, July 1966, National Advisory Committee on Selective Service (NACSS), Box 23, RG 220, National Archives, Washington, D.C.; and Sam Sarkesian, "Who Serves?" *Society* 18 (1981):12.

8. See M. R. D. Foot, *Men in Uniform: Military Manpower in Modern Industrial Societies* (New York: Praeger, 1961), pp. 9, 16, and Van Doorn, *Soldier*, pp. 54–55.

9. McNamara interview, 7 November 1966, copy in NACSS, Box 23, RG 220; William L. Hauser, *America's Army in Crisis: A Study in Civil-Military Relations*, (Baltimore, Md.: Johns Hopkins, 1973), pp. 50–51; and Blair Clark, "The Question Is What Kind of Army?" *Harpers*, 1 September 1969, p. 82. Milton Friedman, a defender of the AVF, insisted that coups came from officers rather than volunteer enlisted men. But the draft also ensured civilian-like officers through pressure to enter the ROTC; see Milton Friedman, "Session on Recruitment of Military Manpower Solely by Voluntary Means," in Sol Tax, ed., *The Draft* (Chicago: University of Chicago, 1967), p. 367, and Rockefeller quote, Harpers, 16 April 1970. See also ibid., 23 February 1970 and 18 March 1970, Anderson file, Box 39, RMN.

10. Adam Yarmolinsky, *The Military Establishment: Its Impact on American Society*

(New York: Harper and Row, 1971), p. 400; Zeb B. Bradford, Jr., and F. J. Brown, *The United States Army in Transition* (Beverly Hills, Calif.: Sage, 1973), p. 40; John Lovell, "Military Service, Nationalism and the Global Community," in Michael L. Martin and E. S. McCrate, eds., *The Military, Militarism, and the Polity: Essays in Honor of Morris Janowitz* (New York: Free Press, 1984), p. 72; Reedy, *Who Will Do Our Fighting for Us?*, pp. 14–15; and DOD draft study, July 1966, NACSS, Box 23, RG 220, NA.

11. Norman L. Dodd, "Voluntary Recruiting in Great Britain," *Military Review* 53 (June 1973):77; Paul Wollstadt to Kelley, 14 January 1970, Anderson file, Box 37, WHCF, RMN; *New York Times*, 3 January 1971; and *Dallas Morning News*, 5 June 1970.

12. Michael Useem, *Conscription, Protest, and Social Conflict* (New York: Wiley, 1973), p. 116; Thomas D. Morris, "Department of Defense Report on Study of the Draft," in Martin Anderson, ed., *The Military Draft* (Stanford, Calif.: Hoover Institution, 1982), p. 560; Robert P. Friedman and Charles Liestner, eds., *Compulsory Service Systems* (Columbia, Mo.: Artcraft Press, 1968), p. 181; Clark, "Question," p. 80; John Helmer, *Bringing the War Home: The American Soldier in Vietnam and After* (New York: Free Press, 1974), p. 5; George H. Gallup, ed., *The Gallup Poll: Public Opinion, 1935–1971*, 3 vols. (New York: Random House, 1972), 3:1938, 2255; U.S. Congress, Senate, Subcommittee on Employment, Manpower, and Poverty, *Hearings, Manpower Implications of Selective Service*, 90th Cong., 1st sess., 6 April 1967, pp. 244–46; John F. Morse to David J. Callard, 27 October 1969, President's Commission on an All-Volunteer Force (PCAVF), Box 4, RG 220, NA; and David J. Callard to Robert Odle, 11 March 1970, Anderson file, Box 37, WHCF, RMN.

13. Gerald F. Linderman, "Commentary on "Roots of American Military Policy," in Garry D. Ryan and T. K. Nenninger, eds., *Soldiers and Civilians: The U.S. Army and the Amerian People* (Washington, D.C.: National Archives, 1987), p. 41, and Harrington quote in News Analysis by SAFAAR, 17 March 1970, Anderson file, Box 39, WHCF, RMN.

14. Donald Smith, "The Volunteer Army," in Anderson, *Military Draft*, p. 122; Anderson to R. Nixon, n.d., Anderson file, Box 11, WHCF, RMN; and Nixon speech, 17 October 1968, ibid., Box 25.

15. Quote in Robert K. Griffith, Jr., "About Face? The U.S. Army and the Draft," *Armed Forces and Society* 12 (Fall 1985):123; *New York Times*, 31 January 1969; press release, 27 March 1969, PCAVF, Box 5, RG 220; ibid., 6 June 1969; and Enke to Anderson, 12 January 1970, Anderson file, Box 38, WHCF, RMN.

16. Gates quote in Gates speech, 6 June 1966, copy in NACSS, Box 54, RG 220. Membership of the committee consisted of Thomas Gates, chair; Thomas Curtis; Fred Dent; Milton Friedman; Crawford Greenewalt; Alan Greenspan; Alfred Gruenther; Stephen Herbits; Theodore Hesburgh; Jerome Holland; John Kemper; Jeanne Noble; Lauris Norstad; W. Allen Wallis; and Roy Wilkins. Hesburgh to E. Paul Weaver, 3 November 1969, PCAVF, Box 4, RG 220; Minutes of PCAVF meeting, 15 May 1969, Anderson file, Box 38, WHCF, RMN, and 20 December 1969, PCAVF, Box 2, RG 220; and David J. Callard to Anderson, 18 September 1969, Box 5, ibid.

17. Minutes of PCAVF, 28 June 1969, PCAVF, Box 1, RG 220; DOD briefing for commission, n.d., Anderson file, Box 38, WHCF, RMN; and Bradford and Brown, *United States Army*, pp. 41–42.

18. Hauser, *America's Army*, p. 195; MG James F. Cantwell to Gates, 25 November 1969, PCAVF, Box 4, RG 220; Statement of NG Association of US, 25

November 1969, Anderson file, Box 37, WHCF, RMN; Margaret Mealey to Gates, 27 October 1969, PCAVF, Box 4, RG 220; Resolution by 70th Convention of Veterans of Foreign Wars, 15 August 1969, ibid.; Frank Pace, Jr., to Gates, 16 September 1969, ibid.; Fount L. Robinson to Collard, 21 October 1969, ibid.; Raymond P. Neal to Gates, 26 September 1969, ibid.; Paul B. Porter to Gates, 28 March 1969, Box 6, ibid.; Irving F. Laucks to Gates, 17 September 1969, Box 3, ibid.; Gus Tyler, "Prospects and Problems," in June A. Willenz, *Dialogues on the Draft* (Washington, D.C.: American Veterans Commission, 1967), p. 7; Califano in Anderson, p. 531; AFL-CIO Ex. Council Resolution, n.d., ibid., Box 3; and speech by Gen. Bruce C. Clarke, n.d., Anderson file, Box 40, WHCF RMN.

19. *Selective Service Newsletter* (hereafter cited as *SSN*), September 1966, p. 4; Morris, "Department of Defense," pp. 558–60; James A. Huston, "Selective Service as a Political Issue," *Current History* 55 (1968): 220–21; Samuel H. Hays, "A Military View of Selective Service," in Tax, ed., *The Draft*, p. 19; and Wilson A. Swanker to Gates, 26 November 1969, PCAVF, Box 4, RG 220. Anthony C. Fisher, "The Cost of Draft and the Cost of Ending the Draft," *American Economics Review* 59 (1969):239, 252, concluded that only $5 million to $7.5 billion annually would buy the AVF.

20. Anderson to Nixon, n.d., Anderson file, Box 11, WHCF, RMN; Clark, "Question," p. 81; and James M. McConnell, "European Experience with Volunteer and Conscript Forces," study for PCAVF, RG 220, pp. 2–7.

21. Randall C. Teague to Gates, 17 September 1969, PCAVF, Box 3, RG 220; Glenna B. Johnson to Gates, 3 October 1969, ibid.; Nelson C. Jackson to Gates, 6 October 1969, ibid.; Sanford Gottlieb to Gates, 3 November 1969, ibid.; and Resolution of ADA convention, 1969, ibid.

22. U.S. Senate, *Hearing, Manpower Implications of Selective Service*, 6 April 1967, pp. 232–38, 240–43.

23. Minutes, 28 June 1969, PCAVF, Box 1, RG 220; ibid., 12 July 1969; quote from Friedman memo on cost of draft, 31 January 1970, ibid., Box 2; clip of article by Friedman, n.d., Anderson file, Box 11, WHCF, RMN; and Minutes of PCAVF, 20 December 1969, PCAVF, Box 2, RG 220.

24. Minutes, 28 June 1969, 12 July 1969, PCAVF, Box 1, RG 220; and minutes, 6 December 1969, 31 January 1970, ibid., Box 2.

25. U.S., President Commission on All-Volunteer Armed Force, *Report* (Washington, D.C.: USGPO, 1970) (hereafter cited as Gates report), pp. 5–7, 9, 46, 97, 115, 119, 137; Vincent Davis, "Universal Service: An Alternative to All Volunteer Service," in Stephen E. Ambrose and James A. Barber, eds., *The Military and American Society* (New York: Free Press, 1972), p. 222; and Jack W. Carlson, OMB, to Director, 22 September 1970, Anderson file, Box 37, WHCF, RMN. See also James C. Miller and Robert Tollison, "The Implicit Tax on Reluctant Military Recruits," *Social Science Quarterly* 51 (1971):929, for the commission's method of figuring the cost of the AVF.

26. Anderson to Dwight Chapin, 2 February 1970, Anderson file, Box 11, WHCF, RMN, and Anderson memo for President's file, 21 February 1970, ibid., Box 39.

27. White House Press conference, 21 February 1970, PCAVF, Box 5, RG 220.

28. Friedman to Laird, 23 February 1970, Box 37, Anderson file, WHCF, RMN. In September 1970, Jack W. Carlson of the Budget Office agreed with Friedman that an AVF could be achieved for only $895 million the first year, a figure considerably below that of the Gates estimate. Under this plan pay raises went only to enlisted

men in their first and second years of duty; see Carlson to Director of Budget, 22 September 1970, Anderson file, Box 37, WHCF, RMN.

29. National Council to Repeal the Draft to Anderson, 26 February 1970, Anderson file, Box 37, WHCF, RMN, and Spock statement, ibid.

30. *Army Magazine*, 1 April 1970; Califano quote in Joseph Califano, "Doubts about an All-Volunteer Army," in Anderson, *The Military Draft*, p. 538; and Hauser, *America's Army*, pp. 148–49. On the greater expendability of professionals than draftees, see Bradford and Brown, *United States Army*, p. 42; wire service story by Alsop, 24 August 1970, Anderson file, Box 39, WHCF, RMN; statement by Tarr, 9 December 1970, ibid.; and *New York Times*, 15 January 1970.

31. *SSN*, January 1964, p. 3; Griffith, "About Face?" p. 124; *SSN*, August 1969, p. 2; and quote in ibid., September 1969, p. 2.

32. Paul Wollstadt to Kelley, 14 January 1970, Anderson file, Box 37, WHCF, RMN, and Kelley to Deputy Chiefs of Staff, etc., 22 January 1970, ibid.

33. Transcript, "Meet the Press," 22 February 1970, copy in Anderson file, Box 37, WHCF, RMN.

34. Laird to President, 11 March 1970, Subject file: CF, Box 43, WHCF, RMN.

35. Quotes in *U.S. News and World Report*, 9 March 1970; *New York Times*, 15 March 1970; and *SSN*, March 1970, p. 2.

36. Report on survey by *Christian Science Monitor*, 27 February 1969 and 20 November 1969, Anderson file, Boxes 11 and 39, WHCF, RMN; memo of meeting of Gates, David Callard, and Senator Stennis, 30 January 1970, ibid., Box 37; statement by Sen. Margaret C. Smith, 25 February 1970, ibid.; Meckling memo to Anderson, 6 February 1970, ibid.; and transcript of "Face the Nation" broadcast, 22 February 1970, ibid.

37. Mark O. Hatfield to President, 13 March 1970, Anderson file, Box 38, WHCF, RMN; memo by Jon Rose on Hatfield bill, 7 April 1970, ibid.; Steiger and Lowenstein news release, 23 July 1970, ibid., Box 37; and *New York Times*, 4 February 1970.

38. Kelley to Anderson, 27 February 1970, Anderson file, Box 37, WHCF, RMN.

39. Cole memo for Ziegler, 14 March 1970, Anderson file, Box 37, WHCF, RMN; Kissinger talking points for Nixon, 22 March 1970, ibid., Box 39; Mayo to President, 26 March 1970, ibid., Box 37; and Lamar Alexander to Bryce Harlow, 3 April 1970, Subject file: CF, Box 43, WHCF, RMN.

40. Donald Smith, "The Volunteer Army," p. 123; Kelley press conference, 23 April 1970, Anderson file, Box 40, RMN; Report to secretary of defense by project volunteer, 17 August 1970, ibid., Box 37; and Kelley press conference, 14 October 1970, ibid., Box 40.

41. Griffith, *Men Wanted*, p. xiii; Hauser, *America's Army*, pp. 132, 141; Janowitz, *Military Conflict*, pp. 249, 253; and Kelley news conference, 14 October 1970, Anderson file, Box 40, WHCF, RMN.

42. Griffith, *Men Wanted*, p. 220; Thomas H. Etzold, *Defense or Delusion: America's Military in the 1980s* (New York: Harper, 1982), pp. 31–32, 35, 39, 48. See Smith, "The All Volunteer Army," p. 119, for charges of sabotage, and for a recent defense see Martin Anderson, "L'armée de métier americaine, 1973–1991: un succes," in Bernard Boene and Michel Louis Martin, eds., *Conscription & armée de métier* (Paris: FEDN, 1991), pp. 34–53.

43. Curtis W. Tarr, *By the Numbers: The Reform of the Selective Service System, 1970–1972* (Washington, D.C.: National Defense University Press, 1981), p. 149; Harry A. Marmion, "Against the All-Volunteer Force: It Just Isn't Working," in

Jason Berger, ed., *The Military Draft* (New York: Wilson, 1981), pp. 23–24; and James Webb, "Why the Army Needs It" (draft), in ibid., p. 88.

44. Hauser, *America's Army*, p. 141; Califano, "Doubts," pp. 532–33, 536; editorial from *The Economist*, "Today's American Army," in Berger, *Military Draft*, p. 49; Marmion, "Against the All-Volunteer Force," p. 22; Charles C. Moskos, Jr., "National Service and the All-Volunteer Force," in Berger, *Military Draft*, pp. 33–34, 38; Murray Polner, "Opening Pandora's Box," in ibid., p. 43; Webb, "Why the Army Needs It," p. 94; Moskos, "The Citizen Soldier and the All Volunteer Force, in Martin and McCrate, eds., *The Military*, p. 144; *New York Times*, 20 February 1985, p. 8, and 15 May 1988, p. 13. The number of married men at lower enlisted levels doubled from 1964 to 1979. For the contribution of women to the quality level of the AVF see Ellen C. Collier, "Women in the Armed Forces," CRS Issue Brief IB79045, 9 October 1984 (Washington, D.C.: Library of Congress, 1984).

45. Quote in Berger, *Military Draft*, p. 101; James B. Jacobs, "Punishment or Obligation," *Society* 18 (1981):54–55; and Moskos, "Citizen Soldier," p. 140.

46. Moskos, "National Service," pp. 34, 36; staff in Berger, *Military Draft*, p. 45; Etzold, *Defense*, p. 36; Roger Kelley, "Reply to Califano," in Anderson, *Military Draft*, p. 535; Kurt Lang, "Service Inequality," *Society* 18 (1981):41; and *New York Times*, 16 October 1988, 4:5.

47. Hauser, *America's Army*, p. 141; Janowitz, *Military Conflict*, p. 257; Moskos, "Citizen Soldier," p. 141; Juan Cameron, "It's Time to Bite the Bullet on the Draft," in Berger, *Military Draft*, p. 99; and Etzold, *Defense*, p. 38.

48. Etzold, *Defense*, p. 38; Webb, "Why the Army Needs It," pp. 83–90; and *New York Times*, 8 July 1986, p. 19.

49. Hauser, *America's Army*, pp. 83, 136–37; staff in Berger, *Military Draft*, p. 51; Marmion, "Against the All-Volunteer Force," pp. 22–23; Moskos, "National Service," p. 37; and Moskos, "Citizen Soldier," pp. 144, 147. Some critics have suggested that the little ability and stability that existed in the AVF was owing to the increased number of female volunteers, which jumped from 43,000 in 1973 to 150,000 in 1980 for all services; see Christopher A. Kojm, "Military Readiness, Manpower and the Draft," in Berger, *Military Draft*, p. 18.

50. Kojm, "Military Readiness," p. 17, and Will cited in Polner, "Opening Pandora's Box," p. 41.

51. Yarmolinski, *Military Establishment*, pp. 400–1, 335, 324–25, and Charles C. Moskos, Jr., *The American Enlisted Man: The Rank and File in Today's Military* (New York: Sage, 1970), pp. 7, 75–76.

52. Gates Report, p. 151; Tax, *The Draft*, p. 342; Yarmolinski, *Military Establishment*, p. 401; and Peter Karsten, *Soldiers and Society: The Effect of Military Service and War on American Life* (Westport, Conn.: Greenwood, 1978), pp. 204–5.

53. Tax, *The Draft*, p. 342; James Fallows, "What Did You Do in the Class War, Daddy?" *Washington Monthly* 7 (October 1975):8.

54. *Studies Prepared for the President's Commission on an All-Volunteer Armed Force (PCAVF)*, (Washington, D.C.: GPO, 1970), 2:7-3-5. More concrete information appeared when considering the impact of military life on the economic status of the individual. The armed forces were a powerful tool for training individuals, as shown by McNamara's grand experiment with Project 100,000. See McNamara for President, 2 March 1966, WHCF, ND 9-4, Ct. 148, LBJ; Edward B. Glick, *Soldiers, Scholars, and Society* (Pacific Palisades, Calif.: Goodyear, 1971), pp. 1–13; and David Freeman, "Defense Department Expenditures for Civilian Occupation Training," 1 March 1969, Anderson file, WHCF, Box 11, RMN.

55. Paul A. Weinstein, "Occupational Crossover and Universal Military Training," in Tax, *The Draft*, pp. 26–27; *SSN*, August 1962, p. 3; January 1964, p. 3; August 1968, p. 4; and Arthur Marwick, *War and Social Change in the Twentieth Century* (London: Macmillan, 1974), p. 223.

56. Yarmolinsky, *Military Establishment*, pp. 325, 331–32, and Morris Janowitz, *The Professional Soldier: A Social and Political Portrait* (New York: Free Press, 1960), p. 358. Supporters of the draft insisted that a tour of duty enhanced a person's status in society, and at certain levels this was true. People seeking careers in politics recognized that some type of military experience, even a tour with the National Guard, was the sine qua non of election success. In the Eighty-sixth Congress at least 60 percent of both the Senate and House members boasted veteran status. In 1964 the National Opinion Research Center study of 5,000 veterans found that such experience seemed to have a beneficial impact only among people in the lower social positions; for those with high civilian status, service had a negative effect.

57. When the veteran group was narrowed to cover only those who served after 31 January 1955, the spread between the nonveteran median income and veteran median income was almost $2,000. A study in 1964 of 556 registrants in Maryland found that veterans with low AFQT earned $500 a year more than men with the same scores who did not serve. But no difference in income after 10 years was observed for men scoring in the upper categories of the AFQT. Yarmolinsky, *Military Establishment*, p. 331; *SSN*, May 1968, p. 1; David B. Kassing, "Military Experience as a Determinant of Veterans' Earnings", in *Studies PCAVF*, 2:8–1, 8–17.
Several studies released in 1990 found that veterans of World War II outearned nonveterans by 10 to 20 percent, but veterans of Vietnam had earned, to date, 10 to 20 percent less. Even the rehabilitation program of Project 100,000 seemed to have had no lasting effect on civilian earning power; see *New York Times*, 23 May 1990, C2.

58. Kojm, "Military Readiness," p. 16; Janowitz, *Military Conflict*, pp. 275, 286–87; Kelley, "Reply," p. 18; Moskos, "National Service," p. 142; *New York Times*, 16 October 1988, 4:5; and Webb, "Why the Army Needs It," p. 89; Moskos, "National Service," pp. 34–35; staff in Berger, *Military Draft*, p. 51; and Smith, "The Volunteer Army," p. 124. Richard Gabriel said the AVF "is among the most discriminatory social institutions allowed to exist in the United States since slavery"; see Berger, *Military Draft*, p. 101.

59. Marshariki comments in Joseph Kelley, "Behind the Push to Revive the Draft," in Berger, *Military Draft*, p. 20.

60. Quotes in *New York Times*, 1 August 1989, p. 10; Bertram M. Gross, "The Drive to Revive the Draft," in Berger, *Military Draft*, pp. 28–30; *U.S. News and World Report* interview with Sam Nunn in ibid., pp. 54–57; and James B. Jacobs and Dennis McNamara, "Selective Service without a Draft," *Armed Forces and Society* 4 (Spring, 1984):363.

61. Quotes in *New York Times*, 1 August 1989, p. 10; Polner, "Opening Pandora's Box," pp. 41–45. For the Hoover Institution conference see Martin Anderson, ed., *Registration and the Draft* (Stanford, Calif.: Hoover Institution, 1982).

62. Roger Little, "For Choice, Not Chance," *Society* 18 (1981):49.

63. Stephen M. Kohn, *Jailed for Peace: The History of American Draft Law Violators, 1658–1985* (Westport, Conn.: Greenwood, 1986), p. 95; David Shichor and D. R. Ranish, "President Carter's Vietnam Amnesty: An Analysis of a Public Policy Decision," *Presidential Studies Quarterly* 10 (1980):443. Eizenstat quote in Gross, "Drive

to Revive," p. 26; Carter quote in ibid., p. 27; and Webb, "Why the Army Needs It," p. 88. Ford had provided selective clemency for draft resisters.

64. Editorial, in Berger, *Military Draft*, p. 53; ibid., p. 58; Nunn interview in ibid., pp. 54–57; Jacobs and McNamara, "Selective Service without a Draft,," pp. 370, 375; and *Time*, 6 July 1981, p. 44. Ibid., 21 September 1981, p. 19, reported that 93 percent complied in the first registration but only 69 percent did so in the first three months of 1981. Congress prohibited female registration, and the Supreme Court upheld the decision; Collier, "Women in the Armed Forces," pp. 1–15.

65. Jacobs and McNamara, "Selective Service without a Draft," p. 365, and quote in Berger, *Military Draft*, p. 109.

66. Reagan quoted in *New York Times*, 8 January 1982, p. 1.

67. Jacobs and McNamara, "Selective Service without a Draft," pp. 365, 371; Berger, *Military Draft*, p. 109; *New York Times*, 8 January 1981, p. 1, and 1 August 1989, p. 10; and Caspar W. Weinberger, "Foreword," in Anderson, *Military Draft*, p. xiv. On prosecution see *Washington Post*, 27 August 1982, pp. 1, 35, and 17 November 1982, p. 3; *Los Angeles Times*, 20 July 1983, pp. 1, 17; *Chronicle of Higher Education*, 11 August 1982, p. 6; and *New York Times*, 11 March 1984, p. 38.

68. Jacobs and McNamara, "Selective Service without a Draft," p. 377 n.12; Robert L. Goldich, "Return to a Peacetime Draft," Congressional Research Service, Report No. 80-190E, 6 October 1983, pp. 3–11; *New York Times*, 15 May 1988, p. 13, and 16 October 1988, 4:5. Regarding the unworkability of the draft, one scholar pointed out that only 13,580 Americans officially refused to be drafted during the Vietnam war; see Webb, "Why the Army Needs It," p. 95. For summaries of the debate see Robert L. Goldich, *Congressional Research Service Issue Briefs* IB82100 (29 May 1984), IB82101 (15 October 1984), and IB84073 (29 October 1984) (Washington, D.C.: Library of Congress, 1984).

69. *New York Times*, 16 October 1988, 4:5; and 26 February 1989.

70. *New York Times*, 1 August 1989.

Bibliographical Essay

A traditional history, a category for which I hope this work qualifies, must be grounded in archival investigations. Despite the many blessings of electronics—the computer, the modem, the database—the historian has found no substitute for the endless turning of manuscript leaves. In this essay I comment upon only the most valuable primary sources and do not attempt to replicate the material in the preceding notes. In addition, I list useful and accessible books and articles and guides to such material. The most useful guides for this work were Martin Anderson, ed., *Conscription: A Select and Annotated Bibliography* (1976); Robin Higham, ed., *A Guide to the Sources of United States Military History, Plus Supplement 1* (1975); and John E. Jessup, Jr., and R. W. Coakley, eds., *A Guide to the Study and Use of Military History* (1982).

For primary sources on the draft in America I relied upon a variety of collections, all well organized and professionally presented, if of uneven value. The most important collections are the Lewis B. Hershey Papers at the Military History Institute, Carlisle Barracks, Pennsylvania, and the Official Files of the Selective Service System, Record Group 147, at the National Archives in Washington, D.C. In keeping with modern American political tradition, General Hershey took into retirement all of his papers and a vast collection of collateral data on the draft which his office had accumulated over thirty years. The Official Files in Washington are well organized with the exception of some material dealing with the pre-1940 years of the Joint Army-Navy Selective Service Committee.

The National Archives also contains several additional files deposited by the various commissions that were established to study the draft during the Vietnam era. Included are the National Advisory Commission on Selective Service, Record Group 220, and the President's Commission on An All-Volunteer Armed Force, Record Group 220. Also see the files of the office of the secretary of War, Record Group 107, and the files of the Office of the Secretary of Defense, especially the Office of Undersecretary for Manpower, Record Group 330.

In modern times the presidential library has developed into an essential institution. Unlike Thomas Jefferson and many other earlier presidents, the modern chief executive is not satisfied with depositing his papers with the Library of Congress. Instead, a shrine, a monument must be erected, preferably at the president's birth place, to become a center of study. Among the presidential collections I studied, relating to the period of the draft, the most valuable was that of Lyndon B. Johnson in Austin, Texas. Next was the Richard M. Nixon Presidential Paper Project, then held by the

National Archives in Alexandria, Virginia. Since these two men faced the most controversy over the draft, the richness of their files is unsurprising. Other useful collections were the Franklin D. Roosevelt Papers at Hyde Park, New York; the Harry S. Truman Papers at Independence, Missouri; the Dwight D. Eisenhower Papers at Abilene, Kansas; and the John F. Kennedy Papers in Boston.

Several other manuscript collections proved useful. At the Library of Congress in Washington, for instance, are the papers of Robert Taft, whose opposition to the draft offers useful insight. The papers of James W. Wadsworth, an original sponsor of the draft bill, and Robert Patterson, secretary of war, are also found in the manuscript room. Not far away, in Lexington, Virginia, one finds the very useful papers of General George C. Marshall, at the Marshall Research Library. I also use the following: Dee Ingold Papers, in my possession; Frank Keesling Papers, privately held, San Francisco; and Henry Stimson Papers, Yale University Library, New Haven, Connecticut.

One of the advantages, or disadvantages, of writing modern history is the availability of participants who can offer their oral recollections. Although sometimes self-serving and misleading, the material can offer collaboration for written documents. This work benefited from the following interviews. Those in the first group were conducted by me; those in the second by professionals associated with various archives:

Group One:

Averill, William. Tupelo, Miss. 27 July 1978.
Barber, John W. Arlington, Va., 6 Aug. 1977; San Francisco, 29 Dec. 1978.
Clark, Ramsey. Letter to author, 14 July 1980.
Franck, Bernard. Arlington, Va., 1 Sept. 1977.
Hebert, F. Edward. New Orleans, La., 19 July 1978.
Hershey, Lewis B. Bethesda, Md., 26 May 1975.
Ingold, E. D. Alamagordo, N.M., 15–16 Aug. 1978.
McGill, Kenneth. Abilene, Kans., 17 Aug. 1978.
Rose, Jonathan. Alexandria, Va., 16 Nov. 1977.
Slatinshek, Frank M. Alexandria, Va., 31 Aug. 1977.
Vaughan, Harry H. Alexandria, Va., 29 Aug. 1977.

Group Two:

Anderson, Clinton P. LBJ Library, 20 May 1969.
Clark, Ramsey. LBJ Library, Oct. 1968, Feb.-Jul. 1969.
Hesburgh, Theodore. LBJ Library, 1 Feb. 1971.
Taylor, Maxwell D. LBJ Library, Jan.-Feb. 1969.
Thurmond, Strom. LBJ Library, 7 May 1979.
Vinson, Carl. LBJ Library, 24 May 1970.
Westmoreland, William C. LBJ Library, 8 Feb. 1969.
Wheeler, Earle G. LBJ Library, Aug. 1969, May 1970.
Wilkins, Roy. LBJ Library, 1 Apr. 1969.

There are many valuable published records on the operations of government agencies and commissions. The *Congressional Record* is the most obvious of sources for any study involving a political institution such as the draft; but even more valuable are the various congressional hearings conducted on conscription and related topics. The hearings listed below represent the most useful record of congressional oversight of Selective Service:

U.S. Congress, House, Armed Services Committee. *Review of Selective Service Administration.* Washington, D.C.: GPO, 89th Cong. 2d sess., 22 June 1966.

U.S. Congress, House, Committee on Post Office and Civil Service, Subcommittee on Civil Service. *Hearings on Compensation for Selective Service System Employees.* Washington, D.C.: GPO, 89th Cong, 2d sess., 18 April 1966.

U.S., House, Military Affairs Committee. *Selective Service Extension.* Washington, D.C.: GPO, 79th Cong. 2d sess., 21 March 1946.

U.S. Congress, Senate, Committee on Appropriations. *Hearings on Independent Offices Appropriations.* Washington, D.C.: GPO, 89th Cong., 1st sess., May-June 1965.

———. *Hearings on Independent Office Appropriations.* Washington, D.C.: GPO, 89th Cong, 2d sess., 25 May 1966.

U.S. Congress, Senate, Committee on Judiciary, Subcommittee on Administrative Practices and Procedures. *Hearings; Right of Counsel in the Selective Service System.* Washington, D.C.: GPO, 90th Cong., 2d sess., 16 May 1968.

U.S. Congress, Senate, Military Affairs Committee. *Hearings on Demobilization.* Washington, D.C.: GPO, 79th Cong., 1st and 2d sess., 18 January 1946.

———. *Selective Service Extension.* Washington, D.C.: 79th Cong. 2d sess, 5, 28 March 1946.

U.S. Congress, Senate, Subcommittee on Employment, Manpower, and Poverty of the Committee on Labor and Public Welfare. *Manpower Implications of Selective Service, Hearings.* Washington, D.C.: GPO, 90th Cong., 1st sess., 20–23 March, 4–6 April 1967.

Besides congressional hearings, several reports by various government departments and commissions also offer insights into the operation of the draft:

Advisory Commission on Universal Training. *A Program for National Security, Report.* Washington, D.C.: GPO, 1947.

Civilian Advisory Panel on Military Manpower Procurement. *Report to the Committee on Armed Services, House of Representatives, 90th Cong, 1st sess.* Washington, D.C.: GPO, 1967.

Commission on an All-Volunteer Armed Force. *Report.* Washington, D.C.: GPO, 1970.

———. *Studies Prepared for the President's Commission on an All-Volunteer Armed Force.* Washington, D.C.: GPO, 1970.

Committee on Higher Education. *Higher Education for American Democracy.* Washington, D.C.: GPO, December 1947.

Compton, Karl P., ed. *A Program for National Security.* Washington, D.C.: GPO, 1947.

Military Manpower Task Force. *A Report to the President on Selective Service Registration.* Washington, D.C.: GPO, 1981.

National Advisory Commission on Selective Service. *In Pursuit of Equity: Who Serves When Not All Serve?* Washington, D.C.: GPO, 1967.

Report of the Commission of Physicians Appointed to Examine the Requirements for Admission to the Army, Navy, and Marine Corps. Washington, D.C.: GPO, 29 February 1944.

Task Force on Manpower Conservation. *One-Third of a Nation: A Report on Young Men Found Unqualified for Military Service.* Washington, D.C.: GPO, 1964.

U.S., Bureau of the Budget. *History of Office of Health and Welfare in World War II.* Washington, D.C.: GPO (microfilm) 1943.

Department of Commerce. *Historical Statistics of the United States: Colonial Times to 1970,* 2 pts. Washington, D.C.: GPO, 1975.

Department of Health, Education, and Welfare, Office of Education. *Survey of the Draft Status of First and Second Year Science Graduate Students.* Washington, D.C.: GPO, 1968.

Department of Labor. *Report to President.* Washington, D.C.: GPO, 1 May 1964.

Department of the Army, Medical Department. *Personnel in World War II.* Washington, D.C.: Department of Army, 1963.

Without question, however, the most valuable government information on conscription is found in the official reports issued by the Selective Service System. Although one must be wary of information generated by an agency frequently battling to justify its existence, the variety of sources, the fulsomeness of the data and the unconscious evidence of the testimony all make this source indispensable. See the following reports:

Annual Report of the Director of Selective Service, 1951. Washington, D.C.: GPO, 1952.

Annual Report of the Director of Selective Service, 1952. Washington, D.C.: GPO, 1953.

Annual Report of the Director of Selective Service, 1953. Washington, D.C.: GPO, 1954.

Annual Report of the Director of Selective Service, 1954. Washington, D.C.: GPO, 1955.

Conscientious Objection: Special Groups. Special Monograph No. 10. 2 vols. Washington, D.C.: GPO, 1953.

Selective Service and Victory: 4th Report of the Director of Selective Service, 1944–1947. Washington, D.C.: GPO, 1948.

Selective Service as the Tide of War Turns: 3rd Report of the Director of Selective Service. Washington, D.C.: GPO, 1945.

Selective Service in Peacetime: First Report of the Director of Selective Service, 1940–1941. Washington, D.C.: GPO, 1942.

Selective Service in Wartime: Second Report of the Director of Selective Service, 1941–1942. Washington, D.C.: GPO, 1943.

Selective Service Monthly Newsletter. Washington, D.C.: SSS, August 1951–April 1970.

Selective Service under the 1948 Act. Washington, D.C.: GPO, 1951.

Selective Service under the 1948 Act Extended. Washington, D.C.: GPO, 1953.

One recurring theme in any history of the draft is the strange relationship between the conscription agency and the defense establishment. After the American Civil War experience, the draft agency, Selective Service, became independent and supposedly civilian directed. During World War I national headquarters consisted of military officers and policy came from the provost marshal general's office, but civilians ran the local boards and regional boards. Although the military influence in the agency was always strong, serious disagreements emerged repeatedly. The following works deal with the conflicts. Martin Anderson, ed., *The Military Draft* (Stanford, Calif.: Hoover Institution, 1982) is a collection of essays by experts in the field of military manpower. George Q. Flynn, *The Mess in Washington: Manpower Mobilization in World War II* (Westport, Conn.: Greenwood, 1979), treats the rivalry among the Selective Service, the War Department, and the War Manpower Commission. A comprehensive study of governmental debate over conscription is James M. Gerhardt, *The Draft and Public Policy* (Columbus: Ohio State, 1971). William L. Hauser, *America's Army in Crisis: A Study in Civil-Military Relations* (Baltimore, Md.: Johns Hopkins, 1973) focuses upon the problems created for the army by the draft protest during Vietnam. And I. B. Holley, Jr., *General John M. Palmer: Citizen Soldiers and the Army of a Democracy* (Westport, Conn.: Greenwood, 1982), offers insights into the career of the chief military proponent of a citizens' army serviced by conscription.

Several articles also give insight into the relationship between the armed forces and Selective Service. To appreciate the evolution in historical studies of the military see the important essay by John W. Chambers II, "The New Military History: Myth and Reality," *Journal of Military History* 55 (July 1991):395–400. Also useful for post-Vietnam trends is Robert K. Griffith, Jr., "About Face? The U.S. Army and the Draft," *Armed Forces and Society* 12 (Fall 1985):114–19. For information on the problems of mobilization for Korea, see John M. Kendall, "An Inflexible Response: United States Army Manpower Mobilization Policies, 1945–1957 (Ph.D. dissertation, Duke University, 1982), and Rocco M. Paone, "The Last Volunteer Army, 1946–1948," *Military Review* 49 (December 1969).

I followed internal operations of the Selective Service System—which became the focus for draft protest in the 1960s—through several studies, beginning with the annual reports listed above. See also Albert A. Blum, *Drafted or Deferred: Practices Past and Present* (Ann Arbor:University of Michigan, 1967), which was written under the influence of the Vietnam War but is a valuable study. Other studies that reveal more of the antimilitary pressure of the 1960s include Harry A. Marmion, *Selective Service: Conflict and Compromise* (New York: Wiley, 1968), and Gary L. Wamsley, *Selective Service and a Changing America* (Columbus, Ohio: Merrill, 1969). Later works include the excellent study of the origins of Selective Service by J. Garry Clifford and Samuel Spencer, Jr., *The First Peacetime Draft* (Lawrence: University Press of Kansas, 1986), and George Q. Flynn, *Lewis B. Hershey: Mr. Selective Service* (Chapel Hill: University of North Carolina, 1985).

For useful articles on various phases of draft operations see Albert A. Blum and J. D. Smyth, "Who Should Serve: Pre–World War II Planning for Selective Service," *Journal of Economic History* 30 (February 1970):379–404; Robert K. Griffith, Jr., "Conscription and the All-Volunteer Army in Historical Perspective," *Parameters* 10 (1980):61–69; Lawrence M. Hepple, "Differential Selective Service Rejection Rates for the Rural Area of Missouri," *Rural Sociology* 12 (December 1947):388–94; I. B. Holley, Jr., "To Defend the Nation: Conscription and the All-Volunteer Army: Historical Perspective," *Public Historian* 61:1 (1984):65–71; James B. Jacobs and Dennis McNamara, "Selective Service without a Draft," *Armed Forces & Society* 4 (Spring 1984):361–79; Hobart B. Pillsbury, Jr., "Raising the Armed Forces," *Armed Forces & Society* 14 (Fall 1987):65–84; Herbert C. Puscheck, "Selective Service Registration," *Armed Forces & Society* 10 (Spring 1983):5–25; and Mapheus Smith, "The Differential Impact of Selective Service Inductions on Occupations in the United States," *American Sociological Review* 11 (October 1946):567–72. Donald D. Stewart has also written a series of fine pieces on the administration of Selective Service: "Local Boards: A Study of the Place of Volunteer Participation in Bureaucratic Organization" (Ph.D. dissertation Columbia University, 1950); "The Dilemma of Deferment," *Journal of Higher Education* (April 1953); and "Selective Service Appeal Boards," *Southwestern Social Science Quarterly* 31(June 1950).

Many works on the draft emerged under the pressure of protest over Vietnam. Lawrence M. Baskir and William A. Strauss, *Chance and Circumstance: The Draft, the War, and the Vietnam Generation* (New York: Knopf, 1978) is useful for information on the differential impact of the system but weak on the mechanics of operation. The most recent and comprehensive study of antiwar activities by two scholars in sympathy with the idea is Charles DeBenedetti and C. Chatfield, *An American Ordeal: The Antiwar Movement of the Vietnam Era* (Syracuse, N.Y.: Syracuse University, 1990). Also valuable are John Helmer, *Bringing the War Home: The American Soldier in Vietnam and After* (New York: Free Press, 1974), and Melvin Small, *Johnson, Nixon, and the Doves* (New Brunswick, N.J.: Rutgers, 1988). Stephen M. Kohn, *Jailed for Peace: The History of American Draft Law Violators, 1658–1985* (Westport, Conn.: Greenwood, 1986) is wide ranging but confused over draft operations. A valuable history of the entire decade is Allen J. Matusow, *The Unraveling of America: A History of Liberalism in the 1960s* (New York: Harper and Row, 1984). Other useful studies include the following: Michael Useem, *Conscription, Protest, and Social Conflict: The Life and Death of a Draft Resistance Movement* (New York: John Wiley and Sons, 1973); Milton Viorst, *Fire in the Streets: America in the Sixties* (New York: Simon and Schuster, 1979); and Nancy Zaroulis and G. Sullivan, *Who Spoke Up? American Protest against the War in Vietnam, 1963–1975* (New York: Doubleday, 1984).

Several valuable articles have also appeared: Henry Anderson, "The Folklore of Draft Resistance," *New York Folklore Quarterly* 28 (1972):135–50; James Burk, "Debating the Draft in America," *Armed Forces and Society* 15 (Spring 1989):431–48; Charles DeBenedetti, "On the Significance of Citizen Peace Activism: America, 1961–1975," *Peace and Change* 9 (Summer 1983):6–20; James Fallows, "What Did You Do in the Class War, Daddy?" *Washington Monthly* 7 (October 1975):5–19; Saul V. Levine, "Draft Dodgers: Coping with Stress, Adapting to Exile," *American Journal of Orthopsychiatry* 42 (1 April 1972):431–39; Paul T. Murray, "Local Draft Board Composition and Institutional Racism," *Social Problems* 19 (1971):129–36; Kenneth O'Reilly, "The FBI and the Politics of the Riots, 1964–1968," *Journal of American History* 75 (June 1988):91–114; Patti M. Peterson, "Student Organizations and the Antiwar Movement in America, 1900–1960," *American Studies* 13 (Spring 1972):131–47; Stuart Showalter, "American Magazine Coverage of Objectors to the Vietnam War," *Journalism Quarterly* 53 (1976):648–53, 688; and John D. Stuckey and Joseph H. Pistorius, "Mobilization for the Vietnam War: A Political and Military Catastrophe," *Parameters* 15 (Spring 1985):26–38.

An issue that attracted considerable attention in the 1960s was the relative impact of the draft upon different racial groups. Some black leaders insisted that the draft, like America society, was racially biased in operation, but the preceding pages point to the dangers of accepting this charge at its most simplistic. For further reading one should begin with Richard M. Dalfiume, *Desegregation of the U.S. Armed Forces* (Columbia: University of Missouri, 1969). Selective Service produced a useful monograph on blacks in the draft: *Special Groups*, Special Monograph No. 10, 2 vols.

(Washington, D.C.: GPO, 1953), and another government-sponsored publication of value is Ulysses G. Lee, *The United States Army in W.W. II: Special Studies: The Employment of Negro Troops* (Washington, D.C.: GPO, 1966). The problem of merging black and white troops is covered in Richard J. Stillman, *Integration of the Negro in the U.S. Armed Forces* (New York: Praeger, 1968); for the larger question of the draft and society see Morris Janowitz, *The Professional Soldier: A Social and Political Portrait* (New York: Free Press, 1960); Adam Yarmolinsky, *The Military Establishment: Its Impact on American Society* (New York: Harper and Row, 1971); and Jacques Van Doorn, *The Soldier and Social Change* (Beverly Hills, Calif.: Sage, 1975).

For articles of interest see the following: Alison R. Bernstein, "Walking in Two Worlds: American Indians and World War Two" (Ph.D. dissertation, Columbia University, 1986); Caroline Bird, "Let's Draft Women, Too!" *Saturday Evening Post* 239 (18 June 1966):10–11; Roy K. Davenport, "Implications of Military Selection and Classification in Relation to Universal Military Training," *Journal of Negro Education* (Fall 1946):594; George Q. Flynn, "Selective Service and American Blacks During World War II, *Journal of Negro History* 69 (Winter 1984):14–25; Ulysses Lee, "The Draft and the Negro," *Current History* 55 (July 1968):28–33, 47–48; Duane E. Leigh and R. E. Berney, "The Distribution of Hostile Casualties on Draft Eligible Males with Differing Socioeconomic Characteristics," *Social Science Quarterly* 51 (March 1971):932–40; Albert J. Mayer and Thomas F. Hoult, "Social Stratification and Combat Survival," *Social Forces* 34 (1 December 1955):155–59; Phillip McGuire, "Judge William H. Hastie and Army Recruitment, 1940–1942," *Military Affairs* 42 (April 1978):75–79; Lawrence J. Pasyet, "Negroes and the Air Force, 1939–1949," *Military Affairs* 31 (Spring 1967):1–9; and A. J. Street, "Hasty Marriage and the Draft," *Journal of Social Hygiene* 27 (May 1948):228–31.

One of the most difficult and recurring problems facing officials of the draft grew out of the desire by the government and society to both respect religious conviction and punish draft evaders. The literature bearing on the theme of conscientious objection and religion is vast. Michael Noone, ed., *Selective Conscientious Objection* (Boulder, Colo.: Westview, 1989), offers several essays on the fruitless quest for this special recognition. A valuable work covering the period before World War II is Charles Chatfield, *For Peace and Justice: Pacifism in America, 1914–1941* (Knoxville: University of Tennessee, 1971), and Selective Service offers the official response to the problems of conscious and valuable statistics in *Conscientious Objection*, Special Monograph No. 11, 2 vols. (Washington, D.C.: GPO, 1950). Two sympathetic scholars have written a work covering the World War II experience: Mulford Q. Sibley and Philip Jacob, *Conscription of Conscience: The American State and the Conscientious Objector, 1940–1947* (Ithaca, N.Y.: Cornell, 1952); for developments after World War II see Lawrence S. Wittner, *Rebels against War: The American Peace Movement, 1941–1960* (New York: Columbia University, 1969). Charles DeBenedetti and C. Chatfield cover religious protest and much more in *An American Ordeal*.

The literature found in journals is very comprehensive. Some of the more interesting pieces are the following: Leo P. Crespi, "Attitudes toward Conscientious Objectors and Some of Their Psychological Correlates," *Journal of Psychology* 18 (July 1944):81–117; Nathan Eliff, "Jehovah's Witnesses and the Selective Service Act," *Virginia Law Review* 31 (September 1945):811–834; George Q. Flynn, "Lewis Hershey and the Conscientious Objector: World War II," *Military Affairs* 47 (February 1983):1–6; Walter S. Griggs, Jr., "The Selective Conscientious Objector: A Vietnam Legacy," *Journal of Church and State* 21 (January 1979):91–107; Patricia McNeal, "Catholic Conscientious Objection during World War II," *Catholic Historical Review*

61 (1975):222–42; R. R. Russell, "Development of Conscientious Objector Recognition in the United States," *George Washington Law Review* 20 (1951–1952):409–48; and John K. Walkup, "Swords into Plowshares: Alternative Requirements for CO," *Harvard Civil Rights–Civil Liberties Law Review* 6 (1 May 1971):505–24.

The draft had a double-edged impact on American education, protecting and encouraging it with deferments but also causing apprehension among students and educators. A definitive monograph remains to be written on this topic, but see the following reports: Vannevar Bush, *Science: The Endless Frontier; Report for the President on a Program for Postwar Science Research* (Washington, D.C.: GPO, 1945), discusses the need to defer scientists; John Masland and Lawrence I. Radway, *Soldiers and Scholars* (Princeton, N.J.: Princeton University, 1957), deal with military educational needs; National Manpower Council, *Student Deferment and National Manpower Policy* (New York: Columbia University, 1952), and M. H. Trytten, *Student Deferment in Selective Service* (Minneapolis: University of Minnesota, 1952), describe the deferment plan established by Selective Service; and President's Commission on Higher Education, *Report, Higher Education for American Democracy*, 6 vols. (Washington, D.C.: GPO, 1947) is a comprehensive study forming the basis of federal action for the post–World War II era.

For useful periodical literature see the following representative sample: Howard L. Bevis, "The Challenge of Deferment," *Journal of Higher Education* 22 (1 October 1951):353–58; Albert A. Blum, "The Army and Student Deferments during the Second World War," *Journal of Higher Education* 31 (1 January 1960):41–45; George Q. Flynn, "The Draft and College Deferments during the Korean War," *The Historian* 50 (May 1988):369–85; E. T. Katzoff, and A. R. Gilliland, "Student Attitudes on the World Conflict," *Journal of Psychology* 12 (October 1941):227–33; Patti M. Peterson, "Student Organizations and the Antiwar Movement in America, 1900–1960," *American Studies* 13 (Spring 1972):131–47; D. Wolfle, "Draft, Deferment and Scientists," *American Psychologist* 5 (August 1950):432–34; and George F. Zook, "How the Colleges Went to War," *Annals* of the American Academy of Political and Social Science 231 (January 1944):1–7.

The draft, of course, reflected the physical state of American youth, so American medicine and health were involved in operations. Several useful general overviews exist: John Duffy, *The Healers: A History of American Medicine* (Chicago: University of Chicago, 1979), and Paul Starr, *The Social Transformation of American Medicine* (New York: Basic Books, 1982), are two of the best. John H. McMinn and Max Levin, *Personnel in World War II*, ed. Charles M. Wiltse (Washington, D.C.: Office of Surgeon General DA, 1963), is an official history but valuable. William D. Tribble, *Doctor Draft Justified?* (San Antonio, Tex.: National Biomedical Labs, 1968), discusses this issue from the viewpoint of the profession; U.S. President's Task Force on Manpower Conservation, *One-Third of a Nation: A Report on Young Men Found Unqualified for Military Service* (Washington, D.C.: GPO, 1964), is important for figures on draft rejectees, and U.S., Bureau of the Budget, *History of Office of Health and Welfare in World War II* (Washington, D.C., 1943, microfilm) is old but a good overview.

There are literally hundreds of articles bearing on the theme of health and the draft. The scholar should consult the relevant chapter notes, but a representative sample follows: Robert A. Bier, "The Physician in Selective Service," *Medical Annals of the District of Columbia* 10 (4 April 1941):1–3; George Q. Flynn, "American Medicine and Selective Service in World War II," *Journal of the History of Medicine and Allied Sciences* 42 (July 1987):305–26; Marcus S. Goldstein, "Physical Status of Men Examined Through Selective Service in World War II," *Public Health Reports* 66 (11 May 1951):587–609; Lawrence M. Hepple, "Selective Service Rejectees in Rural Missouri, 1940–1943," *Research Bulletin 439, U. of Missouri, College of Agriculture* (1 April 1949):1–19; Bernard D. Karpinos, "Evaluation of the Physical Fitness of Present-Day Inductees," *Armed Forces Medical Journal* 4 (1 Mar. 1953):415–30; and Richard H. Kohn, "The Social History of the American Soldier: A Review and Prospectus for Research," *American Historical Review* 86 (June 1981):553–67, is a valuable guide to research.

Conscription functioned within an evolving political and legal context, and several important studies focus upon these themes. June A. Willenz, *Dialogue on the Draft* (Washington, D.C.: American Veterans Commission, 1967) contains several useful essays, and the previously mentioned J. Garry Clifford and Samuel R. Spencer, Jr., *The First Peacetime Draft* is excellent on political context during the debate in 1940. John W. Chambers II, *To Raise an Army: The Draft comes to Modern America* (New York: Free Press, 1987), is very good on placing the draft within the context of American modernization; also useful is William F. Levantrosser, *Congress and the Citizen-Soldier* (Columbus: Ohio State University, 1967).

Helpful articles include the following: James Burk, "Debating the Draft in America," *Armed Forces and Society* 15 (Spring 1989):431–48; Joseph M. Cormack, "The Universal Draft and Constitutional Limitations," *Southern California Law Review* 3 (June 1930):361–83; Charles DeBenedetti, "On the Significance of Citizen Peace Activism: America, 1961–1975," *Peace and Change* 9 (Summer 1983):6–20; Philip A. Grant, Jr., "The Kansas Congressional Delegation and the Selective Service Act of 1940," *Kansas History* 2 (1979):196–205; Samuel P. Huntington, "Interservice Competition and the Political Roles of the Armed Services," *American Political Science Review* 55 (1 March 1961):40–51; James A. Huston, "Selective Service as a Political Issue," *Current History* 55 (1968):218–23, 244–45; Kenneth O'Reilly, "The FBI and the Politics of the Riots, 1964–1968," *Journal of American History* 75 (June 1988):91–114; David Shichor and D. R. Ranish, "President Carter's Vietnam Amnesty: An Analysis of a Public Policy Decision," *Presidential Studies Quarterly* 10 (1980):443–50; Melvin Small, "The Impact of the Antiwar Movement on Lyndon Johnson, 1965–1968: A Preliminary Report," *Peace and Change* 10 (Spring 1984): 1–22; and Glenn H. Smith, "Senator William Langer and Military Conscription, 1945–1959," *North Dakota Quarterly* 37 (Autumn 1969):14–24.

Through the principal of selection and the apparatus of deferment Selective Service had a continuing impact on the economy. During the Vietnam period the economic aspects of the draft became a major debating point for opponents. M. R. D. Foot, *Men in Uniform: Military Manpower in Modern Industrial Societies* (New York: Praeger, 1961), is useful, but much more can be gleaned from periodical literature. See especially George Q. Flynn, "Drafting Farmers in World War II," in John Wunder, *At Home on the Range: Essays on the History of Western Social and Domestic Life* (Westport, Conn.: Greenwood, 1985); Robert Evans, Jr., "The Military Draft as a Slave System: An Economic View," *Social Science Quarterly* 50 (1969):535–43; Samuel Hays, "What is Wrong with Induction Procedures?" *Military Review* 50 (May 1970):3–7; James C. Miller and Robert Tollison, "The Implicit Tax on Reluctant Military Recruits," *Social Science Quarterly* 51 (1971):924–31; Rainer Schickele and Glenn Everett, "The Economic Implications of Universal Military Training," *Annals, American Academy of Political and Social Science* 241 (September 1945):102–12; and Paul Weinstein, "Comments on Papers by Altman, Fechter, and Oi," *American Economic Review: Papers and Proceedings* (1 May 1967):63–70.

For a chronological view of American conscription, the reader is again referred to the relevant notes in the foregoing chapters, but the following list is a selection of the most important and most available works. For the period before and during World War II one should begin with John W. Chambers II, *To Raise an Army*, which consists of a detailed treatment of the World War I draft filled with insights on modern America; also critical for the 1940 debate over the draft is J. Garry Clifford and Samuel R. Spenser, Jr., *The First Peacetime Draft*. Of value for understanding the home front are the following: John M. Blum, *V Was for Victory* (New York: Harcourt Brace Jovanovich, 1976); Gerald T. Dunne, *Grenville Clark: Public Citizen* (New York: Farrar Strauss, 1986), a biography of the leading civilian promoter of conscription; George Q. Flynn, *The Mess in Washington: Manpower Mobilization in World War II* (cited earlier); Lee Kennett, *G.I.: The American Soldier in World War II* (New York: Scribner's Sons, 1987); Michael Pearlman, *To Make Democracy Safe for America: Patricians and Preparedness in the Progressive Era* (Urbana: University of Illinois, 1984); and Victor Vogel, *Soldiers of the Old Army* (College Station: Texas A.&M., 1990).

Of the hundreds of articles that have appeared, the following proved most useful to me: Leo P. Crespi, "Attitudes toward Conscientious Objectors and Some of Their Psychological Correlates," *Journal of Psychology* 18 (July 1944):81–117; George Q. Flynn, "Selective Service and American Blacks during World War II," *Journal of Negro History* 69 (Winter 1984):14–25; and George Q. Flynn, "Lewis Hershey and the Conscientious Objector: World War II," *Military Affairs* 47 (1983):1–6. Also useful are two dissertations: John S. Brown, "Draftee Division: A Study of the 88th Infantry Division, First All Selective Service Division into Combat in World War II" (Ph.D. dissertation, Indiana University, 1983), and Roger B. Fosdick, "A Call to Arms: The American Enlisted Soldier in World War II," (Ph.D. dissertation, Claremont Graduate School, 1985).

From 1945 to 1960 the draft functioned as a means of containing communism. Active during the Korean War, it fell into the doldrums during the Eisenhower period and developed the elaborate deferment and channeling system that received much criticism during the 1960s. For general histories of the Korean War see especially the following: Joseph C. Goulden, *Korea: The Untold Story of the War* (New York: McGraw-Hill, 1983); Clay Blair, *The Forgotten War: America in Korea 1950–1983* (New York: Times Books, 1987); and Bruce Cumings, *The Origins of the Korean War* (Princeton, N.J.: Princeton University Press, 1987). Other useful works on the same period include Jack S. Ballard, *The Shock of Peace: Military and Economic Demobilization after World War II* (Washington, D.C.: University Press of America, 1983); Robert J. Donovan, *Tumultuous Years: The Presidency of Harry S. Truman, 1949–1953* (New York: Norton, 1982); and John M. Kendall, "An Inflexible Response: United States Army Manpower Mobilization Policies, 1945–1957" (Ph.D. dissertation, Duke University, 1982).

For journal literature see the entire issue of American Academy of Political and Social Science, *Annals* 24 (1 September 1945), but especially the following: Mary Earhart, "The Value of Universal Military Training in Maintaining Peace," pp. 46–57; Robert A. Graham, "Universal Military Training in Modern History," pp. 8–14; Hajo Holborn, "Professional Army Versus Military Training," pp. 123–30; Halford L. Hoskins, "Universal Military Training and American Foreign Policy," 58–66; John J. McCloy, "The Plan of the Armed Services for Universal Military Training," pp. 26–34; and Rainer Schickele and Glenn Everett, "The Economic Implications of

Universal Military Training," pp. 102–12. See also the article by George Q. Flynn, "The Draft and College Deferments during the Korean War," mentioned previously.

The literature on the 1960s and Vietnam grows more massive daily. Although some of the earlier works suffered as a consequence of political passion, more detached treatments are now appearing. I found the following books useful for a study of the draft, but the reader should also consult items mentioned earlier under protest and opposition to conscription. There are several edited collections of essays which are valuable: Martin Anderson, ed., *The Military Draft*, mentioned earlier in connection with conflicts regarding the draft, is also a comprehensive work focusing on public policy; John B. Keeley, *The All Volunteer Force and American Society* (Charlottesville: University of Virginia, 1978), evaluates the system that replaced the draft; and Sol Tax, ed., *The Draft: A Handbook of Facts and Alternatives* (Chicago: University of Chicago, 1967) is the best of many anthologies generated by the Vietnam war protest. Michael L. Martin and E. S. McCrate, eds., *The Military, Militarism, and the Polity: Essays in Honor of Morris Janowitz* (New York: Free Press, 1984), offer the views of sociologists on the military, and Stephen E. Ambrose, *Nixon*, 3 vols. (New York: Simon and Schuster, 1987–1992) is the best and most scholarly study we have of that complex man. The work by Lawrence M. Baskir and William A. Strauss, *Chance and Circumstance: The Draft, the War and the Vietnam Generation* is a valuable but uneven work by two men involved in public evaluation of the draft; see also their earlier work, *Reconciliation after Vietnam* (Notre Dame, Ind.: Notre Dame University, 1977).

The most valuable books on the military and Vietnam for this study were the following: Arthur T. Hadley, *The Straw Giant: Triumph and Failure: America's Armed Forces* (New York: Random House, 1986); John Helmer, *Bringing the War Home*; and George C. Herring, *America's Longest War: The United States and Vietnam, 1950–1975* 2d ed. (New York: Knopf, 1986). For the views of two insiders in the ending of the draft see Richard Nixon, *No More Vietnams* (New York: Arbor House, 1985), and Curtis W. Tarr, *By the Numbers: The Reform of the Selective Service System, 1970–1972* (Washington: National Defense University Press, 1981). Both works are self-serving and must be used with caution. U.S. National Advisory Committee on Selective Service, *In Pursuit of Equity: Who Serves When Not All Serve?* (Washington, D.C.: GPO, 1967), is the Marshall report done under Johnson, and U.S., President, Commission on an All-Volunteer Armed Force, *Report* (Washington, D.C.: GPO, 1970), is the Gates report done under Nixon. For protest see general histories of the 1960s such as William L. O'Neill, *Coming Apart: An Informal History of America in the 1960's* (New York:Times Books,1971); Milton Viorst, *Fire in the Streets*; and Nancy Zaroulis and G. Sullivan, *Who Spoke Up? American Protest against the War in Vietnam, 1963–1975.*

Journal literature is extensive. The following proved useful to me, and are accessible, but also see chapter notes: Charles DeBenedetti, "On the Significance of Citizen Peace Activism: America, 1961–1975," *Peace and Change* 9 (Summer 1983):6–20; Daniel C. Hallin, "The Media, the War in Vietnam, and Political Support: Critique of Thesis on an Oppositional Media," *Journal of Politics* 46 (February 1984):2–24; Lawrence W. Lichty, "The War We Watched on Television," *American Film Institute Report* 4 (Winter 1973):30–37; Michael Mandelbaum, "Vietnam: The Television War," *Daedalus* 111 (Fall 1982):157–69; Paul T. Murray, "Local Draft Board Composition and Institutional Racism," *Social Problems* 19 (1971):129–36; Ronald Sinaiko, "The Last American Draftees," *Armed Forces and Society* 16 (Winter

1990):241–50; Melvin Small, "The Impact of the Antiwar Movement on Lyndon Johnson, 1965–1968: A Preliminary Report," *Peace and Change* 10 (Spring 1984):1–22; John D. Stuckey and Joseph H. Pistorius, "Mobilization for the Vietnam War: A Political and Military Catastrophe," *Parameters* 15 (Spring 1985):26–38; and Jacques Van Doorn, "The Decline of the Mass Army in the West," *Armed Forces and Society* 1 (February 1975):147–57.

Index

Abernathy, Ralph, 267
Absenteeism, 84
Academic leaders, 76, 181
Academic performance, 107
ACE. See American Council on Education
Acheson, Dean, 112
ACLU. See American Civil Liberties Union
Adjutants general, 21, 24, 58
Advisory boards: and blacks, 42-43, 99; on
  draft rules, 21; role of, 60, 107, 141; role
  of women, 31;
Afghanistan, 277, 278
AFL-CIO, 13, 16, 36, 37, 67, 83, 264
Age: and classification, 30, 56, 69, 76, 86; as
  factor in rejection, 32, 40, 49; impact on
  draft operation, 230, 261; impact on qual-
  ity of soldier, 71, 86; and manpower pool,
  16, 62, 73; and size of draft call, 92, 94
Age cohort, 230-32, 281
Agriculture: deferment for work force, 59,
  65, 117, 253; impact of studies in, 75; and
  Korean mobilization, 130; labor draft for,
  66; wage structure and draft, 131. See also
  Farmers
Agriculture, Department of, 35, 66, 131
Air force, 229, 253; black percentage of,
  206; and equity debate, 194; and father
  draft, 73; and need for, 97, 113, 118, 135;
  opinion of draftees, 269; reliance on vol-
  unteers, 109, 207; and Vietnam, 249
Aircraft industry, 81
Alabama, 15, 209, 210
Alcoholism, 273
Alexander, Clifford L., Jr., 274, 276
Algeria, 112
Ali, Muhammad, 206, 210
All Volunteer Force (AVF), 4, 96, 166, 188,
  189, 249, 251, 259, 282, 327n47,
  334n21, 339n71, 343n9, 345n28,
  347n49; Congress and, 257, 269, 277;
  cost of and economy, 190, 196-97, 252-

53, 261, 264-65, 267, 270, 272, 280-81;
  creation of, 228, 238, 252, 258, 263-64,
  268; critics and debate on, 101, 163, 196,
  198, 252, 262, 265-69, 272, 273; and
  draft, 174, 178, 240, 251-52, 254-56,
  265-66; and elections, 164, 226; Nixon
  and, 225-26, 261, 263, 271; and politics,
  250, 261, 263, 279, 281; problems with,
  271-74, 279, 281; public opinion on,
  197, 237, 263, 267; racism and, 265,
  274-76; recruiting quality, 234, 262, 272,
  273, 277
Alternate service, 201, 224; cost of, 140; for
  COs, 19, 47, 117, 128; and 1968 campaign, 225; problems with, 47
American Association for the Advancement
  of Science, 106
American Bar Association, 182
American Chemical Society, 39, 76, 79, 107,
  304n68
American Civil Liberties Union (ACLU),
  196, 199, 211
American Council of Education (ACE), 39,
  40, 106, 222
American Legion, and father draft, 73; and
  local boards, 24, 58; promotes draft, 11,
  29, 49
American Medical Association (AMA), 31-
  32, 40, 156, 157-60, 316n91; cooperates
  with rehab, 34; and doctors draft, 157-60;
  on induction standards, 33
Americans for Democratic Action, 265
Amnesty Review Board, 173
Anderson, Martin, 225, 238, 245, 252, 263,
  265
Antiwar protest, 181, 215, 243, 262, 268;
  causes of decline, 236-37; character of,
  237, 250; in Congress, 186, 270; and draft
  extension, 204, 256-57; effect of, 270;
  and Johnson, 214; and lottery, 245; and

Antiwar protest, *continued*
    Nixon, 236, 239, 246, 249–50; and public
    opinion, 185. *See also* Protest
Appeal system, 19, 183, 202; agents of, 43,
    99, 205; boards organized, 13, 29, 36, 60;
    for different wars, 13, 60, 120–21, 180,
    182; effect of, 60, 120–21, 150, 181–82,
    184, 202, 240, 250; system at work, 19–
    20, 47, 60, 61, 133, 180, 191
Aptitude tests, 78, 234
Armed forces: assignment policies, 47, 194–
    95; blacks and, 15, 99–100, 102–4, 129,
    206; changes in character, 227; character-
    istics of, 5, 86, 126, 202, 227, 233; classi-
    fication for, 117; cost of recruiting
    volunteers, 228; evolution of character,
    227; expansion of, 108, 170–71; formula
    for calling men, 120; impact of Nixon's re-
    forms, 240; needs of, 14, 47, 77, 79, 91,
    153, 159; public opinion and, 93, 262;
    size and volunteers, 97, 111, 228, 252,
    264, 268; special calls for health person-
    nel, 159; standards for induction, 31, 64,
    153, 170, 172; strength and cost, 48, 62–
    63, 67–68, 100, 110, 139, 159, 227, 255,
    272. *See also* Military
Armed Forces Qualification Test (AFQT),
    153, 208, 227, 233–34, 348n57
Armed Forces Voluntary Recruiting Act, 261
Armed Services Committees, 203–4. *See also*
    House Armed Services Committee; Senate
    Armed Services Committee
Army: and antiwar movement, 236, 250; as-
    signments and education, 194, 234; and
    AVF, 269, 274; and blacks, 43, 103, 105,
    276–77; draft calls for, 13, 18, 44, 48, 64,
    90, 92, 97, 114–16, 159, 171, 259; draft
    extension and, 49, 89, 94; and education,
    3, 78, 141, 200, 233; mobilization plans,
    13, 21, 52, 91, 113; recruiting for, 54, 96,
    108–9, 118–19, 229, 234, 240, 271–73,
    281; reserve callups, 114–15; secretary of,
    103–5; and specialists, 78, 106, 154, 157;
    standards for, 32–33, 49, 90, 109, 274;
    strength levels change in, 48, 62, 96, 100,
    113–14, 137, 139, 159, 163, 167, 234.
    See also Armed forces; Military
Army airforce, 10
Army Magazine, 267
Army Medical Corps, 32, 154, 316n89
Army Ready Reserve, 272
Army Specialized Training Program (ASTP),
    77, 78–79, 154–55
Army-Navy Union, 73
Asia, 29, 49, 112, 116, 123, 199

Association of American Colleges, 77
Association of American Universities, 122
Atomic bomb, 79, 90, 94, 106, 109, 111,
    123, 133, 149, 160, 262
Austin, Warren, 84, 95
Australia, 263
Authoritarianism, 275
Averill, Ernest L., 44

Bankhead bill, 67–68
Baruch, Bernard, 74
Baseball: deferments for, 20, 27, 54, 62;
    owners and, 27; players affected, 27–28
Berlin, 108, 137, 138, 168, 281
Berrigan, Philip, 176
Berrigan brothers, 184
Berry plan, 158–60, 316nn89, 91
Birthrate, 164, 227, 265. *See also*
    Demography
Black Panthers, 237
Blacks, 15, 32, 43–44, 99, 100, 113, 177,
    210, 302n43, 312n37, 329n80; AVF and,
    226, 265, 274, 276, 281; CO status of,
    99; induction rate of, 15, 43–44, 49, 86,
    99, 231–32, 328n69; Korean war and,
    129; leadership of, 15; opinion of draft,
    61, 98, 100, 102–3, 176, 206, 219, 231;
    reenlistment of, 207–8; rejections and re-
    hab, 207–9, 232, 328n72, 335n26; role in
    draft system, 42–43, 99, 104, 193, 206,
    209–10, 242–43; in service, 15, 43, 86,
    99, 102, 105, 193, 206, 277; Vietnam war
    and, 206–7, 209, 231; volunteers, 42, 99,
    105, 129, 207
Blanket deferment, 13, 29, 35, 41, 77, 79,
    107, 147, 204
Bombing, 97, 135, 182, 250
Boston University, 144
Bradley, Omar, 103, 113, 136
Brandt, Joseph A., 77
Brewster, Kingman, 178, 185, 191, 203,
    217–18, 324n9
Bribes, 29, 59
Britain, 9, 50, 53, 94–95, 263
Brown, Edmund (Jerry), 278
Brown, Harold, 277, 278
Brown, Rap, 276
Brown University, 200, 217
Budget, 110–11, 128, 137, 252, 270
Burke-Wadsworth bill, 16
Bush, George W., 278, 281
Bush, Vannevar, 105–7
Byrnes, James F., 16, 64, 82, 94

Califano, Joseph C., 185, 190–91, 201–2,
    216–18, 267

Callups, 24, 62, 168. *See also* Draft calls; Inductions
Cambodia, 249, 340n80
Campus Crusade for Christ, 240–41
Canada, 179, 224
Carmichael, Leonard, 133, 147–48, 223
Carmichael, Stokeley, 206, 276
Carter, Jimmy, 277–79
Cash bonus, 90, 256, 261
Casualty rates, 194, 262, 308n47, 319n20, 325n20; and class bias, 126, 193; and draftees, 28, 63, 72, 116, 169; and race, 206, 231
Central Committee for Conscientious Objectors, 176
Centralization, 284n14; in draft theory, 53–58, 60–61, 87, 198, 202, 260; opposition to, 57, 192; in World War II, 54, 56, 57. *See also* Decentralization
Chemistry, 304n68, 313n55; professionals in, 61, 105, 149; students and, 76, 79, 106–7, 223
Chicago, 40, 193, 198, 239
China, 51, 109, 115, 122, 133, 137
Churches, 14, 45–46, 47, 177, 179, 195
CIA, 215
Citizenship, 2, 90, 196, 280
Citizen-soldiers, 2, 3
Civilian Conservation Corps (CCC), 18, 34, 47
Civilians: control of draft, 20, 58, 61; health of, 154–55, 157; labor of, 13, 56, 72, 74, 80, 90, 92, 96, 117, 151; military and, 86, 96, 220, 227
Civilian Volunteer Effort, 10
Civil libertarians, 28, 46, 99, 182
Civil rights, 100, 242, 274; protest and, 177, 178, 182, 187, 190, 236
Civil War, 15, 77, 81, 108, 183, 212, 277; draft in, 5–6, 60, 80, 167, 211
Clark, Grenville, 11–13, 17, 20
Clark, Ramsey, 186, 210, 212, 215–18, 329n84. *See also* Justice Department
Class bias, 80, 126, 145, 187, 189–90, 193–95, 197, 224, 230–31. *See also* Social class
Classifications, 37, 57–58, 66, 117, 126, 140; appeals of, 19, 29, 60, 120–21; criticism and reform of, 29, 45, 50, 61, 69–70, 126, 186, 191, 201, 204, 215, 220, 248; procedure of, 19, 21, 25, 29, 41, 58–62, 109, 117, 139; specific, 25, 80, 85, 93, 117, 128, 139, 143–44, 152, 192, 224, 228, 233; statistics of, 48, 59, 68, 127, 169, 192; students and, 40, 142, 144, 147, 151

Cold War, 97, 113, 124, 137–39, 170, 177–78, 281; deferments and, 132, 141, 165; draft reform and, 93, 98, 164
Colleges, 168, 176–77, 224, 240, 342n97; administrators of and SS, 25, 76–77, 120, 142, 148, 200, 216, 218, 223, 251; dropouts, 172, 194, 200; enrollments, 39–41, 78–79, 145, 147, 172, 231–32, 260; faculty of, 39–40, 183, 200, 233; graduates of, 171, 194, 221–22, 229; and military training, 39, 72, 76–78; and veterans, 106. *See also* Universities
College students: and deferments, 25, 38–41, 76–77, 79, 108, 117, 124, 137, 140–43, 145, 165, 181, 186, 191, 198–99, 202, 205, 245, 256; and Korea, 144, 200; and military service, 86, 141, 144–45, 200, 201, 232–33, 273, 276; public opinion and politics of, 145, 148, 178, 204, 219, 256; SSCQT and, 142, 147; statistics of, 75, 133, 144, 147, 150, 169; Vietnam and, 172, 184–85, 199–201, 220; women as, 47. *See also* Deferments
Collins, J. Lawton, 97, 115
Columbia University, 40–41, 135, 141, 150, 175, 200, 217, 224
Combat assignments, 126, 194, 227, 275; and class, 194–95, 234; inductees and, 234–35, 266, 268; and race, 207, 209, 276; volunteers for, 228–29, 256, 266; and youth, 64, 71
Commerce, Department of, 132, 149, 252
Commission on National Service, 190
Commission on Physical Rehabilitation, 33
Committee against Jim Crow in Military Service, 102
Communism, 112, 122, 224, 277; deferments and, 132–33, 148; draft acts and, 93, 108, 111, 123, 158; politics and, 109, 162, 281
Communist party, 101, 333n4, 340n80
Community, 24, 35–36, 57, 59, 83–84, 212
Compulsory military training, 12, 34, 40, 50
Conant, James Bryant, 11, 76, 135, 141–42
Congress, 348n56; armed forces and, 9, 71–72, 88, 90, 161–62, 208, 261; and AVF, 269–70, 273; blacks and racism and, 15, 102, 207–8; debates on draft, 8, 16–17, 45, 49, 51, 55, 71, 88, 91–96, 103, 107–8, 110–12, 116, 121, 124, 168, 203, 254–56; and deferments, 39, 40, 49, 62, 68, 70–73, 79, 137, 256; and demobilization, 92, 135; and draft reform, 89, 137, 140, 164, 191, 198, 202–5, 207, 211, 220, 239, 244, 246; farmers and, 65–67, 82;

Congress, *continued*
    Korea and, 112–13, 116, 131; labor and,
    37, 55–57, 66, 80, 82–85; physicians draft
    and, 154, 156, 158–59; protest and, 178,
    181–86, 204–5, 216, 218; UMT and, 37,
    91, 124, 135, 161, 164, 195; volunteers
    and, 96, 118. *See also* House Armed Ser-
    vices Committee; Politics; Senate Armed
    Services Committee
Conscientious objection, 15, 19–20, 140,
    321n44; blacks and, 99, 206; draft resis-
    tance and, 178–79, 201; problems with,
    20, 117, 120, 193, 224, 254; recognition
    of, 14, 19, 45–47, 128, 204, 224. *See also*
    Alternate service; Religion
Constitution, 16, 28, 51, 196, 211, 283n7
Containment, 96, 98, 101, 109, 123, 177,
    190
Convictions, 126, 173, 214, 330n85
Cordiner report, 163, 261
County Agricultural Mobilization Commit-
    tees, 66, 131
Courts, 158, 212, 340n82, 341n82; and
    blacks, 43, 206; and COs, 179, 204, 224,
    258; doctor draft and, 151; power of over
    SS, 28, 126, 251, 254, 265; resisters and,
    28, 180, 182, 185–86, 211, 213, 216,
    250. *See also* Supreme Court
Cultural values, 7, 47, 127, 236, 260
Czechoslovakia, 101, 108

Decentralization, 116, 129, 133, 245, 249;
    critics of, 61, 203, 211, 220; and draft op-
    erations, 6–7, 20, 29, 35, 260; farmers
    and, 65, 68. *See also* Centralization
Defense, Department of, 109, 123, 162, 189,
    199; AVF and, 229, 252, 254, 261, 264,
    266, 268–69, 271, 277; budget issues,
    114, 162, 262, 270–72, 281; deferments
    and, 40–41, 106, 138, 221, 251–52; draft
    reform and, 122, 187; economy and, 34–
    38, 81, 136, 138; health and rejectees,
    154–55, 158–59, 208–9; induction calls
    by, 114–15, 223, 257, 269; induction
    standards, 139, 153, 156–57, 172, 227;
    lottery and, 244–45; mobilization plans of,
    110, 160; and need for draft, 121, 163,
    189, 238, 252–56, 268–69; science and,
    106, 122; UMT and, 161. *See also* Pen-
    tagon; War Department
Defense, secretary of, 109, 156
Deferments, 7, 58, 93, 169, 313n55,
    341n92, 342n97; and age, 49, 52; criti-
    cism of, 194, 224, 270; and culture, 27–
    28, 49, 54, 62, 127; during Korean War,
    113–14, 116, 121, 123–24, 125, 128,

130–31, 136, 143; during Vietnam War,
    171–72, 221, 248; during World War II,
    64, 68, 82, 106, 120; economy and, 80,
    129; and educators, 75–76, 122, 222,
    232; and family, 14, 20, 30, 69, 73–74,
    127–28, 136, 138; and farmers, 65–68,
    130–31; and graduate school, 151, 221–
    23; for hardship, 41, 42, 52, 58, 127, 128;
    and industry, 37, 80–83, 106, 132, 149;
    and labor, 13, 35, 38, 55–56, 85, 151;
    protests of, 76, 145, 182–84, 189–90,
    215, 220, 251, 265; and public opinion,
    54, 61; and race, 207, 209; reforms of, 64,
    79, 137, 149, 189–93, 197, 199, 246,
    251–52, 260, 269; and religion, 20, 128;
    and science and health, 33, 75, 77, 79,
    106–7, 133, 141, 151, 153, 159–60; so-
    cial bias, 35, 49, 231; and students, 14,
    19, 39–42, 75–76, 106, 124, 141, 144,
    168
Deferments, law and policy of, 13, 18–19,
    29–30, 35, 38, 40, 54, 60, 108, 124, 137,
    161; categories of, 58, 69, 72, 81, 106,
    117–18, 169, 189, 194; procedures of, 38,
    85, 140–42, 147, 170, 173; and rate and
    size, 24, 30, 49, 57, 62, 86, 137–38, 140,
    164, 169, 192, 228, 231
Delinquency, draft, 229, 340n82; definition
    of, 117, 183, 218; and Korea, 119, 125;
    punishment of, 172, 183–84, 215, 251;
    rate and cause of, 174, 250; and Vietnam,
    182; and World War II, 184–85
Demobilization, 50, 60, 122, 135; after Ko-
    rea, 115, 261; after World War II, 89, 92,
    98, 100
Democratic party, 134, 278; AVF and, 261,
    263; and draft, 17–18, 39, 51, 98–99,
    121, 127, 164, 168, 240; and elections,
    193, 205, 215; Nixon and, 236, 258; re-
    forms and, 202, 241
Demography, 86, 141, 160, 188, 192, 198,
    236, 272
Dentists, 32–33, 153, 154–59, 315n84,
    316n91
Dependents, 14, 74, 272; Congress and, 70;
    deferments for, 30, 57–58, 68, 70, 72,
    127, 136, 137, 138, 180; definition of,
    24–25, 30, 69–70, 117; economy and, 35,
    37, 56, 70; Korea and, 115, 127, 143;
    public opinion of, 61; reform of, 72, 74,
    138, 202, 205; size and statistics on, 62,
    139, 169, 228; students and, 76, 145
Desertion rate, 274, 336n33
Dick Act, 6
Director, Selective Service, 19, 23–24, 46–
    47, 140. *See also* Hershey, Lewis B.

Discrimination, 18, 42–44, 76, 103, 107, 129, 190, 193. *See also* Blacks
Disqualification for draft, 58, 115, 117, 228, 230
Divinity students, 14–15, 19, 28, 117, 128, 178, 256
Divorce rate, 27, 68, 75
Doctors, draft of, 155–59, 315nn76, 84, 316n89. *See also* Physicians
Dodds, Harold W., 11, 142
Draft board. *See* Local boards
Draft calls: blacks and, 43–44, 105; deferments and, 72, 125; deficits in, 48, 64; Eisenhower and, 137–39; for Korean War, 114–16, 120, 123; procedures, 117; for Vietnam War, 170–72, 199, 223, 228; volunteers and, 161, 228; for World War II, 63–64, 70, 72, 81, 89, 92
Draft card, 28, 175, 181, 186, 215
Draft extension: of 1945, 88–91; of 1946, 95; of 1950, 110; of 1971, 254, 256–57, 268
Draft legislation: of 1917: 44, 55; of 1940: amendments, 50; Congress and, 16; COs and, 46–47; deferments of, 19, 38–39, 65, 75; economy and, 19, 55, 154; liability under, 18, 30, 50; opposition to, 36, 45; racism and, 15, 42–43, 99, 102–3; Roosevelt and, 17; theory of, 19, 54, 58; War Department and, 12; of 1948: 103–4, 116, 127, 129, 154; of 1950: 127, 129, 132; of 1951: 122–24, 127–28, 136–37, 151, 153, 164; of 1967: 202, 204, 329n77; of 1971: 339n73
Draft pool, 48–49, 63–64, 73, 77, 89, 93–94, 115, 120, 137, 139, 142, 147, 152, 171, 207, 227–28, 232, 246
Draft protest, 176–82, 204. *See also* Protest
Draft reform: Congress and, 186, 201–3, 270; debate on, 197–98, 269; and JFK, 189; and LBJ, 190, 193, 201, 205; and Nixon, 237, 239–41, 243, 251, 270. *See also* National Advisory Commission on Selective Service
Draft resistance. *See* Protest; Resistance
Drugs, 235, 273, 274
Dulles, John Foster, 91, 95, 137
Dykstra, Clarence, 20, 23–24, 31, 34–36, 43

Economics, 347n54; and class and draft, 27, 30, 80, 231, 242; cost of SS, 11, 110, 193, 235, 260, 278–79; deferments and, 6, 13–14, 30, 35, 54, 82, 125; and Korean War, 127, 129, 131; mobilization and, 13, 16, 34, 53–54, 56, 80; Vietnam and, 166; volunteers and, 48, 96, 196, 265, 272

Education, 327n47; and assignments in military, 126, 195, 201, 207, 234; classification and calls, 24, 59, 76–77, 126, 137, 141–42, 144, 203; deferments for, 38, 79, 93, 127, 148, 169, 194, 222, 232, 257, 264; and Korean War, 125, 127, 129, 143; and military participation rate, 127, 144, 194–95, 200, 231–33; military service and, 78, 119, 126, 173, 195, 207, 227, 233, 235, 275; race and, 86, 208, 210, 276; reaction to draft, 15–16, 39–42, 71, 75–79, 98, 102, 106–7, 133, 141, 145, 148, 164, 195, 199, 203, 222, 232; volunteers and, 234, 273. *See also* Colleges; Students
Egalitarianism, 6–7, 28–29, 75, 86, 105, 107, 140, 145, 167, 221, 230, 262
Ehrlichman, John R., 237, 270
Eisenhower, Dwight D., 91, 141, 164, 169, 277; and cuts to military, 137–38, 163, 227; draft reform and, 133, 135–38, 142–45, 149, 158–61, 164, 168, 190, 251; election campaigns of, 136, 162, 225; Korea and, 134–35, 153; on need for draft, 88, 94–95, 97, 134–35, 139, 160–62, 259; on UMT, 91, 135–36, 161; on volunteers, 96, 135, 163, 261; on Vietnam, 165, 167, 170
Elections: 1940, 21; 1952, 135–36; 1946, 99; 1956, 162, 261; 1960, 164, 263; 1964, 186; 1968, 223, 225, 244, 266; 1972, 253, 258, 270; 1980, 278–79; 1988, 280
Eligibility standards, 30, 58, 108, 116, 120, 139, 169, 209. *See also* Inductions; Liability
Elites, 106, 141, 160, 167, 181, 222
Engineers, 313n55; deferments for, 39, 41, 76, 79, 106, 140–41, 149, 151; schools, 76–78, 133; shortages of, 140, 149–50, 221
England, 2, 11, 13, 17, 49, 113, 128, 168, 263
Enke, Stephen, 245, 251–52, 254, 339n73
Enlisted men: blacks and, 99, 105, 129, 206–7, 231; and draft, 95, 97, 118–19, 189, 224, 228–29; education level of, 86, 141, 200, 227, 233–34; motivation of, 118, 260–61, 264, 274, 281; quality of, 109, 118–19, 234, 266, 273; sources of, 118–19, 171, 272, 274
Equality. *See* Egalitarianism
Essential activities, 56, 58, 74, 81, 129, 132, 149, 203
Estep v. U.S., 1951, 126

Executive Order 9981, 100
Executive Order 10469, 138
Exemptions, 6, 19, 45, 94, 116, 130, 151, 179, 240, 251

Fallows, James, 193, 246
Family, 14, 30, 54, 59, 62, 68–69, 72, 74, 79, 92, 127, 138
Farmers: deferments for, 19, 63, 65–68, 71, 93, 130–31, 138, 251; inductions of, 35, 41, 64–68, 86, 123, 126, 129–31, 231; lobby of, 60, 64–68, 74; productivity of, 56, 64, 68, 130. *See also* Agriculture
Fathers: calls for, 61, 70–74, 82; Congress and, 70, 72–73, 82; deferments for, 14, 20, 36, 64, 68, 72, 74, 106, 127–28, 136–38, 230; economy and, 70, 72; exemptions, 95; Korea and, 127–28; local boards and, 70, 72–73, 83; Vietnam and, 172. *See also* Dependents
FBI, 148, 173, 176, 182, 215, 236, 237, 250
Females, 22, 31, 74, 78, 127, 278. *See also* Women
First Amendment, 186
Fish, Hamilton, 15, 16
Fishbein, Morris, 32, 33
Flanigan, Peter, 239, 242–43, 245, 248–49
Fleming, Arthur S., 138–39, 161
Ford, Gerald R., 118, 186, 258
Foreign policy, 88–89, 95, 101, 178, 191, 265, 266
Forrestal, James, 91, 102
4-A classification, 117
4-B classification, 117
4-D classification, 117, 128
4-F classification, 25, 80, 85, 93, 117, 139, 143–44, 152, 192, 224, 228, 233
France, 2–3, 9–10, 12, 17, 20, 49, 79, 112, 113, 138, 168, 230, 318n3, 334n21
Friedman, Milton, 196, 225, 235, 260, 265–67, 343n9, 344n16, 345n28

Gallup poll, 11, 51, 61, 100, 278; on deferments, 38–39, 61, 128; on fathers, 70, 73; on military, 93, 226, 275; on Vietnam, 219, 226, 237. *See also* Public opinion
Gates, Thomas S., 192, 238, 252, 254, 266–67, 324n9, 339n71
Gates committee, 250, 252–53, 255–56, 266–67, 269–71
General Accounting Office (GAO), 272, 280, 281
Germany, 2, 9, 17–18, 49–51, 53, 56, 63, 88–89, 114, 259
GI bill, 96
Goldwater, Barry, 170, 186, 189, 225, 256

Governors, 21, 24, 60, 105, 205, 210
Graduate students, 311n30, 332n119; deferments for, 76, 145, 147, 149–51, 198, 200, 202, 205, 221–23, 239; degrees and enrollment, 78, 149–50, 222–23; military service and, 127, 145, 149, 200, 231–32
Graham, Billy, 240–41
Grammar school, 127, 147, 200
Great Britain. *See* England
Greece, 95–97, 108–9
Greenewalt, Crawford, 264, 266, 344n16
Gruening, Ernest, 204, 267
Gruenther, Alfred M., 266, 344n16
Guerrilla warfare, 111–12, 225
Gulf of Tonkin resolution, 106
Gutknecht v. U.S., 250–51

Haldeman, H. R., 239, 241–42, 245, 249, 258
Hannah, John, 126, 161
Harlem, 182, 206, 209, 328n69
Harrington, Michael, 263, 325n20
Harvard, 40, 76, 122, 135, 141, 193, 196, 203, 217, 219, 222, 239, 246
Hatfield, Mark, 204, 218, 256, 270, 278
Healing Arts Committee, 141, 153. *See also* Health; Physicians
Health, 275; civilians and, 31–32, 95, 151, 153; deferments for, 75–75, 155, 202, 221; military personnel and, 151, 154–56, 158, 256; and SS, 59–60. *See also* Doctors, draft of; Physicians; Rejectees
Health, Education, and Welfare, Department of, 252
Hebert, F. Edward, 186, 204–5, 256
Hershey, Lewis B., 62–63, 92, 140, 253; appeals and, 60, 182; economy and labor and, 35, 37–38, 53, 55, 83–85, 132; farmers and, 66–68, 131; fathers, family, and, 30–31, 68, 70–74, 82; Korea and, 114, 116; lottery and, 22, 220, 243; ministers, COs, and, 46, 128, 240; politics, Congress, and, 89, 92–94, 121, 215, 225; protesters and, 175, 182, 184–86, 211, 215–18; public opinion and, 61, 219; racism and, 42, 44, 103–4, 210; reform of draft and, 40, 81, 92, 187, 190, 198, 201–3, 210, 220, 241; rejectees, pool, and, 32–34, 48–49, 63–64, 71, 93, 159; removal of, 239, 242–43; and SS, 12, 17, 23, 36, 41, 54, 58, 61, 139–40, 188, 311n21; science and, 106, 145, 223; student deferments and, 40–41, 76, 107, 141, 149, 222–23
Hesburgh, Theodore, 264, 267, 344n16
High school students, 98, 144, 147; AVF

and, 272–73, 281; deferments for, 106, 117, 143–44, 147; MPR of, 86, 119, 144, 194, 200, 227, 232–33; opinion of service of, 136, 148, 169, 186, 196, 219
Hoffman, Anna Rosenberg, 192, 324n9
Hoover, Herbert, 53, 134
Hoover, J. Edgar, 215, 237
Hope, Bob, 25, 245, 246
House Armed Services Committee, 89, 108, 111, 114, 154, 186, 198, 202, 211
House Committee on Small Business, 82
House Military Affairs Committee, 93
House of Representatives, 51; debate on draft, 15–17, 51–52, 94, 96, 98, 124, 204, 256–57, 278; on deferments, 49, 68, 72–74, 84; on protest, 186
House Rules Committee, 108
House Un-American Activities Committee, 332n4
Humphrey, Hubert, 164, 223, 225–26

Illiteracy, 32, 72, 76, 93
Imperialism, 88, 177, 178, 260
Imprisonment, 19, 115, 173. *See also* Prosecution
Income, 121, 126, 231, 276, 325n20
Inductions, 25, 61, 88, 108, 114, 170, 200, 206–7, 224, 248, 342n97; acceleration of, 59, 67, 71, 183; age and, 55, 67, 71, 77, 124, 192; appeals of, 60, 120; courts and, 251; delays in, 43, 48, 64, 120; marriage and, 68, 69, 73, 138, 180; opposition to, 28, 111, 124, 167, 176, 212, 251; procedure of, 31, 111, 117, 158, 160, 163, 169, 170, 187, 201, 256, 278, 328n72; race and, 43, 64, 99, 206, 207, 231; rate of, 48, 63–64, 85, 89, 131, 139, 147, 168–69, 171, 184; standards for, 5, 32–33, 64, 68, 81, 93, 139, 152–53, 156, 162, 194, 207; World War II and, 60, 85
Industry: deferments for, 19, 34, 59, 65, 79–82, 121, 132, 147; Korea and, 130–32; labor and, 64–67, 72, 82; mobilization of, 19–20, 34, 65, 80, 81, 95, 99, 141; and SS, 35, 54, 81–82, 132
Infantry, 25, 55, 77, 119, 171, 235, 273
Integration of armed forces, 100, 102–3, 105
Interagency Advisory Committee, 221–22
Iran, 95, 277, 279
Iraq, 281
Isolationism, 9, 12, 17, 51–52, 96
Italy, 9, 63–64, 73

JANSSC. *See* Joint Army Navy Selective Service Committee
Japan, 9, 34, 49–53, 81, 88–90, 95, 112,

113–14, 168
Jeffersonianism, 20, 29
Jehovah's Witnesses, 45, 173, 214, 240, 250
Jews, 45, 237
Jim Crow, 15, 42–43, 99, 103, 109, 129
Job deferments, 25, 54, 59, 63, 65, 81, 82, 84, 120, 147, 169, 202, 207
Johnson, Campbell, 42–44, 99, 100
Johnson, Louis, 109, 111, 113, 135, 228
Johnson, Lyndon B., 84, 136, 168, 170, 204, 209, 228, 238, 242, 245, 268, 330n88, 334n18; deferments and, 116, 221–23; lottery and, 197–98, 220, 244; politics and, 170, 187, 189, 218–19, 224; protesters and, 166, 174, 178, 181–82, 185–86, 205, 211, 214–18, 224, 236, 249; reforms draft, 2, 4, 187, 189–91, 198, 201–5, 210, 220, 261
Joint Army Navy Selective Service Committee (JANSSC), 10, 12, 13, 14, 19, 183
Joint Chiefs of Staff, 63, 97, 107, 123, 170, 277
Joint Induction Centers, 62
Judiciary, 126, 213. *See also* Courts
Judiciary committee, 37
Junior college students, 200, 341n92
Justice Department, 29, 125–26, 173, 175, 183, 186, 204–5, 211–15, 218, 224, 240, 248, 250, 279, 329n84, 340n82
Juvenile delinquency, 74

Kelley, Roger, 268, 270
Kennan, George, 101
Kennedy, Edward, 202–3, 218, 221, 242, 244, 248, 256, 270, 278, 325n20
Kennedy, John F., 164–65, 168, 170, 172, 188–89, 208, 209, 334n18
Kennedy, Robert, 224, 325n20
Kent State University, 40, 249
Kilday, Paul J., 67, 72–73, 82, 89, 154
Kilday-May bill, 72–73, 82
King, Martin Luther, Jr., 177, 206, 214, 224
Kissinger, Henry, 247, 248, 250–51, 258, 270, 340n82
Knox, Frank, 54, 84
Korean War, 5, 113, 122–25, 137, 140–41, 149, 153, 157, 164–65, 169–70, 173, 191, 199, 220–21, 225, 316n91, 336n33; appeals in, 120, 180–81; armistice in, 138, 140; blacks and, 113, 129; class bias of, 126–27, 143, 200; COs and, 128, 321n44; deferments and calls for, 112–15, 121, 127, 129, 133, 140, 142–43, 149, 171; demobilization and, 162, 166; Eisenhower and, 135; farmers and, 130; LBJ and, 136; mobilization for, 111–16, 123,

Korean War, *continued*
129, 135–36, 143, 160, 227; public opinion and protest of, 121, 125, 144, 174, 182, 219, 220, 340n80; physicians draft for, 154, 158; rejectees and, 152; Truman and, 112–14, 116, 121, 129, 220; volunteers for, 118–20, 261

Labor, 84, 196, 235; attitude to draft, 16, 36, 98; control of, 13, 16, 38, 65–66, 81, 83, 85; relations with SS, 35–36, 83, 85; shifts in, 14, 66; shortages of, 56, 66, 80, 129, 132; unrest of, 36–37, 98. *See also* Strikes
Labor, Department of, 131, 149, 188, 208–9
La Guardia, Fiorello H., 49, 56, 73
Laird, Melvin, 245, 252, 254, 257–58, 264, 267–71, 339n73
Lemke bill, 68
Lewis, John L., 16, 36, 38, 84, 85, 98
Liability, 13, 18, 29, 30, 94, 95, 108, 116, 124, 147, 158, 167–68, 252, 256, 342n97
Liberal arts, 39–40, 76, 78
Liberals, 214, 256, 267
Limited war, 112, 121, 125, 220, 282
Local boards, 19, 27, 35, 60, 82, 118, 124, 184, 210, 248, 260, 340n82; appeals and, 19, 60, 120–21; COs, religion, and, 46, 128, 179, 240; courts and, 126, 216, 251; and deferments, 13, 41, 49, 62, 79, 83, 133, 137, 140, 172, 316n91; family, fathers, and, 14, 30, 68–73, 136; farmers and, 65–67, 131; labor, economy, and, 13–14, 35–38, 59, 81–85, 132; lottery and, 21–22, 244–47, 257; minorities and, 15, 42–44, 99, 103, 105, 129, 206–211, 220; personnel for, 24, 26, 29, 35–36, 49, 57–59, 61, 66, 81, 116, 182, 188, 193, 198, 210, 220, 241–42, 329n77; power and theory of, 19, 20, 35–36, 57–58, 61, 69, 108, 204, 231, 260; procedures and classifications, 19–21, 24–25, 29–32, 35, 48–49, 52, 58–60, 62, 69–70, 109–10, 117, 120, 147, 173, 183, 220, 228, 248; protesters and delinquents, 29, 117, 174, 176, 182–84, 189, 199, 213–16, 240, 250; public opinion of, 13, 61, 75, 121, 191, 219; reforms and criticism of, 49, 60, 138, 173, 189, 193, 198, 201–3, 241, 245, 248, 254, 256; rejectees and, 32, 33, 170; students and, 39–42, 77, 79, 127, 142, 145, 148–49, 193, 199–200, 222; Vietnam and, 170, 172, 243
Lottery, 339n71; Congress, politics, and, 21, 202, 204–5, 225, 245–46; debate on, 197, 201–4, 220, 239, 245–46, 250, 252; effect of, 5, 50, 246, 249, 264; Nixon and, 239, 243–46, 249, 256–57; procedure and problems of, 22, 48, 197, 245, 247–49, 253, 269; as reform, 198, 252, 257. *See also* Reforms of draft

MacArthur, Douglas, 10, 88, 95, 112–16, 123, 135
McCarthy, Eugene, 224, 225
McCone, John A., 192, 324n9
McCrocklin, James H., 324n9
McDermott, Arthur V., 56, 81
McGovern, George, 256, 258, 267, 270
Machinists, 81, 132
McNamara, Robert, 166, 189–90, 196, 201, 203, 208–9, 221, 228, 232, 262, 280, 347n54
McNutt, Paul, 33–34, 56, 64, 72–74, 78, 81–82
Male age cohort, 30, 86, 137, 167, 231–32
Male population, 61–62, 69, 86, 147, 206. *See also* Demography
Management, 35–36, 38, 53, 66, 80, 83, 86, 116, 126
Manpower: management of, 3, 6, 10, 13, 34, 38, 48, 54, 75, 107, 120, 125, 141, 203, 230, 281, 301n28; mobilizing, 52, 54, 57, 65, 105, 109, 120, 122, 125, 129, 195, 262; policy and planning, 68, 74, 121, 139–40, 160, 162, 164–65; pool of, 62, 70–72, 76, 92, 117; shortages of, 1, 34, 64, 71, 94, 260
Mansfield, Mike, 186, 257
Marines, 109, 118, 206, 229, 231, 233, 281
Market economy, 196, 235, 260
Marriage, 14, 69, 75; deferments for, 14, 20, 30, 67, 69, 123, 127–28, 137, 172, 180, 202, 222; and draft calls, 62, 68–69, 71–72, 172–73; and economy, 69, 82; rate of service, 36, 68, 72, 80, 86, 127, 136, 168, 180, 272
Marshall, Burke, 191–92, 195, 198, 201–2
Marshall, George C., 10, 12, 17, 50–52, 64, 67, 74, 76–77, 79, 88, 91–92, 97, 101, 108, 115, 118, 122–23, 127, 135–36, 155, 191
Marshall commission. *See* National Advisory Commission on Selective Service
Marshall Plan, 101, 102, 108, 112
Mass armies, 2, 3, 4–6, 139, 161, 235, 259, 262, 282
May, Andrew J., 70, 73, 89
May Second Movement, 177
Mechanics, 82, 132
Medicine, 31–32; and advisory boards, 32, 157; and deferments, 41, 49, 77, 79, 106,

159; and examinations, 20, 32, 53, 152; and military reserve corps, 114, 154–57, 159–60; schools of, 33, 40, 75, 141, 153, 316n89, 316n91. *See also* American Medical Association; Health; Physicians

Mental qualifications, 335n26; AVF and, 273; rejections for, 31, 119, 152, 169; standards for, 124, 162, 180, 207, 227, 230, 232

Meyerhoff, Howard A., 106, 148, 223

Michigan, 49, 118, 151, 173, 183–85, 192

Michigan State University, 178

Michigan, University of, 144, 176, 183

Militarism, 3, 16, 20, 88, 230

Military: assignments in, 126, 234; budget and pay, 51, 95, 110, 196, 226, 236, 253, 256, 260–61, 263, 264, 266, 267, 271–72, 279, 281; draft calls for, 40, 62, 71, 74, 82, 90, 111, 121, 155; expansion and strength, 9, 52, 72, 77, 91–92, 101–2, 109, 165, 168, 199, 271, 281; leadership of, 90, 101, 127, 268; life in, 80, 90, 118, 191, 200, 208, 222, 268–69, 271, 274–76; mobilization plans, 5, 36, 62, 80, 93, 97, 101, 108, 116, 122, 167; morale and training, 1, 18, 77–78, 90, 94, 97, 122, 137, 142, 274; participation rate (MPR), 5, 126, 130, 139, 141, 143, 144, 162, 194–95, 200, 206, 230, 231–33; politics, 13, 85, 89–92, 110, 191, 262, 265; recruiting and volunteers, 48, 54, 56, 96, 100, 263, 268–69, 281; SS and, 36, 61, 65, 90, 111, 188, 193, 220. *See also* Armed forces; *individual branches*

Military Training Corps Association, 58

Militia, 1, 5, 14, 89–90

Miners, 84, 85, 98

Ministers, 14–15, 19–20, 44–45, 117, 120, 128, 206, 240. *See also* Religion

Minorities, 104, 219–20, 273

Mitchell, John, 250, 340n82

Mobilization, 284n17; and cold war, 97; impact of, 39, 105; for Korea, 112–13, 121, 123, 125; plans, 53, 58, 87, 122, 140; problems of, 1, 13–15, 44, 47, 54, 56, 230, 279; for Vietnam, 170; World War II and, 5, 10, 21, 47–48, 53, 64

Modernization, 3, 7, 57, 80, 87, 253, 260–61

Morale, 119, 182, 198

Moratorium Day, 246

Morse, Wayne, 102, 103, 204

Moses, John, 65, 66

Moynihan, Daniel Patrick, 209, 238, 245

MPR. *See* Military: participation rate

Murray, John C., 191, 324n9

National Academy of Science, 79, 248

National Advisory Commission on Selective Service (NACSS; Marshall commission), 190–91, 192–93, 195, 197–98, 201–3, 205, 222, 244, 261

National Association for the Advancement of Colored People (NAACP), 99, 103, 206

National Association of State Universities, 39

National draft calls, 252–54, 256, 269

National Council to Repeal the Draft, 267

National Defense Mediation Board, 38

National Farmers Union, 66, 124, 130

National Guard, 1, 5–6, 9–10, 24, 50, 52, 58, 62, 90, 101, 123, 163, 166, 168, 170–71, 193, 207, 229, 231, 233, 249, 264–65, 348n56

National Security Act, 129

National Security Council (NSC), 68, 110–11, 160, 205, 221–22, 253, 270

National Security Resources Board (NSRB), 129, 133

National Security Training Commission, 124, 136, 160

National Security Training Corps (NSTC), 124, 136

National Selective Service Appeal Board (NSSAB), 140, 150, 239–40, 241, 311n21

National service, 54–57, 80, 82–83, 190–91, 195–96, 198, 280

National service bill, 18, 54–56, 80, 84

National Service Board for Religious Objectors, 128

National Student Association, 218

NATO. *See* North Atlantic Treaty Organization

Navy, 10, 50, 154; blacks in, 15, 206; reserves, 229; secretary of the, 77, 266; use of draft, 62, 64, 82, 89; volunteers in, 48, 54, 97, 109, 118, 207, 229, 272–73

Nelson, Gaylord, 270, 325n20

New Deal, 31, 34, 47, 80

New Left, 236

Newspapers, 11, 51, 62, 228

New York City, 18, 24, 26, 28–29, 39, 49, 56, 73, 76, 82, 175, 199, 260

New York Times, 11, 25, 27, 92, 107, 218, 240, 268

Nixon, Richard, 166, 210, 211, 223, 250, 259, 266, 269; attitude toward the draft, 162, 164, 223, 225–26, 229, 234–35, 249, 252, 261, 271; extends the draft, 245, 251, 253–57, 268, 270–71, 333n4; Hershey and, 242–43; lottery and, 244–

Nixon, Richard, *continued*
46, 248, 339n71; and politics, 225–26,
236, 239, 249, 258; on protesters, 236,
246, 249, 267, 341n82; reforms the draft,
227, 236–41, 249, 251–53, 255–57,
341n92; supports an AVF, 226, 238,
262–63, 267–71; and Vietnam strategy,
249–50, 269, 271
Noble, Jeanne, 324n9, 344n16
Noncombat duty, 47, 227
Nondeferrable jobs, 72, 82
Norstad, Lauris, 266, 344n16
North Africa, 56, 63–64, 72
North Atlantic Treaty Organization (NATO),
112, 164
NSSAB. *See* National Selective Service Appeal Board
Nuclear arms, 7, 112, 160, 161, 163, 226,
259
Nunn, Sam, 277, 278, 280, 281

Occupational deferments: classification of,
13, 24, 35, 59, 61, 81, 173, 327n57; fathers and, 128; for Korean War, 130, 138,
143; problems of, 37, 62, 81, 85, 96, 136,
231; reforms of, 205, 251, 253; Vietnam
and, 171. *See also* 2-A classification
Occupation forces, 89, 91, 93, 95, 106
Office of Civilian Defense Mobilization, 163
Office of Defense Mobilization (ODM), 131,
138, 139
Office of Selective Service Records (OSSR),
96, 108
Office of War Information (OWI), 61, 72
Office of War Mobilization, 64, 82
Office of War Mobilization and Reconversion (OWMR), 92, 107
Officers, 227, 229, 261, 266, 272
Oi, Walter Y., 196–97, 235, 266
1-A classification, 27, 59, 66, 77, 140, 144,
149, 340; appeals from, 120, 171, 180;
definition of, 24, 117, 199; and draft protest, 175, 178, 184; reclassification of, 59;
and strikers, 85–85; and students, 40, 75
1-A pool: distortions in, 169, 228; and lottery, 247; and MPR by education, 233
1-S classification, 117, 143–44, 232
1-Y classification, 117, 172–73
Operation Overlord, 64, 79
Order of call, 44, 58, 69, 172, 245
Organized labor. *See* Unions

Pacifism, 14–16, 46, 75, 98, 176, 179, 259
Parolees, 29, 93, 201
Parsons, Charles L., 39, 79
Patriotism, 36, 178, 181, 266

Patterson, Robert, 11, 39–40, 50, 55, 91–94,
96–98, 106–7, 109, 111
Patton, James G., 66, 124, 130
Peace churches, 15, 19, 45, 47, 176
Peace Corps, 164, 191, 204
Peacetime draft, 18, 91, 93, 96, 98–99
Peace treaties, 89, 95
Pearl Harbor, 34, 42, 45–47, 52–55, 62, 69,
75, 82, 83
Pentagon, 101–2, 104, 154–55, 164, 175,
190, 199, 214, 246, 263, 267, 281. *See
also* Defense, Department of
Personnel management, 140, 230
Physical qualifications, 86, 222, 246,
341n82; disqualified for, 33, 40, 169,
172, 180, 224; examination for, 31–32,
117, 152, 208; standards for, 24, 49, 85,
117, 119, 152, 157, 169, 180, 207, 230,
232. *See also* Inductions
Physicians, 39, 43, 99; draft of, 152–60; in
military, 154–56, 158, 229; role in SS,
31–33, 40, 99, 152. *See also* Doctors, draft
of
Physicists, 76, 79, 105, 106, 140, 148, 223,
313n55
Plumbers, 81, 84, 105
Policemen, 28, 49, 59, 73
Politics, 348n56; and the AVF, 226, 261–65,
276; blacks and, 100, 206; deferments
and, 74, 105, 127, 130, 138, 145, 251;
draft renewal and, 91, 95–96, 102, 110,
124, 162, 192, 202, 229, 256, 260; Korean war and, 113, 121, 128, 130, 135;
protest and, 140, 166–67, 178, 181, 186,
236; reform and, 189–90, 195, 203, 205,
236, 238, 270; reserves and, 115, 168; SS
and, 7, 52, 57–58, 65, 87, 98, 181, 225,
241, 243, 259. *See also* Congress: protest
and; Protest; Public opinion
Population, 5, 15, 100, 169, 231, 275. *See
also* Demography
Pre-induction physicals, 117, 152–53, 180,
228
Premed students, 33, 153
Presidential appeal board, 60, 120–21
Presidential commission on induction, 64, 68
Presidential Committee on an All-Volunteer
Force (PCAVF), 263, 264–67, 274,
324n9, 344n16
President's Advisory Committee on UMT,
97
Press, 25, 27, 94, 205, 239, 241, 267
Princeton University, 133, 190, 217
Prison, 73, 93, 201, 214
Productivity, 37, 66, 130

Professional army, 2–3, 89, 101, 135, 268
Professors, 182, 185
Project 100,000, 209, 232, 347n54, 348n57
Project Volunteer, 254, 264, 268
Prosecution, 29, 117, 126, 173, 184, 186, 212, 214, 218, 240, 250, 256, 279, 329n84
Protest, 66–67, 98, 124, 134, 174, 196, 250, 266; blacks and, 206; causes, 220, 266; characteristics of, 125, 167, 176, 224; Congress and, 186, 216; FBI and, 215, 236; impact of, 168, 175, 181–82, 184, 199, 219, 240, 243; Korea and, 125–27; LBJ and, 181–82, 190, 201, 205, 214; Nixon and, 220, 236, 238, 242, 246, 249, 340n80; public opinion on, 184, 216; reaction and prosecution, 182, 184–86, 199, 205, 211, 215–16, 218, 250; tactics and targets, 124, 130, 175–76, 187, 215, 279; Vietnam War and, 173–74, 183, 202, 207, 211, 214, 225
Provost Marshall General, 167, 173
Public health, 19, 38, 153, 208
Public Law 54, 89
Public Law 779, 154
Public opinion, 11, 25, 51–52, 75, 92, 126–127, 165, 169, 220, 262, 275, 278, 282; on AVF and volunteers, 118, 197, 226, 237, 263, 267; on deferments, 28, 54, 62, 94, 132, 138; on the draft and extensions of it, 8, 17, 25, 28, 54, 61, 88, 92–94, 96–97, 102, 108, 165, 168–69, 206, 237, 282; on farmers, 67–68, 131; on fathers and family, 70–73, 83, 127, 136; on Korean War, 121, 135, 144; on labor, 37–38, 83; on protesters, 185, 219; on Russia, 93–94; on SS operations, 61–62, 65, 100, 219, 242, 339n71; on student deferments, 39, 143, 178; on UMT, 80, 135; on Vietnam War, 185–86. *See also* Gallup poll
Public relations, 40, 42–43, 60–61, 115, 118, 249
Pyramiding deferments, 127, 138, 145, 147

Quotas, 18, 20, 48

Race, 193, 197, 205, 219, 230–31, 276, 328n72; in armed forces, 43, 90, 103, 105, 126; and AVF, 208, 265, 269, 276; Congress and, 15, 208; deferments and, 190, 207; and draft calls, 42–44, 100, 102–3, 129, 209; protest and, 206, 237; rejection rate and, 48, 207–8; in SS, 42, 44, 205, 242. *See also* Blacks; Minorities
Randolph, A. Philip, 100, 102–3

Random selection system, 21–22, 197, 202, 243, 246–47, 254. *See also* Lottery
Rayburn, Sam, 50–51, 116
Ready Reserve, 161
Reagan, Ronald, 272, 278–79, 281
Reclassifications, 27, 38, 56, 83–85, 120–21, 140, 149, 183–85, 190, 199, 215–16, 218, 251. *See also* Classifications
Recruiting, 54, 91, 95, 97, 108, 134, 157, 263; and AVF, 16, 54, 91, 271, 273–74, 276–77, 279–81; cost of, 118, 228, 267–72; draft and, 18, 110, 118–19, 207, 228; protest over, 176, 204, 215–17, 224; standards, quality, and 48, 96, 139, 229, 273, 281; success of, 54, 108, 161, 165, 171, 228, 266, 271, 281; tactics of, 93, 111, 262, 272
Reedy, George, 185, 192, 197, 202, 219, 324n9
Reemployment, 19–20, 35–36
Reenlistment, 89–90, 119, 197, 231, 261, 272, 319n20
Reforms of draft, 49, 138, 181, 198, 210, 236, 327n47
Regional appeal boards, 35, 193
Registration, 278–79, 349n64; appeals in, 60, 120; classification in, 24–25, 59, 69, 120, 132, 139, 144; delinquency of, 19, 117, 125, 174–75, 183, 186, 204, 218; inductions and, 24, 117, 144; liability under, 13, 16, 18, 21, 48, 57, 71, 108–9, 117, 141, 168, 278; lottery and, 22; pool size and, 48, 62, 71, 114, 116, 138, 147, 169, 172, 199, 228, 246; race and, 15, 42–44, 99; rejection rate and, 32
Regular Army, 5–6, 9–10, 90, 109
Rejectees, 25, 63, 169; effect of, 32, 34, 48, 62, 64, 71, 80, 93, 173, 233; race and, 207–8; rate of, 31, 33, 116, 139, 143, 152–53, 162, 172, 180, 224, 228; reasons for, 27, 32–33, 40, 49, 145, 152, 208; rehabilitation of, 33–34, 76, 208–9, 232, 348n57
Religion, 44, 103; attitude toward draft, 16, 22, 44–45, 127, 179, 214; recognition of, 14–15, 19–20, 44–47, 128. *See also* Conscientious objection
Replacements, 82, 88–92, 227
Republicans, 17, 49–51, 99, 102, 110, 121, 127, 135, 138, 164, 186–87, 190, 202, 236, 241, 263, 278
Reserve Forces Act, 161–62, 313n55, 316n94
Reserve Officers Training Corps (ROTC), 117, 126, 137, 142, 147, 171, 197, 215,

Reserve Officers Training Corps (ROTC),
  continued
  224, 229, 265, 271
Reservists, 316n94, 324n18; call up of, 112–
  15, 123, 129, 137, 160, 165, 168, 170,
  221, 229; obligations of, 97, 108, 122,
  124, 136–37, 161; size of, 109, 163, 165,
  168, 171, 229, 233, 261, 272
Resisters. *See* Protest
Retention rate, 268, 272–74, 280
Reuther, Walter, 38, 189
Riots, 91–92, 167
Rivers, Mendell, 186, 198, 202, 205, 216,
  218
Rockefeller, Nelson, 27, 225, 226, 244
Roosevelt, Eleanor, 30–32, 77
Roosevelt, Franklin D.: on age of draftees,
  49, 71, 85; on college students, 39–42,
  76–77; on deferments, 64, 67–68, 71, 74,
  79, 82, 85; on draft, 2, 10–12, 17–18, 88;
  on labor and strikes, 37–38, 56, 66, 80,
  84–85; racism and, 15, 42, 44, 99; reject-
  ees and rehab, 31–34; role in SS, 20–24,
  36, 49, 60; on volunteers, 18, 48, 54, 56
Rose, Jonathan, 241, 243
Rosenberg, Anna M., 115–16, 118, 122, 128
Royall, Kenneth C., 101, 103
Rural areas, 192, 230. *See also* Farmers
Rusk, Howard A., 155, 315nn76, 88
Russell, Richard, 103, 135–36, 186, 198,
  202, 205
Russell-Overton bill, 37
Russia, 49–50, 51, 53, 93–95, 97, 101, 109,
  111, 123, 133, 137, 148, 150, 278

Saigon, 170, 254
SANE (National Committee for a Sane Nuclear Policy), 265
Science, 291n92; advisers for SS, 79, 133,
  141, 144–45, 147–48, 221; attitude toward draft, 39, 79, 95, 98, 102, 105, 106,
  129, 143, 145, 149, 167, 223; deferments
  for, 28, 75, 79, 105–7, 132–33, 141, 149,
  151, 313n55; foreign policy and, 133,
  141, 149; military service and, 91, 105–6,
  147–49, 221, 223; mobilization and, 5,
  91, 93, 105–7, 122, 125, 149, 260; students in, 105–7, 133, 149–50, 221, 223
Scientific Manpower Commission, 148, 223
Segregation, 15, 43, 99–100,102–3, 209
Selective conscientious objection, 179, 191,
  224, 258
Selective Service Act. *See* Draft legislation
Selective Service College Qualification Test
  (SSCQT), 142–43, 147, 150, 180, 184,
  199, 220, 311n29

Selective Service System (SS): management
  theory of, 3–4, 7, 13, 20, 28, 54–58, 62,
  140; national headquarters of, 20, 23, 33,
  44–46, 49, 57–60, 70; operations of, 19,
  21–22, 34, 54, 58, 62, 92, 181, 188; personnel of, 4, 31, 42, 99, 116; prosecution
  by, 29, 183; public opinion of, 25, 61, 62.
  See also Deferments; Hershey, Lewis B.;
  Local Boards
Senate, U.S., 16–17, 23, 49–51, 66–67, 74,
  76, 89, 94, 96, 99, 103, 124, 186, 203–4,
  244, 256–57
Senate Armed Services Committee, 135,
  204, 243
Senate Military Affairs Committee, 72
Senate Subcommittee on Demobilization,
  92–93
Servicemen's Dependents Allowance Act, 70
Seymour, Charles, 39, 142
Shipyards, 81–83
Single men, 30, 55, 61, 68–69, 70–74, 82–
  83, 172
Sit-ins, 176, 181, 183–84
Six-month reserve program, 161–62, 313n55
Smith, Margaret Chase, 243, 257, 338n59
Smith-Connally Act, 85
SNCC (Student Nonviolent Coordinating
  Committee), 177, 206
Social class, 126, 145, 176, 194–95, 209,
  219, 231, 242, 277
Socialist party, 28, 51, 88, 95, 177
Soldiers. *See* Enlisted men
Southeast Asia, 168, 177
Soviet Union, 138, 95, 97, 101–2, 108, 110,
  135, 277–78, 281. *See also* Russia
Special Training Enlistment Program, 208
Spock, Benjamin, 179, 267–68
Sputnik, 148–49
SSCQT. *See* Selective Service College Quali-
  fication Test
State, Department of, 94, 101, 110
State appeal boards, 36, 120–21
Stennis, John, 186, 243, 254, 256–57, 269,
  277
Stevenson, Adlai, 162, 225, 261, 262
Stimson, Henry, 11–12, 22–23, 33, 37, 42,
  44, 54–55, 62, 67–68, 72, 78, 84–85, 90
Strikes, 13, 36–38, 83–85, 98, 100, 183
Student deferments, 14, 29, 38–42, 71, 78,
  107, 128, 145, 151, 200, 314n60; abuse
  of, 136, 138, 145, 185, 199; defense of,
  76, 107, 140, 145, 147, 180, 222, 252;
  Korea and, 123, 142–43; opposition to,
  40, 137, 141, 143, 187; public opinion of,
  39, 143–44, 219; reforms of, 79, 191–92,

198, 201–3, 205, 222, 252–53; requirements for, 40–41, 78, 133, 141–42, 144,
184, 204; Vietnam and, 172, 183–84,
199. *See also* 2-S classification
Student Nonviolent Coordinating Committee
(SNCC), 177, 206
Student Peace Union, 175–76
Students, 19, 40, 144–45, 147, 183; classifying and ranking, 25, 40–41, 78, 107, 123,
142–43, 169, 200, 311n29; and draft
pool, 39, 118, 144, 147, 228; enrollment
of, 16, 232; local boards and, 75, 173,
193; military service of, 161, 201; opinions of, 39, 143, 148; protest and opposition, 28, 75, 176–77, 181, 184–85, 200,
217, 222, 243, 249, 340n80
Students for a Democratic Society (SDS),
178, 184, 237, 325n20
Supreme Court, 28, 126, 179, 250, 279,
349n64
Surgeon General of the Army, 157
Symington, Stuart, 129, 164

Taft, Robert, 50–51, 61, 68, 70, 73, 99, 102,
124
Taft-Hartley Act, 99
Tarr, Curtis, 243, 249–50, 253–54, 257, 268
Teachers, 39, 75, 151, 172, 200, 222–23,
327n57
Television, 164, 228, 274
Test scores, 109, 199–200, 221, 273
Third World, 177, 196, 269
Thomas, Norman, 28, 51, 88, 89
3-A classification, 68–69, 72, 117, 127, 132,
137–39
3-B classification, 69
Total war, 53, 87, 109
Truman, Harry S., 98, 133, 135, 170, 240;
and blacks, 100, 102–3, 129; cold war
and, 91, 95–98, 101–2, 109–10, 123, 170;
deferments and, 68, 73, 105–7, 128, 131–
33, 142, 314n21; doctors draft and, 155–
56; extends draft, 88–98, 101–2, 105,
107–8, 110–12, 122, 124, 135; Korea
and, 112–14, 116, 121, 129, 220; military
cuts and, 90, 101, 114; UMT, volunteers,
and, 90, 92, 96–97, 118, 123–24, 334n18
Truman doctrine, 101, 108, 112
2-A classification, 25, 75–76, 117, 130–32,
142, 149, 151, 200, 251
2-B classification, 58, 75–76
2-C classification, 117, 130–31, 251
2-S classification, 117, 127, 130, 132, 138–
45, 147, 199–200, 222, 232, 251
Tydings amendment, 67, 71

Unemployment, 25, 34, 80–81, 166, 228,
263–64, 271, 276, 279, 280–81
Unions, 13, 36, 45, 66, 67, 80, 83, 85, 95,
98–99
United Auto Workers (UAW), 38, 190
United Mine Workers, 98
United Nations, 94–95, 259
Universal military service (UMS), 135, 136
Universal Military Training (UMT), 3, 49,
90–91, 94, 97–98, 100–102, 107–8, 122–
24, 135–37, 161, 191, 195–96, 198,
316n94
Universal Military Training and Selective
Service Act, 1951, 122, 124, 168. *See also*
Draft legislation, 1951
Universal service, 14, 55, 64, 86, 163–64,
167
Universities, 39, 78, 106, 203, 222. *See also*
Colleges
Urban areas, 4, 61, 86, 182, 230

Vance, Cyrus, 185, 190
Vandenburg, Arthur H., 49, 96
Veterans, 36, 89, 94, 145, 231, 264, 275,
348nn56, 57; classifications and, 22, 96,
106, 109, 117, 131, 138, 142, 169, 222,
228, 264; on draft, 94, 196, 256; Korea
and, 113–16, 123, 135, 137; on protest,
185, 216; SS and, 29, 46, 116, 193, 242–
43
Veterans Administration, 275
Veterans of Foreign Wars, 216
Vietnam War, 112, 170, 172, 188–89, 191,
193–94, 214, 224, 242, 249, 275, 278;
AVF and, 228, 268–69; blacks and, 177,
206–7, 209, 231; COs and, 179, 221,
227, 234; draftees and, 5, 165, 167, 171,
204, 221, 227, 234–35, 258, 266, 268,
316n91, 319n24, 334n18; impact on SS,
165–68, 173, 180–81, 194, 199, 243–44,
254, 260; MPR for, 194–95, 220, 231,
257, 336n33; Nixon and, 226, 238–39,
251, 258, 271; politics and, 166, 170,
186, 220, 225, 256, 258, 269; protest
over, 174, 176–79, 181–82, 184, 211–12,
214, 220, 250, 325n20, 329n84; public
opinion and, 186, 200, 219–20, 236–37.
See also Johnson, Lyndon B.
Vinson, Carl, 103, 111
Vinson, Fred, 185, 186, 204
Violators of draft, 19, 173, 184, 201, 211,
217–18
VJ Day, 89, 92–93
Volunteers, 4, 5, 7, 25, 35, 97, 125, 165,
262–63; armed forces and, 10, 48, 89, 96–
98, 109, 111, 118, 189, 196, 252, 264,

Volunteers, *continued*
  271; cost of, 18, 108, 110, 119, 196, 228,
  265–66, 274; doctors and, 155–56, 159;
  draft effect on, 16, 18, 25, 28, 48, 60, 93–
  96, 109–11, 117–18, 139, 163, 168, 172,
  189, 227–28, 240, 254, 306n23, 334n13;
  economy and, 13, 48, 68, 81, 131, 189,
  260, 301n28; Korea and, 17, 113, 116,
  118; politics and, 18, 162, 181, 204, 260,
  279; problems of, 11, 49, 54, 194; profile
  of, 31, 71, 109, 118–19, 118, 126, 171,
  195–96, 201, 219, 231–34, 261–62, 268,
  275; race of, 15, 207, 274; rate of, 48, 54,
  91–92, 96, 101, 120, 189, 197, 246, 252,
  254, 271; recruitment of, 54, 89, 91, 96,
  100, 108, 112, 228, 261, 264; students
  and, 13, 40, 75, 144, 185, 263; Vietnam
  and, 165, 171, 226, 268

Wadsworth, James W., 11, 84
Wallace, George, 210, 225, 329n80
War, Department of, 10, 21, 36, 91, 106;
  deferments and, 28, 40, 42, 67, 78–79,
  81, 107; demobilization and, 92–93; draft
  calls of, 20, 24, 52, 92–93, 96, 118; in-
  duction standards of, 33, 93; labor and,
  35, 38, 66, 81; race and, 42–43; relations
  to SS, 11–13, 17–18, 20–25, 49, 95–96.
  See also Defense, Department of
War industries, 36, 56, 68, 75–76, 83, 129
War jobs, 56, 69–70, 72, 82
War Manpower Commission, 56, 72, 81–82,
  84–85, 129
War workers, 81–82, 84
West Germany, 95, 101, 277

Westmoreland, William, 3, 170, 214
Wheeler, Burton, 51, 72–74
Wilkins, Roy, 99, 344n16
Willkie, Wendell, 18, 21
Wisconsin, University of, 23, 176, 184, 200
Women, 24, 30–31, 61, 69–70, 82–83, 86,
  127, 132, 205, 210, 242, 272, 347nn44,
  49, 349n64
Workers, 34, 81–82, 195; classification of,
  34, 59, 81; control of, 35, 37, 38, 65–66,
  80, 98–99; deferments for, 13, 20, 29, 35,
  37, 80–81, 129; shortages of, 82, 86. *See
  also* Labor
"Work or fight," 56, 66, 72, 85
World War I, 6, 11, 13–16, 19, 22, 28, 31,
  38, 66, 60, 74, 78, 85, 90, 101, 125, 134,
  173, 202, 230
World War II, 6, 61, 98, 102, 103, 109,
  111, 113, 116, 118, 121, 126–30, 134,
  136, 140, 154–55, 157, 167, 169, 173,
  180, 188, 191, 216, 234, 242, 259, 260,
  261–62, 281; blacks and, 103, 129,
  328n69; deferments for, 54, 132, 145,
  180–81; inductions for, 62, 85, 100, 118,
  120, 171, 194–95, 197, 227; mobilization
  for, 5, 20, 38, 54–55, 57–58, 64, 125,
  132, 336n33; protest and public opinion
  during, 121, 125, 173–74, 182–83, 185,
  213, 219; social effect of, 51, 81, 154,
  220, 274

Yale University, 39, 185, 203, 217
Young Republicans, 225, 236
Youth Advisory Committees, 241, 246